THE POLITICS OF SOCIAL PSYCHOLOGY

Social scientists have long known that political beliefs bias the way they think about, understand, and interpret the world around them. In this volume, scholars from social psychology and related fields explore the ways in which social scientists themselves have allowed their own political biases to influence their research. These biases may influence the development of research hypotheses, the design of studies and methods and materials chosen to test hypotheses, decisions to publish or not publish results based on their consistency with one's prior political beliefs, and how results are described and dissemination to the popular press. The fact that these processes occur within academic disciplines, such as social psychology, that strongly skew to the political left compounds the problem. Contributors to this volume not only identify and document the ways that social psychologists' political beliefs can and have influenced research, but also offer solutions towards a more depoliticized social psychology that can become a model for discourse across the social sciences.

Jarret T. Crawford is a Professor of Psychology at The College of New Jersey. He is the author of over 50 publications on political psychology and intergroup attitudes.

Lee Jussim is a Professor of Psychology at Rutgers University. He has authored or edited six books and over 100 articles and chapters, focusing primarily on social perception and scientific integrity.

Frontiers of Social Psychology

Series Editors:

Arie W. Kruglanski, University of Maryland at College Park
Joseph P. Forgas, University of New South Wales

Frontiers of Social Psychology is a series of domain-specific handbooks. Each volume provides readers with an overview of the most recent theoretical, methodological, and practical developments in a substantive area of social psychology, in greater depth than is possible in general social psychology handbooks. The editors and contributors are all internationally renowned scholars whose work is at the cutting edge of research.

Scholarly, yet accessible, the volumes in the *Frontiers* series are an essential resource for senior undergraduates, postgraduates, researchers, and practitioners and are suitable as texts in advanced courses in specific subareas of social psychology.

Published Titles

Goal-directed Behavior
Aarts & Elliot

Social Judgment and Decision Making
Krueger

Intergroup Conflicts and their Resolution
Bar-Tal

Social Motivation
Dunning

Social Cognition
Strack & Förster

Social Psychology of Consumer Behavior
Wänke

Computational Social Psychology
Vallacher, Read, & Nowak

Forthcoming Titles

For continually _gy s_ ▮formation about published and forthcoming titles in the *Frontiers of* ▮eries, please visit: https://www.routledge.com/psychology/se

THE POLITICS OF
SOCIAL PSYCHOLOGY

*Edited by Jarret T. Crawford
and Lee Jussim*

Routledge
Taylor & Francis Group

NEW YORK AND LONDON

First published 2018
by Routledge
711 Third Avenue, New York, NY 10017

and by Routledge
2 Park Square, Milton Park, Abingdon, Oxon, OX14 4RN

Routledge is an imprint of the Taylor & Francis Group, an informa business

Library of Congress Cataloging-in-Publication Data
Names: Crawford, Jarret T., editor. | Jussim, Lee J., editor.
Title: The politics of social psychology / Jarret T. Crawford and Lee Jussim, editors.
Description: NewYork, NY: Routledge, 2017. |
Series: Frontiers of social psychology
Identifiers: LCCN 2017009846 |
ISBN 9781138930599 (hardback: alk. paper) |
ISBN 9781138930605 (pbk.: alk. paper) |
ISBN 9781315112619 (ebook)
Subjects: LCSH: Social psychology—Political aspects.
Classification: LCC HM1033 .P654 2017 | DDC 302—dc23
LC record available at https://lccn.loc.gov/2017009846

ISBN: 978-1-138-93059-9 (hbk)
ISBN: 978-1-138-93060-5 (pbk)
ISBN: 978-1-315-11261-9 (ebk)

Typeset in Bembo
by codeMantra

CONTENTS

CONTRIBUTORS

Anglin, Stephanie M., Department of Social and Decision Sciences, Carnegie Mellon University

Blanton, Hart, Department of Psychology, University of Connecticut

Brandt, Mark J., Department of Social Psychology, Tilburg University

Buss, David M., Department of Psychology, The University of Texas at Austin

Campbell, W. Keith, Department of Psychology, University of Georgia

Ceci, Stephen J., Department of Human Development, Cornell University

Contrada, Richard, Department of Psychology, Rutgers University

Crawford, Jarret T., Psychology Department, The College of New Jersey

Duarte, Jose, Psychology Department, University of Arizona

Edlund, John, Department of Psychology, Rochester Institute of Technology

Holzer, Nissan, Yeshiva University

Ikizer, Elif G., Department of Psychology, University of Connecticut

Jussim, Lee, Department of Psychology, Rutgers University

Labrecque, Jennifer S., Department of Psychology, University of Southern California

Lelkes, Yphtach, Annenberg School for Communication, University of Pennsylvania

Malka, Ariel, Department of Psychology, Yeshiva University

Martin, Chris C., Emory University

Mitchell, Gregory, University of Virginia School of Law

Motyl, Matt, Department of Psychology, The University of Illinois at Chicago

Navarrete, C. David, Department of Psychology, Michigan State University

Reyna, Christine, Department of Psychology, DePaul University

Sowden, Walter, Department of Psychology, University of Michigan

Spälti, Anna Katarina, Department of Psychology, Tilburt University

Stern, Charlotta, Department of Sociology, Stockholm University

Stevens, Sean T., Stern School of Business, New York University

Terbeck, Sylvia, Department of Psychology, Plymouth University

Tybur, Joshua M., Department of Experimental and Applied Psychology, Vrije Universiteit Amsterdam

Von Hippel, William, School of Psychology, University of Queensland

Welch, Cheryl Alyssa, Department of Psychology, James Madison University

Williams, Wendy M., Department of Human Development, Cornell University

Winegard, Benjamin, Department of Psychology, Carroll College

Winegard, Bo, Department of Psychology, Florida State University

1

INTRODUCTION TO THE POLITICS OF SOCIAL PSYCHOLOGY

Jarret T. Crawford and Lee Jussim

Science is an endeavor to discover truths. It provides a method for observing and measuring phenomena and drawing conclusions about how the world works and why. Scientific discoveries and innovations offer windows into the workings of time, space, and society.

But what happens when the tools of the scientific method are used, intentionally or not, to advance and confirm one's political beliefs and values rather than to discover truth? The problem of confirmation bias in science, wherein researchers skew the questions they ask, the way they seek to answer them, and their interpretations of results in order to vindicate their hypotheses, preferences, or values, is well known (Jussim, Crawford, Stevens, & Duarte, 2016; Lilienfeld, 2010; MacCoun, 1998). Philosophers of science have noted the importance of attempting to disconfirm rather than confirm one's predictions (Popper, 1934/2002). Although strict falsification has its limitations and critics (e.g., Meehl, 1990), many scientists believe that falsification and skepticism, however imperfect, have important roles in science (e.g., Jussim et al., 2016; Merton, 1942; Teo, 2016). But what happens when one's scientific hypotheses are enmeshed with one's outlook on life, society, and politics?

There is no question that social scientists have more in common than simply their disciplinary interests. Specifically, many surveys indicate that social scientists across various disciplines tend to hold to more liberal/leftist points of view than the wider population. An accumulating scholarly literature has documented ways in which that skew has led to political discrimination and undermined the credibility and validity of scholarship (Inbar & Lammers, 2012; Jussim, 2012; Pinker, 2003).

Duarte et al. (2015) recently argued for increased political diversity within the field of social psychology. That paper made four key arguments: (1) social psychology is ideologically homogenous; (2) such ideological homogeneity sometimes harms scientific inquiry; (3) increasing political diversity would reduce some of this damage; and (4) some portion of ideological homogeneity within social psychology is due to hostile work climate and discrimination. That article invited 33 commentaries from social scientists from multiple disciplines and backgrounds, and most commentators agreed on all four of these arguments, although there was substantial disagreement with the third argument.

The present volume represents an extension of this conversation about the politics of social psychology. That social psychology is overwhelmingly liberal is established fact (Inbar & Lammers, 2012; Chapter 2). The authors of the present chapters focus now on highlighting the ways in which such homogeneity can harm social psychological science. Chapters 2–5 address how politicized social psychology can restrict the types of theories employed to understand human social behavior and the types of hypotheses that researchers test. Von Hippel and Buss suggest that social psychologists are reluctant to use evolutionary theory to generate social psychological hypotheses because of misperceptions regarding supposed "conservative" implications of evolutionary theory. Brandt and Spälti note that norms among social psychologists (of which politically liberal outlooks is one of them) influence the kinds of questions they seek to test. The next two chapters consider how unanswered questions in gender equity research (Stern; Martin) and intergroup relations research (Martin) can distort scientific conclusions.

Chapters 6–8 focus on how a politicized social psychology can impact decisions in research design. Reyna highlights how political beliefs can influence scale creation and use, leading to misinterpretations of measurements. Crawford focuses on how measures of prejudice limited to historically marginalized and disadvantaged groups can mask people's understanding of the nature of prejudice itself. Malka, Lelkes, and Holzer identify suboptimal methodological practices in research on ideological differences in psychological rigidity that are influenced by researchers' prior beliefs.

Chapters 9–11 address how politics can distort how not only researchers but also other science communicators and an engaged public interpret research conclusions. Mitchell addresses the consequences of the dissemination of research conclusions that are not properly vetted for their external validity, especially when those research conclusions purport applicability to policy debates (and almost always favor left-wing conclusions). Ceci and Williams highlight how people's political disagreements with scientific conclusions can lead them to draw unfounded critiques of methods and motivations of the researchers themselves. Blanton and Ikizer address how scientists' simplifications of their conclusions for general audiences, both to increase exposure and dissemination of the findings, can have unintended political consequences.

Chapters 12 and 13 address consequences of a politicized social psychology for its practitioners or would-be practitioners. Winegard and Winegard review problems associated with a lack of political diversity in social psychology and discuss the consequences for hostile climate. Stevens et al. highlight how nonliberal social psychologists, or even liberal social psychologists who reject politically infused theoretical orthodoxies, experience hostility and discrimination against them, personally, and against their research and scholarship.

Finally, this volume ends with insights into how to reduce the politicization of social psychological science. In Chapter 14, Tybur and Navarette not only present evolutionary psychology as a paradigm through which social psychologists might understand psychological phenomena but also, more importantly, argue that "big theories" such as evolutionary theory can provide a buffer against subjectively biased interpretations of research conclusions that are currently possible because of the lack of strong theory in most social psychology research.

In the final chapter, we the editors conclude by succinctly summarizing the specific suggestions offered both within and outside this volume on how to depoliticize social psychology. Our hope is that this final chapter (Jussim and Crawford) will provide an informative guidepost to those who wish to make greater efforts to improve the quality of their teaching, mentorship, research, and, indeed, the quality of social psychology by limiting the unwarranted effects of their political beliefs and values in their professional work. We hope that readers of this volume will learn more about the ways that politics can influence social psychological research and be inspired to be part of the solution to depoliticize the field.

References

Duarte, J., Crawford, J. T., Stern, C., Haidt, J., Jussim, L. & Tetlock, P. E. (2015). Political diversity will improve social psychological science. *Behavioral and Brain Sciences*, *38*, 1–13. doi:10.1017/S0140525X14000430.

Inbar, Y. & Lammers, J. (2012). Political diversity in social and personality psychology. *Perspectives on Psychological Science*, *7*, 496–503.

Jussim, L. (2012). *Social perception and social reality: Why accuracy dominates bias and self-fulfilling prophecy*. New York: Oxford.

Jussim, L., Crawford, J. T., Stevens, S. T., Anglin, S. M. & Duarte, J. L. (2016). Good morals gone bad: Can high moral purposes undermine scientific integrity? In J. Forgas, P. van Lange & L. Jussim (Eds.), *The Social Psychology of Morality* (pp. 173–195). New York: Routledge.

Lilienfeld, S. O. (2010). Can psychology become a science? *Personality and Individual Differences*, *49*, 281–288.

MacCoun, R. J. (1998). Biases in the interpretation and use of research results. *Annual Review of Psychology*, *49*, 249–287.

Meehl, P. (1990). Appraising and amending theories: The strategy of Lakatosian defense and two principles that warrant it. *Psychological Inquiry*, *1*, 108–141.

Merton, R. K. (1942). A note on science and democracy. *Journal of Legal and Political Sociology*, *1*, 115–126.

Pinker, S. (2003). *The blank slate: The modern denial of human nature*. New York: Penguin.

Popper, K. (1934/2002). *The logic of scientific discovery*. New York: Routledge.

Teo, T. (2016). *Three cheers for methodological terrorists*. Retrieved on November 18, 2016 from: www.psychologytoday.com/blog/rabble-rouser/201610/three-cheers-methodological-terrorists.

PART I

How Politicized Social Psychology Undermines Theory Generation and Hypothesis Testing

2

DO IDEOLOGICALLY DRIVEN SCIENTIFIC AGENDAS IMPEDE THE UNDERSTANDING AND ACCEPTANCE OF EVOLUTIONARY PRINCIPLES IN SOCIAL PSYCHOLOGY?

William von Hippel and David M. Buss

This is an exciting time to be a social psychologist. Our journals are full of fascinating findings that attract the attention of our colleagues and the media. The breadth and eclectic nature of our discipline—along with the centrality of social and personality psychology to human experience—have made our theories and findings foundational to many other social sciences. Unfortunately, that breadth and eclecticism come at a cost, as social research is more aptly described as a thousand points of light than as a coherent beam illuminating the empirical landscape. Although our field contains hundreds of fascinating findings and an abundance of mini-theories, it lacks a cogent meta-theoretical framework that unifies its diverse elements.

This lack of coherence makes it difficult to organize the field in ways that are clear for our students and compelling for policymakers and fellow scientists. It can also obscure the relevance and applicability of new ideas from one area to another. But these costs need not be borne by our discipline. A widely accepted meta-theory with the potential to inform many of the important aspects of human existence was first proposed over 150 years ago, when Darwin included humans within the purview of evolutionary theory. This chapter considers a possible reason this meta-theory has yet to play a major organizing role in our discipline, why its adherents often toil on the periphery of social/personality psychology rather than at its center, and why some members of our discipline might prefer it that way.

An evolutionary approach might or might not be emphasized in the study of a particular social psychological problem for many reasons, depending on which aspects of which problems are being studied. But no matter the problem, it is always relevant to consider *why* people behave as they do—that is, to consider function. Indeed, social psychology has many theories that address the *why* question, and they are typically along the lines of "people do X to increase their self-esteem, happiness, sense of control or justice, relationship satisfaction, and so on."

Nevertheless, most of these theories provide only partial explanations, because they do not consider why people want to increase their self-esteem, happiness, sense of control or justice, relationship satisfaction, and so on. From an evolutionary perspective, the proper function of psychological processes cannot be these internal end-states. If people want to enhance their self-esteem, then enhanced self-esteem is likely to have aided them in solving one or more adaptive problems, such as increased effectiveness at negotiating hierarchies, attracting mates, or ensuring the success of one's coalition. Evolution has crafted specific motivations in people because those motivations historically led their bearers to experience greater reproductive success, so it is worth considering what outcomes psychological states such as self-esteem, happiness, and a sense of control evolved to support.[1] In this sense, an evolutionary perspective does not take anything away from existing social psychological theories but rather adds an important level of explanation to them. An evolutionary perspective also provides guidance and constraints on our theorizing and integrates it with the rest of the life sciences.

This proliferation of seemingly unrelated partial explanations in social psychology leads us to the central question of this chapter: Why do social psychologists spend their careers studying problems that are central to survival and reproduction (e.g., close relationships, inter-group relations, persuasion) but without availing themselves of the theoretical advantage that can be gained by considering the only known theory of *why* that exists in the life sciences? We propose that at least *part* of the answer to this question lies in the left-leaning political ideology of most social psychologists. We spend the remainder of this chapter outlining how and why ideologically driven scientific goals might play a role in limiting the understanding and acceptance of evolutionary principles in social psychology.

Important caveat. If what you have read so far is already raising your ire or blood pressure (as it did for a few of our reviewers), please keep in mind that we are not arguing that ideology is the only thing preventing all social psychologists from becoming evolutionary psychologists. People adopt a particular theoretical orientation for many reasons,[2] and the goal of this chapter is to explore one of them. If this chapter convinces you that ideology explains some of the variance in some people's conceptual misunderstandings and negative attitudes toward evolutionary psychology, then our goal in writing it will have been achieved.

A Survey of 335 Well-Established Social Psychologists

The arguments articulated in this chapter are based primarily on data collected from members of the Society of Experimental Social Psychology (SESP) in an IRB-approved survey conducted in July of 2015. These results are supplemented by several decades of our observations and inferences from interactions with fellow social psychologists. Membership in SESP is limited to people who are five years post-PhD and are judged to have made a significant contribution to social psychology. There are slightly more than 1,000 SESP members, most of whom are North American. We surveyed 901 of these members, avoiding people known to have significant administrative duties, known to be retired and no longer actively involved in social psychology, and known to emphasize an evolutionary perspective in their own work. We received 335 responses to our survey, for a response rate of 37.2%. Of these respondents, 33.4% were female (which is representative of the gender distribution of the society itself), the average age was 51.5 years, and the average time since completing the PhD was 22.8 years. The complete survey and the raw data are available at https://osf.io/ebvtq/.

The first question we consider is how do members of SESP view evolutionary psychology? To address this question, we included three key items in the survey. First, participants were asked to respond on a scale from 0% to 100% how likely it is that *Darwin's ideas of evolution are true and that plants, animals, and humans all evolved through similar causal processes across hundreds of millions of years.* The mean response to this item was 87.6% (modal response was 100%), suggesting overwhelming endorsement of evolutionary theory as applied to life on Earth. Next, participants indicated how likely it is that *most of Darwin's ideas about evolution are true BUT that humans were an exception and were not a product of evolution.* The mean response to this item was 6.9% (modal response 0%). These findings indicate that almost all members of SESP believe evolutionary theory applies to humans, and very few believe that humans are an exception to evolutionary principles.

The critical issue for this chapter is the degree to which this endorsement of evolutionary theory manifests in a belief in the evolution of the social mind. To examine this question, we asked participants to indicate how likely it is that *Darwin's ideas of evolution apply to the human mind and that many of our social attitudes and preferences evolved across millions of years.* In contrast to the highly skewed responses to the prior two questions, responses to this item were almost equal across the entire scale range, and the mean response was 54.8% (with a mode of 50%).

There are at least two ways to interpret this 33% gap between the mean levels of endorsement of evolutionary biology and evolutionary social psychology (or the 50% gap between the modes). First, it is possible that SESP members are skeptical that slow-moving evolutionary processes could play an important role in the context of incredibly fast-moving cultural and technological changes. Consistent with such a possibility, an eminent member of SESP wrote the following email along with his/her response to the survey: *"Frankly I'm pretty skeptical of evolutionary psychology. From my point of view, cultural evolution proceeds at a much faster pace than biological evolution, and that's where we should focus our explanatory efforts."* We disagree with this intellectual position for two reasons. First, cultural evolution is based on a foundation of evolved psychological mechanisms from which it cannot be fully divorced (Tooby & Cosmides, 1992). Second, models of gene-culture co-evolution are essential to understanding some phenomena (more on this later), and we see no reason to deprive social psychology of this powerful theoretical tool. Nevertheless, it is reasonable to focus one's efforts on factors that are expected to have the greatest explanatory power, and thus a focus on cultural factors is both scientifically defensible and ideologically neutral.

It is also possible, however, that ideological factors play an important role in this 33–50% gap and that motivational biases prevent social psychologists from learning about and exploiting evolutionary psychology in their own work. Most of the arguments in the remainder of this chapter examine this ideological/motivational possibility. As our first piece of evidence, we consider the remainder of the email from this same eminent member of SESP. After expressing skepticism about the importance of evolutionary psychology, he/she asked us to consider this (slightly abbreviated) list that he/she shares with his/her students.

It does not take much reading between the lines to infer from these questions that there may be more to this psychologist's rejection of evolutionary psychology than concerns about the pace of biological evolution. Addressing all the apparent misunderstandings of the field would require more space than is available in this chapter, but we would be remiss if we did not briefly point out some of the confusions that seem evident in this list of questions (for longer expositions about these and related confusions, we refer readers to Confer et al., 2010, and to Lewis, Al-Shawaf, Conroy-Beam, Asao & Buss, 2017).[3]

TABLE 2.1 Questions to Ask Your Local Evolutionary Psychologist

Do you eat meat? If so, do you eat it raw? If not, why not?

Does your wife have a 5:7 waist-to-hip ratio? Are her breasts symmetrical? If not, why are you still with her?

Has she reached menopause? If yes, why haven't you divorced her?

Do you practice any form of birth control? If so, why?

Other than your wife, how many attractive young women are you currently having sex with?

If you have divorced and remarried, have you killed your new wife's children from her earlier marriage—or at least kicked them out of the house with no financial support? If not, why not?

Do you ever have sex when your partner isn't ovulating? If yes, why?

Do you engage in any form of sexual activity other than vaginal intercourse? If yes, why?

Question 1 implies a lack of awareness that substantial human evolution took place after we learned to control fire. Indeed, our large brain-to-gut ratio is enabled by the fact that we cook our food and thus extract more nutrients than would be available if we ate it raw—an excellent example of gene-culture co-evolution (Wrangham, 2009). *Question 2* confuses evolved preferences with the degree to which those preferences can be translated into actual mating decisions; as Mick Jagger famously noted, "you can't always get what you want." Moreover, this question implies that one aspect of physical appearance should trump all others—a position contrary to evolutionary psychological theories of mating (e.g., Buss, 2015; Schmitt, 2015).

Questions 3, 4, 7, and 8 imply that humans evolved to want to have children or to maximize their reproductive success—positions explicitly repudiated by evolutionary psychologists (e.g., Confer et al., 2010; Tooby & Cosmides, 1990). Rather, humans evolved sexual drives and sexual attraction to partners displaying reliable cues to fertility. In combination, these desires have led to reproduction, with no need for a desire for children (which would obviously be irrelevant in our ancestral species that did not understand the link between sex and reproduction). In other words, humans likely evolved to want sex rather than to want children and then to feel nurturant to those children who came along as a consequence.

Question 5 implies a common confusion between evolved goals and their expression in overt behavior. Men can be attracted to a variety of women but choose not to act on those attractions for a host of reasons: love and commitment to their partner, lack of ability to attract these women, concerns about a loss of status within their social group, and so on. A great deal of evolutionary psychology is concerned with when and how people subvert one set of goals (e.g., desire for sexual variety) to another set of goals (e.g., long-term relationship maintenance) or values (e.g., beliefs in the immorality of infidelity).

Question 6 implies similar confusion between competing goals. Although men tend to invest less in stepchildren than they do in their biological children (Anderson, Kaplan, & Lancaster, 1999), and being a stepchild does pose an increased risk of being killed by one's stepparents (Daly & Wilson, 1988), many men invest in stepchildren, partially as an effort to attract and retain their mother as a romantic partner. For good reason, a man's willingness to invest in a woman's children enhances his attractiveness to her.

Question 7 implies two confusions. First, it mistakenly assumes that the evolved function of sex in humans is solely fertilization, thereby ignoring the role of sexual behavior in promoting long-term pair bonding. Second, it ignores the evolutionary literature on why women evolved concealed ovulation, with one plausible function being to promote sexual interest across the fertility cycle and thereby promote long-term bonding and close companionship (e.g., Strassman, 1981; Thornhill & Gangestad, 2008).

Lastly, these questions raise an interesting irony when juxtaposed with comments from several reviewers regarding the issue of falsifiability. These questions all imply that the observations they contain falsify certain evolutionary psychological hypotheses. For example, Question 2 implies that men who partner with women without a low waist-to-hip ratio falsify the hypothesis that men have evolved an attraction to this well-document fertility cue. Question 5 implies that men who are not having sex with numerous young attractive women falsify the hypothesis that men have evolved a desire for sexual partner variety. The irony is that some critics imply that certain evolutionary hypotheses have been falsified while simultaneously claiming that they are unfalsifiable. We refer interested readers to more extensive discussions of specific evolutionary hypotheses that have been falsified (e.g., the kin investment hypothesis about male homosexuality) and why this frequently repeated yet clearly erroneous claim lacks scientific warrant (e.g., Confer et al., 2010; Lewis et al., 2015).

It is true that this email is only an anecdote, and it is also possible that the individual asking these questions is well aware of the misunderstandings that are implied but feels that they are worthwhile discussion points. Thus, these questions may not reflect the level of understanding of evolutionary psychology that is broadly held by social psychologists. Unfortunately, our experience suggests otherwise. Our guess (and our experience at talks and faculty meetings) is that many members of SESP would find these questions and their implied answers to be damning to the evolutionary enterprise, or at least to prominent evolutionary psychological hypotheses. If so, it seems that many social psychologists have fundamental misconceptions about the basic tenets and theories of evolutionary psychology and consequently reject a view of evolutionary psychology that evolutionary psychologists have explicitly and repeatedly rejected (e.g., Confer et al., 2010).

The interesting question is why would experienced and highly influential social psychologists harbor so many fundamental misconceptions about the theories and findings of evolutionary psychology? We believe that ideological discomfort with the evolutionary enterprise deters many scholars from engaging with it seriously and thereby prevents them from learning a body of theories and empirical research that is much more informative (and much less inflammatory) than they might think.

Why Are Social Psychologists Uncomfortable with Evolutionary Psychology?

Many scholars have argued that social psychologists are on the political left (Haidt, 2011; Inbar & Lammers, 2012; Redding, 2001), and our survey of SESP members corroborates this claim. When asked whom they had voted for (or would have voted for) in the 2012 U.S. presidential election, 305 of our respondents chose Barack Obama (the candidate on the political left), and only 4 chose Mitt Romney (the candidate on the political right). The sample was also skewed with regard to opinions about issues such as abortion and gun control; the mean response was within two points of the liberal end of an 11-point scale and only five individuals (less than 2% of our sample) scored on the conservative side of the scale midpoint.[4]

Such skewed responses make it difficult to correlate SESP members' political positions with their attitudes toward evolutionary issues, but the logic is not difficult to follow. First, as can be seen in the example provided in Table 2.1, social psychologists often perceive evolutionary psychology through the lens of genetic determinism, believing that if people have an evolved tendency to do X, then they have little choice but to do X or are likely to do X regardless of context. If genes did have such a powerful and environmentally independent influence on human behavior, then any social problem that emerged from evolved predispositions would indeed be intractable. An evolved tendency for people to be violent (Archer, 2004) would mean that violence is inevitable, and an evolved tendency for men to prefer sexual variety (Symons, 1979) would mean that monogamy is impossible. This misperception about genetics and psychological adaptations might account for part of the reason that members of SESP showed bimodal distributions in their perceptions of the likelihood that humans have a genetic tendency to be violent ($M = 58\%$, modes at 20/30% and 60%) and that men evolved to have more difficulty than women being sexually faithful ($M = 49\%$, modes at 10 and 50%). A substantial proportion of SESP members might be rejecting these possibilities on ideological grounds.

The theoretical framework of evolutionary psychology reveals why such inferences are mistaken. First, evolved psychological adaptations are context-dependent, designed to produce contingent responses to specialized classes of environmental problems. Second, in most cases, humans have multiple strategies for solving the same adaptive problem. For example, if the adaptive challenge is obtaining a scarce resource, taking it by force may be one option, but engaging in cooperative exchange is another. Third, environmental factors can eliminate or greatly reduce the likelihood of specific strategies by ramping up their costs. Indeed, that is precisely what has happened over the past few centuries with violence, which has steadily declined in much of the world (Pinker, 2011). Fourth, humans also evolved the capacity for self-control (e.g., to delay gratification, to prioritize goals, to subvert one goal in the service of other goals) and thus can choose not to aggress or be sexually unfaithful even if they are tempted to do so. The key point is that the inference that violence and infidelity are inevitable if they evolved is simply erroneous; nor is that inevitability implied by modern evolutionary psychological hypotheses.

The second source of discomfort with evolutionary psychology appears to emerge from the bias that what is natural is good. This has been dubbed the naturalistic fallacy, or the "is–ought" fallacy: If something evolved in nature, it ought to exist. For example, if men have evolved to prefer sexual variety

(Buss & Schmitt, 1993; Schmitt, 2005; Symons, 1979), then philandering by men is at least excusable. Nature is full of undesirable stuff, however, at least according to most human value systems. Diseases are natural, but we deem them undesirable and spend billions trying to eradicate them. Similarly, violence is natural—indeed violent competition for mates or resources is common across the animal kingdom—but we have developed a professional police force and criminal justice systems to reduce the expression of this proclivity in humans. Humans have also evolved context-dependent adaptations to refrain from aggression when resource acquisition and social conflicts can be resolved with less risky strategies, when an opponent is more physically formidable, when reputational costs are too high, and so on (see Buss, 2005; Pinker, 2011).

As Pinker notes,

> Many intellectuals have averted their gaze from the evolutionary logic of violence, fearing that acknowledging it is tantamount to accepting it or even approving of it. Instead, they have pursued the comforting delusion of the Noble Savage, in which violence is an arbitrary product of learning ... But denying the logic of violence makes it easy to forget how readily violence can flare up, and ignoring the parts of the mind that ignite violence makes it easy to overlook the parts that can extinguish it. With violence, as with so many other concerns, human nature is the problem, but human nature is also the solution.
>
> *(Pinker, 2003, p. 336)*

Thus, rather than viewing what is natural as good, it would behoove social psychologists to remember that what is natural is often distinctly unpleasant, and the advantage of human society is that we can choose to inhibit or promote the expression of psychological tendencies in manifest behavior regardless of whether those tendencies have been selected by evolutionary processes.

Opposition to Politically Inconvenient Discoveries: I. Evolved Gender Differences

Gender equality emerged as a strong political movement in the 1960s and 1970s. A critical concern was that women were discriminated against in the workplace (as indeed they were and often still are). Against this backdrop, some psychologists decided that it was essential to view men and women as psychologically monomorphic, possessing identical abilities, dispositions, interests, and proclivities. According to this view, evolved gender differences might be used to justify unequal treatment of women and gender discrimination. As an example, consider a recent commentary in *Psychological Science*, in which Harris, Chabot, and Mickes (2014) failed to replicate some of the menstrual cycle effects on women's political preferences found by Durante, Rae, and Griskevicius

(2013). Concern about the potential misuse of Durante et al.'s results appears evident in Harris et al.'s commentary, titled, *Women can keep the vote: No evidence that hormonal changes during the menstrual cycle impact political and social religious beliefs*.[5] Regardless of the scientific merits of the original empirical study, the conflation of a scientific issue (are there menstrual cycle effects on political beliefs?) with a political issue (gender equality in political participation) is troubling. This is not a lone example, as similar concerns can be seen in Rudman and Fetterolf's (2015) *Psychological Science* commentary, titled, *Why sexual economics theory is patriarchal*,[6] and no doubt a broader search would reveal many others.

We believe that such political concerns have often led to the rejection of evidence for evolved psychological sex differences.[7] Although it is obvious that scientific knowledge can be misused, we argue that this particular concern is misplaced for several key reasons. First, achieving gender equality is a legitimate and worthy moral goal regardless of what the scientific evidence reveals about evolved gender differences. As Pinker (2003) notes,

> equality is not the empirical claim that all groups of humans are interchangeable; it is the moral principle that individuals should not be judged or constrained by the average properties of their group … If we recognize this principle, no one has to spin myths about the indistinguishability of the sexes to justify equality. Nor should anyone invoke sex differences to justify discriminatory policies (p. 340).

Second, evolved gender differences are expected only in domains in which men and women have faced recurrently different adaptive problems over the long course of human history (Buss, 1995a, b). In domains in which they have faced similar adaptive problems—which are in fact most domains—the genders are predicted to be psychologically similar. Nevertheless, some evidence exists for different intellectual profiles between the genders, with women typically showing better verbal abilities than men and men typically showing better spatial rotation abilities (translating into better quantitative skills) than women. There are numerous explanations for these gender differences, and it is unknown whether (and if so, to what degree) genetic or other biological factors underlie these effects (Halpern, 2012).

To examine SESP members' opinions regarding the sources of these differences, we included two questions in our survey. In the first, we asked members to indicate how likely they thought it was that *women's brains had evolved in a manner that led women to be more verbally talented than men*. In the second question, we asked members to indicate how likely they thought it was that *men's brains had evolved in a manner that led men to be more mathematically talented than women*. The mean response to the first item was 40.3%, and the mean response to the second item was 30.2% (a significant difference). Of course, it is possible that the female verbal advantage is more likely to have evolved than the male spatial/mathematical advantage, but it is also possible that left-leaning desires to support women who have faced so much discrimination across our history are playing a role in these perceptions. As one of our respondents wrote, *"I found it curious how contradictory I was in responding! For instance, when science ostensibly reveals that the majority group has certain advantages, I say it's 'bad,' but when the minority group has certain advantages, I say it's 'good!'"* We hope that our findings contribute more generally to the self-insight reflected in this comment, as the field becomes more reflective about the unintended biases we all carry.

Opposition to Politically Inconvenient Discoveries: II. Some People Have More Desirable Traits than Others

Liberal political ideology strongly stresses human equality. According to modern democratic principles, all people should be treated equally regardless of ethnicity, gender, sexual orientation or identity, age, amount of body fat, and so on. Political movements toward equality have made great progress and have expanded most people's moral circles to include groups that had previously been perceived as legitimate targets of discrimination. Partly because of this political ideology, many psychologists are uneasy about theories and empirical findings that suggest that humans have evolved to value some people more than others.

A prime example centers on evolutionary theories of attractiveness. Beauty, according to many in the social sciences, is entirely in the eyes of the beholder. According to this view, standards of attractiveness are arbitrary and culturally variable, and beauty itself is only skin-deep. You can't judge a book by its cover, the cliché goes, and the content of our character is more important than surface appearances. As a consequence of these beliefs, the hypothesis that humans have evolved standards of attractiveness, which some people embody more fully than others, has been met with a great deal of uneasiness by social psychologists. This uneasiness is reflected in the response of SESP members to our survey question that asked how likely it is that there are universal standards of attractiveness for facial features and body shape, such that there are ideal appearances for men and women. SESP members thought this possibility was 51% likely, and consistent with many other items, that average was in the context of a bimodal distribution, with the two modes at 10% and 70/80%.

This uneasiness on the part of some social psychologists (which we believe is reflected in SESP members' bimodal responses) is exacerbated by three key factors. First, beauty is undemocratically distributed; some people have more of it than others due to luck of the draw.[8] Second, beauty appears to be something over which people have limited capacity for improvement, although the multi-billion dollar beauty products, cosmetic surgery, and fitness industries are strong testaments that people try to improve their attractiveness. Third, people endowed with beauty get better treatment; they are more popular, are preferentially hired in many jobs, earn higher incomes, and obtain a variety of social benefits (although there are also drawbacks, such as being perceived as snobbish and sexually unfaithful; Singh, 2004).

The uneasiness of many social scientists with taking attractiveness seriously resulted in it being virtually ignored for most of the history of social psychology (with the exception of a few pioneers, such as Berscheid & Walster, 1974). Evolutionary psychologists have extended this early work and in so doing have marshaled three sets of (admittedly disquieting) findings. First, physical attractiveness is a quality that is more valued in women than in men in the context of mate selection (Buss, 1989). Second, beauty is anchored not in arbitrary social customs but rather in biologically important qualities such as health and fertility (e.g., Buss, 1987; Symons, 1979; Williams, 1975). This line of research has also discovered cues to beauty that were previously unknown to the scientific community, such as waist-to-hip ratio (Singh, 1993), facial symmetry (Gangestad & Thornhill, 1998), thickness of the limbal ring (the outer edge of the iris, which lightens and thins with age; Peshek, Semmaknejad, Hoffman, & Foley, 2011), and lumbar curvature (Lewis, Russell, Al-Shawaf & Buss, in press). Third, the value people place on beauty manifests in more than just mating decisions. Physically attractive people are also more desired as friends, coalition partners, and even kin (Sugiyama, 2005). So beauty is not only unfair, but the unfairness also extends to our most important social relationships.

We confess that these findings are disturbing, and we can offer only two observations. First, and perhaps most obviously, denying the problem does not change the underlying reality. In his memoir *Ugly* (2013), Robert Hoge (the self-described "ugliest person you've never met") decries the widespread tendencies to pretend that beauty doesn't matter and that ugly ducklings inevitably transform into beautiful swans. Hoge argues that we will only make progress in dealing with the undemocratic distribution of attractiveness by first acknowledging it and then moving on to note that attractiveness is not the only human quality that is important and that it need not be self-defining. Hoge's advice could have been written by a clinical psychologist, who would suggest that it is important not to deny unpleasant aspects of reality but not to catastrophize or ruminate on them either. Second, the more we understand the causes and effects of attractiveness, the better placed we are to deal with them. Our role as social psychologists is not to search for social phenomena as we would like them to be but rather to document social phenomena that exist in the world so that we might better prepare people to address them.

Opposition Based on Religious Grounds

Consistent with SESP members' left-leaning politics, concerns about God, religion, and the meaning of life that appear to prevent many people from adopting an evolutionary approach to understanding humanity were not very important to most members of SESP. When asked how often they pray, 63%

of the membership reported that they never pray. Similarly, members of SESP thought it 66% likely that life has no intrinsic meaning or purpose (with the modal response to this item being 90/100% likely) and 73% likely that there is no God or higher power, soul, or continuing existence after death (with the modal response being 90% likely).

How Do the above Concerns Coalesce into SESP Members' Attitudes toward Evolutionary Psychology?

In this chapter, we have proposed a variety of reasons left-leaning social psychologists (i.e., nearly all of us) might be ideologically predisposed to dislike and avoid contact with evolutionary psychology. At this point, it is not possible to disentangle these various sources of antipathy and discomfort, but we can look to our survey of SESP members to provide a tentative answer to which issues play a particularly important role. Recall that SESP members were nearly unanimous in their endorsement of evolutionary theory (judging it as 88% likely to be true, with a mode of 100% likely) but very much on the fence when it comes to evolutionary social psychology (judging it to be 55% likely to be true, with a mode of 50% likely). To gain an initial sense of factors that might play a role in this 33% gap in mean rates of endorsement and 50% gap in the modes, we regressed beliefs in evolutionary social psychology on beliefs in evolutionary theory. We then saved the residuals from this analysis (i.e., the tendency to believe or disbelieve evolutionary social psychology controlling for the underlying tendency to believe in evolutionary theory) and tried to predict these residuals with responses to the various questions discussed above.

The first issue we examined was whether perceptions of evolutionary psychology are tied up in racial/ethnic concerns, perhaps because of some of the ways that evolutionary theory has been misused/misunderstood in the past (e.g., Social Darwinism). To address this issue, we asked SESP members how likely they thought it was that members of some ethnic groups were genetically more intelligent (Mean = 26.4%, Mode = 10% likely) or athletic (Mean = 45.1%, Modes = 20 and 50% likely) than members of other ethnic groups. Responses to this item did not predict the residual tendency to endorse evolutionary social psychology, suggesting that SESP members are not rejecting evolutionary social psychology because of their concerns regarding research on ethnicity and race.

In contrast, a simultaneous regression revealed independent variance in the residual tendency to endorse evolutionary social psychology was predicted by SESP members' beliefs that well-known gender differences might have a genetic cause ($\beta = 0.120$, $p = 0.033$; bivariate $r = 0.295$, $p < 0.001$), that sex hormones might have an important influence on attitudes and behavior ($\beta = 0.207$, $p < 0.001$; bivariate $r = 0.380$, $p < 0.001$), that humans might have a genetic tendency to be violent ($\beta = 0.126$, $p = 0.024$; bivariate $r = 0.308$, $p < 0.001$), and that there might be universal standards of attractiveness ($\beta = 0.208$, $p = 0.001$; bivariate $r = 0.398$, $p < 0.001$).Thus, it seems that members of SESP who do not accept a role for genetics and hormones in sex differences, who do not accept the possibility that the dark side of human nature might have evolved, and who do not accept that there are universal standards of attractiveness that some people meet better than others are also unlikely to embrace evolutionary psychology, despite believing in evolutionary theory.

These findings bring us back to the question with which we began this chapter: What role does ideology play in the acceptance of these possibilities and the more general acceptance of evolutionary explanations for social behavior? We largely abandoned analysis of the political ideology items once we noted the extreme skew in the political attitudes of SESP members, but these findings clearly raise the question of whether ideology might be involved. To test this possibility, we correlated SESP members' averaged responses to these four items with their self-reported liberalism to conservatism and found a small positive relationship($r = 0.20$, $p < 0.001$).[9] This relationship seems to emerge from the fact that people across the political spectrum are equally likely to perceive these possibilities as highly probable, but only people on the far left are likely to believe that there is virtually no chance that these possibilities are true (see Figure 2.1).

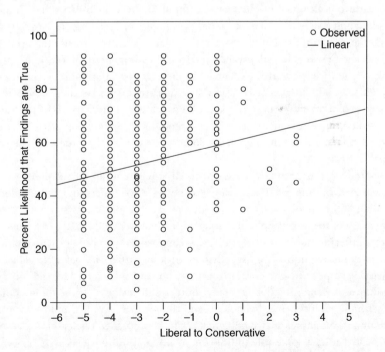

FIGURE 2.1 Relationship Between Self-Reported Political Orientation and Perceived Likelihood that Four Critical Evolutionary Findings Might Be True.

A common assumption often stated among our colleagues is that evolutionary psychologists are more conservative than their nonevolutionary counterparts. The findings in Figure 2.1 suggest that such an ideological difference is neither necessary nor likely. The most liberal respondents in the SESP survey were also the most divided on whether these four key findings are likely to be true, with many of these highly liberal respondents indicating that these possibilities are nearly 100% likely. This finding is consistent with the results of surveys of PhD students in evolutionary psychology (Tybur, Miller, & Gangestad, 2007) and evolutionary anthropology (Lyle & Smith, 2012), which reveal that evolutionary students are just as politically liberal as their fellow PhD students in other areas of psychology and anthropology.

Conclusions

It is neither a novel insight nor a secret that ideology, politics, and religious beliefs sometimes influence science. Darwin's theory of natural selection has been vigorously opposed for religious and ideological reasons. This opposition to evolutionary theory continues in modern times primarily among people on the religious right, as most people on the left accept it as scientifically valid. In this chapter, we have proposed that the ideologically driven goals of our left-leaning colleagues might play an important role in limiting the understanding and acceptance of evolutionary principles in social psychology. We are by no means claiming that ideology is the sole, or even necessarily the primary, factor that prevents social psychology from availing itself of the conceptual tools of the most powerful explanatory framework in the life sciences. Other key causes include lack of educational exposure to the fundamental principles of evolutionary biology in psychology graduate curricula and (ironically) evolved cognitive mechanisms such as essentialism and teleology that interfere with people's understanding of the logic of evolutionary processes (Legare, Lane, & Evans, 2013).

Moreover, there are healthy scientific disagreements about the precise ways in which evolutionary theory can best be used to understand human social conduct. One involves disputes about the relative domain-specificity versus generality of social psychological adaptations (Confer et al., 2010). Another involves differing models of the links between evolved psychological adaptations and cultural evolution (e.g., see chapters in the 2016 *Handbook of Evolutionary Psychology*, especially the contrasting positions of Pinker and Henrich on cultural group selection). Clearly, many sources of healthy scientific disagreement exist about evolutionary psychology and the precise ways it should be applied to humans. Nonetheless, we hope that we have persuaded readers that ideology has played at least some role in limiting its integration in social psychology.

Substantial social psychological research shows that many people would rather not learn about bad news that cannot be fixed (e.g., Dawson, Savitsky, & Dunning,

2006; Lerman, Croyle, Tercyak, & Hamann, 2002), but this understandable tendency should not stand in the way of our scientific enterprise. Evolutionary psychology clearly has given us some bad news, but it has given us a lot of good news, too. People have evolved tendencies to be selfish, suspicious, hostile, and prejudiced but also to be friendly, cooperative, and altruistic. The public image of evolutionary psychology is that it tends to focus on the dark side of human nature, and it is true that sexual treachery, violence, and warfare are central topics of study. It seems less widely known among social psychologists that empathy, cooperation, altruism, friendship, love, and morality are also the focus of a great deal of evolutionary psychological theorizing and research (e.g., Bloom, 2012; Buss, 2006; de Waal, 2008; Tooby & Cosmides, 1996). And just as important, evolutionary psychology has shown us many times that people have an evolved capacity to override their evolved tendencies, to activate some and deactivate others, and thereby to behave in a manner of their own choosing. Just as we can create low-friction physical environments to prevent activation of our callus-producing adaptations, we can create low-friction social environments to prevent activation of our adaptations for discrimination and violence. Furthermore, societies can create social structures that overpower or suppress some of our evolved mechanisms and in so doing create more peaceful and just communities (Nowak, Gelfand, Borkowski, Cohen, & Hernandez, 2016). Indeed, by examining the contexts that activate, deactivate, and override evolved tendencies, evolutionary psychology gives greater leverage to social psychologists who use their scientific research to pursue social justice goals.

In closing, we see two reasons to be optimistic about a fuller, more integrative, evolutionary social psychology. One is that mainstream social psychology and evolutionary psychology agree fundamentally about the power of the situation. Social psychologists have a deep and rich history of showing the power of the situation in classic studies such as Milgram's experiments on obedience to authority and Latane's studies of the effects of group size on social loafing. Evolutionary psychology, despite the stereotype of it being a genetic determinist framework, comports well with this emphasis on the power of the situation. Examples include the effects of income inequality on homicide rates (Daly & Wilson, 1988) and the effects of attractive women on testosterone production and male risk-taking (Ronay & von Hippel, 2010). Social psychological adaptations evolved precisely to respond to situation-specific social challenges. Thus, the context-dependent adaptations at the core of evolutionary psychology and social psychology's emphasis on the power of the situation are intrinsically compatible.

The second encouraging note is that many of the most powerful evolutionary theories focus on important domains of social behavior. These include kin selection theory (Hamilton, 1964), the theory of reciprocal altruism (Trivers, 1971), sexual selection theory (Darwin, 1871), sexual conflict theory (Parker, 1979), as well as a host of more specialized evolutionary theories designed to account for coalitional psychology, opposite-sex friendships, mating strategies, cognitive biases, status hierarchies, costly social signaling, social learning, cultural evolution, and many others (see the 51 chapters in the 2016 *Handbook of Evolutionary Psychology*). Social psychology and evolutionary psychology, in short, are natural scientific allies. Both stand to benefit from a fuller scientific integration.

Acknowledgments

We thank Kelly Asao, Roy Baumeister, Paul Conway, Jarret Crawford, Alice Eagly, David Funder, Al Goethals, Jon Haidt, Geoffrey Leonardelli, Greg Mitchell, Mike Norton, Janet Ruscher, Anna Sedlacek, Todd Shackelford, Virginia Slaughter, Thomas Suddendorf, Kathleen Vohs, Ladd Wheeler, Michael Wohl, and Leslie Zebrowitz for helpful comments on an earlier draft of this manuscript.

Notes

1 For example, see section titled "Happiness, confidence, optimism, and guilt are interpersonal" in von Hippel & Trivers (2011, p. 42).

2 A psychologist might be skeptical of an evolutionary approach for other reasons than ideology. To quote one of our commentators, the criticism "I hear most often is the 'it's not falsifiable' issue, which usually takes the form of, 'If a man is sleeping with lots of women, that's because he evolved to be attracted to many mates to enhance chances of reproduction; but if he is monogamous with one woman forever, that's *also* because he evolved to be faithful to continue to have access to that one woman.'" The problem with this criticism is that it skips levels of analysis. If research revealed that men are no more interested in sexual variety than women, that would disconfirm an evolutionary hypothesis. But such a finding would not disconfirm *evolutionary psychology* any more than finding that a particular situation doesn't matter would disconfirm *social psychology*. Evolutionary hypotheses are just as falsifiable as any others, are just as likely to be moderated by contextual factors, and are just as likely *not* to apply to a particular individual.

3 We would also be remiss if we didn't acknowledge that we had many similar misconceptions when we first engaged with the literature in evolutionary psychology and biology. The pitfall is that evolutionary logic seems seductively simple, but the predictions that arise from it are often anything but simple, leading many people to think that they understand it when they do not.

4 For a more thorough discussion of these data, see Jonathan Haidt's blog at http://heterodoxacademy.org/2016/01/07/new-study-finds-conservative-social-psychologists/.

5 Alternatively, perhaps this title was meant to be tongue-in-cheek, and the authors were noting that hormonal effects on voting—reliable or not—are immaterial to voting rights.

6 For further discussion of this issue, see Baumeister & Vohs (2004) and Vohs & Baumeister (2015).

7 Perhaps this is why members of SESP believe that it is only 33% likely that well-known gender differences in nurturance and aggression might have a stronger basis

in genetics than in socialization or cultural factors (or perhaps not; at this point, we have no clear answer to this question).

8 Of course, the same holds for intelligence, as a great deal of evidence points to its high heritability. Nevertheless, in intellectual domains it is readily apparent that accomplishments are achieved through hard work, whereas it is easy to forget how much effort models and movie stars exert to maintain their perfect physiques.

9 When we residualize their answers to these questions by first removing the variance accounted for by beliefs in Darwinian evolution, the unexplained residual variance in these four critical items also correlates with self-reported liberalism to conservatism ($r = 0.23$, $p < 0.001$). It is important to note, however, that these relationships do not emerge with the index of political issues.

References

Anderson, K. G., Kaplan, H. & Lancaster, J. (1999). Paternal care by genetic fathers and stepfathers I: Reports from Albuquerque men. *Evolution and Human Behavior*, *20*, 405–431.

Archer, J. (2004). Sex differences in aggression in real-world settings: A meta-analytic review. *Review of General Psychology*, *8*, 291–322.

Baumeister, R.F. & Vohs, K. D. (2004). Sexual economics: Sex as female resource for social exchange in heterosexual interactions. *Personality and Social Psychology Review*, *8*, 339–363.

Berscheid, E. & Walster, E. (1974). Physical attractiveness. *Advances in Experimental Social Psychology*, *7*, 157–215.

Bloom, P. (2012). Religion, morality, evolution. *Annual Review of Psychology*, *63*, 179–199.

Buss, D. M. (1987). Sex differences in human mate selection criteria: An evolutionary perspective. In C. Crawford, D. Krebs & M. Smith (Eds.), *Sociobiology and psychology: Ideas, issues, and applications* (pp. 335–352). Hillsdale, NJ: Erlbaum.

Buss, D. M. (1989). Sex differences in human mate preferences: Evolutionary hypotheses tested in 37 cultures. *Behavioral and Brain Sciences*, *12*, 1–14.

Buss, D. M. (1995a). Evolutionary psychology: A new paradigm for psychological science. *Psychological Inquiry*, *6*, 1–30.

Buss, D. M. (1995b). Psychological sex differences: Origins through sexual selection. *American Psychologist*, *50*, 164–168.

Buss, D. M. (2005). *The murderer next door: Why the mind is designed to kill*. New York: Penguin.

Buss, D. M. (2006). The evolution of love. In R. J. Sternberg (Ed.), *The new psychology of love* (pp. 65–86). New Haven: Yale University Press.

Buss, D. M. (2015). *Evolutionary psychology: The new science of the mind*. Boston: Allyn & Bacon.

Buss, D. M. (Ed.) (2016). *The handbook of evolutionary psychology*, (Vol. 2: Integrations). Hoboken: John Wiley & Sons.

Buss, D. M. & Schmitt, D. P. (1993). Sexual strategies theory: An evolutionary perspective on human mating. *Psychological Review*, *100*, 204–232.

Confer, J. C., Easton, J. A., Fleischman, D. S., Goetz, C. D., Lewis, D. M., Perilloux, C. & Buss, D. M. (2010). Evolutionary psychology: Controversies, questions, prospects, and limitations. *American Psychologist*, *65*, 110–126.

Daly, M. & Wilson, M. (1988). *Homicide.* Livingston, NJ: Transaction Publishers.

Darwin, C. (1871). *The descent of man, and selection in relation to sex.* London: J. Murray.

Dawson, E., Savitsky, K. & Dunning, D. (2006). "Don't tell me, I don't want to know": Understanding people's reluctance to obtain medical diagnostic information. *Journal of Applied Social Psychology, 36,* 751–768.

de Waal, F. B. (2008). Putting the altruism back into altruism: The evolution of empathy. *Annual Review of Psychology, 59,* 279–300.

Durante, K. M., Rae, A. & Griskevicius, V. (2013). The fluctuating female vote: Politics, religion, and the ovulatory cycle. *Psychological Science, 24,* 1007–1016.

Gangestad, S. W. & Thornhill, R. (1998). Menstrual cycle variation in women's preferences for the scent of symmetrical men. *Proceedings of the Royal Society of London B: Biological Sciences, 265,* 927–933.

Haidt, J. (2011). "The bright future of post-partisan social psychology." Talk given at the annual meeting of the Society for Personality and Social Psychology. San Antonio, TX.

Halpern, D. F. (2012). *Sex differences in cognitive abilities* (4th ed.). New York: Psychology Press.

Hamilton, W. D. (1964). The genetical evolution of social behaviour. I, II. *Journal of Theoretical Biology, 7,* 1–52.

Harris, C. R., Chabot, A. & Mickes, L. (2014). Women can keep the vote: No evidence that hormonal changes during the menstrual cycle impact political and religious beliefs. *Psychological Science, 25,* 1147–1149.

Hoge, R. (2013). *Ugly: My memoir.* Sydney: Hachette Australia.

Inbar, Y. & Lammers, J. (2012). Political diversity in social and personality psychology. *Perspectives on Psychological Science, 7,* 496–503.

Legare, C. H., Lane, J. D. & Evans, E. M. (2013). Anthropomorphizing science: How does it affect the development of evolutionary concepts? *Merrill-Palmer Quarterly, 59,* 168–197.

Lerman, C., Croyle, R. T., Tercyak, K. P. & Hamann, H. (2002). Genetic testing: Psychological aspects and implications. *Journal of Consulting and Clinical Psychology, 70,* 784–797.

Lewis, D. M., Russell, E. M., Al-Shawaf, L. & Buss, D. M. (2015). Lumbar curvature: A previously undiscovered standard of attractiveness. *Evolution and Human Behavior, 36,* 345–350.

Lewis, D. M. G., Al-Shawaf, L., Conroy-Beam, D., Asao, K., & Buss, D. M. (2017). Evolutionary psychology: A how-to guide. *American Psychologist, 72,* 353–373.

Lyle III, H. F. & Smith, E. A. (2012). How conservative are evolutionary anthropologists? *Human Nature, 23,* 306–322.

Nowak, A., Gelfand, M. J., Borkowski, W., Cohen, D. & Hernandez, I. (2016). The evolutionary basis of honor cultures. *Psychological Science, 27*(1), 12–24.

Parker, G. A. (1979). Sexual selection and sexual conflict. In M. S. Blum & A. N. Blum (Eds.), *Sexual selection and reproductive competition among insects* (pp. 123–166). London: Academic Press.

Peshek, D., Semmaknejad, N., Hoffman, D. & Foley, P. (2011). Preliminary evidence that the limbal ring influences facial attractiveness. *Evolutionary Psychology, 9,* 147470491100900201.

Pinker, S. (2003). *The blank slate: The modern denial of human nature.* New York: Penguin.

Pinker, S. (2011). *The better angels of our nature: The decline of violence in history and its causes.* New York: Penguin.

Redding, R. E. (2001). Sociopolitical diversity in psychology: The case for pluralism. *American Psychologist, 56,* 205.

Ronay, R. & von Hippel, W. (2010). The presence of an attractive woman elevates testosterone and physical risk taking in young men. *Social Psychological and Personality Science, 1,* 57–64.

Rudman, L. A. & Fetterolf, J. C. (2015). Why sexual economics theory is patriarchal: Reply to Vohs and Baumeister's (2015) comment on Rudman and Fetterolf (2014). *Psychological Science, 26,* 1524–1525.

Schmitt, D. P. (2005). Sociosexuality from Argentina to Zimbabwe: A 48-nation study of sex, culture, and strategies of human mating. *Behavioral and Brain Sciences, 28,* 247–275.

Schmitt, D. P. (2015). Fundamentals of human mating strategies. In D. M. Buss (Ed.), *The handbook of evolutionary psychology.* Hoboken: John Wiley & Sons.

Singh, D. (1993). Adaptive significance of female physical attractiveness: Role of waist-to-hip ratio. *Journal of Personality and Social Psychology, 65*(2), 293.

Singh, D. (2004). Mating strategies of young women: Role of physical attractiveness. *Journal of Sex Research, 41,* 43–54.

Sugiyama, L. S. (2005). Physical Attractiveness: An adaptationist perspective. In D. M. Buss (Ed.), *The handbook of evolutionary psychology.* Hoboken: John Wiley & Sons.

Symons, D. (1979). *The evolution of human sexuality.* New York: Oxford University Press.

Thornhill, R. & Gangestad, S. W. (2008). *The evolutionary biology of human female sexuality.* Oxford: Oxford University Press.

Tooby, J. & Cosmides, L. (1990). The past explains the present: Emotional adaptations and the structure of ancestral environments. *Ethology and Sociobiology, 11,* 375–424.

Tooby, J. & Cosmides, L. (1992). Psychological foundations of culture. In J. Barkow, L. Cosmides & J. Tooby (Eds.), *The adapted mind: Evolutionary psychology and the generation of culture* (pp. 19–136). New York: Oxford University Press.

Tooby, J. & Cosmides, L. (1996). Friendship and the banker's paradox: Other pathways to the evolution of adaptations for altruism. In *Proceedings-British Academy* (Vol. 88, pp. 119–144). Oxford: Oxford University Press.

Trivers, R. L. (1971). The evolution of reciprocal altruism. *Quarterly Review of Biology, 46,* 35–57.

Tybur, J. M., Miller, G. F. & Gangestad, S. W. (2007). Testing the controversy: An empirical examination of adaptationists' attitudes toward politics and science. *Human Nature, 18,* 313–328.

Vohs, K. D. & Baumeister, R. F. (2015). Correcting some misrepresentations about gender and Sexual Economics Theory: Comment on Rudman and Fetteroff (2014). *Psychological Science, 26,* 1522–1523.

von Hippel, W. & Trivers, R. (2011). Reflections on self-deception. *Behavioral and Brain Sciences, 34,* 41–56.

Williams, G. C. (1975). *Sex and evolution* (No. 8). Princeton: Princeton University Press.

Wrangham, R. (2009). *Catching fire: How cooking made us human.* New York: Basic Books.

3

NORMS AND EXPLANATIONS IN SOCIAL AND POLITICAL PSYCHOLOGY

Mark J. Brandt and Anna Katarina Spälti

Explanation is a core part of science. Scientists observe patterns in nature and then explain why those patterns occur. Because individual scientists choose which patterns to explain and what explanations to test, it is important to understand what types of explanations scientists are most likely to gravitate toward and, by extension, what types of explanations scientists are most likely to miss (i.e., unidentified research opportunities). Prior work suggests that prevailing norms determine what we attempt to explain (Hegarty & Pratto, 2001; Kahneman & Miller, 1986; Miller, Taylor, & Buck, 1991), such that people often attempt to explain things that they see as non-normative. Our idea is that social psychologists are no different. The key issue that this chapter aims to raise is that the norms of social psychology influence the explanations social psychologists seek to test when they construct theories, construe research questions, and design studies.

The norms of social psychologists are relatively liberal, progressive, and left-wing (Duarte et al., 2015). Because people have a tendency to search for explanations for aberrant events, people, and groups, we would expect that theories in social psychology tend to focus on explaining people on the right side of the political spectrum rather than those on the left. This tendency can not only produce incomplete explanations for human behavior but may also affect how social psychologists and the general public perceive conservatives and the relative "neutrality" of our explanations. We build on research from sociology, psychology, and cultural studies to analyze the norms of social psychology and make predictions about what types of explanations social psychologists are likely to find, which types of explanations they are likely to miss, and how these hits and misses can affect the perception of social psychology.

Where Do Norms Come From?

People construct norms by retrieving past, salient information about events and stimuli from memory (Kahneman & Miller, 1986). A "normative" representation of the event or stimulus is then formed by compiling an aggregate of all the retrieved information. As such, "an abnormal event is one that has highly available alternatives whether retrieved or constructed; a normal event mainly evokes representations that resemble it" (Kahneman & Miller, 1986, p. 137). Similarly, people construct category or group norms by aggregating all the salient and relevant information about all the group members that come to mind. Thus, when we call a specific category to mind, for example, people from New Jersey, we retrieve salient information about people from New Jersey, and from this information, we construct a notion of what a "normal" person from New Jersey is.[1] Consequently, people considered different and non-representative of people from New Jersey differ from this aggregate.

A key piece of information for figuring out what is normative or which category memberships are perceived as normal is to figure out what information— be it events or category members—is likely to be salient. One possibility is that people who are viewed as normative are more likely to be visible in society. Members of majority and high-status social groups tend to occupy highly visible places in society. High-status groups (i.e., whites, men, middle-aged, etc.) make up disproportionate majorities of politicians (Arceneaux, 2001), people on television (Mastro & Stern, 2003), and people in films (Erigha, 2015). Thus, when constructing norms of what is normal in society, people are likely to draw on these sources of information. Consequently, high-status groups, including men (Bem, 1993; Eagly, Wood, & Diekman, 2000; Pratto, Sidanius, & Levin, 2006), heterosexual people (Hegarty & Pratto, 2001; Herek, 2000; Simoni & Walters, 2001), and whites (Bonilla-Silva, 1997; Branscombe, Schmitt, & Schiffhauer, 2007; McIntosch, 1988), all seem to represent norms in (American) society. Furthermore, these high-status groups are often attributed culturally valued characteristics. In one recent study, Cuddy, Wolf, Glick, Crotty, Chong, and Norton (2015) found that people believe men (i.e., the high-status group) to be more individualistic than women (i.e., the low-status group) in cultures that score high on individualism. However, in cultures that score high on collectivism, people believe men are more collectivistic than women. Majority and high-status groups are therefore more likely to be perceived as the norm and as having normative characteristics in a society.

People can also draw on other sources of information to construct norms. Social sampling posits that when people make judgments about a population, they infer this information from a small sample of people in their environment: their social circle (Fiedler, 2000; Galesic, Olsson, & Rieskamp, 2012; Pachur, Rieskamp, & Hertwig, 2005). Social sampling may result from direct conversations about people's attitudes and beliefs, but it can also be inferred from other sources, such as people's behaviors (e.g., Paluck & Shepherd, 2012, Prentice & Miller, 1996). A quote commonly misattributed to the late film critic Pauline Kael is a good example of social sampling: "I don't know how Richard Nixon could have won. I don't know anybody who voted for him."[2] Similarly, when asked to make judgments about the average income of people in the U.S., people's estimations were influenced by the perceived average income of the people in their social circle (Dawtry, Sutton, & Sibley, 2015). Similarly, when highly connected people hold a particular attitude, even if they are the minority (Lerman, Yan & Wu, 2015), it becomes more visible to the social network as a whole, resulting in its spread (Paluck, Shepherd, & Aronow, 2016). As such, characteristics and group memberships overrepresented in a social circle might be perceived as more normative within the population as a whole than is warranted by a more representative sample.

The makeup of our social networks and information that makes particular people salient can cause misconceptions about what is normative in a population. For example, if the people from New Jersey in our social network are primarily highly accomplished university professors,[3] in our construction of the "people from New Jersey norm," we will likely draw on these salient examples resulting in a norm that assumes that people from New Jersey are very accomplished and perhaps even professors. If these university professors were also particularly well connected, this would lead to the widespread norm that people from New Jersey are quite accomplished. Although we do not want to insult the people of New Jersey, we suspect that this proposed norm of people from New Jersey as accomplished university professors is not widespread. If people draw other norms from visible examples of people from New Jersey, such as current politicians like Chris Christie and Cory Booker, formerly popular television shows like *Jersey Shore* or *The Sopranos*, or instances when New Jersey is discussed in the news, then the constructed norm for people from New Jersey will likely be different.

What Are the Norms of Social Psychology?

Our discussion of the source of norms can be applied to social and political psychology.[4] Social psychologists are affected by the same sources of information as the participants in the studies summarized above when they construct their norms of people and their social environments. That is, by consulting representations in society overall (i.e., the media) and the attitudes and behaviors of their social networks, social psychologists construct their ideas of what is normative.

There is no data, to our knowledge, on the social networks of social psychologists, but it is possible to make reasonable predictions. People are more likely to associate with and include in their social networks people who are similar to themselves on a number of dimensions, including race/ethnicity, education, age, religion, and politics (McPherson, Smith-Lovin, & Cook, 2011). Political similarity is one of the most robust traits that predicts affiliation (Alford, Hatemi, Hibbing, Martin, & Eaves, 2011). Social psychologists, like other academics in the social sciences and humanities (Duarte et al., 2015), tend to be politically liberal, especially when it comes to social issues, but also on economic and foreign policy issues (Inbar & Lammers, 2012). Based on this evidence, one would predict that social psychologists are more likely to have social networks, including partners, friends, and colleagues, that are politically liberal.[5,6] The political attitudes and behaviors of people in their social networks will influence their idea of what is normative politically. When large majorities of our colleagues are political and socially liberal, this is likely taken as the normal political position.

Social psychologists may also develop liberal norms from their observations of broader society. People tend to tune into media that confirms their prior held beliefs, including political beliefs (Burke, 2008). This tendency to consume attitude-consistent media likely reinforces the social network effects hypothesized above. Furthermore, the media may also present an ideological bias. Researchers who examine media bias often find that liberal points of view are more likely to be represented (Groseclose & Milyo, 2005). This research has its critics with some studies refuting the idea of a liberal media bias altogether (D'Alessio & Allen, 2006). Even assuming no media bias, if people tune into attitude-consistent media, then it is very likely that social psychologists' exposure to broader society via the media will also lead social psychologists to construct liberal norms.

People having skewed norms about the population at large is not necessarily a bad thing. Most people probably do, and those norms are likely functional for navigating their immediate social environments. However, the scientific task of social and political psychologists is to understand people's social and political worlds. If the norms that researchers intuitively construct are skewed toward liberalism, it suggests that psychologists' intuitive understanding of people may be slightly askew as well. Psychologists, however, do not rely on an intuitive understanding of people. They conduct careful experiments, surveys, and archival studies to test their hypotheses about human behavior, and these studies constrain their reasoning about people. From this perspective, the skewed norms of social and political psychologists are not a problem.

Explanation as a Consequence of Norms

Although the methodological rigor of social and political psychologists may not be affected by a liberal skew, the questions we ask and, consequently, the explanations we seek may be affected by the belief that political liberalism is normative. Norms have consequences for the explanations we test and use to explain phenomena. There is a pervasive tendency for people to take the norm for granted (Bem, 1993; McIntosch, 1988) and to seek explanations for things that are non-normative (Hegarty & Pratto, 2001; Kahneman & Miller, 1986). If the norm is that people from New Jersey are professors, then people from New Jersey who hold other professions need explanation. If liberal social and political attitudes are the norm, then conservative social and political attitudes are non-normative attitudes that need explanation. A number of research literatures report evidence for people's tendency to explain the non-normative.

Based on careful observation and keen insight into the experience of gender, Bem (1993) suggested that people take the normative category (i.e., men) for granted, which shifts the focus to explaining the non-normative category (i.e., women). The norm (i.e., men), and all things similar to it, becomes the reference point from which all things "other" (i.e., women) are judged. Empirical work backs up this claim. Miller and colleagues (1991) found that people picture the typical voter as a man (i.e., the norm), and consequently, when they explain gender gaps in voting, they are more likely to generate potential explanations for female voting preferences rather than the reverse. In other situations, where women are the norm (i.e., primary school teachers), people generate more possible explanations for the behavior of men. The effects of norms go beyond gender, as people are more likely to provide explanations for gay men (i.e., non-normative category) compared to straight men (i.e., normative category; Hegarty & Pratto, 2001).

These empirical findings are consistent with norm theory (Kahneman & Miller, 1986), which predicts that abnormal stimuli or categories evoke the feeling of surprise when it becomes clear that they differ significantly from the norm. This surprise highlights the failure to make sense of an experience and prompts people to be vigilant and search for an explanation (Anderson, Krull, & Weiner, 1996; Heine, Proulx, & Vohs, 2006; Mendes, Blascovich, Hunter, Lickel, & Jost, 2007). Because normal events do not evoke surprise, there is no need to question them or search for an explanation.

Explanations in Social and Political Psychology

We expect that the relatively liberal, progressive, and left-wing norms of social psychology (Duarte et al., 2015) influence the explanations social psychologists seek to test. Just like people tend to search for explanations for aberrations in their environment, we expect social psychological theories to do the same and to therefore focus on explaining people on the right side of the political spectrum rather than those on the left (see also Lilienfeld, 2015). That is, social psychology tries to explain groups outside of social psychology's norms. To illustrate this idea, we focus on several broad theoretical perspectives. The goal is not to highlight every possible theoretical perspective or each empirical study but rather to capture the representative gist of the perspectives and the explanations of human behavior they employ. The goal is also not to single out these theories. In many cases, these theories are successful and generative. They have helped guide our own research, and the studies present interesting and insightful data. We aspire to such influence in our own work. However, we also believe that it is possible to ask better questions that will help us develop a broader understanding of social and political psychology.

Explaining Conservatism

As a first example, we turn to theories that aim to understand political belief systems, in particular, conservatism and other traditional belief systems (e.g., right-wing authoritarianism, religious fundamentalism). Many models and theories are constructed to explain the adoption of conservative, right-wing, and traditional beliefs rather than liberal, left-wing, and progressive beliefs. Theories about the psychological underpinnings of political ideology represent some of the earliest work in political psychology (Adorno, Frenkel-Brunswik, Levinson, & Sanford, 1950) and have been some of the most successful exports of political psychology to psychology, political science, and the broader media landscape. These theories typically posit that some psychological trait or state leads people to adopt conservative and right-wing political beliefs.

For example, the motivated social cognition model (Jost, Glaser, Kruglanski, & Sulloway, 2003) and its extension, the threat-uncertainty model (Jost et al., 2007) test how epistemic (e.g., uncertainty) and existential (e.g., death) threats are associated with conservative political views. The theories suggest—and the meta-analysis confirms (Jost et al., 2003)—that people adopt conservative views as a method for fulfilling these epistemic and existential needs. The focus of these papers and the research following from them is almost entirely concerned with why people adopt conservative political views and the motivations that conservatism serves (for a highly similar account, see Hibbing, Smith, & Alford, 2015).

Other work in political psychology tries to understand the basis of authoritarianism and, in particular, right-wing authoritarianism (Adorno et al., 1950; Altemeyer, 1981, 1988, 1996; Stenner, 2005). With thousands of empirical studies on the causes and consequences of right-wing authoritarianism, it is one of the most popular topics in political psychology. For example, Altemeyer's original trio of books on the topic have each been cited more than 1,700 times.[7] One of the biggest controversies in authoritarianism research is the best way to measure authoritarianism, with scales being developed and redeveloped over the last 60 years. In the last ten years, there have been at least five different published measures of authoritarianism. This highlights the intense interest political psychologists have in understanding right-wing authoritarianism, but by omission it also highlights psychologists' disinterest in understanding authoritarianism's converse: freedom and autonomy (i.e., liberal values).[8]

Perhaps the focus on conservatives and authoritarians compared to liberals can be seen most clearly in the title of the 2003 paper that reads, "Conservatism as motivated social cognition" (Jost et al., 2003). In many ways, this title works. It is memorable (we did not need to look it up to quote it here), short, and to the point. Moreover, the data in the meta-analysis are consistent with the hypothesis that conservatism is motivated social cognition, and similar findings have been conceptually replicated in empirical studies (e.g., Matthews, Levin, & Sidanius, 2009) and in additional meta-analyses (e.g., Onraet, Van Hiel, Dhont, & Pattyn, 2013; Sibley & Duckitt, 2008; Sibley, Osborne, & Duckitt, 2012). This is largely a win. However, the title implies that liberalism—or any other, non-conservative ideology—is not the result of motivated social cognition (or, at least, might not be the result). However, the data do not support this inference. Many measures of ideology in the meta-analysis are bipolar measures with liberals at one end and conservatives at the other. Similarly, many of the measures of motivated social cognitive are bipolar and contrast one motivation (e.g., need for closure) with another (e.g., need to avoid closure). A positive correlation is consistent with the hypothesis that conservatism is motivated, that liberalism is motivated, or that both ends of the liberal/conservative continuum (and possibly those places in the middle) are motivated. The key difference, of course, is the type of motivation.[9]

Mapping the motivations that drive diverse ideological beliefs is an important research activity for a full psychological understanding of ideology. It helps scholars understand why some people feel a pull for conservative ideas and other people a pull for liberal ideas. However, by framing conservatism as the ideology that needs explanation, research has largely ignored the motivations that underlie liberalism, libertarianism, and other ideologies. This leads to a relatively impoverished understanding of the diversity of ideological beliefs and has the possibility of creating the perception that conservatism is motivated whereas these other ideological beliefs are not.

There are exceptions to the tendency for psychologists to explain conservatism. These studies represent important steps for a fuller understanding of political ideology. One example is work that distinguishes between conservatism and liberalism and measures each ideology with its own scale (Choma, Hafer, Dywan, Segalowitz, & Busseri, 2012, see also Choma, Busseri, & Sadava, 2009). These studies find, by measuring each ideology individually, that these are two different belief systems rather than mirror images of each other and that different values and motivations correlate with each belief system. Other studies (van der Toorn, Napier, & Dovidio, 2014) have experimentally tested how intergroup interdependence leads to greater political liberalism. There are other examples scattered throughout the literature, such as work on incidental disgust and left-wing economic attitudes (Petrescu & Parkinson, 2014), threats to personal control and support for a controlling government (Kay, Gaucher, Napier, Callan, & Laurin, 2008), and the diversity of associations between personality, motivations, and political ideology across political domains and countries (Malka, Soto, Inzlicht, & Lelkes, 2014). Combined, these studies highlight that a psychological and motivational understanding of ideology requires a psychological understanding beyond conservatism. The successful theories of ideology in the future will be able to incorporate these types of results to understand and explain the psychology of a diversity of ideologies.

Explaining Conservatives

Just as psychologists construct theories to explain why people adopt conservatism, theories in social and political psychology often aim to explain the actions of conservatives. This might include why conservatives oppose affirmative-action policies (e.g., Reyna, Henry, Korfmacher, & Tucker, 2005), oppose help for people facing foreclosure (e.g., Brandt, 2013), and oppose government help for the poor (e.g., Weiner, Osborne, & Rudolph, 2011). These questions are important for understanding the psychology of real-world political issues and are valuable contributions to the literature, but so too would be research programs devoted to understanding why liberals support affirmative-action policies, foreclosure aid, and helping the poor that (in some cases) go against their own self-interest. Because social psychologists do not typically ask these questions, we do not have a much better answer than "liberals have opposite values of conservatives." This is incomplete.

A version of this issue ties in closely to our own work, namely, the tendency for social and political psychologists to explain why conservatives express prejudice. There is a long line of research testing and probing the correlation between conservativism and prejudice. Some of the founders of social psychology, such as Gordon Allport, were interested in this correlation over 85 years ago (Allport, 1929). Since then, a number of research programs have explored this relationship, from work on authoritarianism (Adorno et al., 1950; Altemeyer, 1996) to work on symbolic racism (Sears & Henry, 2003), social dominance (Sidanius & Pratto, 2001) and more. Social psychologists have delineated the motivational, personality, and cognitive components that make up conservatives' prejudices (for reviews, see Dhont & Hodson, 2014; Roets & Van Hiel, 2011; Sibley & Duckitt, 2008) and have accrued substantial knowledge in this domain.

For example, we know that the need for closure (and related cognitive styles; Roets & Van Hiel, 2011), (low) openness to experience (Sibley & Duckitt, 2008), (low) cognitive ability (Dhont & Hodson, 2014), perceptions of a dangerous world (Duckitt, Wagner, du Plessis, & Birum, 2002), and perceived competitiveness (Duckitt et al., 2002) all play a role in the prejudices of conservatives. We also know that some forms of conservative political ideology, such as right-wing authoritarianism, are related to prejudice toward groups who threaten societal norms and that other forms of conservative political ideology, such as social dominance orientation, are related to prejudice toward groups who are low status and competitive over resources (Duckitt, 2006; Duckitt & Sibley, 2007). A meta-analysis suggests that the association between ideology and prejudice ranges between $r = 0.46$ and $r = 0.58$ depending on the measure of ideology or prejudice used (Sibley & Duckitt, 2008). These findings are important and highlight consistent and replicable effects.

This line of research on the relationship of political ideology suggests that conservatives are more prejudiced than liberals because of the variety of motivational, personality, and cognitive differences between conservatives and liberals, described above, that predispose conservatives to express prejudice. The picture painted by the wealth of knowledge on conservatives' prejudices overshadows our knowledge of liberals' prejudices. Until 2012, virtually no papers carefully examined the groups or situations where liberals might show more prejudice compared to conservatives (for an exception, see Murno, Lasane, & Leary, 2010). That is, social and political psychologists did not ask when and why liberals might be prejudiced or if they might even be more prejudiced than conservatives in some situations.

After 2012, several groups began working on exactly this sort of question. In short, these groups find that liberals and conservatives both show approximately equal levels of prejudice toward groups they disagree with (for an initial review, see Brandt, Reyna, Chambers, Crawford, & Wetherell, 2014; for another deep dive, see Crawford, Chapter 7, this volume). The results are consistent across student (Chambers, Schlenker, & Collisson, 2013; Wetherell, Brandt, & Reyna, 2013), community (Crawford, 2014; Crawford & Pilanski, 2014; Wetherell et al., 2013), and representative samples (Chambers et al., 2013; Iyengar & Westwood, 2015) of participants. They also replicate using implicit (Iyengar & Westwood, 2015), explicit (Chambers et al., 2013; Crawford, 2014; Crawford & Pilanksi, 2014; Wetherell et al., 2013), and behavioral (Gift & Gift, 2015; Iyengar & Westwood, 2015) measures of prejudice. Studies focusing on mediators of these associations find that symbolic or value-based threats are typically the most robust, but rights threats (i.e., intolerance of intolerance) and more realistic threats can also play a role (Crawford, 2014; Wetherell et al., 2013). This work is very consistent overall in showing that people are prejudiced toward dissimilar others (i.e., Byrne, 1969), and that this is the case for both liberal and conservative participants (for similar findings in the domain of religious fundamentalism, see Brandt & van Tongeren, 2017).

Because social and political psychology has primarily tried to explain the prejudices of conservatives, it has missed instances where liberals show prejudices in equal force. This is problematic because it makes it difficult to tease apart what effects of ideological differences in prejudice are due to cognitive and motivational processes of conservatives, what effects represent the same general mechanism across both liberals and conservatives, and what conditions are most likely to elicit prejudice from conservatives or from liberals. These are important questions for a complete understanding of ideology, prejudice, and belief systems broadly. These questions are missed when the focus is on explaining conservatives.

Lest we think that this problem is unique to the prejudice side of the literature, it is important to highlight that similar dynamics have played out in research on attributions and ideology. Much of this work finds that conservatives are more likely to make internal attributions (e.g., Brandt, 2013; Reyna et al., 2005; Zucker & Weiner, 1993; for a review, see Weiner et al., 2011), presumably because conservatives put an emphasis on personal responsibility. The bulk of this work focuses on explaining why conservatives make punitive attributions. However, an equally interesting question is why liberals are not particularly punitive. Is it because they are making thoughtful moral judgments or because they are reflexively following their ideological beliefs (it's likely the latter; see Skitka & Tetlock, 1993)? Similarly, one could ask whether there are situations when liberals make more internal attributions than conservatives do. The answer is yes, because both liberals and conservatives make internal attributions for the bad actions of people they do not value (Morgan, Mullen, & Skitka, 2010). For example, liberals make more internal attributions for bad actions of people in the military than do conservatives. Notably, these counter-examples to research that focuses on why conservatives make more attributions that are punitive primarily come from one lab group. If more researchers focused on this sort of question, we could have as rich of an understanding of liberals' attributions as we do of conservatives'.

Perceptual Consequences of Norms and Explanations

Social psychology's norms, and the explanations they elicit, affect the completeness of social psychology's theories of human behavior. To us, this is enough of a consequence to be taken seriously by researchers motivated by theoretical rigor. However, there is another likely consequence of social psychology's tendency to explain conservatism and the behavior of conservatives: It can affect people's perceptions of conservatives and of the explanations and underlying assumptions of social psychologists. Norms affect explanations, but explanations can also affect norms. Explanations have a type of conversational logic to them (Blanton & Christie, 2003). We explain only the things that need explanation. When a person explains something, it conveys to the audience that it was in need of explanation. If people associate explanations with non-normative behaviors or people, then the mere focus of explaining conservatives would convey that conservatives are a non-normative group. Consistent with this idea, when a persuasion campaign explains why condom use is smart, people think low levels of condom use is the norm, but when the campaign explains why not using a condom is irresponsible, then people think condom use is the norm.

Social psychology's explanations of conservatives then might have the external effect of conveying to both other researchers and people outside of the field that conservatives are not the norm and are not "one of us." This is a problem. It will perpetuate the tendency for researchers to explain conservatives as a non-normative group, turn off potentially talented students who detect biases via explanations, and further the stereotype that our field primarily produces politically biased findings and is not worthy of taxpayer funding (see, e.g., attempts to defund political science research at the National Science Foundation, Ferenstein, 2013). The effects of different but potentially equivalent explanations on people's perceptions of social psychology deserve study. How does "conservatism as motivated social cognition" compare to "liberalism as motivated social cognition" or "political beliefs as motivated social cognition?"

Solutions

We've suggested that the norms of social and political psychology (unintentionally) constrain the questions we ask and the explanations we seek. To avoid this problem, we offer three suggestions.

1   Understand what our own norms are so that we do not take them for granted. Seek out people, situations, and information sources with different norms and solicit their intuitions on psychological questions. It is easy to operate within our own social and work groups with norms that we know and are familiar with; however, we do not need to limit ourselves to our own norms. Consulting websites, discussion forums, newspapers, Twitter feeds, and people with diverse ideological beliefs, from conservatism to libertarianism, communism, and beyond, will help bump us out of our normative rut.

2   Explicitly ask our collaborators, our lab mates, and ourselves why the normative group performs the behavior or expresses the attitudes. Studies of norms demonstrate that explicitly asking people to consider explanations for the normative group increases explanations for these groups (Hegarty & Pratto, 2001). In other words, rather than just ask, "why do conservatives support X?," also ask, "why do liberals oppose X?" A broader version of this approach (for ideology-related questions) requires that researchers identify a list of belief systems held in the population of interest and then identify explanations across those belief systems. Some explanations may be similar across belief systems, suggesting general processes, whereas other explanations might be unique to particular beliefs systems, suggesting the psychological uniqueness of some belief systems.

3   Look for conditions where a typical finding can reverse. The perspectivist approach to psychological research that many social psychologists encounter in their graduate training suggests that the opposite of a great truth is also true (McGuire, 1973). Purposefully searching for the conditions where the opposite is also true leads to creative questions and answers that are

not possible when only considering the norms. For example, conservatives tend to report higher levels of need for closure (Jost et al., 2003). Under what conditions do liberals report higher levels of need for closure?

We integrated solutions #2 and #3 into a perspectivist grid in Table 3.1 (cf., McGuire, 1983). For any research question on ideologically related behavior, a research team can generate and test multiple explanations for multiple belief systems. Then, the research team can generate and test multiple situations that could reverse the typical effect, followed by the generation and testing of multiple explanations for the reversal. In total, our three suggestions do not guarantee that we won't be affected by the norms that surround us; however, they should help reduce the pervasive influence of norms

TABLE 3.1 A Perspectivist Grid for Generating Hypotheses and Explanations for Multiple Belief Systems

	Step 1: Generate multiple possible explanations for multiple possible belief systems.	Step 2: Generate possible situations where the relationship could reverse.	Step 3: Generate multiple reasons why the relationship could reverse.
Example Questions	Why might people with these beliefs _____? (e.g., support/oppose a policy, have a particular motivation, etc.)	When do they do the opposite?	Why do they do the opposite?
Liberals			
Conservatives			
Feminists			
Tea Party Supporters			
Libertarians			
Socialists			
Black Lives Matter Supporters			
Atheists			
Christian Fundamentalists			
Catholics			
Muslims			
Buddhists			
Hindus			
Etc.			

on explanations by prompting researchers to consider different explanations and different norms (for a helpful methodological checklist, see Washburn, Morgan, & Skitka, 2015).

Of course, these solutions may provide solutions only to a problem psychologists are not incentivized to solve. Part of the reason people generate explanations for non-normative behaviors and people is that these explanations are surprising and more interesting; they are explanations for things that attract our attention. By implication, generating explanations for normative behavior and groups is unlikely to spark the imagination of reviewers and editors, which may make it less likely for reviewers and editors to accept a paper studying liberals and their behavior. For example, political and social psychologists have written a lot on how conservatives are prejudiced; however, we expect that explaining the reverse, why liberals are tolerant, would not attract the same type of attention from journal editors and the media. Similarly, researchers have examined whether conservatives are more sensitive to threat. The framing suggests that this is an abnormal type of behavior and that an optimal level of functioning would be to be less sensitive to threat. However, the enterprising researcher could use the same data to examine whether liberals are less sensitive to threat. Given the dynamics discussed above, this alternative framing implies that liberals should be *more* sensitive to threat, but we suspect that this framing would not have the same publication potential. Our hope is that our suggestions in this paragraph are wrong.

Conclusion

Norms affect the explanations people seek, and social and political psychology's norms are no different. Researchers need to question their norms to build a more complete picture of humans' social and political world. A reader might see our description of the field as a (yet another) critique of social psychology, but we think this would be a mistake. Just as the field has amassed substantial data and developed refined theories on the psychology of conservatives, the field can also amass data and develop refined theories on the psychology of liberals, libertarians, and any other belief system. By questioning our own personal norms and the theoretical norms in the field, researchers can prompt new investigations that test new explanations that current norms miss. The current chapter, rather than being a negative critique of the field, is a call to action to test these unexplored explanations with new, rigorous, and generative lines of research.

Acknowledgments

Hart Blanton provided helpful comments on this chapter.

Notes

1 In this example, the norm is also similar to a stereotype, but this does not always need to be the case.
2 This version of the quote paints Kael as insular; however, the real quote in context highlights her awareness of her limited social circle: "I live in a rather special world. I only know one person who voted for Nixon. Where they are I don't know. They're outside my ken. But sometimes when I'm in a theater I can feel them."
3 Such as the editors of this book.
4 It is possible to extend this analysis to other similar disciplines; we refrain from that here because social and political psychology are our home disciplines.
5 Based on other demographic characteristics of social psychologists, we might also predict that their social networks are overwhelmingly white, for example. Another chapter could be written about how this influences the norms and explanations of social psychologists. We hope this issue is also taken seriously.
6 We use *liberal* here as a convenient shorthand but urge readers to assume a broader definition of *liberal* that includes not only the American liberal but also progressive and left-wing politics in general. Similarly, we use *conservative* to mean not only the American conservative but also tradition-minded and right-wing politics in general.
7 Data from Google Scholar, last checked December 16, 2015.
8 This example highlights another unexamined norm in social psychology: Freedom and autonomy are the norm in Western democracies, which could also explain why social psychologists generally seek to understand authoritarianism, obedience, and conformity rather than freedom and autonomy.
9 Interestingly, theorists, including the primary proponent of the conservatism as motivated social cognition approach, have pointed out that liberalism may be motivated, too, but by motivations for curiosity, openness, and system challenge (e.g., Jost, Federico, & Napier, 2013). However, this has not clearly translated into research or the focus of explanation.

References

Adorno, T., Frenkel-Brunswik, E., Levinson, D. & Sanford, R. (1950). *The authoritarian personality.* Oxford: Harpers.

Alford, J., Hatemi, P., Hibbing, J., Martin, N. & Eaves, L. (2011). The politics of mate choice. *The Journal of Politics, 73*(2), 362–379. doi: 10.1017/S0022381611000016.

Allport, G. (1929). The composition of political attitudes. *American Journal of Sociology, 35*(2), 220–238.

Altemeyer, B. (1981). *Right-wing authoritarianism.* Winnipeg: University of Manitoba Press.

Altemeyer, B. (1988). *Enemies of freedom: Understanding right-wing authoritariansim.* San Fransisco: Jossey-Bass.

Altemeyer, B. (1996). *The authoritarian specter.* Cambridge: Harvard University Press.

Anderson, C., Krull, D. & Weiner, B. (1996). Explanations: Processes and consequences. In E. Higgins & A. Kruglanski (Eds.), *Social psychology: Handbook of basic pricinples* (pp. 271–296). New York: Guilford.

Arceneaux, K. (2001). The "gender gap" in state legislative representation: New data to tackle an old question. *Political Research Quarterly, 54*(1), 143–160. doi: 10.1177/106591290105400108.

Bem, S. (1993). *The lenses of gender: Transforming the debate on sexual inequaltiy*. New Haven: Yale University Press.

Blanton, H. & Christie, C. (2003). Deviance regulation: A theory of identity and action. *Review of General Psychology*, 7(2), 115–149.

Bonilla-Silva, E. (1997). Rethinking racism: Toward a structural interpretation. *American Sociological Review, 62*(3), 465–480.

Brandt, M. (2013). Onset and offset deservingness: The case of home foreclosure. *Political Psychology, 34*(2), 221–238.

Brandt, M. & van Tongeren, D. (2017). People both high and low on religious fundamentalism are prejudiced towards dissimilar groups. *Journal of Personality and Social Psychology, 112*, 76–97.

Brandt, M., Reyna, C., Chambers, J., Crawford, J. & Wetherell, G. (2014). The ideological-conflict hypothesis: Intolerance among both liberals and conservatives. *Psychological Science, 23*(1), 27–34. doi: 10.1177/0963721413510932.

Branscombe, N., Schmitt, M. & Schiffhauer, K. (2007). Racial attitudes in response to thoughts of white privilege. *European Journal of Social Psychology, 37*, 203–2015. doi: 10.1002/ejsp.348.

Burke, J. (2008). Primetime spin: Media bias and belief confirming information. *Journal of Economics and Management Strategy, 17*(3), 633–665. doi: 10.1111/j.1530-9134.2008.00189.x.

Byrne, D. (1969). Attitudes and attraction. *Advances in Experimental Social Psychology, 4*, 35–89.

Chambers, J. R., Schlenker, B. R. & Collisson, B. (2013). Ideology and prejudice: The role of value conflicts. *Psychological Science, 24*(2), 140–149.

Choma, B., Busseri, M. & Sadava, S. (2009). Liberal and conservative political ideologies: Different routes to happiness? *Journal of Research in Personality, 43*(3), 502–505.

Choma, B., Hafer, C., Dywan, J., Segalowitz, S. & Busseri, M. (2012). Political liberalism and political conservatism: Functionally independent? *Personality and Individual Differences, 53*(4), 431–436.

Crawford, J. (2014). Ideological symmetries and asymmetries in political intolerance and prejudice toward political activist groups. *Journal of Experimental Social Psychology, 55*, 284–298.

Crawford, J. & Pilanski, J. (2014). Political intolerance, right and left. *Political Psychology, 35*(6), 841–851.

Cuddy, A., Wolf, E., Glick, P., Crotty, S., Chong, J. & Norton, M. (2015). Men as cultural ideals: Cultural values moderate gender stereotype content. *Journal of Personality and Social Psychology, 109*(4), 622–635.

D'Alessio, D. & Allen, M. (2006). Media bias in presidential elections: A meta-analysis. *Journal of Communication, 50*(4), 133–156. doi: 10.1111/j.1460-2466.2000.tb02866.x.

Dawtry, R., Sutton, R. & Sibley, C. (2015). Why wealthier people think people are wealthier, and why it matters: From social sampling to attiudes to redistribution. *Psychological Science, 26*(9), 1389–1400. doi: 10.1177/0956797615586560.

Dhont, K. & Hodson, G. (2014). Does lower cognitive ability predict greater prejudice? *Current Directions in Psychological Science, 23*(6), 455–459.

Duarte, J., Crawford, J., Stern, C., Haidt, J., Jussim, L. & Tetlock, P. (2015). Political diversity will improve social psychological science. *Behavioral and Brain Sciences, 38*, 1–58, e130. doi: 10.1017/S0140525X14000430.

Duckitt, J. (2006). Differential effects of right wing authoritarianism and social dominance orientation on outgroup attitudes and their mediation by threat from and competitiveness to outgroups. *Personality and Social Psychology Bulletin, 32*(5), 684–696.

Duckitt, J. & Sibley, C. (2007). Right wing authoritariansim, social dominance orientation and the dimensions of generalized prejudice. *European Journal of Personality, 21*(2), 113–130.

Duckitt, J. & Sibley, C. (2009). A dual-process motivational model of ideology, politics, and prejudice. *Psychological Inquiry, 20*(2–3), 98–109.

Duckitt, J., Wagner, C., du Plessis, I. & Birum, I. (2002). The psychological bases of ideology and prejudice: Testing a dual process model. *Journal of Personality and Social Psychology, 83*(1), 75–93.

Eagly, A., Wood, W. & Diekman, A. (2000). Social role theory of sex differences and similarities: A current appraisal. In T. Eckes & H. Trautner (Eds.), *The developmental social psychology of gender.* Mahwah: Erlbaum.

Erigha, M. (2015). Race, gender, Hollywood: Representation in cultural production and digital media's potential for change. *Sociology Compass, 9*(1), 78–89. doi: 10.1111/soc4.12237.

Ferenstein, G. (2013, February 12). Former political scientist to congress: Please defund political science. *The Atlantic.* Retrieved from: https://web.archive.org/web/20160410213323/http://www.theatlantic.com/politics/archive/2013/02/former-political-scientist-to-congress-please-defund-political-science/273060/.

Fiedler, K. (2000). Beware of samples: A cognitive-ecological sampling approach to judgement biases. *Psychological Review, 107*(4), 659–676. doi: 10.1037//0033-295X.107A659.

Galesic, M., Olsson, H. & Rieskamp, J. (2012). Social sampling explains apparent biases in judgments of social environments. *Psychological Science, 23*, 1515–1523.

Gift, K. & Gift, T. (2015). Does politics influence hiring? Evidence from a randomized experiment. *Political Behavior, 37*(3), 653–675.

Groseclose, T. & Milyo, J. (2005). A measure of media bias. *The Quarterly Journal of Economics, 120*(4), 1191–1237. Retrieved from: www.jstor.org/stable/25098770.

Hegarty, P. & Pratto, F. (2001). The effects of social category norms and stereotypes on explanations for intergroup differences. *Journal of Personality and Social Psychology, 80*(5), 723–735.

Heine, S., Proulx, T. & Vohs, K. (2006). The meaning maintenance model: On the coherence of social motivations. *Personality and Social Psychology Review, 10*(2), 88–110.

Herek, G. (2000). The psychology of sexual prejudice. *Current Directions in Psychological Science, 9*(1), 19–22.

Hibbing, J., Smith, K. & Alford, J. (2015). Liberals and conservatives: Non-convertible currencies. *Behavioral and Brain Sciences, 38*, e145.

Inbar, Y. & Lammers, J. (2012). Political diversity in social and personality psychology. *Perspectives on Psychological Science, 7*(5), 496–503.

Iyengar, S. & Westwood, S. (2015). Fear and loathing across party lines: New evidence on group polariyation. *American Journal of Political Science, 59*(3), 690–707.

Jost, J., Federico, C. & Napier, J. (2013). Political ideologies and their social psychological functions. In M. Freeden (Ed.), *Oxford Handbook of Political Ideologies* (pp. 232–250). New York: Oxford University Press.

Jost, J., Glaser, J., Kruglanski, A. & Sulloway, F. (2003). Political conservatism as motivated social cognition. *Psychological Bulletin, 129*(3), 339–375.

Jost, J., Napier, J., Thorisdottir, H., Gosling, S., Palfai, T. & Ostafin, B. (2007). Are needs to manage uncertainty and threat associated with political conservatism or ideological extremity? *Personaltiy and Social Psychology Bulletin, 33*(7), 989–1007.

Kahneman, D. & Miller, D. (1986). Norm theory: Comparing reality to its alternatives. *Psychological Review, 93*(2), 136–153.

Kay, A., Gaucher, D., Napier, J., Callan, M. & Laurin, K. (2008). God and the government: Testing a compensatory control mechanism for the support of external systems. *Journal of Personality and Social Psychology, 95*(1), 18–35.

Lerman, K., Yan, X. & Wu, X. (2015). The majority illusion in social networks. *arXiv*, 1–10. arXiv:1506.03022.

Lilienfeld, S. (2015). Lack of political diversity and the framing of findings in personality and clinical psychology. *Behavioral and Brain Sciences, 38*, 31–32.

Malka, A., Soto, C., Inzlicht, M. & Lelkes, Y. (2014). Do needs for security and certainty predict cultural and economic conservatism? A cross-national analysis. *Journal of Personality and Social Psychology, 106*(6), 1031–1051.

Mastro, D. & Stern, S. (2003). Representations of race in television commercials: A content analysis of prime-time advertising. *Journal of Broadcasting and Electronic Media, 47*(4), 638–647. doi: 10.1207/s15506878jobem4704_9.

Matthews, M., Levin, S. & Sidanius, J. (2009). A longitudinal test of the model of political conservatism as motivated social cognition. *Political Psychology, 30*(6), 921–936.

McGuire, W. (1973). The yin and yang of progress in social psychology. *Journal of Personality and Social Psychology, 26*(3), 446–456.

McGuire, W. (1983). A contextualist theory of knowledge: Its implications for innovation and reform in psychological research. *Advances in Experimental Social Psychology, 16*, 1–47.

McIntosch, P. (1988). *White privilege and male privilege: A personal account of coming to see.* Working Paper Wellesley Center for Women Publications, no. 189.

McPherson, M., Smith-Lovin, L. & Cook, J. (2011). Birds of a feather: Homophily in social networks. *Annual Review of Sociology, 27*, 415–444. doi: 10.1146/annurev. soc.27.1.415.

Mendes, W., Blascovich, J., Hunter, S., Lickel, B. & Jost, J. (2007). Threatened by the unexpected: Physiological responses during social interactions with expectancy-violating partners. *Journal of Personality and Social Psychology, 92*(4), 698–716. doi: 10.1037/0022-3514.92.4.698.

Miller, D., Taylor, B. & Buck, M. (1991). Gender gaps: who needs to be explained? *Journal of Personality and Social Psychology, 61*(1), 5–12. doi: 10.1037/0022-3514.61.1.5.

Morgan, G., Mullen, E. & Skitka, L. (2010). When values and attributions collide: Liberals' and conservatives' values motivate attributions for alleged misdeeds. *Personality and Social Psychology Bulletin, 36*(9), 1242–1254.

Murno, G., Lasane, T. & Leary, S. (2010). Political partisan prejudice: Selective distortion and weighting of evaluative categories in college admissions applications. *Journal of Applied Social Psychology, 40*(9), 2434–2462.

Onraet, E., Van Hiel, A., Dhont, K. & Pattyn, S. (2013). Internal and external threat in relationship with right-wing attitudes. *Journal of Personality, 81*(3), 233–248.

Pachur, T., Rieskamp, J. & Hertwig, R. (2005). The social circle heuristic: Fast and frugal decisions based on small samples. In K. Forbus, D. Gentner & T. Regier (Eds.), *Proceedings of the Twenty-Sixth Annual Conference of the Cognitive Science Society* (pp. 1077–1082). Mahwah: Erlbaum.

Paluck, E. & Shepherd, H. (2012). The salience of social referents: A field experiment on collective norms and harassment behavior in a school social network. *Journal of Personality and Social Psychology, 103*(6), 899–915.

Paluck, E., Shepherd, H. & Aronow, P. (2016). Changing climates of conflict: A social network experiment in 56 schools. *Proceedings of the National Academy of Science, 113*(3), 556–571.

Petrescu, D. & Parkinson, B. (2014). Incidental disgust increases adherence to left-wing economic attitudes. *Social Justice Research, 27*(4), 464–486.

Pratto, F., Sidanius, J. & Levin, S. (2006). Social dominance theory and the dynamics of intergroup relations: Taking stock and looking forward. *European Review of Social Psychology, 17*, 271–320. doi: 10.1080/10463280601055772.

Prentice, D. & Miller, D. (1996). Pluralistic ignorance and the perpetuation of social norms by unwitting actors. *Advances in Experimental Social Psychology, 28*, 161–209.

Reyna, C., Henry, P., Korfmacher, W. & Tucker, A. (2005). Examining the principles in principled conservatism: The role of responsibility stereotypes as cues for deservingness in racial policy decisions. *Journal of Personality and Social Psychology, 90*(1), 109–128.

Roets, A. & Van Hiel, A. (2011). Allport's prejudiced personality today: Need for closure as the motivated cognitive basis of prejudice. *Current Directions in Psychological Science, 20*(6), 349–354.

Sears, D. & Henry, P. (2003). The origins of symbolic racism. *Journal of Personality and Social Psychology, 85*(2), 259–275.

Sibley, C. & Duckitt, J. (2008). Personality and prejudice: A meta-analysis and theoretical review. *Personality and Social Psychology Review, 12*(3), 248–279.

Sibley, C., Osborne, D. & Duckitt, J. (2012). Personality and political orientation: Meta-analysis and test of a threat-constraint model. *Journal of Research in Personality, 46*(6), 664–677.

Sidanius, J. & Pratto, F. (2001). *Social dominance: An intergroup theory of social hierarchy and oppression.* Cambridge: Cambridge University Press.

Simoni, J. & Walters, K. (2001). Hetersexual identity and heterosexism. *Journal of Homosexuality, 41*(1), 157–172. doi: 10.1300/J082v41n01_06.

Skitka, L. & Tetlock, P. (1993). Providing public assistance: Cognitive and motivational processes underlying liberal and conservative policy preferences. *Journal of Personality and Social Psychology, 65*(6), 1205–1223.

Stenner, K. (2005). *The authoritarian dynamic.* Cambridge: Cambridge Unviersity Press.

van der Toorn, J., Napier, J. & Dovidio, J. (2014). We the people: Intergroup interdependence breeds liberalism. *Social Psychological and Personality Science, 5*(5), 616–622.

Washburn, A., Morgan, G. & Skitka, L. (2015). A checklist to facilitate objective hypothesis testing. *Brain and Behavioral Sciences, 38*, 42–43.

Weiner, B., Osborne, D. & Rudolph, U. (2011). An attributional analysis of reactions to poverty: The political ideology of the giver and the perceived morality of the receiver. *Personality and Social Psychology Review, 15*(2), 199–213.

Wetherell, G., Brandt, M. & Reyna, C. (2013). Discrimination across the ideological divide: The role of value violations and abstract values in discrimination by liberals and conservatives. *Social Psychology and Personality Science, 4*(6), 658–667.

Zucker, G. & Weiner, B. (1993). Conservatism and perceptions of poverty: An attributional analysis. *Journal of Applied Social Psychology, 23*(12), 925–943.

4

DOES POLITICAL IDEOLOGY HINDER INSIGHTS ON GENDER AND LABOR MARKETS?

Charlotta Stern

The leftist character of sociology cannot be disputed. In surveys and voter-registration studies, the ratio of Democrats to Republicans in American sociology ranges between 59 to 1 and 19.5 to 1 (Klein & Stern, 2009a; see also Klein & Stern, 2006). One survey reports more self-identified Marxists (25.5%) than self-identified Republicans (5.5%) in sociology (Gross & Simmons, 2007), and another finds that more sociologists are comfortable with the prospect of working with a Communist colleague than a Republican or a hard-core Christian (Yancey, 2011).[1]

More disputed is whether the near monopoly of the left is problematic. Most people would agree that ideological monopoly is a problem if the one-sidedness (a) creates a culture where ideological beliefs are treated as self-evidently true, (b) stunts theorizing and understanding by shunting research into certain ideas or topics, or (c) leads researchers to ignore inconvenient knowledge or plausible alternative explanations.

In this chapter, I argue that all three problems surface in the sociological study of gender differences in the labor market (henceforth sometimes referred to as gender sociology).[2] I also argue that the problems emanate from the particular definition of equality embraced by the left and thus are causally related to one another and greatly overlap.

How Left-Feminist Ideology and Classical Liberal Feminism Differ

Before looking at each of these problems, I wish to compare the perspective that dominates sociological studies of gender differences in the labor market and the classical liberal alternative. The dominant sociological perspective is left-feminist. In left-feminism,[3] gender equality means that labor-market outcomes for men and women should be about the same. A truly equal society, this thinking goes, is a society where couples "engage symmetrically in employment and caregiving" (Gornick & Meyers, 2009, p. 4). Inequality ends when virtually no differences occur between men and women in their care for children, choices of work, and labor market results (England, 2010; Ridgeway, 2009; Ridgeway & Correll, 2004), or, in other words, "slim-outcome differences."

In envisioning such a society, left-feminism is bold, to say the least, since no society known to us shows such slim differences between men and women. It is also collectivist in that the end goal of slim-outcome differences encompasses everyone. If women (and men) do not (yet) prefer, aspire, or choose the lifestyles defined as equal, they are unwilling victims of culture and oppression (examples of this argument include Charles & Grusky, 2007; Ridgeway, 2009; West & Zimmerman, 1987). The victimhood stands in contrast to, among others, corporate men (and women), who strive to hold onto the power and privilege vested in patriarchy (England, 2010).

In contrast, classical liberal feminists share a belief in equal value of and equal rights for women and men but differ on what counts as equality.[4] In classical liberal feminism, equality means that men and women have the same rights to pursue happiness in ways they see fit, assuming that they do not infringe on anyone else's right to do the same (Hoff Sommers, 1995; Ingelhardt & Welzel, 2005; McElroy, 1982, 2002; Pinker, 2002; Taylor, 1992). An individualistic feminism favors a society where women and men are free to express their different preferences, aspirations, and lifestyles. Classical liberal feminism is humble rather than bold; it does not presume that all individuals share the same goals. It is also stern, a feminism that strongly believes in reason and toleration and presumes that individuals themselves are responsible for and best able to judge their pursuit of life goals.[5]

While simplified, this depiction of two feminist ideologies highlights one indication of how the near monopoly of left-wing feminist ideology in gender sociology assumes that equality means slim-outcome differences. In this view, an equal society is a society in which women and men share parenting equally, strive equally for positions of status and power, and prefer occupations in a similar fashion. Had there been more ideological diversity in the field, I hypothesize, there would have been more discussion and debate about whether it is reasonable to assume that all men and women share the goals of slim-outcome differences. For instance, under this presumption, it would seem that a traditional lifestyle is incompatible with equality as well as incompatible with being a feminist. But with more ideological diversity, alternative definitions of equality, such as free (formally unlimited) choice and movement, a classical liberal definition of equality, would be acceptable (see also Winegard, Winegard & Geary, 2015).

A Culture Where Ideological Beliefs Are Seen as Self-Evidently True

On the surface, the sociology study of gender differences in the labor market seems heterogeneous; there are devaluation theory (England, 2010), cognitive frame theory (Ridgeway, 2009), structural theory (Risman, 2004), and doing gender (West & Zimmerman, 1987), to name a few. In fact, however, the ideology of slim-outcome differences limits scholars in the field to acknowledge only social constructivist theorizing.

This is despite the fact that evolutionary science continues to amass knowledge about how the reproductive differences between men and women have co-evolved with corresponding hormonal, cognitive, and physiological differences between men and women (Baron-Cohen, 2003; Campbell, 2013; Pinker, 2002). Examples of studies showing plausible biological differences include hormone studies showing that "male" testosterone affects dominance, whereas "female" oxytocin affects social bonding (see studies cited in Croft, Schmader & Block, 2015). Similarly, as a result of such hormonal differences, competition studies show that men are more willing to compete than are women (Niederle & Vesterlund, 2011). Men are also more inclined to take risks than are women (Byrnes, Miller & Schaffer, 2009). This willingness to compete and take risks often stems from overconfidence rather than actual competence (Niederle & Vesterlund, 2011). Personality studies find that women are more agreeable and more neurotic than are men (Costa, McCrae & Holland, 1984; Costa, Terracciano & McCrae, 2001). Intelligence studies show that men, on average, score higher on spatial ability, and women, on average, score higher on verbal ability (Halpern, 2012; Kimura, 1999; for Sweden, see Madison, 2016). Also, fewer women seem to be in both the top and bottom of the IQ distribution (Johnson, Carothers & Deary, 2008; Wai, Putallaz & Makel, 2012), suggesting that overall women are more "normal" than men.

Evolution may thus have shaped average differences in preferences between men and women, differences that seem relevant to consider when trying to understand gender differences in the labor market. For example, occupational preference studies show that women are more likely to prefer occupations dealing with people, and men are more likely to prefer occupations dealing with inanimate things, and it is thought that these preferences are partly hard-wired and partly due to gender socialization (Baron-Cohen, 2003; Browne, 2006; Gottfredson, 1999; Holland, 1959, 1997; Johnson, 2008). In sociology, preference theory stipulates that whereas men overall prefer a lifestyle centered on work and career, women prefer three different types of lifestyles: A minority of women prefer a lifestyle centered on the household, another minority of women prefer a lifestyle centered on work and career, while most women prefer a mixed lifestyle, balancing work and family life (Hakim, 1995, 2000, 2002, 2008).

These differences between men and women in competitiveness, personality, IQ, and preferences are common findings in some parts of sociology and in neighboring fields. All of them are reported as stable results over time and contexts. Yet in sociological studies of labor market differences between men and women, they are ignored. Hypotheses about biological sex differences are rarely engaged (exceptions exist; see, e.g., Lueptow, Garovich-Szabo & Lueptow, 2001; Udry, 1995, 2000).[6]

Instead of acknowledging these biological differences, scholars in the field write about gender differences in preferences as "essentialist ideology," which they say perpetuates erroneous stereotypes about natural male and female characteristics (Charles & Grusky, 2007; England, 2010). Explaining the essentialist ideology from their perspective, Charles and Grusky write:

> Although prevailing characterizations of male and female traits are complex and multifaceted, a core feature of such characterizations is that women are *presumed* to excel in personnel service, nurturance, and interpersonal interaction, and men are *presumed* to excel in interaction with things (rather than people) and in strenuous or physical labor. These *stereotypes about natural male and female characteristics* are disseminated and perpetuated through *popular culture and media*, through *social interaction* in which significant others (parents, peers, teachers) implicitly or explicitly support such interpretations, and through *micro-level cognitive processes* in which individuals pursue and remember evidence consistent with their preexisting stereotypes and ignore, discount, or forget evidence that undermines those stereotypes.
>
> *(Charles & Grusky, 2007, p. 333, Italics added)*

A careful examination of this quotation reveals how a seemingly multifaceted characterization is really just depicting one theme—that gender is socially constructed (highlighted by added italics). Charles and Grusky (2007) go on to argue that "essentialist" presumptions are internalized by employers, who practice "essentialist discrimination" and allocate men and women in accordance with them, and by workers, who aspire to occupations that satisfy "essentialist preferences" (ibid.). The concept "essentialist ideology" treats evolutionary differences as little more than cultural stereotypes.[7]

In a related paper studying cross-national occupational gender segregation, Charles and Bradley (2009) discuss gendered preferences and claim to define it "in its broadest sense here, to encompass values socialized and internalized at the individual level, as well as the performative enactment of cultural scripts" (p. 928). Yet "the broadest sense" includes only socially constructed mechanisms as underlying preferences. In a footnote following the definition, they do acknowledge that some social scientists have treated differences in preferences as in some sense genetic, citing Baron-Cohen's (2003) book

The Essential Difference. This book presents research regarding how men's and women's brains are hard-wired differently so that, on average, more women are "empathizers" whereas more men are "systemizers." But nothing more is mentioned in the article about this alternative explanation of preferences.

The Constructivist Theoretical Monopoly Limits the Quality of Scholarship

Above, Charles and co-authors illustrate how sociologists studying labor market differences in gender exclude all but socially constructed mechanisms from theorizing. In scholarship, such neglect of the potential impact of hard-wired differences between men and women is unfortunate. Taking differences seriously could potentially yield new insights regarding gender stratification. One could speculate that average differences between individuals in terms of empathy or risk taking affect choices in the labor market, choices that over time translate into average differences in career paths. Since sociologists are inherently interested in understanding mechanisms underlying social stratification, it seems damaging to expel such relevant and potent input.

Partly, of course, a focus on social constructivism in theorizing is a valid disciplinary choice in that sociology as a discipline deals with the social web of humans (see Horowitz, Yaworsky & Kickham, 2014). A sociologist myself, I am not suggesting that socialization and discrimination are unimportant social mechanisms. The radical changes of the last 200 years have extended available roles, norms, identities, and choices for women (and men). The pre-modern state-backed subjection of women to male rule is an equally clear illustration of how important gender discrimination has been.

Even so, theorizing that socialization and discrimination are the main, or even the sole, explanations for gender differences remaining, seems scientifically dubious given knowledge about evolutionary differences.[8] The slim-outcome difference definition of equality coupled with the lock-in of social constructivist theorizing locks in a culture of blank-slate scholarship (Pinker, 2002), that is, scholarship that presumes the mind is free from innate traits, a *tabula rasa* shaped by experience or perception (Stern, 2016).

What Gender Sociology Leaves Out

In this section, my aim is to give a few examples of how the domination of left-feminism limits what hypotheses are tested and what alternative explanations there could be for empirical findings. In what follows, gender equality in Sweden is used as a background to illustrate the limitation.

Sweden is often touted as one of the most gender-equal countries in the world (see, for instance, World Economic Forum, 2015; UNDP Human Development Report, 2015). Swedish culture is the most "feminine" culture in the world (Hofstede, Hofstede & Minkov, 2010). Typically, a feminine culture values social relations and quality of life. In a feminine culture, gender roles are more fleeting, with small differences between male and female roles.[9] Sweden is also the country with the most secular-rational citizens with strong post-materialist values of self-expression, as seen in Figure 4.1, which maps each country's location on two dimensions. On the vertical axis, the dimension called traditional versus secular-rational values indexes a number of questions relating to how important religion, traditional family values, and deference to authority, etc., are among people in a country. On the horizontal axis, the dimension called survival versus self-expression indexes a number of questions relating to the importance of economic and physical security, etc. Cultures ranking high on self-expression are high-trust cultures, with tolerance toward others, and high regard for individual freedom (Ingelhardt & Welzel, 2005).

It should come as no surprise then that most Swedes have gender-egalitarian attitudes (Jakobsson & Kotsadam, 2010) and are positive toward gender equality at home (Bernhardt, Noack, & Lyngstad, 2008).

In 1974, Sweden became the first country to implement state-supported parental leave. Swedish parents can freely share 12 months of paid parental leave

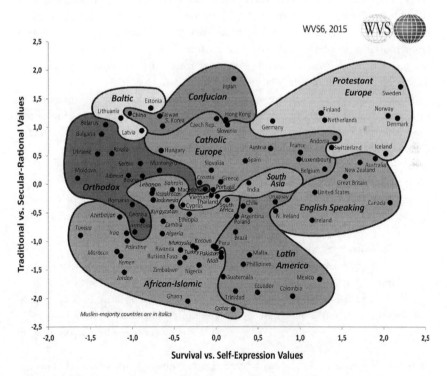

FIGURE 4.1 Inglehardt-Welzel's Cultural Map of the World.
Source: www.worldvaluessurvey.org/images/Cultural_map_WVS6_2015.jpg.

(Duvander, Ferrarini, & Thalberg, 2005). Sweden has tax-funded and heavily subsidized preschools available to all children over 1 year of age, and Swedish children are on average enrolled in preschool by the time they are 1.5 years old (Duvander, 2006). These state-supported family policies have often been credited for Sweden's success in combining a (relatively) high fertility rate with high female labor force participation rates (Duvander et al., 2005).

Swedish men and women participate in the labor market to almost the same extent (89% of males and 83% of females; Statistics Sweden, 2014). Less than 5% of women are homemakers (ibid.). As in most wealthy Western countries, Swedish women outperform men in school grades and in educational achievement (Statistics Sweden, 2014).

Still, when making choices in the educational system, women tend to choose educational fields that lead to occupations dealing with people, and men tend to choose educational fields leading to occupations dealing with things (Statistics Sweden, 2014; see also Gottfredson, 1999). This pattern has been quite stable since the 1970s (Jonsson, 2004). The result is a gender-segregated labor market (Halldén, 2014; Kumlin, 2010), and, as it turns out, up until the 1990s, Swedish women and men were more segregated into different occupations than women and men in the United States, Germany, Portugal, and Italy (Blackburn, Jarman & Brooks, 2000; Charles & Grusky, 2004). Today, Sweden is a mid-level segregated country, partly because of changes in the Swedish labor market and partly because some Eastern European countries and some Southern European countries have more segregated labor markets than they did in the end of the 1990s (Halldén, 2014).

Overall, while traditional gender socialization and anti-female discrimination have withered, gender segregation in the labor market has not. One of the most influential attempts to understand the stability in Sweden and worldwide is Charles and Grusky's (2004) book *Occupational Ghettos*. To understand the "failure of egalitarianism" (Charles & Grusky, 2007, p. 329; see also Charles, 2008; Charles & Bradley, 2009; Charles & Grusky, 2004), an explanation is put forth based on the coexistence of "liberal egalitarian values" with an "essentialist ideology." According to their theory, gender segregation persists in Sweden because:

> Normative mandates for self-expression and the associated celebration of individual choice encourage sex segregation because males and females draw upon different cultural schemas and different social resources as they seek to realize and express their true "selves," and because they anticipate that others will hold them accountable to established gender scripts.
>
> *(Charles & Bradley, 2009, p. 929)*

It is fair to say that the Swedish state has encouraged dual-earner/dual-care families (or slim-outcome-difference feminism) in both policy and ideology.[10] In spite of this, it also seems that Swedish culture tolerates and even supports the individual's freedom to choose a lifestyle relatively free from traditional values so that men and women would be exceptionally empowered to explore choices that express their interests and preferences.[11] If social context matters for outcomes, it makes little sense to explain Sweden's occupational segregation as merely a product of "essentialist ideology." Such an explanation would seem to lack an answer to how such "essentialist ideology" is sustained when traditionalist norms are eroded and government policy militates against outcome differences.

The stability of occupational gender segregation in the Swedish context suggests that alternative hypotheses informed by evolutionary-based preference differences between men and women would be fruitful. In gender sociology, however, such readily available alternative explanations are not tested or even considered. Understanding informed by evolutionary science would open up new avenues of research and push knowledge further. It would also question whether a labor market characterized by slim-outcome difference, called "full integration" and "complete equality" in Charles and Grusky's terminology, is a desirable social state.

Other Examples of Untested Hypotheses and Underexplored Alternative Explanations

To summarize, for the most part, gender sociologists assume that absent structural and cultural constraints, such as glass ceilings and "essentialist" attitudes about household labor, there would be slim-outcome differences between men and women (i.e., a left-feminist version of equality). Seldom is it seriously discussed whether the slim-difference assumption is a reasonable expectation.

The purpose of the following section is to outline some examples of untested hypotheses and underexplored explanations to give some concrete examples of potential knowledge lost due to missing explorations into differences between men and women informed by evolutionary science. Explorations of such gender differences, in combination with traditional variables, would get us closer to discerning how much of the success gap is driven by present-day differences between women and men and how much is driven by different treatment of women and men. For instance, occupational positions that yield high incomes and power are assumed to be stressful, competitive, and demanding. A difference-informed sociology would explore whether fewer women than men find such positions attractive. Perhaps fewer women may thrive in a competitive climate, be willing to tolerate the stress and acrimony of being a boss, and prefer to take up occupations that are most likely to present leadership opportunity, etc. All of these are testable hypotheses that, as far as I know, have remained untested.

I hypothesize that such difference-informed theorizing is rare because it would challenge the slim-difference outcome hypothesis and open the possible conclusion that fewer women aspire to and compete for recognition and status in the workplace.

Similarly, very few studies investigate the potential impact of gender differences in productivity on success. Wages and promotions are partially determined by productivity, broadly defined. We rarely measure such differences in on-the-job productivity directly because it is hard to measure. However, one area where productivity can be measured is in academic publishing. Studies of academic publishing tend to find average gender differences in publishing, differences that used to be large (Cole & Zuckerman, 1984; Long, 1992) but are declining (Xie & Shauman, 1998). One source of the mean difference in publishing is that top producers are more likely to be male (Cole & Zuckerman, 1984; Long, 1992).

Productivity differences between men and women have also been found in matched employer-employee data from Denmark, where women on average are found to be less productive than men (Gallen, 2015). Gallen finds that mothers are paid much lower wages than men, but according to her findings, mothers' estimated productivity gap completely explains their pay gap (Gallen, 2015, p. 1).

Large-scale studies in sociology and economics where productivity is estimated with more easily observed approximations, such as tenure, workplace experience, education, and on-the-job training, show that differences in productivity explain part of the gender wage gap.[12] The gender wage gap, however, is never "fully explained." The "never fully explained" part can be interpreted as cultural discrimination against women (England, 1992, 2010) or unmeasured productivity differences (Becker, 1985), or a combination of the two. In cultural explanations, wage gaps between mothers and fathers are theorized as due to stereotypes of mothers being less committed to work and fathers as serious breadwinners. The latter explanation is found in studies of "daddy bonuses" (Hodges & Budig, 2010) and "motherhood penalties" (Correll, Benard, & Paik, 2007; see also Anderson, Binder & Krause, 2003; Budig & England, 2001). In contrast, Becker (1985) theorized that mothers, on average, may be less productive because they use more of their energy caring for children.[13]

It seems likely that both productivity and cultural explanations have merit, and therefore the small amount of attention aimed at exploring gender differences in productivity is unfortunate. After all, men and women behave very differently in their division of time between household and labor markets.[14] One hypothesis rarely tested is whether the stereotypical view of mothers and fathers is empirically correct, on average. Stereotypes are often found to be empirically accurate in studies in social psychology (see Jussim, 2012).

A Difference-Informed Explanation of Labor Market Success

Asking questions informed by potential differences could further our understanding of the persistence in gender differences in the labor market. Interestingly, a difference-informed alternative has been available in sociology at least since the 1990s. In a number of articles and books, Catherine Hakim has put forth a preference theory that calls the slim-outcome-difference ideology into question. Hakim has discussed persistent differences in lifestyle preferences among women and men in their career and family orientation (briefly introduced above and outlined in Hakim, 1995; 2000; 2002; 2008). With a title of "Five Feminist Myths about Women's Employment" published in 1995 in *British Journal of Sociology,* Hakim is clearly trying to engage gender scholars. Her impact in *Gender & Society* is more than meager; her work on preference differences has been cited twice in the journal.[15] It is hard to know the reason for so little impact, but one speculation is that feminists refuse to engage Hakim's work because her theorizing is difference-informed.

The Intolerance of the Left toward a Difference-Informed Feminist Ideology

Gender sociology's insistence on a "proper" lifestyle choice fosters a culture of intolerance toward alternative lifestyle choices that may appeal to some men and women—such as a traditional lifestyle with a male breadwinner and a female caretaker. We should all share the slim-outcome difference lifestyle, according to gender sociology. But even in Sweden, one will find a minority of religious, conservative, and traditionalist families. Fewer than in other cultures, and probably[16] more stigmatized, these families tend to prefer a traditional lifestyle. In other Swedish families, women take most of the responsibility for the household and parenting when children are small. About half of Swedish mothers take advantage of the entire state-subsidized parental leave period, except the weeks earmarked for the father of the child (Eriksson, 2016). More women also work part-time while the children are small.[17] From a left-feminist perspective, these choices are nefarious because they reproduce differences between women and men. If families continue on this path, the slim-outcome difference will remain distant. From a classical liberal standpoint, these choices are less problematic. What a truly feminist society would look like is unknown, and the goal is not to cohere on a particular lifestyle but to allow all women (and men) to pursue their own path in life.

Conclusion

The sociology of gender is blinded by taboos of a left-feminist ideology (Martin, 2016). The left-feminists' domination of gender sociology has resulted in a strong norm to explain differences between men and women only in terms of culture, broadly defined, and to ignore or gloss over biological or preference explanations, and hence to interpret differences in outcome as resulting from socialization into gender roles or to discrimination of various sorts. The taboo is kept in place by a groupthink mentality where it seems scholars fear that even a slight dissension from the constructivist view would cause expulsion and charges of anti-feminism (on groupthink in academia, see Klein & Stern, 2009b). As a result, the field is impoverished. It excludes from its imagination the complexity of human life. Humans are social and cultural beings, to be sure, but also biological creatures. When gender feminists ignore the persistent evidence of a biological imprint on humankind, they are embracing ideologically biased science.

Now, one can question whether differences in preferences between the average man and the average woman are significant enough to cause the differences observed in the labor market. Many gender sociologists would doubt that. There are examples of situations where small differences in preferences can produce large results, with Schelling's (1978) segregation dynamics and tipping points as a relevant example. I hypothesize that small gender differences in preferences, coupled with reproductive differences, will continue to impact labor market success and occupational choice.

One could argue that the taboos and blindness are means that gender sociology scholars use to undermine what they conceive to be the prevailing essentialist ideology. Ignoring differences is a way to provide an alternative constructivist interpretation to help erode our patriarchal past. Thus, gender sociologists feel the need to exaggerate the near sameness of men and women and to free men and women from the sex stereotypical shackles of the past. Questioning the status quo and critically examining conventional beliefs is indeed in line with the scientific approach. Ignoring potentially relevant knowledge, however, is not.

Lastly, scientists always choose perspectives and theoretical lenses in studying society, and such perspectives and lenses are always colored by the scientist's ideological stance (see Myrdal, 1969; Weber, 1949). Gender sociology, then, it might be argued, has chosen the lens of social constructivism to study gender relations; social constructivism is a valid theoretical perspective and is well suited for challenging notions of individual behavior free from social constraints. But constructivists risk overstating the causal force of social constraints, in ways analogous to how rationalists overstate free choice. Indeed, in gender sociology, this risk is no mere possibility; rather, it has reached a point where scholars overstate the extent to which women (and men) are ruled by socialization in making their choices. In social science, theories should be used to make sense of reality, but they also need to respond to and be kept in check by empirical reality. Holding on to an oversimplified theory of gender is damaging and will continue to hurt the long-standing reputation of sociology.

Appendix

I made a small investigation of the impact of Pinker's attack on gender sociology by going through the two most highly cited articles between 2004 and 2014, which in turn cited *Doing Gender* (1987) by West and Zimmerman

(Stern, 2016). *Doing Gender* is the most highly cited article ever published in *Gender & Society*, a top journal in the field as well as in general sociology (Jurik & Siemsen, 2009). The purpose was to get an indication of the extent to which the field remains stuck in what Pinker labeled a "blank slate mentality" (Pinker, 2002). Among the 23 articles, I found one article that discussed evolutionary theory. Although the journal features scholars and experts on gender, it is remarkable how little awareness there seems to be toward the advances in evolutionary theory.

Sociology textbooks, too, tend to present a view of sociobiology as mired in reductionism and genetic determinism (Machalek & Martin, 2004, cited in Horowitz et al., 2014). An investigation of 18 sociology theory books found that only two covered sociobiology or evolutionary psychology (Horowitz et al., 2014). Surveys of sociologists' views on evolutionary theory find a mixed bag; the most common perception is "I am open to considering evolutionary ideas, but I am not sure that much of human social behavior and organization can be explained by evolutionary processes" (49% of survey respondents, reported in Horowitz et al., 2014). Forty-one percent agree or strongly agree with the view that sociologists have allowed ideology to blind them to the major significance of evolutionary biological processes in shaping human social behavior and organization (Horowitz et al., 2014). Horowitz et al. (2014) also find that 81.2% of the surveyed sociological theorists find it plausible or highly plausible that differences in intelligence has biological roots, 70.2% find it plausible or highly plausible that sexual orientation has biological roots, and 42.8% find it plausible or highly plausible that gender differences in communication and spatial reasoning has biological roots. Overall, Horowitz et al. (2014) conclude "that sociological theorists are most inclined to reject evolutionary reasoning when it is employed to explain behavioral differences between women and men" (ibid., p. 499). Overall, two surveys of sociologists in 1992 and 1999 find that the more radical sociologists are, the more likely they are to reject evolutionary theory (Sanderson & Ellis, 1992; Lord & Sanderson, 1999; who are cited in Horowitz et al., 2014). Describing oneself as a feminist theorist, too, is correlated with a rejection of evolutionary theory (Horowitz et al., 2014).

Notes

1 The left-wing character is also true of Sweden, where the largest political party among academic sociologists is the former Communist party (Berggren, Jordahl, & Stern, 2009). Sweden has a proportional political system, and in 2009 Swedish politics had eight political parties. In the electorate, the Social Democratic Party and the Moderate Party (right liberal) are the largest parties overall. The Left Party (the former Communist party) is one of the smallest parties.

2 The focus of the chapter is the sociological study of gender differences in the labor market, and I use the term *gender sociology* to make reading a bit easier and to distinguish the field from general stratification research, which also studies gender stratification. Gender sociology is more specialized, and, ideal typically, scholars in the field are gender-studies scholars (sociologists who specialized in gender topics).

Typically, they are scholars who read and publish in *Gender & Society*, a top journal in the field of women's studies and in sociology overall (Jurik & Siemsen, 2009).

3 Dividing feminists into two kinds is a simplification: there are Marxist, socialist, critical, constructivist feminism, post-modern feminists (see Tong, 1989).

4 It seems common to describe the feminist movement as evolving from classical liberal feminism, the first wave, into the modern left-wing feminism, the third wave. Such descriptions seem to suggest that classical liberal feminism somehow is obsolete and an ideology of the past. Perhaps this is because the classical liberal definition of a feminist encompasses an ideology most people of the West agree upon; most Westerners think it is obvious that women and men should have equal rights. In that sense, we are all feminists.

5 The ideal typical presentation of the feminist ideologies is reminiscent of the stereotypical depiction of the difference betwen economics and sociology; "economics is all about how people make choices; sociology is all about how people have no choice." A related criticism of left-wing feminism's insistence on social constructivism is thus that it presents us with an oversocialized view of women being pushed by culture (whereas men with power seem to be able to practice "rational choice" in their suppression of women).

6 The hostility of sociologists toward biology and evolutionary principles is not unique to the field of labor markets and gender; about half doubt that evolutionary factors affect gender difference (see Horowitz et al., 2014 and the references therein). See also Winegard and Deaner (2014) on how evolutionary psychology is misrepresented in sex and gender textbooks. (For more information, please see the appendix at the end of this chapter.)

7 The left-feminist stance also shines through when Charles and Grusky (2004, p. 340) present the tradition of classical liberalism as a problem in reaching equality: "...the second revolution will face many obstacles, not the least of which is an entrenched tradition of classical liberalism that celebrates individual choice and thus supports and sustains those forms of inequality that can be represented as consistent with it." One fears to think of their alternative to the classical liberal tradition of celebrating choice.

8 Personally, I also find it quite demeaning toward women (and men). I also find that the portrayal of modern societies as oppressive to women is so widespread that young women (and men) grow up thinking that their situation in the labor market is marked by unfairness and hostility. Such portrayal fosters an attitude among women that they need ever more government intervention to even the odds.

9 In contrast, a masculine culture values competitiveness, assertiveness, and material well-being, whereas masculine cultures hold more strictly divided gender roles with larger differences between male and female roles (ibid.).

10 From an ideological point of view, it is interesting to note that Statistics Sweden defines gender equality as "women and men have equal power to shape society and their own lives. This implies the same opportunities, rights and obligations in all spheres of life" (SCB, 2014, p. 2). The definition touches both the classical liberal and the left-wing feminist vision. Statistics Sweden then goes on to state that "the quantitative aspect (of gender equality) implies *an equal distribution of women and men in all areas of society*, such as education, work, recreation and positions of power. If a group comprises more than 60% women, it is women-dominated. If men make up more than 60% of a group, it is men-dominated. Qualitative gender equality implies that the knowledge, experiences and values of both women and men are given equal weight and are used to enrich and direct all spheres of society"(SCB, 2014, p. 2, italics added).

11 The choice in a self-expressive culture would mean choosing what one deems a meaningful occupation, not necessarily an occupation that gives the highest monetary rewards.

12 Occupational segregation also explains part of the wage gap (Meyersson Milgrom, Petersen & Snartland, 2001).

13 Sociologists also theorize gender gaps as due to statistical discrimination (see Moro, 2009).

14 Returning to the Swedish context, for instance, we find that the opportunities to share parental leave time equally among parents has had a small but increasing effect on parental choice. On average, women take 75% of the parental leave. When they return to work, women with small children work part-time. Swedish women do more household work than their spouses (ibid.). On average, we also find that Swedish women are absent from work about twice as much due to sickness than are men and stay home from work to take care of sick children more often than fathers (Eriksson, 2011). On average, women, especially mothers with small children, may very well be or be seen as less productive at work. Given their larger responsibilities for childcare, it would almost be astonishing if they were not.

15 A SSCI search yields that Hakim (1995) is cited 145 times, 24 times in *Women's studies* (a collection of journals categorized by SSCI), and zero times in *Gender & Society* (a major journal of the field). Hakim (2000) is cited 70 times, 8 times in *Women's* studies, and zero times in *Gender & Society*. Hakim (2002) is cited 138 times, 13 times in *Women's* studies, 2 times in *Gender & Society*.

16 I write *probably*, although I find Swedes to be intolerant toward traditional lifestyles. However, I am not knowledgeable of data with questions about "conservative lifestyle" values; it seems most value studies are interested in "modern lifestyle" values, such as attitudes toward working mothers, divorce, homosexuality, etc.

17 The glass is actually half full, because in the other half of Swedish families, parents share parental leave—although it is not exactly equally divided between woman and man, it is clear that many Swedish fathers take active care of their children when small (ibid.). The nurturing father being a strong norm in Sweden is not surprising, given the world's most feminine culture!

References

Anderson, D., Binder, M. & Krause, K. (2003). The motherhood wage penalty revisited: Experience, heterogeneity, work effort, and work-schedule flexibility. *Industrial and Labor Relations Review, 56*(2), 273–294.

Baron-Cohen, S. (2003). *The essential difference. The truth about the male and female brain.* New York: Basic Books.

Becker, G. S. (1985). Human capital, effort and the sexual division of labor. *Journal of Labor Economics, 3*, 33–58.

Berggren, N., Jordahl, H. & Stern, C. (2009). The political opinions of Swedish social scientists. *Finnish Economic Papers, 22*(2), 75–88.

Bernhardt, E., Noack, T. & Lyngstad, T. (2008). Shared housework in Norway and Sweden: Advancing the gender revolution. *Journal of European Social Policy, 18*, 275–288.

Blackburn, R. M., Jarman, J. & Brookes, B. (2000). The puzzle of gender segregation and inequality: A cross-national analysis. *European Sociological Review, 16*, 119–135.

Browne, K. R. (2006). Evolved sex differences and occupational segregation. *Journal of Organizational Behavior, 27*(2), 143–162.

Budig, M. & England, P. (2001). The wage penalty for motherhood. *American Sociological Review, 66*(2), 204–225.

Byrnes, J., Miller, D. & Schaffer, W. (2009). Gender differences in risk-taking: A meta-analysis. *Psychological Bulletin, 125*, 367–383.

Campbell, A. (2013). *A mind of her own. The evolutionary psychology of women* (2nd ed.). Cambridge: Oxford University Press.

Charles, M. (2008). Culture and inequality: Identity, ideology, and difference in "Postascriptive Society." *Annals of the American Academy of Political and Social Science, 619*, 41–58.

Charles, M. & Bradley, K. (2009). Indulging our gendered selves? Sex segregation by field of study in 44 countries. *American Journal of Sociology, 114*(4), 924–976.

Charles, M. & Grusky, D. B. (2004). *Occupational ghettos. The worldwide segregation of women and men.* Stanford: Stanford University Press.

Charles, M. & Grusky, D. B. (2007). Egalitarianism and gender inequality. In D. B. Grusky & S. Szelényi (Eds.), *The inequality reader: Contemporary and foundational readings in race, class, and gender* (pp. 327–342). Boulder: Westview Press.

Cole, J. R. & Zuckerman, H. (1984). The productivity puzzle: Persistence and change in patterns of publication of men and women scientists. *Advances in Motivation and Achievement, 2*, 217–258.

Correll, S. J., Benard, S. & Paik, I. (2007). Getting a job: Is there a motherhood penalty? *American Journal of Sociology, 112*(5), 1297–1339.

Costa, P. T., McCrae, R. R. & Holland, J. L. (1984). Personality and vocational interests in an adult sample. *Journal of Applied Psychology, 69*, 390–400.

Costa P. T., Terracciano, A. & McCrae, R. R. (2001). Gender differences in personality traits across cultures: Robust and surprising findings. *Journal of Personality and Social Psychology, 81*, 322–331. www.ncbi.nlm.nih.gov/pmc/articles/PMC2031866/.

Croft, A., Schmader, T. & Block, K. (2015). An underexamined inequality: Cultural and psychological barriers to men's engagement with communal roles. *Personality and Social Psychology Review, 19*(4), 343–370.

Duvander, A. Z. (2006). *När är det dags för dagis? En studie om vid vilken ålder barn börjar på förskola och föräldrars åsikt om detta.* (When is it time for pre-school? A study of at what age children start pre-school and parental views about it) (p. 2). Stockholm: Arbetsrapport, Institutet för Framtidsstudier.

Duvander, A. Z., Ferrarini, T. & Thalberg, S. (2005). *Swedish parental leave and gender equality—achievements and reform challenges in a European perspective.* Stockholm: Arbetsrapport, Institutet för Framtidsstudier.

England, P. (1992). *Comparable worth.* New York: Aldine De Gruyter.

England, P. (2010). The gender revolution. Uneven and stalled. *Gender & Society, 24*(2), 149–166.

Eriksson, H. (2011). The gendering effects of Sweden's gender-neutral care leave policy. *Population Review, 50*(1), 156–169.

Eriksson H. (2016). Taking turns or halving it all: Care strategies of dual-caring couples. Submitted manuscript. Paper presented at Department of Sociology, Stockholm University.

Gallen, Y. (2015). The gender productivity gap. Working Paper available at: http://yanagallen.com/Gallen_Yana_JMP.pdf. Accessed April 26, 2017.

Gornick, J. C. & Meyers, M. (2009). *Gender equality: Transforming family division of labor.* London: Verso Books.

Gottfredson, L. S. (1999). The nature and nurture of vocational interests. In M. L. Savickas & A. R. Spokane (Eds.), *Vocational interests: Their meaning, measurement, and use in counseling.* Palo Alto: Davies-Black Publishing.

Gross, N. & Simmons, S. (2007). *The Social and Political Views of American Professors.* Working paper presented at the Harvard University Symposium on Professors and Their Politics, Cambridge, MA, October 6, 2007.

Hakim, C. (1995). Five feminist myths about women's employment. *British Journal of Sociology*, *46*, 429–455.

Hakim, C. (2000). *Work-lifestyle choices in the 21st century: Preference theory*. Oxford: Oxford University Press.

Hakim, C. (2002). Lifestyle preferences as determinants of women's differentiated labor market careers. *Work and Occupations*, *29*(4), 428–459.

Hakim, C. (2008). Diversity in tastes, values, and preferences: Comment on Jonung and Ståhlberg. *Econ Journal Watch*, *5*(2), 204–218.

Halldén, K. (2014). Könssegregering efter yrke på den svenska arbetsmarknaden år 2000–2010. [Gender Segregation after Occupation in the Swedish Labor Market during 2000–2010]. In A. Kunze & K. Thorburn (Eds.), *Yrke, karriär och lön— kvinnors och mäns olika villkor på den svenska arbetsmarknaden. SOU* (p. 81). Stockholm: Fritzes.

Halpern, D. F. (2012). *Sex differences in cognitive abilities* (4th ed.). New York: Psychology Press.

Hodges, M. & Budig, M. (2010). Who gets the daddy bonus? Organizational hegemonic masculinity and the impact of fatherhood on earnings. *Gender & Society*, *24*, 717–745. doi: 10.1177/0891243210386729.

Hoff Sommers, C. (1995). *Who stole feminism? How women have betrayed women*. New York: Simon & Schuster.

Hofstede, G. H., Hofstede, G. J. & Minkov, M. (2010). *Cultures and organizations: Software of the mind*. New York: McGraw Hill.

Holland, J. L. (1959). A theory of occupational choice. *Journal of Counseling Psychology*, *6*, 35–45.

Holland, J. L. (1997). *Making vocational choices: A theory of vocational personalities and work environments* (3rd ed). Odessa: Psychological Assessment Resources, Inc.

Horowitz, M., Yaworsky, W. & Kickham, K. (2014) Whither the blank slate? A report on the reception of evolutionary biological ideas among sociological theorists. *Sociological Spectrum*, *34*(6), 489–509.

Ingelhardt, R. & Welzel, C. (2005). *Modernization, cultural change, and democracy. The human development sequence*. Oxford: Cambridge University Press.

Jakobsson, N. & Kotsadam, A. (2010). Do attitudes toward gender equality really differ between Norway and Sweden? *Journal of European Social Policy*, *20*(2), 142–159. doi: 10.1177/0958928709358790.

Johnson, J. A. (2008). Preferences underlying women's choices in academic economics. *Econ Journal Watch*, *5*(2), 209–226.

Johnson, W., Carothers, A. & Deary, I. J. (2008). Sex differences in variability in general intelligence. A new look at the old question. *Perspectives on Psychological Science*, *3*(6), 518–531.

Jonsson, J. O. (2004). Könssegregeringen inom utbildningssystemet: Förändringar och förklaringar. [Gender segregation within the Educational System: Changes and Explanations]. In Löfström (Ed.) *Den könsuppdelade arbetsmarknaden, bilaga 6, s.* (pp. 339–366). Stockholm: Fritzes.

Jurik, N. C. & Siemsen, C. (2009). "Doing gender" as canon or agenda: A symposium on West and Zimmerman. *Gender & Society*, *23*(1), 72–75.

Jussim, L. (2012). *Social perception and social reality: Why accuracy dominates bias and self-fulfilling prophecy*. New York: Oxford University Press.

Kimura, D. (1999). *Sex and cognition*. Cambridge: MIT Press.

Klein, D. B. & Stern, C. (2006). Sociology and classical liberalism. *The Independent Review. v, XI*(1), 37–52.

Klein, D. B. & Stern, C. (2009a). By the numbers: The ideological profile of professors. In R. Maranto, R. E. Redding & F. M. Hess (Eds.), *The Politically Correct University*. Washington, D.C.: The AEI Press.

Klein, D. B. & Stern, C. (2009b). Groupthink in academia. Majoritarian departmental politics and the professional pyramid. The independent review. *A Journal of Political Economy, 13*(4), 586–600.

Kumlin, J. (2010). *Har kvinnor och män blivit mer jämnt fördelade över yrken, organisationer och arbetsplatser i Sverige under perioden 1990–2003?* [Have women and men become more evenly divided over occupations, organizations, and workplaces in Sweden during the period 1990–2003] (p. 8). Stockholm: Arbetsrapport, Institutet för Framtidsstudier.

Long, J. S. (1992). Measures of sex differences in scientific productivity. *Social Forces, 7*(1), 159–178.

Lord, J. & Sanderson, S. (1999). Current Theoretical Perspectives of Western Sociological Theorists. *The American Sociologist, 30*, 42–66.

Lueptow, L., Garovich-Szabo, L. & Lueptow, M. (2001). Social change and the persistence of sex typing: 1974–1997. *Social Forces, 80*(1), 1–36.

Machalek, R. & Martin, M. (2004). Sociology and the Second Darwinian Revolution: A Metatheoretical Analysis. *Sociological Theory, 22*, 455–476.

Madison, G. (2016). *Sex Differences in Adult Intelligence in Sweden*. Working Paper, Department of Psychology, Umeå University, Sweden.

Martin, C. C. (2016). How ideology has hindered sociological insight. *The American Sociologist, 47*(1), 115–130.

McElroy, W. (1982). *Freedom, feminism, and the state*. Washington, D.C.: Cato Institute.

McElroy, W. (2002). *Liberty for women: Freedom and feminism in the twenty-first century*. Chicago: Ivan R. Dee.

Meyersson Milgrom, E. M., Petersen, T. & Snartland, V. (2001). Equal pay for equal work? Evidence from Sweden and a Comparison with Norway and the U.S. *Scandinavian Journal of Economics, 103*, 559–583. doi: 10.1111/1467-9442.00260.

Moro, A. (2009). Statistical discrimination. In S. N. Durlauf & L. E. Blume (Eds.), *The New Palgrave Dictionary of Economics* (Online Edition). Palgrave Macmillan. Accessed February 29, 2016. www.dictionaryofeconomics.com/article?id=pde2009_S000544. doi: 10.1057/9780230226203.1905.

Myrdal, G. (1969). *Objectivity in social research*. New York: Pantheon Books.

Niederle, M. & Vesterlund, L. (2011). Gender and competition. *Annual Review of Economics, 3*, 601–630.

Pinker, S. (2002). *The blank slate: The modern denial of human nature*. New York: Penguin Books.

Ridgeway, C. L. & Correll, S. J. (2004). Unpacking the gender system: A theoretical perspective on gender beliefs and social relations. *Gender & Society, 18*(4), 510–533.

Ridgeway, C. L. (2009). Framed before we know it. How gender shapes social relations. *Gender & Society, 23*(2), 145–160.

Risman, B. J. (2004). Gender as social structure: Theory wrestling with activism. *Gender & Society, 18*(4), 429–450.

Sanderson, S. & Ellis, L. (1992). Theoretical and Political Perspectives of American Sociologists in the 1990s. *The American Sociologist, 23*(2), 26–42.

Schelling, T. C. (1978). *Micromotives and macrobehavior*. New York: Norton.

Statistics Sweden. (2014.) Women and men in Sweden. Facts and figures 2014. Statistics Sweden. Örebro: SCB Tryck.

Stern, C. (2016). Undoing insularity: A small study of gender sociology's big problem. *Econ Journal Watch, 13*(3), 452–466. https://econjwatch.org/1044.

Taylor, J. K. (1992). *Reclaiming the mainstream: Individualist feminism reconsidered.* Amherst: Prometheus Books.

Tong, R. (1989). *Feminist thought. A comprehensive introduction.* London: Routledge.

Udry, J. R. (1995). Sociology and biology: What biology do sociologists need to know? *Social Forces, 73*(4), 1267–1278.

Udry, J. (2000). Biological limits of gender construction. *American Sociological Review, 65*(3), 443–457.

UNDP Human Development Report (2015). *Work for Human Development.* Available at at: http://hdr.undp.org/sites/default/files/2015_human_development_report.pdf. Accessed February 28, 2017.

Wai, J., Putallaz, M. & Makel, M. C. (2012). Studying intellectual outliers: Are there sex differences, and are the smart getting smarter? *Current Directions in Psychological Science, 21*(6), 382–390.

Weber, M. 1904 [1949]. "Objectivity" in social science and social policy. In E. Shils & H. Finch (Eds.), *The methodology of social sciences.* Glencoe: Free Press.

West, C. & Zimmerman, D. H. (1987). Doing gender. *Gender & Society, 1*, 125–151.

Winegard, B. M. & Deaner, K. A. (2014). Misrepresentations of evolutionary psychology in sex and gender textbooks. *Evolutionary Psychology: An international Journal of Evolutionary Approaches to Psychology and Behavior, 12*, 474–507.

Winegard, B., Winegard, B. & Geary, D. C. (2015). Too paranoid to see progress: Social psychology is probably liberal, but it doesn't believe in progress. *Behavioral and Brain Sciences, 38*, 43.

World Economic Forum (2015). *The Global Gender Gap Report.* Geneva, Switzerland: World economic Forum. Available at: http://reports.weforum.org/global-gender-gap-report-2015/the-global-gender-gap-index-results-in-2015/. Accessed February 28, 2017.

Xie, Y. & Shauman, K. A. (1998). Sex differences in research productivity revisited: New evidence about an old puzzle. *American Sociological Review, 63*, 847–870.

Yancey, G. (2011). *Compromising scholarship. Religious and political bias in American Higher Education.* Waco: Baylor University Press.

5

NEGLECTED TRADE-OFFS IN SOCIAL JUSTICE RESEARCH

Chris C. Martin

Much social activism, both within academia and outside it, proceeds as though certain trade-offs do not exist. It assumes all desirable goals are simultaneously attainable, an assumption that conflicts with reality. In this chapter, I illustrate two trade-offs that applied psychologists and other social scientists who are interested in social justice must consider. The first trade-off is between unity and proportionality in the management of interethnic relationships. Much applied work promotes a color-conscious ideology, based on the compensatory treatment of minorities in proportion to the harm they suffer. Such promotion of a proportionality-based model requires the demotion of a unity-based model, in which all people regardless of ethnicity are considered members of one larger community. The second trade-off is between distributional parity and intrinsic fulfillment in attempts to increase female representation in science and math. Attempts to create parity can involve pulling women out of fields that they are intrinsically motivated to pursue, which could diminish their happiness. The neglect of these trade-offs leads to biased research.

The Model Problem: Inconsistency between Unity and Proportionality

I begin this section with an overview of relational models theory, which posits four modes of interchange: unity, hierarchy, equality, and proportionality. I then explain the tension between unity and proportionality, after which I present one successful example and one unsuccessful example of acknowledging this tension.

According to relational models theory, four models of human interaction exist: unity (communal sharing), hierarchy (authority ranking), equality (equality matching), and proportionality (market pricing; Fiske, 1992). The terms in parentheses are the labels Fiske uses in his earlier work. For this chapter, just two models—unity and proportionality—are relevant. Under *unity*, there is a sense that all individuals are combined into one cohesive entity, and distinctions between individuals are unimportant. The modern nation-state rests on a model of unity. That unity often fades into the background, but it comes to the fore during major positive events like the Olympic Games or negative events like terrorist attacks, where the salient entity is the nation itself. Romantic couples, clans, tribes, and certain religious communities are also unity-based inasmuch as they construe themselves as united or joined and feel collective emotions (Fiske, 2004). Proportionality is based on ratios of exchange value. Purchases in a market are based on ratios. Goods are priced at unambiguous rates, and to compute the total cost, one multiplies the rate by the quantity. Compensation is also based on ratios. Wrongdoers must compensate victims in proportion to their injury. A victim who suffers a bruise will get less compensation than a victim who breaks a limb.

Factor analyses have shown that unity and proportionality are polar opposites (Haslam, 2004) and more broadly that the intrusion of proportionality into non-proportional systems evokes moral opprobrium. For instance, vignette-based studies have shown that people feel moral disgust toward the buying and selling of the right to become a U.S. citizen and the right to a jury trial (Tetlock, Kristel, Elson, Green, & Lerner, 2000; see also Tetlock, McGraw, & Kristel, 2008). In these vignettes, something that is shared on a communal or equal basis, like nationality or civil rights, turns into something that is exchanged on a proportional basis, an exclusive privilege that must be purchased at the going rate. My interpretation of these findings is that unity is a warm inclusive model, based on sharing, where no member of the in-group is rejected, whereas proportionality is a cold exclusive model, where anyone who cannot pay the going rate must face rejection. To understand this warmth-coldness distinction, imagine a city government that decided to stop public parks from being free and instead charged for their use on an hourly basis. Or imagine a country at war in which the armed forces are not deployed to defend all parts of the nation but only areas where people can afford to pay them at a weekly rate. Indeed, the political philosopher Michael Sandel has argued, in *What Money Can't Buy: The Moral Limits of Markets*, that it is immoral to push proportionality-based models—where money is the medium—into life domains where other models have traditionally operated.

The contrast between unity and proportionality mirrors the contrast between subjectively natural and artificial arrangements. Much sociological discourse has revolved around the distinction between the pre-modern society where Gemeinschaft (organic social collaboration) prevailed, and the modern society, where Gesellschaft (explicitly contracted collaboration) has encroached upon many life domains (Tönnies, 1887; Weber, 1968). One possible reason for the seeming naturalness of unity (and hierarchy) is that these models can be found in the animal kingdom, and the feelings they arouse may activate evolutionarily ancient parts of our mind (Fiske, 2004). In the course of development, children also understand unity very early. As they grow older, they incrementally learn new models, and proportionality comes last in the sequence (Fiske & Schubert, 2012).

Given the tension between unity and proportionality, which model should people instantiate to create harmony between ethnic groups? In a unity-based model, members of different ethnic groups, despite their distinctions, can relate to one another as co-citizens of a larger community.[1] However, if injustice is salient, proportionality may be preferred, particularly by victims who seek compensation in proportion to the amount of injustice that they have suffered. Some applied researchers recognize this trade-off; others produce biased research by treating the imposition of a unity-based model as blind to proportional reparation—*color*blind in the racial case—and therefore prejudiced. In the case of race scholarship, there are good and bad instances of managing this trade-off.

The social psychologist Jack Dovidio exemplifies how one can acknowledge the trade-off and address the problem of choosing a model. In research on *common group identity* and the *dual identity model*, Dovidio and his collaborators have explored the potential of both unity-based and proportionality-based models in promoting intergroup harmony (although Dovidio himself does not use the terms *unity* and *proportionality*). In early work, Dovidio assessed the impact of a common in-group identity that covers all group members regardless of ethnicity (Gaertner & Dovidio, 2000). A common in-group identity imposes a unity-based model: Members of diverse ethnic groups re-categorize themselves as belonging to a more inclusive superordinate group. Empirical work showed that under these conditions, people are more likely to develop positive intergroup attitudes and engage in helping and personal disclosure across group boundaries (Gaertner & Dovidio, 2000). Because unity blurs the distinctions between individuals, these outcomes are expected in a unity-based model.[2] However, further research by Dovidio's lab revealed a trade-off. A common identity can be problematic because minorities may experience unique victimization for which collective action is warranted, but such action becomes less likely when the minority has no distinct ethnic identity (Ufkes, Calcagno, Glasford, & Dovidio, 2016). Dovidio's early propagation of the common in-group identity model has thus gradually made way for the dual-identity model, where the common identity is complemented by a distinct ethnic identity. Although Dovidio and colleagues do not draw on relational models theory, their findings comport with its axioms. The common in-group identity model is an example of unity, because distinctions are diminished and the fusion of people into one larger unit is emphasized. The dual-identity model is an example of alternating between unity and other models.[3] Its first component, the common identity, relies on unity. Its next component, the distinct ethnic identity, cannot be easily classified, but it is *not* unity-based because it emphasizes distinctions.

Research on the dual-identity model appears to falsify the idea that there is a trade-off, but Dovidio has acknowledged that a model that is entirely based on unity has unique advantages, and thus a trade-off does exist. He reveals this when suggesting how to manage the trade-off, which entails determining when unity-based models are appropriate and when non-unity-based models are appropriate. These are subjective moral judgments to some degree, but they show that researchers *can* recognize the trade-off. In the following excerpt, Dovidio uses the terms *colorblindness* for a unity-based model where distinctions based on skin color do not matter and *multicultural* for a model where unity, equality, and proportionality are blended.

> The meaning of "improving intergroup relations" varies as a function of the nature of the group relations and the goals of people who may still identify with different groups. When groups are in conflict or intergroup relations are characterized by tension, achieving group harmony through colorblindness that emphasizes common identity may be an important immediate goal and effective strategy for beginning to improve intergroup relations. When relations become more stable, members of minority groups may be less concerned about systematic exclusion and become more focused on achieving the promised inclusion in society, being treated fairly, and being respected for what makes them different as well as what they have in common with the majority group. From this perspective, Martin Luther King, Jr.'s goal to have his children not "judged by the color of their skin but by the content of their character" was an insightful and strategic one in the midst of the intense racial conflicts of the 1960s. However, in the current racial climate, in which overt bigotry is much less common but the promise of full racial equality remains unfulfilled, adopting a multicultural perspective in race relations, which recognizes both components of a dual identity, may be a more desirable, appropriate and effective goal in intergroup relations.
>
> *(Dovidio, Gaertner, Ufkes, Saguy, &*
> *Pearson, 2016, pp. 37–38)*

Dovidio's evaluation of the advantages and disadvantages may not be perfect, but it represents an acknowledgment that is missing elsewhere. Many sociologists of race fail to recognize the trade-off and are blind to the costs of rejecting unity. Consider the sociologist of race Eduardo Bonilla-Silva (2013), who treats proportionality-based reparative policies, like affirmative action, as the *only* appropriate form of anti-racism. He equates opposition to these policies as a manifestation of colorblind racism. As Bonilla-Silva rightly notes, members of different racial groups in the U.S. have, on average, different opportunities and outcomes, which provide unfair structural advantages to whites. But there are many remedial options, and rather than consider alternatives, Bonilla-Silva takes it as axiomatic that proportionality-based reparative policies, like affirmative action, are correct.

Bonilla-Silva's lopsided evaluation is evident in his survey and interview research, in which he and his collaborators explore colorblind ideology, which emphasizes unity. He notes that some whites espouse unity but oppose policies like affirmative action because of how those policies affect them. In a survey sample of college students (N = 410), 25.8% of respondents said that they would support an anti-affirmative-action proposition at the state level, and in an interview sample (N = 41), 37.5% also stated that they would support that kind of proposition (Bonilla-Silva & Forman, 2000). Because of Bonilla-Silva's methodology, it is difficult to ascertain why. A desire for racial hierarchy motivates some individuals to oppose affirmative action (Federico & Sidanius, 2002), but other motivations such as unity may also be influential. Bonilla-Silva does not attend to this difference—in his world, opposition to affirmative action (proportionality) equates to colorblind racism.

Bonilla-Silva's work is biased in other ways. In his most influential book, *Racism without Racists,* Bonilla-Silva excluded Asian-white contrasts in income and education (Bonilla-Silva, 2003). The inclusion of these contrasts, which would have shown higher median household income and higher educational attainment among Asians would, by Bonilla-Silva's conventions, warrant that whites are victims of structural racism (Sakamoto, Goyette, & Kim, 2009). This is a paradoxical finding requiring a reassessment of what *structural racism* means. In the second edition, Bonilla-Silva remedied this omission to some degree but still selectively excluded Asians when convenient. For instance, he adopted the contrived term "blacks and dark-skinned racial minorities" in an explication of white racial advantage. This artifice ("dark-skinned") allowed him to exclude Asians. This issue of Asian exclusion, which has been covered in more detail elsewhere (Sakamoto et al., 2009; Sakamoto, Takei, & Woo, 2012; Sakamoto & Wang, 2015), allows proponents of proportional reparations to selectively eliminate evidence that whites, in some situations, are structurally disadvantaged, and that Asians, in some situation, are privileged, at least according to conventional sociological definitions of disadvantage and privilege.

Returning to the trade-off, colorblind attitudes could indeed be a veneer for racist attitudes. But consider this claim, extracted from Barack Obama's 2004 convention speech: "There is not a black America and a white America and Latino America and Asian America; there's the United States of America." Should we be concerned that Barack Obama is racist (cf., Arkes & Tetlock, 2004)? Or should we acknowledge that Bonilla-Silva's bipartite classification is inadequate to the ideological diversity in the world? Add at least one more ideology to that model, colorblind unity, and you go some way toward acknowledging that both unity-based and proportionality-based models can be anti-racist (Apfelbaum, Stephens, & Reagans, 2016). That acknowledgment opens the door to an unbiased evaluation of models, which in turn helps activists decide whether they want unity or proportionality in a particular situation.

The Missing Source Problem: Recruiting More Women into Science and Technology

Whereas the previous section considered the trade-off between two relational models, this section considers a trade-off between costs and benefits in programs that promote gender parity in academic fields. Applied psychologists and sociologists who advocate for greater female representation in certain fields do not see that moving women into one field involves pulling them from another field, and they further neglect a trade-off—women who have autonomously chosen to pursue that other field due to intrinsic motivation may need to pushed into a field where they have less intrinsic motivation. This blindness leads to a biased evaluation of how programs to promote female representation may diminish well-being.

In recent decades, social scientists have attempted to recruit more women into academic fields where they comprise less than half of the population (De Cohen & Deterding, 2009; Marx & Roman, 2002; Stout, Dasgupta, Hunsinger, & McManus, 2011). These interventions hinge on the belief that "protected" groups, a category that includes women, should be represented at least on par with their base rate in the population (e.g., De Cohen & Deterding, 2009).[4] Proponents of these interventions have generally ignored the research on sex differences in interests (Pinker, 2002) and researchers who *have* drawn attention to the interest difference have not had a strong theoretical basis for showing that a trade-off exists (Holden, 2000). My goal in this section is to leverage self-determination theory, a well validated psychological theory, to illustrate a trade-off in well-being, which likely occurs when women who are more interested in a field like psychology are recruited into science and technology. I also show how the elision of this trade-off results in problematic research methodologies.

Self-determination theory differentiates motives on the basis of whether they are intrinsic or extrinsic (Ryan & Deci, 2000). Intrinsic motivation directly arises from an individual's interests and values. When a person is intrinsically motivated to act, the pleasure of engaging in the activity is the primary source of motivation. Extrinsic motivation arises from secondary factors, such as incentives or punishments, which are not fundamental to an activity itself. For instance, if a person does homework out of authentic interest in a subject, he or she is intrinsically motivated. If a person does homework for the purpose of completing a lucrative degree, he or she is extrinsically motivated. Fundamental to self-determination theory is the principle that people derive greater joy from the pursuit of intrinsically motivated goals (Sheldon & Kasser, 2001). Adding extrinsic rewards to pursuits that are intrinsically motivated diminishes this joy (Deci, Koestner, & Ryan, 1999).

Self-determination theory suggests that men and women should be expected to find fulfillment in different careers if they are intrinsically interested in different things. Vocational research consistently shows such a difference—on average, men are intrinsically interested in things, and women are intrinsically interested in people. On the Strong Interest Inventory, a vocational guidance instrument, women and men have consistently separated along the People-Things dimension (for a review, see Su, Rounds, & Armstrong, 2009). The magnitude of this gap remained almost constant from the 1930s to the 1980s (Hansen & Campbell, 1985) despite appreciable changes in gender stereotypes (Duehr & Bono, 2006) and increased support for gender equality (Bolzendahl & Myers, 2004). A recent meta-analysis of Strong Interest Inventories, drawing on data from more than 500,000 respondents, found an effect size of $d = 0.93$ for this gender difference (Su et al., 2009), an effect that is large by conventional standards (Cohen, 1962). It also found high stability across age cohorts. Studies conducted after this meta-analysis showed the same gender distinction (Diekman, Clark, Johnston, Brown, & Steinberg, 2011; Lippa, Preston, & Penner, 2014; Robertson, Smeets, Lubinski, & Benbow, 2010; Wang, Eccles, & Kenny, 2013; Woodcock et al., 2013). Furthermore, research on sex hormones has revealed that atypical exposure to typically male sex hormones (among females) is associated with more interest in things relative to people (Beltz, Swanson, & Berenbaum, 2011; Berenbaum & Beltz, 2011; Berenbaum, Bryk, & Beltz, 2012). These findings have been replicated in a different but extensive stream of research on autism, where the sex difference is described as being between empathizing (women) and systematizing (men; Baron-Cohen, 2005; Nettle, 2007). The discovery of interest differences does not imply that gender-specific socialization has no effect, but they do reveal two crucial things: (1) Socialization may be a minor cause, and (2) socialization may be *evoked* by innate differences. Indeed, the evidence of temporal stability in some prestigious "masculine" fields involving things (e.g., engineering) but increasing female representation in other prestigious "masculine" fields involving people (e.g., law and medicine) suggests that interest differences are more influential than socialization regarding which fields are "appropriate" for women (Pinker, 2002). In an assessment of relative impact, two leading scholars in the area of gender and education have cited the interest difference as one of the three major factors causing women to be in the minority in math-intensive fields (Ceci & Williams, 2011).

The issue of intrinsic motivation is often neglected in research on recruitment and retention of women in science, technology, engineering, and math (STEM). Rather than acknowledging innate differences, women and men are treated as inanimate particles in a pipeline, which carries people from early education through the professoriate (Goulden, Mason, & Frasch, 2011; Miller & Wai, 2015). The pipeline is considered leaky because some women diverge from the "ideal" path. Even in mathematical terms, the leaky pipeline metaphor falls short. Among STEM bachelor's degree earners in the 1970s and 1980s, women were less likely than men to later earn a doctorate, but this gap closed in the 1990s; there is no leak at this transitional phase (Miller & Wai,

2015). This means that the sex ratio at the doctoral level now mirrors the sex ratio at the undergraduate level in STEM. Nevertheless, the pipeline may still be considered leaky at other transitional stages, and administrators can adopt the pipeline metaphor and modify the flow by targeting transitional phases such as the first year of college (Atkin, Green, & McLaughlin, 2002).

Given the research showing that women and men are not, in fact, interchangeable when it comes to intrinsic interests, the persistence of the pipeline metaphor is an unambiguous manifestation of political bias. Of course, one reason for hesitation in calling attention to intrinsic interest differences is that people may get accused of biological determinism. For instance, in a guest post for *The Curious Wavefunction*, a *Scientific American* blog run by chemist Ashutosh Jogalekar, I revisited Steven Pinker's six explanations for the gender gap in science (Pinker & Spelke, 2005). Although I criticized some of Pinker's argument, my assessment overall was that Pinker got several things right, one of which was intrinsic interest differences as a cause of discipline choice. The piece garnered many thoughtful comments, some supportive and some critical.[5] Notably, Stephen Ceci, a leader in psychological research on gender and education, criticized two minor points in my argument yet praised the overall piece: "I enjoyed this summary of the sex differences literature very much. It seems fair to me and it is refreshing to see such even-handedness." Nevertheless, about 20 users on Twitter, with dubious scientific expertise, were angered, which led to the retraction of the piece, a subsequent restoration of the piece with a disclaimer, and the firing of Ashutosh Jogalekar from *Scientific American* (Farhi, 2014).

For a similar sanctioning due to research on sex differences, see the case of Helmuth Nyborg, a Danish IQ researcher who was suspended after publishing a *peer-reviewed* article showing that average male and female IQs slightly differ (American Association for the Advancement of Science, 2006). Nyborg was re-instated, but cases like this undoubtedly have a chilling effect on junior researchers. This political silencing is unnecessary. Social scientists could acknowledge that every woman—and every man—is an individual. Every man and woman can and should be assessed through individual testing rather than generalization from group averages, unless there are extenuating circumstances like time scarcity. Simultaneously, social scientists could acknowledge that the average woman differs from the average man in interests, so pulling women into the "correct" path to create parity involves redirecting some of them from majors and careers they are pursuing out of intrinsic interest. Even among officially undeclared majors, undergraduate women are likely leaning toward some set of majors, and if those majors are non-STEM, women must be pulled away from it.

This *hidden-source* problem persists because interventions are not labeled honestly. They are called "programs to increase the number of women in X" rather than "programs to increase the number of women in X by taking them from Y." Such biased framing keeps people from seeing that women must be drawn from some source. Admittedly, the source may not have mattered in an earlier era, when women aimed for low-status majors like home economics. However, the source is relevant today—today's college women are enrolled in high-status majors, ones that relate more to empathizing than systematizing, like psychology, sociology, anthropology, education, and medicine (National Science Board, 2012). Thus, new women in STEM must come from the pool of women who are leaning toward or currently majoring in those fields.

Some objections to my argument deserve consideration. First, there is the fact of increasing female enrollment in post-secondary education (American Council on Education, 2010). If this trend were to continue, there would be "enough" women in STEM, but the trend is not continuing, with female enrollment remaining steady at approximately 57% (American Council on Education, 2010). Second, one might postulate that women who are pulled into STEM fields through extrinsic incentives will eventually develop an intrinsic interest in their field. However, self-determination research shows that such integration (an SDT term meaning development of intrinsic interest) occurs only for *some* people under such circumstances (Deci, Eghrari, Patrick, & Leone, 1994). Among the rest, some weaker form of internalization occurs.

If the average woman is more intrinsically motivated to pursue a person-centered major, like psychology, her pursuit of that major will likely be affectively rewarding (Ryan & Deci, 2000). If this woman is then recruited to a different major to address the gender gap in science, researchers ought to measure whether this woman feels some dissatisfaction relative to a comparable woman who stayed in the person-centered major. The literature is currently biased because the possibility of dissatisfaction is hardly ever considered in empirical work. Moreover, some incentives to switch fields involve financial incentives like scholarships, such as the Association for Women Geoscientists scholarship, the Clare Boothe Luce scholarship, and the Lou Henry Hoover Girl Scout Scholarship (in the sciences); the Admiral Grace Murray Hopper Scholarship, the Association for Women in Mathematics scholarship, and the Michigan Council of Women in Technology scholarship (in technology); and the Alpha Omega Epsilon Engineering and Technical Science Achievement Scholarship, the Anne Maureen Whitney Barrow Memorial Scholarship, and the B. J. Harrod Scholarship (in engineering; Larkin & Heinzelman, 2016). These scholarships may be awarded to women who are majoring in STEM already, but they otherwise act as extrinsic incentives to major in STEM rather than something else. Such incentives can decrease intrinsic motivation and subsequent satisfaction (Deci et al., 1999; Ryan & Deci, 2000). In rare cases, a STEM field could be marketed so that the average woman finds it more intrinsically appealing. For example, professors could emphasize how computer projects address communal concerns (Diekman, Weisgram, & Belanger, 2015). However, such attempts cannot entirely change the fact that certain fields like physics and chemistry are fundamentally not about communal or personal welfare and should therefore attract unequal proportions of men and women. Gender distributions overlap—there is no field that should exclusively satisfy or dissatisfy all people of a particular gender. Nevertheless, an *average* difference should emerge if interest determines choice.

My argument does not imply that women who are intrinsically interested in physics and math never experience discrimination or discouragement as a result of their gender. Undoubtedly, some professors create a hostile atmosphere for female subordinates, and some parents encourage their daughters to pursue stereotypically feminine careers. However, the elimination of unfair discrimination is different from the creation of representational parity. The first element is procedural, and the second is distributive. An unbiased applied researcher could focus solely on procedural discrimination while acknowledging that interest differences make it problematic to aim for parity. Yet, currently, representational parity seems to be an unalloyed concern, and applied researchers suggest interventions whenever women constitute less than half of some population (e.g., Alvarado & Dodds, 2010; Fisher & Margolis, 2002; Klawe, Whitney, & Simard, 2009). The adoption of this technique does not account for intrinsic interest (see also Richards, 2009). Even worse, it is blind to the fact that if men and women are both *equally* likely to rate their chosen disciplines as very fulfilling, one form of gender equality has been attained. This phenomenon of equal life satisfaction across genders through different career trajectories has been documented (Lubinski, Benbow, & Kell, 2014).

The literature contains many studies in which researchers noted that more men than women are in computer science, but hardly anywhere researchers probed whether women, rather than being excluded, were simply more interested in another discipline. In a literature search, I found only one study where interest in another discipline was explicitly measured (Carter, 2006). Carter constructed a survey to measure high-school students' attitudes toward computer science, and one question on the survey presented students with a list of beliefs that could persuade or dissuade a student from focusing on computer science. Students were asked to select whether the item was persuasive, dissuasive, or irrelevant. The most frequent reason was identical for both men and women—being "completely sold" on *another* major. The survey did not measure *which* other major, but given the statistics mentioned earlier, more women than men were likely "completely sold" on a person-centered major.

A more typical self-report instrument is the one used by Hoegh and Moskal (2009), who sought to explain why students with an aptitude for computer science were majoring in other fields and why there were gender differences in enrollment. Their instrument measured five factors, one of which was interest. (The others were confidence, gender, usefulness, and beliefs about professionals). For *interest*, Hoegh and Moskal used ten items, including "I think computer science is boring," "The challenge of solving problems using computer science appeals to me," and "I think computer science is interesting." However, not a single item measured *relative* interest. Were many students, including those with some interest in computer science, perhaps more interested in other disciplines? We cannot tell. Instruments other researchers have created have the same blind spot (e.g., Beyer, Rynes, Perrault, Hay, & Haller, 2003).

General research on major choice suggests that students choose majors based on the appeal of the subject matter or the associated careers. In a 2013 survey of college students, a question was posed about major choice, and 35.6% of students chose "appeal of subject matter,"; 45.0% chose "career connection"; 11.9%, "chance of employment"; 4.4%, "chance for income"; 1.8%, "good grades"; and 1.2% chose "no reason" (National Association of Colleges and Employers, 2013). This finding bolsters the claim that students choose majors out of intrinsic interest, so applied researchers should measure both absolute and relative interest. The exclusion of such items has political consequences. It creates the illusion that STEM is a singular male-dominated fortress with women outside the gates. Women, for the most part, are not outside the gates of this fortress but happily living in other fortresses. Discrimination and discouragement are operative, but current research suggests that they do not have a major impact on gender differences in STEM participation. The three major reasons for gender differences in STEM are (a) differences in interests, (b) the pairing of high math ability with high verbal ability in girls but not boys, and (c) fertility choices and work–home balance (see Ceci & Williams, 2011, 2015).

Scientific practice involves testing various explanations for a phenomenon. Given the extensive literature on gender differences in interests and abilities (see Ceci & Williams, 2011), it behooves researchers to account for these differences when conducting studies that purport to discover why women are not in some field where one wishes to see them. Adjusting for confounds like interest differences is not hard. It does not involve expensive laboratory equipment or biological testing but rather the addition of a few additional survey items. Relative to their cost, the potential scientific benefit of such measurement improvement is huge, and it would lead to stronger, more valid scientific research on gender differences.

To reiterate, I do not claim that sexist discrimination is completely absent, but I do propose that scientists consistently measure the magnitude of sexism's effect *relative to other effects*. It is entirely possible to find that discrimination has an effect and that the effect of interest is stronger. It is also possible to find that imbalanced gender ratios promote gendered stereotypes but that the cost of creating a gender balance is that men and women are pushed into fields where they lack intrinsic interest. It is even possible to find that both anti-male and anti-female discrimination are operative but that neither explains most of the variance (Ceci & Williams, 2011). If researchers do not acknowledge these possibilities, they will paint a distorted picture of the scientific landscape.

Notes

1 A hierarchical system can also create harmony, if people perceive themselves as followers of a common leader, whose "parentage" unites them. Generalized trust is higher in constitutional monarchies (Bjørnskov, 2006), a phenomenon that may be driven by such solidarity. Experimental work on creating harmony through perceptions of common descent are, to my knowledge, missing from the literature. This absence may reflect a realistic appraisal of the current egalitarian climate in Western countries, which is averse to hierarchical arrangements.
2 Similar findings can be found in experimental work by Kurzban, Tooby, and Cosmides (2001) testing whether race "can be erased," and in findings pertaining to social identity theory (Tajfel & Turner, 1986) contrasting altruism within groups and competition between groups.
3 A more accurate description of the model would also acknowledge that elements of equality are embedded in it, where equality is defined at the population level and the interacting entities are the white population and the black population. Acknowledging this complexity is important overall, but it adds unnecessary complexity to this chapter, so I have elided it.
4 When the group that is underrepresented is not a protected group, social scientists typically appear unconcerned. Despite an extensive online search, I was unable to find any scholarship on the underrepresentation of men in anthropology, sociology, and psychology at the undergraduate level. There is one exception—the field of nursing has an extensive literature on anti-male discrimination in both pedagogy and practice (Kouta & Kaite, 2011).
5 Due to changes in Scientific American's website, the comments are no longer visible on the live page, which is here: http://blogs.scientificamerican.com/the-curious-wavefunction/why-prejudice-alone-doesnt-explain-the-gender-gap-in-science/.
But they can be found on an archived version of the page here:
http://web.archive.org/web/20150526190937/http://blogs.scientificamerican.com/the-curious-wavefunction/why-prejudice-alone-doesnt-explain-the-gender-gap-in-science/.
To see Stephen Ceci's comment, click More Comments at the bottom and scroll down to the comment by sjceci. Stephen first sent me this comment in a personal email, and I requested him to post it on the page for posterity.

References

Alvarado, C. & Dodds, Z. (2010). Women in CS: An evaluation of three promising practices. In *Proceedings of the 41st ACM technical symposium on computer science education—SIGCSE '10* (p. 57). New York: ACM Press. doi:10.1145/1734263.1734281.

American Association for the Advancement of Science. (2006). Newsmakers. *Science*, *314*(5804), 1365.

American Council on Education. (2010). *Gender equity in higher education: 2010*. Washington, D.C. American Council on Education.

Apfelbaum, E. P., Stephens, N. M. & Reagans, R. E. (2016). Beyond one-size-fits-all: Tailoring diversity approaches to the representation of social groups. *Journal of Personality and Social Psychology.* doi:10.1037/pspi0000071.

Arkes, H. R. & Tetlock, P. E. (2004). Target Article: Attributions of implicit prejudice, or "Would Jesse Jackson 'Fail' the implicit association test?" *Psychological Inquiry, 15*(4), 257–278. doi:10.1207/s15327965pli1504_01.

Atkin, A. M., Green, R. & McLaughlin, L. (2002). Patching the leaky pipeline: Keeping first-year college women interested in science. *Journal of College Science Teaching, 32*(2), 102–108.

Baron-Cohen, S. (2005). Sex differences in the brain: Implications for explaining autism. *Science, 310*(5749), 819–823. doi:10.1126/science.1115455.

Beltz, A. M., Swanson, J. L. & Berenbaum, S. A. (2011). Gendered occupational interests: Prenatal androgen effects on psychological orientation to Things versus People. *Hormones and Behavior, 60*(4), 313–317. doi:10.1016/j.yhbeh.2011.06.002.

Berenbaum, S. A. & Beltz, A. M. (2011). Sexual differentiation of human behavior: Effects of prenatal and pubertal organizational hormones. *Frontiers in Neuroendocrinology, 32*(2), 183–200. doi:10.1016/j.yfrne.2011.03.001.

Berenbaum, S. A., Bryk, K. L. K. & Beltz, A. M. (2012). Early androgen effects on spatial and mechanical abilities: Evidence from congenital adrenal hyperplasia. *Behavioral Neuroscience, 126*(1), 86–96. doi:10.1037/a0026652.

Beyer, S., Rynes, K., Perrault, J., Hay, K. & Haller, S. (2003). Gender differences in computer science students. In *Proceedings of the 34th SIGCSE technical symposium on computer science education—SIGCSE '03* (Vol. 35, p. 49). New York: ACM Press. doi:10.1145/611892.611930.

Bjørnskov, C. (2006). Determinants of generalized trust: A cross-country comparison. *Public Choice, 130*(1–2), 1–21. doi:10.1007/s11127-006-9069-1.

Bolzendahl, C. I. & Myers, D. J. (2004). Feminist attitudes and support for gender equality: Opinion change in women and men, 1974–1998. *Social Forces, 83*(2), 759–789. doi:10.1353/sof.2005.0005.

Bonilla-Silva, E. (2003). *Racism without racists: Color-blind racism and the persistence of racial inequality in the United States* (1st ed.). Lanham: Rowman & Littlefield.

Bonilla-Silva, E. (2013). *Racism without racists: Color-blind racism and the persistence of racial inequality in America* (4th ed.). Lanham: Rowman & Littlefield.

Bonilla-Silva, E. & Forman, T. A. (2000). "I am not a racist but...": Mapping White College students' racial ideology in the USA. *Discourse & Society, 11*(1), 50–85. doi: 10.1177/0957926500011001003.

Carter, L. (2006). Why students with an apparent aptitude for computer science don't choose to major in computer science. In *Proceedings of the 37th SIGCSE technical symposium on computer science education—SIGCSE '06* (Vol. 38, p. 27). New York: ACM Press. doi:10.1145/1121341.1121352.

Ceci, S. J. & Williams, W. M. (2011). Understanding current causes of women's underrepresentation in science. *Proceedings of the National Academy of Sciences, 108*(8), 3157–3162. doi:10.1073/pnas.1014871108.

Ceci, S. J. & Williams, W. M. (2015). Why so few women in mathematically intensive fields? In *Emerging Trends in the Social and Behavioral Sciences* (pp. 1–12). Hoboken: John Wiley & Sons, Inc. doi:10.1002/9781118900772.etrds0388.

Cohen, J. (1962). The statistical power of abnormal-social psychological research: A review. *Journal of Abnormal Psychology, 65*(3), 145–153.

De Cohen, C. C. & Deterding, N. (2009). Widening the net: National estimates of gender disparities in engineering. *Journal of Engineering Education, 98*(3), 211–226. doi:10.1002/j.2168-9830.2009.tb01020.x.

Deci, E. L., Eghrari, H., Patrick, B. C. & Leone, D. R. (1994). Facilitating internalization: The self-determination theory perspective. *Journal of Personality, 62*(1), 119–142. doi:10.1111/j.1467-6494.1994.tb00797.x.

Deci, E. L., Koestner, R. & Ryan, R. M. (1999). A meta-analytic review of experiments examining the effects of extrinsic rewards on intrinsic motivation. *Psychological Bulletin, 125*(6), 627–668. doi:10.1037/0033-2909.125.6.627.

Diekman, A. B., Clark, E. K., Johnston, A. M., Brown, E. R. & Steinberg, M. (2011). Malleability in communal goals and beliefs influences attraction to stem careers: Evidence for a goal congruity perspective. *Journal of Personality and Social Psychology, 101*(5), 902–918. doi:10.1037/a0025199.

Diekman, A. B., Weisgram, E. S. & Belanger, A. L. (2015). New routes to recruiting and retaining women in STEM: Policy implications of a communal goal congruity perspective. *Social Issues and Policy Review, 9*(1), 52–88. doi:10.1111/sipr.12010.

Dovidio, J. F., Gaertner, S. L., Ufkes, E. G., Saguy, T. & Pearson, A. R. (2016). Included but Invisible? Subtle bias, common identity, and the darker side of "We." *Social Issues and Policy Review, 10*(1), 6–46. doi:10.1111/sipr.12017.

Duehr, E. E. & Bono, J. E. (2006). Men, women, and managers: Are stereotypes finally changing? *Personnel Psychology, 59*(4), 815–846. doi:10.1111/j.1744-6570.2006.00055.x.

Farhi, P. (2014, July 16). What's going on at Scientific American? Deleted posts, sexism claims, a fired writer. *Washington Post*. Washington, D.C.

Federico, C. M. & Sidanius, J. (2002). Racism, ideology, and affirmative action revisited: The antecedents and consequences of " principled objections" to affirmative action. *Journal of Personality and Social Psychology, 82*(4), 488.

Fisher, A. & Margolis, J. (2002). Unlocking the clubhouse. *ACM SIGCSE Bulletin, 34*(2), 79. doi:10.1145/543812.543836.

Fiske, A. P. (1992). The four elementary forms of sociality: Framework for a unified theory of social relations. *Psychological Review, 99*(4), 689.

Fiske, A. P. (2004). Relational models theory 2.0. In N. Haslam (Ed.), *Relational models theory: A contemporary overview* (pp. 3–24). Mahwah: Lawrence Erlbaum Associates.

Fiske, A. P. & Schubert, L. (2012). How to relate to people: The extraterrestrial's guide to homo sapiens. In O. Gillath, G. Adams & A. Kunkel (Eds.), *Relationship science: Integrating evolutionary, neuroscience, and sociocultural approaches* (pp. 169–195). Washington, D.C: APA.

Gaertner, S. L. & Dovidio, J. F. (2000). *Reducing intergroup bias: The common ingroup identity model*. Ann Arbor: Taylor & Francis.

Goulden, M., Mason, M. A. & Frasch, K. (2011). Keeping women in the science pipeline. *The ANNALS of the American Academy of Political and Social Science, 638*(1), 141–162. doi:10.1177/0002716211416925.

Hansen, J. & Campbell, D. P. (1985). *Manual for the Strong Interest Inventory: Form T325 of the Strong Vocational Interests Blanks* (4th ed.). Stanford: Stanford University Press.

Haslam, N. (2004). Research on the relational models: An overview. In N. Haslam (Ed.), *Relational models theory: A contemporary overview* (pp. 27–57). New York: Routledge.

Hoegh, A. & Moskal, B. M. (2009). Examining science and engineering students' attitudes toward computer science. In *2009 39th IEEE Frontiers in Education Conference* (pp. 1–6). San Antonio, TX: IEEE. doi:10.1109/FIE.2009.5350836.

Holden, C. (2000). Parity as a goal sparks bitter battle. *Science (New York, N.Y.), 289*(5478), 380. doi:10.1126/science.289.5478.380.

Klawe, M., Whitney, T. & Simard, C. (2009). Women in computing—take 2. *Communications of the ACM, 52*(2), 68. doi:10.1145/1461928.1461947.

Kouta, C. & Kaite, C. P. (2011). Gender discrimination and nursing: A literature review. *Journal of Professional Nursing, 27*(1), 59–63. doi:10.1016/j.profnurs.2010.10.006.

Kurzban, R., Tooby, J. & Cosmides, L. (2001). Can race be erased? Coalitional computation and social categorization. *Proceedings of the National Academy of Sciences, 98*(26), 15387–15392.

Larkin, M. & Heinzelman, W. (2016). STEM Scholarships for Women|Affordable Colleges Online. Retrieved from www.affordablecollegesonline.org/women-in-stem/#STEM-Scholarships-for-Women.

Lippa, R. A., Preston, K. & Penner, J. (2014). Women's representation in 60 occupations from 1972 to 2010: More women in high-status jobs, few women in things-oriented jobs. *PLoS One, 9*(5), e95960. doi:10.1371/journal.pone.0095960.

Lubinski, D., Benbow, C. P. & Kell, H. J. (2014). Life paths and accomplishments of mathematically precocious males and females four decades later. *Psychological Science, 25*(12), 2217–2232. doi:10.1177/0956797615575525.

Marx, D. M. & Roman, J. S. (2002). Female role models: Protecting women's math test performance. *Personality and Social Psychology Bulletin, 28*(9), 1183–1193. doi:10.1177/01461672022812004.

Miller, D. I. & Wai, J. (2015). The bachelor's to Ph.D. STEM pipeline no longer leaks more women than men: A 30-year analysis. *Frontiers in Psychology, 6*, 37. doi:10.3389/fpsyg.2015.00037.

National Association of Colleges and Employers. (2013). *The Class of 2013 Student Survey Report.* Bethlehem, PA: NACE.

National Science Board. (2012). *Science and engineering indicators 2012.* Arlington: National Science Foundation (NSB 12-01).

Nettle, D. (2007). Empathizing and systemizing: What are they, and what do they contribute to our understanding of psychological sex differences? *British Journal of Psychology, 98*(2), 237–255. doi:10.1348/000712606X117612.

Pinker, S. (2002). *The blank slate: The modern denial of human nature.* New York: Viking.

Pinker, S. & Spelke, E. (2005). The science of gender and science: Pinker vs. Spelke. Debate held by the Mind, Brain and Behaviour Initiative, Harvard University.

Richards, B. (2009). Representation of women in CS: How do we measure a program's success? *ACM SIGCSE Bulletin, 41*(1), 96. doi:10.1145/1539024.1508901.

Robertson, K. F., Smeets, S., Lubinski, D. & Benbow, C. P. (2010). Beyond the threshold hypothesis: Even among the gifted and top math/science graduate students, cognitive abilities, vocational interests, and lifestyle preferences matter for career choice, performance, and persistence. *Current Directions in Psychological Science, 19*(6), 346–351. doi:10.1177/0963721410391442.

Ryan, R. M. & Deci, E. L. (2000). Self-determination theory and the facilitation of intrinsic motivation, social development, and well-being. *American Psychologist, 55*(1), 68–78.

Sakamoto, A., Goyette, K. A. & Kim, C. (2009). Socioeconomic attainments of Asian Americans. *Annual Review of Sociology, 35*(1), 255–276. doi:10.1146/annurev-soc-070308-115958.

Sakamoto, A., Takei, I. & Woo, H. (2012). The myth of the model minority myth. *Sociological Spectrum, 32*(4), 309–321. doi:10.1080/02732173.2012.664042.

Sakamoto, A. & Wang, S. X. (2015). The declining significance of race in the twenty-first century: A retrospective assessment in the context of rising class inequality. *Ethnic and Racial Studies*, *38*(8), 1264–1270. doi:10.1080/01419870.2015.1016058.

Sheldon, K. M. & Kasser, T. (2001). Goals, congruence, and positive well-being: New empirical support for humanistic theories. *Journal of Humanistic Psychology*, *41*(1), 30–50. doi:10.1177/0022167801411004.

Stout, J. G., Dasgupta, N., Hunsinger, M. & McManus, M. A. (2011). STEMing the tide: Using ingroup experts to inoculate women's self-concept in science, technology, engineering, and mathematics (STEM). *Journal of Personality and Social Psychology*, *100*(2), 255–270. doi:10.1037/a0021385.

Su, R., Rounds, J. & Armstrong, P. I. (2009). Men and things, women and people: A meta-analysis of sex differences in interests. *Psychological Bulletin*, *135*(6), 859–884. doi:10.1037/a0017364.

Tajfel, H. & Turner, J. C. (1986). The social identity theory of intergroup behavior. In W. G. Austin & S. Worchel (Eds.), *The psychology of intergroup relations*, (pp. 7–24). Chicago: Nelson-Hall.

Tetlock, P. E., Kristel, O. V., Elson, S. B., Green, M. C. & Lerner, J. S. (2000). The psychology of the unthinkable: Taboo trade-offs, forbidden base rates, and heretical counterfactuals. *Journal of Personality and Social Psychology*, *78*(5), 853–870. doi:10.1037//0022-3514.78.5.853.

Tetlock, P. E., McGraw, A. P. & Kristel, O. V. (2008). Prescribed forms of social cognition—Taboo trade-offs, Blocked Exchanges, Forbidden Base Rates.pdf. In N. Haslam (Ed.), *Relational models theory: A contemporary overview*, (pp. 247–262). Mahwah: Lawrence Erlbaum Associated.

Tönnies, F. (1887). *Gemeinschaft und Gesellschaft*. Leipzig: Fues's Verlag.

Ufkes, E. G., Calcagno, J., Glasford, D. E. & Dovidio, J. F. (2016). Understanding how common ingroup identity undermines collective action among disadvantaged-group members. *Journal of Experimental Social Psychology*, *63*, 26–35. doi:10.1016/j.jesp.2015.11.006.

Wang, M. T., Eccles, J. S. & Kenny, S. (2013). Not lack of ability but more choice: Individual and gender differences in choice of careers in science, technology, engineering, and mathematics. *Psychological Science*, *24*(5), 770–775. doi:10.1177/0956797612458937.

Weber, M. (1968). *Economy and Society*. New York: Bedminster.

Woodcock, A., Graziano, W. G., Branch, S. E., Habashi, M. M., Ngambeki, I. & Evangelou, D. (2013). Person and thing orientations: Psychological correlates and predictive utility. *Social Psychological and Personality Science*, *4*(1), 116–123. doi:10.1177/1948550612444320.

PART II

How Politicized Social Psychology Distorts Research Methods and Design

6

SCALE CREATION, USE, AND MISUSE

How Politics Undermines Measurement

Christine Reyna

Science, in theory, provides a method for gaining objective knowledge about the world. It is rooted in careful observation and measurement paired with a logical assessment of these observations. When done correctly, science enables us to discover properties and processes that may be hidden from our own experiences and unrevealed by our prior assumptions. However, it also has limitations. Because science is an empirical endeavor, it is bounded by our ability to observe and measure phenomena of interest, and therefore its effectiveness is inextricably tied to our capacity for good measurement.

Pulling the levers of the elegant, dispassionate machine of science is often a very passionate human being. As much as the rapidly changing world needs champions of truth, having passionate agendas can be dangerous for the endeavor of science. People do science, and people can be very biased. Thanks to the science of social psychology, we have learned that we are motivated thinkers whose pre-existing beliefs, assumptions, experiences, and desires can affect every aspect of the perceptual and interpretive process—from the questions we ask, to what we perceive, and how we interpret what we perceive (see Kunda, 1990, for review). This very human quality does not bode well for an epistemology rooted in objective observation and measurement.

Liberal Bias in Social Psychological Measurement

One source of bias that can impact science at every stage is ideological bias. Ideologies are associated with particular worldviews and values that can influence the questions we ask, how we design our research and measure our constructs of interest, how we interpret our data, and what we choose to share with the world (Duarte et al., 2015). Social psychologists are overwhelmingly socially and politically liberal (Inbar & Lammers, 2012), which means that our discipline is vulnerable to liberal biases. Liberals have a particular way of looking at the world. They tend to focus on situational or systemic causes for group-based differences in status (like educational, employment, and wealth disparities) rather than personal causes like low ability or motivation (Skitka, Mullen, Griffin, Hutchinson & Chamberlin, 2002; Zucker & Weiner, 1993). They tend to feel passionate about social justice issues and perceive group-based status differences as a byproduct of injustice (Tetlock & Mitchell, 2008). Liberals also have favored scapegoats for social ills, such as high-status groups like big business, whites, and the wealthy (Pew Research Center, 2014).

In this chapter, I examine how a liberal bias can affect issues of measurement in social psychology. I focus on three primary issues: how liberal biases affect (1) what we measure, (2) how we measure, and (3) how we interpret our measures. Most of this analysis draws from literature on intergroup processes such as prejudice and discrimination, but these measurement limitations can affect many other branches of our field. For example, research in political, personality or community psychology may be especially susceptible to liberal viewpoints that could influence measurement strategies and subsequent conclusions. Finally, the examples that I use are from larger programs of research that have made significant contributions. These examples are not intended to diminish these contributions (on the contrary, they are all theories that I use in my own research) but rather show that even some of our best theories and impactful research programs are not immune to these pitfalls.

A Liberal Bias Can Affect What We Measure

Worldviews present a particular "reality" for people that make certain issues or problems come to the forefront as relevant, important, and real and make others seem less relevant, unlikely, or even nonexistent. In social psychology, liberal bias manifests in particular narratives that frame social issues in ways that influence our theories and science. In intergroup research, the narrative goes something like this:

> High status groups are self-serving and oppressive and low status groups are victims who are not responsible for their plights. As a result, it is our job as social scientists to reveal high status groups' oppression in all its forms, and protect vulnerable low status groups by avoiding tough questions about their contributions to these status differences, instead looking for solutions within the psychology of high status people.
>
> *(see also the paranoid egalitarian meliorist narrative,*
> *Winegard, Winegard, & Geary, 2015)*

Narratives such as this can lead to conceptual blind spots that prevent important questions from being explored.

One salient manifestation is how we study prejudice. Prejudice is a universal human phenomenon, but our literature on the topic is tilted toward a liberal perspective—namely, that prejudice is predominantly a majority group affliction (i.e., those in power, such as whites, men, or heterosexuals). Although a number of important studies have investigated prejudice among people of color (e.g., Judd, Park, Ryan, Brauer, & Kraus, 1995), the vast majority of social psychological research on, and thus our theorizing about, stereotypes and prejudice comes from the perspective of white (and/or male and/or high-status) groups oppressing low-status groups. This narrow focus perpetuates liberal and often paternalistic narratives implying that minorities are only *victims* of prejudice and makes it easier to overlook the consequential outcomes of prejudice perpetuated by members of minority groups. For example, gender oppression and sexual violence (Bermúdez, Sharp, & Taniguchi, 2013; Vandello, Cohen, Grandon, & Franiuk; 2009), heterosexism (Lewis, 2003) and interracial bias (McClain et al., 2006; Mindiola, Niemann, & Rodriguez, 2002) may at times be higher among people of color than among whites. Colorism—defined as discrimination based on skin tone—is prevalent within communities of color and is associated with a host of negative psychological and behavioral outcomes (see Russell-Cole, Wilson, & Hall, 2013, for review). These proximal prejudices that occur in one's immediate communities may at times have a more direct impact on minorities' day-to-day lives than the prejudice of more distant majority groups. Without a more comprehensive investigation of minority prejudice, its full scope and impact will remain unknown.

Social psychologists might be less motivated to study prejudice among people of color for several reasons. The first is convenience—it is easier to recruit white participants in larger numbers, especially if we sample from college campuses or low-cost, online participant recruitment tools like Mturk (that are often majority white; Buhrmester, Kwang, & Gosling, 2011). The second is that social psychologists might believe that majority prejudice is more consequential. People in the majority control resources and modes of social and economic status mobility (however, as suggested above, minority-on-minority prejudice might be more proximal and thus also as, or more, consequential). Another factor might be that most social psychologists are white, and given the history of white prejudice in America, there is something distasteful about whites turning the microscope of prejudice onto groups that have been historically victimized by white-perpetrated prejudice. Finally, minority prejudice does not fit a liberal narrative. To suggest that people of color are responsible for some portion of discrimination and oppression of other minorities suggests that they can be agents of oppression rather than simply victims of it. If our liberal sensibilities prevent us from even pondering this possibility, we will examine only a particular incarnation of prejudice and never truly understand its full manifestations and underpinnings.

Another striking example is the study of ideological prejudice. According to an impressive body of literature, there is a *prejudice gap* between liberals and conservatives, showing that, in general, conservatives are more prejudiced toward a variety of groups than are liberals (see Brandt, Reyna, Chambers, Crawford, & Wetherell, 2014). Theoretical examinations of the underpinnings of this difference include conceptualizations of a "conservative mind" that is more fearful, quick to close itself when confronted with different points of view, and much more ethnocentric (see Jost, Glaser, Kruglanski & Sulloway, 2003, for review). Despite this literature, a growing body of research reveals that the prejudice gap may be an artifact of what researchers choose to measure or not measure. Most of the research on ideological prejudice has measured prejudice toward groups that liberals prioritize—people of color, women, gays and lesbians, immigrants, and the poor. As a result, we see that liberals are much more supportive and open-minded toward these groups than are conservatives (the traditional prejudice gap). However, once we measure attitudes toward groups that conservatives prioritize—born-again Christians, businessmen, and anti-abortionists—we see a complete reversal in the prejudice gap. Now liberals are the ones who are more closed-minded and prejudiced (for a review, see Crawford, Chapter 7, this volume).

The bottom line is that examining social problems through a liberal lens motivates social psychologists to identify certain issues and their etiologies that fit liberal views of the world and prevent researchers from seeing other, sometimes equally prevalent and consequential issues or underlying causes that do not fit easily with this worldview. As a result, we tend to measure only a narrow set of manifestations of the problem. Because science is inherently incremental and iterative, this narrow focus can skew future research on the topic, leading to biased perspectives that can dominate our thinking, and ultimately our field, over time. When we include the perspectives and experiences of other groups (minorities; conservatives) on these issues, we improve the scope and accuracy of our theories and science (e.g., Duarte et al., 2015; Reyna & Zimmerman, 2017).

A Liberal Bias Can Affect How We Measure

When we research ideologically charged issues, such as political or intergroup attitudes, liberal biases can subtly influence how we design our research. It is difficult to put ourselves in the minds of those who have different values and perspectives, so we might not recognize when our research paradigms or measures have a liberal slant.

Framing and context effects. Survey construction is an art form fraught with potential pitfalls. The order of questions, how they are clustered together, and how they are worded all can affect the meaning of questions in unintended ways (Strack & Martin, 1987). Furthermore, the cognitive processes that participants execute in order to complete our measures are vulnerable to influence and bias. Respondents need to encode and interpret questions and retrieve pre-existing information and knowledge frameworks in order to formulate a response. Each of these cognitive steps is highly vulnerable to framing and context effects (Tourangeau & Rasinski, 1988).

Exposing participants to information or contexts at earlier stages of a perceptual sequence can bias how subsequent stimuli are perceived. For example, embedding scenarios of people bringing guns to school with questions about gun laws can increase support for gun control (Haider-Markel & Joslyn, 2001). Using emotionally charged words (e.g., "allow" vs. "forbid"), and/or including partisan positions in questions, can bias participant responses (Krosnick & Schuman, 1988). In our efforts to "disambiguate" questions about complex issues, we often provide additional context in scenarios, instructions, or measurements that could inadvertently change the meaning of the issue and the questions that follow (Chong & Druckman, 2007; Nelson, Oxley, & Clawson, 1997), especially when the contexts and frames we use have a decidedly liberal flavor.

Using ideologically charged wording can "activate" partisan associations with those terms, thereby creating a type of implicit framing effect. For example, framing federal aid as "government assistance to the poor" can dramatically increase support for financial aid policies compared to when the ideologically charged term "welfare" is used (Henry, Reyna, & Weiner, 2004). Terms like "income inequality" or "universal healthcare" impose liberal frames on political issues that are more appealing to liberals (vs. conservatives; Wetherell, Reyna, & Sadler, 2013). When the majority of our college samples lean liberal (see Henry, 2008), these language choices can result in powerful effects that distort scientific conclusions in ways that perpetuate liberal positions.

Researchers with a liberal bias may be more likely to assume that their interpretation of a survey question means the same thing to all participants and therefore may reach conclusions about the meaning of their findings based on this faulty assumption. Liberals and conservatives have different sets of assumptions about social and political issues, so the identical question can mean very different things to a liberal or conservative respondent. For example, one source of evidence for the prejudice gap is that conservatives tend to oppose policies that benefit minorities such as affirmative action. However, we know that when questions are framed broadly ("Do you support or oppose affirmative action?"), participants are more likely to rely on existing knowledge structures to interpret these questions. To liberals, affirmative action means outreach and providing qualified minorities with opportunities. To conservatives, affirmative action means arbitrary quotas and depriving qualified candidates of opportunities (Kravitz et al., 2000). Thus, in the minds of different respondents, these are very different questions, yet we often analyze them as though they mean the same thing for everyone (see also Reyna, Tucker, Korfmacher, & Henry, 2005). This can result in conservatives appearing more prejudiced when researchers assume that participants are responding to their liberal definition of this policy. When we ask about specific manifestations of affirmative action (e.g., "numerical quotas," "increasing recruitment of qualified minorities") liberals' and conservatives' attitudes often converge, especially when merit is made explicit (Haley & Sidanius, 2006, Table 1[1]; Kravitz & Klineberg, 2000), suggesting that our measures, and assumptions surrounding them, may be exaggerating the ideological divide (see Sherman, Nelson, & Ross, 2003).

Using proxy measures. A common practice that we see in the intergroup and prejudice literature is the use of proxy measures. Proxy measures are measures that are designed to measure *Phenomenon A* by using items or scales that actually measure *Phenomenon B*. The rationale is that if *Phenomenon B* is correlated with *Phenomenon A*, then it should be a suitable stand-in. Researchers will measure attitudes toward a policy and then interpret their findings in terms of prejudice; Protestant work ethic will be used as a stand-in for party preference; belief in a just world (BJW) will be labeled a system justifying ideology even though there is not a single mention of "the system" in the BJW scale. Our choice of proxy measures can be heavily influenced by our ideological assumptions. For example, as liberals, if we believe that only prejudiced people would oppose policies that benefit minorities, we are more likely to think that policy questions are suitable proxies for prejudice, when in fact there is a broad array of reasons people oppose policies (with prejudice being one of many; Sniderman, Crosby & Howell, 2000).

Assuming that a proxy measure reflects the actual construct of interest simply because they are associated is erroneous. For example, height and weight are strongly correlated, but to say that one is a suitable measure of the other is absurd. Measures can be correlated for a variety of reasons: certainly due to conceptual overlap but also shared variance that is not related to the concept of interest (e.g., method variance, wording similarity, response bias) and "third variables" that link the (possibly unrelated) proxy measure with our construct of interest, thereby artificially increasing their association. Researchers can increase the likelihood of finding effects that fit their hypotheses by using proxy measures that are more likely to get variance in predictable ways than measuring the construct of interest directly (e.g., we are more likely to get variance on a policy measure than a face-valid measure of prejudice). Unfortunately, this practice can perpetuate ideas that may be overstated or wrong.

One example that has received a lot of attention in the literature is the symbolic racism scale (Sears, 1988). Symbolic racism (SR) is a more indirect measure of racism that is more robust to social desirability effects compared to measures of "old-fashioned" racism. However, this scale came under fire because, according to critics, the indirect measures were actually measures of conservative values like hard work and meritocracy (e.g., "It's really a matter of some people not trying hard enough; if blacks would only try harder, they could be just as well off as whites."), so those who believe that hard work is a viable strategy for success (e.g., conservatives) will be more likely to endorse these items (Sniderman & Tetlock, 1986). The critique is that the SR scale could artificially inflate the perception of anti-black prejudice among people that endorse meritocracy by conflating true racism with race-neutral values.[2]

Proxy measures can also point to processes or mechanisms that might not really be driving our effects. An example is the belief that low-status groups justify the system, often to a greater degree than do high-status groups (Jost & Banaji, 1994). According to system justification theory, people are motivated to justify the status quo in which they live and see inequality as resulting from legitimate processes. Contrary to expectation, those who are most vulnerable in a system (e.g., lower-status groups such as women and minorities) may be the ones most motivated to rationalize it (Jost, Banaji, & Nosek, 2004). However, a thorough test of low-status system justification (LSSJ) was conducted on over 100,000 randomly selected people from all over the world using a variety of conceptually valid measures of system justification (Brandt, 2013). The data failed to confirm the LSSJ hypothesis, suggesting that this phenomenon may rarely exist.[3] So how does this reconcile with evidence supporting LSSJ? Many of the key findings showing examples of low-status system justification use proxy measures such as endorsement of so-called "system justifying ideologies" (e.g., ideologies suggesting that America is a meritocracy). The problem is twofold. First, some of these proxy measures (e.g., Protestant work ethic or meritocracy scales) assess larger beliefs about fairness and meritocracy and rarely if ever reference the American system directly. Second, the wording on many of these scales is ambiguous regarding whether or not agreement constitutes agreement with the overall notion of fairness/meritocracy or agreement that the *American system* is actually fair (e.g., "If people work hard, they almost always get what they want," e.g., Blodorn, O'Brien, Cheryan, & Vick, 2016).

Research using more face-valid questions shows that low-status groups tend to endorse these ideologies more than high-status groups, not because low-status groups think the system is legitimate, but because they are more likely to hold the system accountable for living up to these standards (e.g., that hard work *should* lead to success). When asked whether the system *actually* lives up to these ideals, low-status groups (and to a lesser extent, even high-status groups) say that the system is woefully falling short (Zimmerman & Reyna, 2013; see also Son Hing et al., 2011). Recognizing that low-status groups are keenly aware of the system's shortcomings, and may hold the American system to higher standards, can shed light on the ways in which low-status groups try to change, or even undermine, the status quo. Indeed, in 2014–2015, there were large-scale protests that rocked communities across the nation in response to systemic injustice in communities of color (following police shootings of unarmed Black men; e.g., Fieldstadt, Welker, Winter, & Silva, 2014), suggesting a need for theories that are more directly informed by the low-status perspective, and not just what we assume is their experience (see also "high-low fallacy" on p. 89).

Similar to proxy measures is our field's reliance on subtle (e.g., implicit) measures of what are actually very complex constructs. Although implicit measures are less susceptible to social desirability responding, they are also more vulnerable to violations of construct validity, raising questions about what they are really measuring in the first place. This is especially problematic with implicit measures, such as the IAT, which have inconsistent correspondence with explicit measures of the construct of interest, and even other implicit measures of the same construct. This has prompted concerns about the validity of using these methods as measures of attitudes (Olson & Fazio, 2003). Yet websites like Project Implicit (projectimplicit.com) will inform participants that their IAT scores indicate a "preference" for one group over the other—an assumption based on often small response time differences that could be affected by a host of factors and life experiences (and not necessarily attitudinal *preferences*).We know that well-learned associations can develop for a variety of reasons. For example, racists, but also those who feel empathy about the plight of racial outgroups, might both show stronger associations between racial minorities and negative words (Andreychik & Gill, 2012; Uhlmann, Brescoll & Paluck, 2006). This has fueled critiques about whether these measures should be used to represent attitudes like prejudice (Blanton & Jaccard, 2006). Despite these legitimate grounds for skepticism, social psychologists continue to use these measures to assess attitudes and personality traits. Implicit measures (like the IAT) can inflate the preponderance of more controversial attitudes (like prejudice) in our samples compared to that revealed by explicit measures (Arkes & Tetlock, 2004). If our participants tend to be predominantly majority group members, these inflated ratings can make controversial attitudes seem more prevalent among majority groups than they may actually be.

The hazard of using proxy or subtle measures is that we could be developing a science of erroneous or unlikely effects. If our principal understanding of prejudice stems from proxy measures rooted in ideological bias, false assumptions about the meaning of small response time differences, or the presumed interchangeability of correlated measures, some of our key findings and the theories they generate may be suspect. It is hard to measure controversial attitudes that often shrink under the spotlight of social judgment. However, we could do a better job investigating prejudice in more authentic ways. Not all proxy or subtle measures are erroneous; rather, we need to have more stringent burdens of proof that what we measure is actually what we think we are measuring. These methods need to be coupled with other indicators that prove that our proxies are valid and are free from ideological assumptions. We also need to stop treating unverified methods that have found their way into print as precedent that justifies our perpetuation of questionable measurement practices. Using more conceptually valid measures will enable researchers to uncover new patterns of data that might not always conform to a liberal worldview but may point us to more realistic theories and conclusions.

A Liberal Bias Can Affect How We Interpret Our Measures

When we are developing a research study, we meticulously frame statements to accurately represent our constructs of interests and fuss over instructions and wording to increase clarity, accessibility of language, and avoid unintended error from poorly worded or confusing (double-barreled) questions. We also carefully construct our measurement instruments to translate participants' reactions to our statements/questions into quantifiable values that (to the best of our ability) accurately reflect some internal psychological experience. It can be very frustrating when participants fail to follow our carefully worded instructions. We expect, and need, our participants to pay careful attention to the meaning of our questions and respond appropriately to the scales we use to measure them. Yet, when it comes to interpreting and analyzing those same scales, we often hold ourselves to a different standard, especially when we are wedded to preconceived expectations about what we want to find.

There are many ways in which an ideological bias can impact how we interpret findings.[4] In the following section, I focus on two ways that researchers can neglect the meaning of measures and superimpose pre-ordained assumptions about findings that do not align with the scales' original structure: The first is focusing on relative differences to the neglect of absolute values and, the second is ignoring the psychometric properties of our scales, particularly means and variability. Although these problems are not inherently tied to liberal bias per se, they can be strategies that perpetuate liberal biases by enabling us to see data patterns that conform in superficial ways to our ideological expectations but may actually indicate different processes.

Focusing on relative differences and ignoring absolute values: the high-low fallacy. Often, we focus on relative differences and ignore the absolute values associated with our scales. Take the well-known Likert scale:

1	2	3	4	5	6	7
Completely disagree	Mostly disagree	Somewhat disagree	Neither disagree nor agree	Somewhat disagree	Mostly disagree	Completely disagree

It is clear that one-half of the scale represents one type of attitude (disagreement), and the other half represents the opposite attitude (agreement). So it should be equally obvious that any value lower than a 4 represents varying degrees of disagreement, and values higher than 4 represent varying degrees of agreement. Yet all too often we see researchers treating small *relative* differences that occur at one end of the scale as though they represent values on the other end. For example, if participants are asked whether a particular workplace policy that favors men over women is fair (1 = completely disagree; 7 = completely agree), and female participants provide an average rating of $M = 1.6$, and male participants provide an average rating of $M = 2.3$, this does not mean that men on average are more likely to *agree that the policy is fair*. Neither group on average agrees that the policy is fair, even if there is some variability in disagreement. A more accurate interpretation would be that both men and women disagree that the policy is fair, but women disagree more.[5]

Misinterpretations like this occur often in our literature. Participants' average ratings will bunch up at one end of the scale, but because some discernible (i.e., statistically significant) difference occurs between groups, we treat these group means as though they belong to different measurement categories (e.g., those that are "high" vs. "low" on some quality, those that "agree" vs. "disagree" with some idea). I call this the *high-low fallacy*—or the assumption that statistically significant differences between groups clustered at one end of a scale constitute conceptual differences between groups that are psychometrically represented as opposite ends of the scale. Researchers are especially vulnerable to this mistake if they have pre-ordained assumptions about what participants should do. For example, if the researchers set out to investigate when people might agree with a biased workplace policy, it becomes tempting to treat less disagreement as some agreement.

One possible reason for this mistake is assuming that variability in our measures implies ambivalence—that is, assuming that varying degrees of disagreement imply simultaneous degrees of agreement (or varying degrees of opposition imply varying degrees of support and so on). However, this is an unfounded assumption. Often our agree-disagree scales (to use the example above) are structured such that varying degrees of disagreement are exactly opposite of varying degrees of agreement. This is appropriate because "somewhat disagree" does not necessarily imply "somewhat agree." It could mean that the participant disagrees but not very passionately, or that the participant disagrees with some aspects of the question but is neutral or uncertain about other aspects, and, yes, it could also mean that they might slightly agree and disagree at the same time. The point is there is no way to determine whether true ambivalence (a combination of agreement and disagreement) exists with this type of scale or whether the variability represents something else (see Breckler, 1994, for better ways to measure ambivalence).

Another reason for this common mistake is our field's emphasis on null hypothesis testing as the definitive determinant of our effects (a trend that is diminishing). The quest for small p-values can lead to sloppiness in how we interpret findings. When we see a "statistically significant result," we reject the null hypothesis and assume that the alternative hypothesis is supported, and therefore *however we framed the alternative hypothesis* is supported. So if our alternative hypothesis stated that "men would agree more than would women with biased workplace policies," a mean of $M = 2.3$ starts to look like evidence for agreement. The error is twofold. First, this is not what a significant p-value actually represents. A statistically significant difference suggests only that the slight discrepancy in degrees of disagreement between men and women is not a likely result given the sampling distribution of differences associated with the *null* hypothesis. It says nothing about attitudes. The second error lies in ignoring the actual numbers associated with our findings and their meaning. As this example illustrates, both means suggest strong disagreement, so the *p*-value is pointing to a difference not likely due to chance variability in the null distribution but a difference that may mean something other than what we originally predicted (that both men and women disagree with this policy but women disagree more strongly).

This oversight could result in the propagation of theories or popular data interpretations that become part of the collective thinking and culture of our discipline and can take on a life of their own beyond the actual nuances or even counterevidence embedded within the original numbers. Examples of the high-low fallacy abound in the prejudice literature. Almost across the board, most participants are not very supportive of attitudes and beliefs that disparage other groups en masse or policies, social structures, and systems that disadvantage minority groups (see Ho et al., 2015, Tables 2a, b). Research on hierarchy-enhancing policies and beliefs (attitudes that perpetuate unequal systems) often reveals a strong, overall *distaste* for hierarchies (Pratto et al., 2013). Despite these low overall numbers, hierarchy "enhancing" attitudes (like SDO) are often robustly correlated with support for hierarchy "maintaining" policies (like discriminatory policies; Sidanius & Pratto, 1999). However, a careful interrogation of many of these findings points to the greater probability that egalitarians and their strong opposition to discrimination are driving these correlations and not hierarchy-enhancers and their willingness to oppress others. This error is often driven by a tendency to overlook means and variability, especially when we are swayed by predetermined (e.g., ideological) expectations about what our data *should* look like.

Ignoring variance. We know that the vast majority of our sample (roughly 95%) will fall within ±2 standard deviations (SD) of the mean on our measures (assuming a normal distribution). Therefore, it is fairly easy to determine who is actually driving our results. When we are classifying people into high vs. low on a particular measure, especially personality or individual difference measures, it is important to first determine whether participants really span the range of the scale. In the intergroup literature, we are often dealing with restrictions of range on measures such as prejudice, SDO, Right Wing Authoritarianism, System Justification, and so on. Therefore, we have by and large abandoned the strategy of splitting people into actual groups (those that are actually high vs. low on our measure). First, there often are not enough, if any, people in one of those categories (usually the high prejudice groups), and second, it further restricts already-restricted variance and is thus deemed a less-optimal statistical practice. Instead, we allow our scales to remain unfettered and use correlational techniques to test our effects (e.g., regression, modeling), often probing effects at ±1 SD from the mean to show patterns of data. Although these practices rectify some of the *statistical* challenges with restrictions of range, they can make samples seem more variable than they may actually be. When coupled with a disturbing trend in the prejudice literature of only reporting correlational data and not reporting means and variance at all, readers are unable to know the true nature of the effects.

When we fail to consider the variability surrounding our measures, we can allow highly rare participants (the top or bottom 2.5%), or even outliers, to drive how we interpret our findings. Outliers can be especially problematic if our measure is skewed, which can happen with data that cluster at one end of the scale. Furthermore, reviewers and readers are not likely to take the time to see whether the variability surrounding scale means (when provided) justifies conclusions that (a) there are people who actually span the range of the scale, and (b) that these rare (or nonexistent) participants are likely driving the effects (however, see Crawford, 2014, for when restrictions of range can have the opposite effect).

When the vast majority of our sample is clustered in the low-prejudice, low-dominance, low-justifying (etc.) end of our scale,[6] we need to seriously consider the possibility that, although we set out to investigate oppression, what we may be uncovering is the psychology of egalitarianism. The conclusion that strong egalitarians strongly oppose hierarchy-enhancing beliefs and policies does not align with (liberal) goals to uncover oppression by high-status groups; however, this is more likely what is driving correlations in some of this research. A large-scale study was conducted across the world to better understand the psychometric properties of the Social Dominance Orientation (SDO) scale and its attitudinal correlates (Pratto et al., 2013). The researchers concluded that SDO was consistently right-skewed, and ratings were predominantly below the midpoint of the scale with fairly tight distributions suggesting that most people are predominantly egalitarian. Although the body of SDO research links high SDO with perpetuating inequality and oppression (see Pratto, Sidanius, & Levin, 2006, for review), the data may have been telling an egalitarian tale all along.[7]

These errors in measurement interpretation are not exclusive to a liberal bias; however, they are more likely to occur when we approach our science with preconceived ideas about what we expect to find and how society really works. When we see our data through a liberal lens, we are more likely to arrive at liberal conclusions that are more likely to get published in disciplines dominated by liberal-minded scholars (Duarte et al., 2015). When we take the time to consider alternative perspectives, examine our data more thoroughly, and look beyond our liberal assumptions, we discover that prejudice and oppression are far more nuanced than our science shows, and groups that we normally dichotomize into oppressors and victims have more in common than our data suggest. Although this revelation may not sit well in our predominantly liberal field (Inbar & Lammers, 2012), it challenges us to take bigger risks in our thinking, conduct better science, and broaden our theories to explain more of the variability and nuance in intergroup relations. In short, it makes social psychology more relevant.

Preventing Ideological Bias in Our Measurement

Human beings are constrained by their particular points of view, life experiences, and beliefs about how the world works and why. However, as scientists and reviewers, we can protect our research from these biases and enable the powerful tool of science to uncover important findings and mechanisms not readily revealed by a liberal perspective.

Suggestions for scientists. When it comes to what we measure, we must determine whether or not we are asking one-sided questions that presuppose a particular answer or point of view (e.g., why are conservatives more biased than liberals?). One-sided questions—whether they be research questions or survey questions—are especially vulnerable to ideological presuppositions. Instead, we should frame questions in open-ended ways that allow for multiple possible outcomes or pit one perspective against alternatives and provide measures that fairly test each (e.g., including target groups that liberals dislike and groups that conservatives dislike; Brandt et al., 2014). In so doing, we will be less likely to construct measures that are tilted toward a preconceived outcome.

We must also use measurements that have strong construct and face validity to ensure that we are interpreting our measures in the same way that our participants interpret them. This means avoiding questions that are too broad (and thus require participants to impose their own meaning) or "proxy measures" that participants take at face value but researchers interpret to mean something else. If Construct X is the construct of interest, measure it, not Construct Y. Also, we need to be honest about our scales and what their values actually represent. Data are supposed to reflect our participants' psychological states, so we should take their ratings at face value and not reinterpret their ratings to fit our prior assumptions. If they disagree with something, we should respect that and not reframe it as a version of agreement. We need to do the same with our patterns of results and explore patterns that point to a different interpretation than we expected. They may represent important (and equally publishable) unanticipated findings.

Suggestions for reviewers. As reviewers, our most important job is to ensure that the science of our discipline is sound. We are the gatekeepers that permit new ideas and findings to enter our canon of knowledge and eventually shape our understanding of the world around us. We must avoid getting seduced by clever, engaging, or ideologically appealing narratives and examine the data at face value. We need to read the methods and results sections carefully (or maybe read them first!). What did the researchers intend to measure, and what did they *actually* measure? We should examine the appendix or supplemental materials and the wording of the instructions, manipulations, or response items, carefully paying attention to bias in the wording, ordering, and structure of manipulations or measures. Might they produce a different psychological process—but the same pattern of data—than what the researchers intended? We should not be content to take the authors' word that their manipulations or measures actually manipulate or measure what was intended, and when in doubt, we need to request (demand!) to see these details before rendering judgment.

We must hold researchers accountable for their measurements and findings. If they are studying prejudice, their findings should be about prejudice, not some other, unmeasured (but possibly correlated) phenomenon. Also, we should carefully examine the psychometric properties of the scales and request more detail if not enough is provided. Researchers should not impute characteristics on participants that may be false (e.g., labeling people as "high" and "low" on a measure when in fact all participants are bunched at one end of the scale). As reviewers, we should interrogate the patterns of data carefully and go beyond the text to examine the original numbers. Oftentimes, the key pattern driving an effect is not what the authors focus on and rather is driven by groups or processes not central to their hypotheses. This might suggest an alternative explanation that could point to unexplored phenomena and generate new ideas.

Suggestions for consumers of science. Ultimately, the fate of our theories and research rests in the hands of consumers of science—namely, us. We can do our best to set our biases aside, use best practices for rigorous research, and be discerning reviewers with high standards. But we are still motivated perceivers who are more likely to believe research that fits our worldview. Questionable measurement and interpretive practices will still slip into our literature. It is up to us to be discerning consumers. We should not assume that peer review catches every problem, especially when reviewers might share the same liberal biases that might compromise their objectivity. In the end, we have to arrive at our own conclusions. Being aware of biases and methodological pitfalls will help us look beyond the narrative and consider the data more objectively. If the science is sound, the data will tell their own story regardless of the narrative they are given. These stories point us to perhaps different, but equally important, problems or phenomena that deserve our attention. It is up to us to venture outside of the comfort zone of our prized theories and ideological proclivities to let our data reveal their secrets. When we do, we may discover more authentic phenomena, uncover the inevitable nuance that is part of the complex issues that we study, and develop more insightful and accurate theories.

Notes

1 Across six specific policy frames using a random sample, liberal and conservative attitudes converged on all but two; however, ideology was measured with a combination of party ID and attitudes toward specific social policies. See the hazards of using proxy measures like policy attitudes to measure ideology in this chapter.

2 To be clear, racism is a unique predictor of policy attitudes, even for some conservatives (especially less educated conservatives; e.g., Reyna, Henry, Korfmacher & Tucker, 2006; Sniderman et al., 2000). The point is that proxy measures make it difficult to disentangle the role of racial and race-neutral attitudes on policy opposition.

3 The findings on LSSJ do not invalidate system justification theory broadly, which contains a wide array of propositions about how people perceive systems. Even the founders of SJ acknowledge that system justification happens more often with high-status groups (Jost et al., 2004).

4 The chapter by Ceci and Williams (Chapter 10, this volume) goes into much more detail about liberal bias in data interpretation.

5 Researchers can validate whether groups truly "agree" or "disagree" by testing whether the means of both groups differ significantly from the midpoint.

6 For example, one paper examined multiple versions of SDO scales across six diverse samples, and all means were below a 3.5 on a 7-point scale (with 1 = strongly oppose dominance) with the vast majority of means below 3 (Ho et al., 2015).

7 The SDO literature is large, and there have been a number of samples that yield objectively higher (above the midpoint) SDO scores. However, the majority of SDO studies in the U.S. yield very low SDO scores.

References

Andreychik, M. R. & Gill, M. J. (2012). Do negative implicit associations indicate negative attitudes? Social explanations moderate whether ostensible "negative" associations are prejudice-based or empathy-based. *Journal of Experimental Social Psychology, 48*, 1082–1093.

Arkes, H. R. & Tetlock, P. E. (2004). Attributions of implicit prejudice, or "would Jesse Jackson 'fail' the Implicit Association Test?" *Psychological Inquiry, 15*, 257–278.

Bermúdez, J. M., Sharp, E. A. & Taniguchi, N. (2013). Tapping into the complexity: Ambivalent sexism, dating, and familial beliefs among young Hispanics. *Journal of Family Issues, 36*, 1274–1295.

Blanton, H. & Jaccard, J. (2006). Arbitrary metrics in psychology. *American Psychologist, 61*, 27–41.

Blodorn, A., O'Brien, L. T., Cheryan, S. & Vick, S. B. (2016). Understanding perceptions of racism in the aftermath of hurricane Katrina: The roles of system and group justification. *Social Justice Research.* doi:10.1007/s11211-016-0259-9.

Brandt, M. J. (2013). Do the disadvantaged legitimize the social system? A large-scale test of the status-legitimacy hypothesis. *Journal of Personality and Social Psychology, 104*, 765–785.

Brandt, M. J., Reyna, C., Chambers, J. R., Crawford, J. T. & Wetherell, G. (2014). The ideological-conflict hypothesis: Intolerance among both liberals and conservatives. *Current Directions in Psychological Science, 23*, 27–34.

Breckler, S. J. (1994). A comparison of numerical indexes for measuring attitude ambivalence. *Educational and Psychological Measurement, 54*, 350–365.

Buhrmester, M., Kwang, T. & Gosling, S. D. (2011). Amazon's Mechanical Turk a new source of inexpensive, yet high-quality, data? *Perspectives on Psychological Science, 6*, 3–5.

Chong, D. & Druckman, J. N. (2007). Framing theory. *Annual Review of Political Science, 10*, 103–126.

Crawford, J. T. (2014). Ideological symmetries and asymmetries in political intolerance and prejudice toward political activist groups. *Journal of Experimental Social Psychology, 55*, 284–298.

Duarte, J. L., Crawford, J. T., Stern, C., Haidt, J., Jussim, L. & Tetlock, P. E. (2015). Political diversity will improve social psychological science. *Behavioral and Brain Science, 38*, e130.

Fieldstadt, E., Welker, K., Winter, T. & Silva, D. (December 14, 2014). Thousands March Across Nation to Protest Police Killings of Black Men. www.nbcnews. com/storyline/michael-brown-shooting/thousands-march-across-nation-protest-police-killings-black-men-n267806 (last viewed 5 June 2016).

Haider-Markel, D. P. & Joslyn, M. R. (2001). Gun policy, opinion, tragedy, and blame attribution: The conditional influence of issue frames. *The Journal of Politics, 63*, 520–543.

Haley, H. & Sidanius, J. (2006). The positive and negative framing of affirmative action: A group dominance perspective. *Personality and Social Psychology Bulletin, 32*, 656–668.

Henry, P. J. (2008). Student sampling as a theoretical problem. *Psychological Inquiry, 19*, 114–126.

Henry, P., Reyna, C. & Weiner, B. (2004). Hate welfare but help the poor: How the attributional content of stereotypes explains the paradox of reactions to the destitute in America. *Journal of Applied Social Psychology, 34*, 34–58.

Ho, A. K., Sidanius, J., Kteily, N., Sheehy-Skeffington, J., Pratto, F., Henkel, K. E., Foels, R. & Stewart, A. L. (2015). The nature of social dominance orientation: Theorizing and measuring preferences for intergroup inequality using the new SDO_7 scale. *Journal of Personality and Social Psychology, 109*, 1003–1028.

Inbar, Y. & Lammers, J. (2012) Political diversity in social and personality psychology. *Perspectives on Psychological Science, 7*, 496–503.

Jost, J. T. & Banaji, M. R. (1994). The role of stereotyping in system justification and the production of false consciousness. *British Journal of Social Psychology, 33*, 1–27.

Jost, J. T., Banaji, M. R. & Nosek, B. A. (2004). A decade of system justification theory: Accumulated evidence of conscious and unconscious bolstering of the status quo. *Political Psychology, 25*, 881–919.

Jost, J., Glaser, J., Kruglanski, A. W. & Sulloway, F. (2003). Political conservatism as motivated social cognition. *Psychological Bulletin, 129*, 339–375.

Judd, C. M., Park, B., Ryan, C. S., Brauer, M. & Kraus, S. (1995). Stereotypes and ethnocentrism: Diverging interethnic perceptions of African American and White American youth. *Journal of Personality and Social Psychology, 69*, 460–481.

Kravitz, D. A. & Klineberg, S. L. (2000). Reactions to two versions of affirmative action among Whites, Blacks, and Hispanics. *Journal of Applied Psychology, 85*, 597.

Kravitz, D. A., Klineberg, S. L., Avery, D. R., Nguyen, A. K., Lund, C. & Fu, E. J. (2000). Attitudes toward affirmative action: Correlations with demographic variables and with beliefs about targets, actions, and economic effects. *Journal of Applied Social Psychology, 30*, 1109–1136.

Krosnick, J. A. & Schuman, H. (1988). Attitude intensity, importance, and certainty and susceptibility to response effects. *Journal of Personality and Social Psychology, 54*, 940.

Kunda, Z. (1990). The case for motivated reasoning. *Psychological Bulletin, 108*, 480–498.

Lewis, G. B. (2003). Black-White differences in attitudes toward homosexuality and gay rights. *Public Opinion Quarterly, 67*, 59–78.

McClain, P. D., Carter, N. M., DeFrancesco Soto, V. M., Lyle, M. L., Grynaviski, J. D., Nunnally, S. C., ... Cotton, K. D. (2006). Racial distancing in a southern city: Latino immigrants' views of black Americans. *Journal of Politics, 68*, 571–584.

Mindiola, T., Niemann, Y. F. & Rodriguez, N. (2002). *Black-brown relations and stereotypes*. Austin: University of Texas Press.

Nelson, T. E., Oxley, Z. M. & Clawson, R. A. (1997). Toward a psychology of framing effects. *Political Behavior, 19*, 221–246.

Olson, M. A. & Fazio, R. H. (2003). Relations between implicit measures of prejudice: What are we measuring? *Psychological Science, 14*, 636–639.

Pew Research Center. (June, 2014). "Beyond red vs. blue: The political typology". www.people-press.org/files/2014/06/6-26-14-Political-Typology-release1.pdf.

Pratto, F., Çidam, A., Stewart, A. L., Zeineddine, F. B., Aranda, M., Aiello, A., ... Henkel, K. E. (2013). Social dominance in context and in individuals: Contextual moderation of robust effects of social dominance orientation in 15 languages and 20 countries. *Social Psychological and Personality Science, 4*, 587–599.

Pratto, F., Sidanius, J. & Levin, S. (2006). Social dominance theory and the dynamics of intergroup relations: Taking stock and looking forward. In W. Stroebe & M. Hewstone, (Eds.), *European Review of Social Psychology* (Vol 17, pp. 271–320). New York: Psychology Press.

Reyna, C., Henry, P. J., Korfmacher, W. & Tucker, A. (2006). Examining the principles in principled conservatism: The role of responsibility stereotypes as cues for deservingness in racial policy decisions. *Journal of Personality and Social Psychology, 90*, 109–128.

Reyna, C., Tucker, A., Korfmacher, W. & Henry, P. (2005). Searching for common ground between supporters and opponents of affirmative action. *Political Psychology, 26*, 667–682.

Reyna, C. & Zimmerman, J. L. (2017). I issues of status and power in interracial problems and solutions. In A. Blume (Ed.), *Social issues in living color: Challenges and solutions from the perspective of ethnic minority psychology [3 volumes]*, 231–260.

Russell-Cole, K., Wilson, M. & Ronald, E. Hall. (2013). *The color complex: The politics of skin color in a new millennium*. New York: Anchor.

Sears, D. O. (1988). Symbolic racism. In P. A. Katz & D. A. Taylor (Eds.), *Eliminating racism: Profiles in controversy* (pp. 53–84). New York: Plenum.

Sherman, D. K., Nelson, L. D. & Ross, L. D. (2003). Naïve realism and affirmative action: Adversaries are more similar than they think. *Basic and Applied Social Psychology, 25*(4), 275–289.

Sidanius, J. & Pratto, F. (1999). *Social dominance: An intergroup theory of social hierarchy and oppression*. New York: Cambridge University Press.

Skitka, L. J., Mullen, E., Griffin, T., Hutchinson, S. & Chamberlin, B. (2002). Dispositions, scripts, or motivated correction? Understanding ideological differences in explanations for social problems. *Journal of Personality and Social Psychology, 83*(2), 470.

Sniderman, P. M., Crosby, G. C. & Howell, W. G. (2000). The politics of race. In D. O. Sears, J. Sidanius & L. Bobo, (Eds.), *Racialized politics: The debate about racism in America* (pp. 236–279). Chicago: University of Chicago Press.

Sniderman, P. M. & Tetlock, P. E. (1986). Symbolic racism: Problems of motive attribution in political analysis. *Journal of Social Issues, 42*, 129–150.

Son Hing, L. S., Bobocel, D. R., Zanna, M. P., Garcia, D. M., Gee, S. S. & Orazietti, K. (2011). The merit of meritocracy. *Journal of Personality and Social Psychology, 101*, 433–450.

Strack, F. & Martin, L. L. (1987). Thinking, judging, and communicating: A process account of context effects in attitude surveys. In H. J. Hippler, N. Schwarz & S. Sudman (Eds.), *Social information processing and survey methodology* (pp. 123–148). New York: Springer Verlag.

Tetlock, P. E. & Mitchell, G. (2008). Liberal and conservative approaches to justice: Conflicting psychological portraits. In B. Mellers & J. Baron (Eds.), *Psychological perspectives on justice: Theory and applications* (pp. 234–255). Cambridge: Cambridge University Press.

Tourangeau, R. & Rasinski, K. A. (1988). Cognitive processes underlying context effects in attitude measurement. *Psychological Bulletin, 103,* 299.

Uhlmann, E. L., Brescoll, V. L. & Paluck, E. L. (2006). Are members of low status groups perceived as bad, or badly off? Egalitarian negative associations and automatic prejudice. *Journal of Experimental Social Psychology, 42,* 491–499.

Vandello, J. A., Cohen, D., Grandon, R. & Franiuk, R. (2009). Stand by your man: Indirect prescriptions for honorable violence and feminine loyalty in Canada, Chile, and the United States. *Journal of Cross-Cultural Psychology, 40,* 81–104.

Wetherell, G., Reyna, C. & Sadler, M. (2013). Public option vs. the market: Perceived value violations drive opposition to healthcare reform. *Political Psychology, 34,* 43–66.

Winegard, B., Winegard, B. & Geary, D. C. (2015). Too paranoid to see progress: Social psychology is probably liberal, but it doesn't believe in progress. *Behavioral and Brain Sciences, 38.* doi:10.1017/S0140525X14001332.

Zimmerman, J. & Reyna, C. (2013). The meaning and role of ideology in system justification and resistance for high and low status people. *Journal of Personality and Social Psychology, 105,* 1–23.

Zucker, G. S. & Weiner, B. (1993). Conservatism and perceptions of poverty: An attributional analysis. *Journal of Applied Social Psychology, 23,* 925–943.

7

THE POLITICS OF THE PSYCHOLOGY OF PREJUDICE

Jarret T. Crawford

Beginning with seminal work such as *The Nature of Prejudice* (Allport, 1954) and *The Authoritarian Personality* (Adorno, Frenkel-Brunswik, Levinson, & Sanford, 1950) and continuing into the present, many social psychologists seek to understand the predictors, manifestations, and consequences of prejudice. The study of prejudice and intergroup attitudes is certainly one of the principal areas of scientific inquiry in social psychology. There is an APA division *(Society for the Psychological Study of Social Issues)* and a full section *(Intergroup Processes and Group Relations)* of social psychology's flagship journal *(Journal of Personality and Social Psychology)* largely devoted to its study. Further, a PsychINFO search for "prejudice" finds over 19,000 hits (compared to other social psychological topics, such as "obedience" [2,189], "conformity" [8,933], and "persuasion" [5,911]).

This extensive literature has provided a number of potential individual difference predictors that lead to prejudice. Original empirical research as well as theoretical and meta-analytic reviews have identified political conservatism (Dhont & Hodson, 2014), right-wing authoritarianism, and social dominance orientation (Altemeyer, 1998; Crawford & Pilanski, 2014a; Sibley & Duckitt, 2008; Sidanius & Pratto, 1999), lower cognitive ability (Dhont & Hodson, 2014; Hodson & Busseri, 2012), psychological rigidity (Price, Ottati, Wilson, & Kim, 2015; van Hiel, Pandelaere, & Duriez, 2004), lower openness to experience and agreeableness (Akrami, Ekehammar, & Bergh, 2011; Sibley & Duckitt, 2008), and disgust sensitivity (Crawford, Inbar, & Maloney, 2014; Hodson & Dhont, 2015; Terrizzi, Shook, & Ventis, 2010), to name a few. This body of research has examined prejudice expressed primarily against ethnic minority groups, immigrants, women, sexual minorities, and other disadvantaged and low-status groups (e.g., homeless, overweight, poor, welfare recipients; for meta-analytic reviews, see Hodson & Dhont, 2015; Onraet et al., 2015; Sibley & Duckitt, 2008; Terrizzi, Shook, & McDaniel, 2013).

In this chapter, I discuss emerging evidence that challenges these conclusions about the individual different antecedents of prejudice. Specifically, I review evidence for the *ideological conflict model* (Brandt, Reyna, Chambers, Crawford, & Wetherell, 2014), which views prejudice as stemming from value conflicts between the perceiver and the target group or individual. From an ideological conflict model perspective, the link between some (but perhaps not all) individual differences and prejudice has emerged in the social psychological literature, not because these individual differences or traits predict prejudice per se, but because of value conflicts between adherents to these individual differences and the *particular types of targets groups social psychologists have chosen to study*. Emerging evidence shows that when alternative target groups are examined, the association between these individual difference variables and prejudice toward these alternative targets often either reverses direction or is statistically zero.

Before reviewing the ideological conflict model and evidence for it, I briefly review how prejudice has been defined and operationalized in social psychology and why some target groups have been included (while others excluded) in the study of prejudice.

How Is Prejudice Defined?

Allport (1954, p. 9) defined prejudice as "an antipathy based upon a faulty and inflexible generalization. It may be felt or expressed. It may be directed toward a group as a whole or toward an individual because he is a member of that group." This definition of prejudice has motivated many research approaches and is still often quoted in undergraduate social psychology textbooks (e.g., Myers, 2013, p. 309). However, as Brown (2010) and Crandall and Eshleman (2003) note, this definition is problematic, as it is impossible to objectively or empirically determine whether negative group feelings are erroneous, faulty, inaccurate, or irrational.

Another problem with this definition is that Allport (1954) explicitly defined prejudice in terms of *ethnic* prejudice, primarily emphasizing anti-black and anti-Semitic sentiment in his seminal work. In the over half-century of subsequent research, however, social psychological research on prejudice has extended well beyond ethnic groups to immigrants, women, sexual minority groups, elderly people, overweight people, unmarried people, etc.[1] Thus, a workable definition of prejudice encompassing the breadth of the social psychological literature on prejudice cannot be limited to a certain type of group.

It is for these and other reasons (see Brown, 2010, for a more extensive analysis) that a broader and more inclusive definition of prejudice is necessary. Crandall, Eshleman, and O'Brien (2002, p. 359) provide such a definition, defining prejudice as "a negative evaluation of a group or of an individual on the basis of group membership" (for a similarly inclusive definition, see Brown, 2010). In this chapter, I adopt this broad and inclusive definition of prejudice, the type of which Stangor (2009, p. 2) acknowledges has become normative in social psychology.

How Has Prejudice Been Operationalized?

A discrepancy occurs in the literature between how prejudice is defined and how it is operationalized. As noted above, modern scholars accept broad and inclusive definitions of prejudice. However, prejudice must be directed toward a particular target group or individual. Crandall and Eshleman (2003, p. 415) make the important point that whereas some scholars have argued that prejudice should include only expressions of negativity against groups with low status and power (Inman & Baron, 1996; Walker, 1995), prejudice can be expressed toward (and by) groups from across society. In practice, however, social psychologists focus almost exclusively on prejudice against societally disadvantaged and low-status groups rather than a broader array of groups from across society (for meta-analytic reviews, see Hodson & Dhont, 2015; Onraet et al., 2015; Sibley & Duckitt, 2008; Terrizzi et al., 2013; for an exception, see Crandall et al., 2002).

This emphasis on disadvantaged and low-status groups is consistent with the values and objectives expressed by both individual social psychologists and social psychological organizations in using empirical social psychological research to work toward social changes beneficial to such groups (Allport, 1954, p. 516; Eagly, 2016; Stangor, 2009, p. 1; Unger, 2011, p. 73). There is no question that it is societally important to study prejudice against disadvantaged and low-status groups; the spike in hate crimes against minority groups following Donald Trump's election in 2016 (Lichtblau, 2016) highlights the societal importance of unmasking these forms of prejudice and discrimination. That said, there are several disadvantages to restricting the psychological study of prejudice to such groups. First, it creates an artificial discrepancy between our accepted inclusive definition of prejudice (e.g., Crandall & Eshleman, 2003) and its practical operationalization. As Aronson, Wilson, and Akert (2010, p. 388) note in their social psychology textbook, "Prejudice is a two-way street; it often flows from the minority group to the majority group as well as in the other direction. *And any group can be a target of prejudice*" (emphasis mine; see also Yzerbyt & Demoulin, 2010). Second, it encourages imprecision in our scientific language when we refer broadly to "prejudice," yet our inquiry is restricted to only a subset of potential targets of prejudice.

Third, and most important, this restricted range of targets can lead to spurious correlations between individual difference variables and "prejudice." That is, with a restricted operationalization of prejudice, it may be that some people are prejudiced against all groups; or, it may be that there is something that the groups chosen by social psychologists have in common (e.g., low status and societal disadvantage) that inflates the interrelation of individual difference variables with prejudice toward these groups. These are scientifically untenable circumstances that affect most intergroup attitudes research.

Introduction to the Ideological Conflict Model

It is for all these reasons highlighted above that the *ideological conflict model* (Brandt et al., 2014) marks an important transition in the scientific study of prejudice, as it seeks to explore the expression of negative attitudes toward groups from across society rather than narrowly restricted toward disadvantaged and low-status groups. Based on an extensive body of evidence on the effects of similarity on liking (Byrne, 1971; Heider, 1958), the ideological conflict model assumes that people hold negative attitudes toward groups that are dissimilar in their values and beliefs, especially given that people find belief-inconsistent information and experiences threatening (Proulx & Heine, 2010). This presumption therefore allows anyone to express negativity toward any particular group that he or she finds threatening to his or her values and beliefs, regardless of the perceiver's or target's place in society (e.g., Aronson et al., 2010).

The initial research on the ideological conflict model examined the relationship between political ideology and prejudice. As mentioned above, extant evidence suggested that political conservatism was associated with prejudice (see Hodson & Dhont, 2015, for a review). However, the disadvantaged and low-status groups included in such research tend to be politically liberal themselves or are groups for whom liberals advocate (e.g., African-Americans, gay men and lesbians, welfare recipients; see Brandt et al., 2014, for a review). Thus, although it is possible that political conservatism predicts prejudice toward these groups because of particular types of racial or sexual animus (e.g., toward racial or sexual minorities), it may alternatively (or also) be because these groups are perceived of as ideologically dissimilar (i.e., liberal). Further, this question opened the possibility that if conservative target groups were also examined (e.g., the military, Evangelical Christians, rich people), the ideology-prejudice relationship might even reverse itself, such that political liberalism would predict prejudice against such groups.

This is exactly what these initial studies found. Conducted independently and published within just months of each other, three papers examined the ideology-prejudice relationship using a broad, inclusive, and ideologically heterogeneous array of targets (Chambers, Schlenker, & Collisson, 2013; Crawford & Pilanski, 2014b; Wetherell, Brandt, & Reyna, 2013). These studies relied on nationally representative, student, and community samples, used a variety of operationalizations of prejudice (e.g., feeling thermometer ratings; political intolerance; discriminatory intent; liking judgments), and used different sets of target groups. In each paper, there was no relationship between ideology and prejudice per se. Instead, political conservatism predicted prejudice against liberal groups, replicating previous research, while political liberalism was an equally strong predictor of prejudice against conservative groups. Figure 7.1 illustrates the correspondence between perceived target ideology and the ideology-prejudice relationship observed in Chambers et al. (2013)

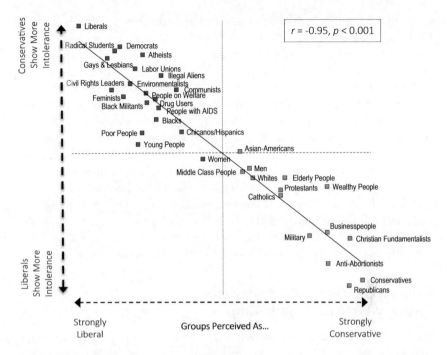

FIGURE 7.1 The more liberal a target group, the stronger conservatism predicts prejudice; the more conservative a target group, the stronger liberalism predicts prejudice.

Study 1, Sample 1—the ideology-prejudice relationship was strongly positive for groups perceived as liberal, and strongly negative for groups perceived as conservative, and the correspondence between perceived target ideology and the ideology-prejudice relationship was nearly perfect ($r = -0.95$). These results underscore the ideological conflict prediction that dissimilarity, and not political conservatism per se, underlies prejudice.

Other recent relevant evidence is consistent with this pattern of findings. Van Prooijen, Krouwel, Boitin, and Eendebak (2015) find in a large Dutch sample that, whereas those on the extreme right derogate groups like atheists and homosexuals, those on the extreme left derogate bankers, millionaires, and soldiers. Iyengar and Westwood (2014) extend Chambers et al.'s (2013) work from ideology to party identification, showing that Republicans prefer fellow Republicans, and Democrats prefer fellow Democrats, regardless of the target's race (see also Waytz, Young, & Ginges, 2014). They find these effects on explicit and implicit prejudice measures, as well as on actual discrimination in the form of a dictator game. Other work shows partisan biases in hiring decisions (Gift & Gift, 2015). This ideological conflict also extends to the left's and right's stereotypes of each other: Crawford, Modri, and Motyl (2013) find that liberals and conservatives ascribe different types of dehumanizing adjectives to each other (i.e., liberals as overly emotional and conservatives as robotic), and Graham, Nosek, and Haidt (2012) find that liberals and conservatives ascribe exaggerated moral stereotypes to each other (i.e., liberals as individual-focused and conservatives as group-focused).

The power of value conflicts appears to not be limited to simple partisan differences. For example, Sidanius, Kteily, Levin, Pratto, and Obaidi (in press) find that among both Christians and Muslims living in Lebanon and Syria, the best predictor of support for fundamentalist violence was a perception of incompatibility between Arab and American cultures. Further, Wetherell, Benson, Reyna, and Brandt (2015) find that value dissimilarity predicts Americans' willingness to withhold foreign aid to some countries but not others.

Research on the ideological conflict model has expanded in two general ways: (a) refining our understanding of the ideology-prejudice relationship, and (b) extending the reasoning of the model to other individual difference variables that have been linked to prejudice. I review this evidence next.

Refining Our Understanding of the Ideology-Prejudice Relationship

The role of threat in predicting negative attitudes. One line of research has examined the different types of threat perceptions that underlie negativity toward ideologically dissimilar others. Two of the original ideological conflict papers identified general threat perceptions (Crawford & Pilanski, 2014b) and threats to values (Wetherell et al., 2013) as mediating the ideology-prejudice relationship. However, neither of these papers compared different types of threats to each other. Crawford (2014) explored the effect of different types of threat perceptions (i.e., symbolic, realistic, safety, and rights threats) on both prejudice and political intolerance (i.e., denying rights to others) and whether there were ideological differences or similarities in these processes. Across three studies, prejudice (as measured with feeling thermometer and social distance ratings) toward both left-wing and right-wing groups was driven by symbolic threats—threats to one's deeply held values and beliefs—but the other types of threats did consistently predict prejudice. This result supports the ideological conflict model argument that value conflicts underlie negative intergroup attitudes and is consistent with other research indicating that symbolic threat is the strongest predictor of prejudice toward dissimilar others (Brandt, Chambers, Crawford, Wetherell, & Reyna, 2015).

Interestingly, however, the left and right differed in the types of threats that underlie their political intolerance. Specifically, whereas threats to physical safety underlie political intolerance toward left-wing target groups, threats to other people's rights underlie political intolerance toward right-wing groups. These results illustrate that those on the left and right express equal levels of political intolerance toward ideological opponents but that the motives underlying this intolerance vary in ways consistent with research on ideological differences in inclinations toward security (among conservatives; Jost, Glaser, Kruglansk, & Sulloway, 2003) and concern for others (among liberals; Graham, Haidt, & Nosek, 2009).

The multi-dimensionality of ideological prejudice. The dual-process motivational (DPM) model of prejudice argues that two related but unique ideological attitude dimensions have different social and personality antecedents and, in turn, have different consequences for intergroup attitudes (Duckitt & Sibley, 2010). Specifically, right-wing authoritarianism (RWA), which captures traditional values and the willingness to obey authorities and to defend those authorities from perceived dissidents, and social dominance orientation (SDO), which captures the belief in the superiority of some groups over others, are related to each other but predict prejudice toward different types of target groups. For example, RWA better predicts prejudice toward groups that violate traditional norms and values ("dissident" or "dangerous" groups; e.g., gay men and lesbians, atheists) whereas SDO better predicts prejudice against groups with low status and power ("competitive" groups, e.g., poor people, welfare recipients; Duckitt & Sibley, 2007; see Duckitt & Sibley, 2010, for a review).

While RWA and SDO strongly predict prejudice (meta-analytic rs of 0.55 and 0.49, respectively; Sibley & Duckitt, 2008), like other extant work, these studies have been limited to disadvantaged and low-status targets. To address this omission, Crawford, Mallinas, and Furman (2015) conducted two studies examining the effects of RWA and SDO on both prejudice and political intolerance toward an ideologically heterogeneous array of targets. Importantly, this work also relied on recent advances in measuring the multidimensionality of the RWA construct (Duckitt, Bizumic, Krauss & Heled, 2010) to examine which dimensions predict negativity toward ideologically dissimilar targets. Consistent with past research, SDO positively predicted prejudice and political intolerance against low-status groups (e.g., pro-affirmative action political activists); however, it negatively predicted prejudice (although not political intolerance) against high-status groups (e.g., anti-affirmative action political activists). Further, and consistent with past research, the traditionalism component of RWA (which captures adherence to traditional morals and values) positively predicted prejudice and political intolerance against groups that threaten traditional morality (e.g., pro-gay rights activists) but negatively predicted prejudice and political intolerance against groups who bolster traditional morality (e.g., anti-gay rights activists). Importantly, the conservatism dimension of RWA (which captures submission and obedience to authority) predicted political intolerance (but not prejudice) toward both right-wing *and* left-wing target groups.

These results provide a number of important contributions. First, they extend ideological conflict model research to ideological attitude measures (RWA and SDO) frequently used by intergroup attitudes researchers. Second, they identify a particular individual difference variable—the submission and obedience to authority component of RWA, i.e., conservatism—that appears to capture the heart of the authoritarianism syndrome, as it predicted political intolerance on both the political right *and* left. Finally, while one dimension of RWA negatively predicted political intolerance of right-wing groups (i.e., traditionalism), another dimension positively predicted political intolerance of these same groups (i.e., conservatism). This is a major problem for a scale that purports to capture political intolerance.

Another recent set of studies (Crawford, Brandt, Inbar, Chambers, & Motyl, 2017) approached the ideology-prejudice relationship in two novel and important ways. First, given evidence that ideology is best conceptualized as related but separate social and economic dimensions (Carmines & D'Amico, 2015; Feldman & Johnston, 2014; Malka & Soto, 2015), it examined the differential effects of social and economic ideologies on prejudice. Second, these studies utilized a variety of operationalizations of prejudice, such as warm/cold ratings, social distance ratings, intergroup emotions, trait attributions, implicit measures (i.e., the Implicit Association Test), and behavioral measures (i.e., the dictator game). These five studies (total $N = 4,912$) offered two important conclusions. First, social and economic ideologies do generally differentially predict prejudice against groups perceived of as varying on the social and economic dimensions, respectively. Thus, for example, social conservatism and liberalism more strongly predict prejudice against atheists and Evangelical Christians, respectively, whereas economic conservatism and liberalism more strongly predict prejudice against welfare recipients and businesspeople, respectively. While these conclusions only partially extended from explicit to implicit measures, they did largely extend to the discrimination measure. Second, consistent with arguments that most political conflict occurs on social issues (Hare & Poole, 2014; Koleva, Graham, Iyer, Ditto, & Haidt, 2012), these effects were generally more robust on the social dimension than on the economic dimension. Thus, ideological conflict is dimension-specific, but people react more strongly to dissimilarities on social than on economic issues.

Does "black" = "liberal?" One of the implicit assumptions of the ideological conflict model is that the reason previous research has found relationships between conservatism and prejudice toward certain groups (e.g., African-Americans; Sears & Henry, 2003) is not necessarily because of group-based animosity (e.g., racism), but because conservatives believe these groups are ideologically dissimilar (i.e., liberal). Chambers et al. (2013) base this argument on results from studies in which participants evaluated targets who varied either in their ethnic group label (i.e., black or white) and their ideology (i.e., liberal or conservative). These studies found that conservatism predicted liking of conservative targets, and liberalism predicted liking of liberal targets, regardless of target race (see Iyengar & Westwood, 2014, for similar effects on party identification).

However, Chambers et al.'s (2013) studies did not include a condition in which the racial target group (black or white) was *not* provided with an ideological label (i.e., simply "black" or "white"), which makes it difficult to conclude that conservatism predicts prejudice against "liberal blacks" as much as it predicts prejudice against "blacks." To explore this question, in a series of studies, Crawford, Brandt, Inbar, and Spälti (2016) examined people's attitudes toward and perceptions of a heterogeneous array of social groups (e.g., blacks, whites, Evangelicals, atheists) who were either labeled "liberal," "conservative," or were not provided an ideological label. Full-throated support for Chambers et al.'s (2013) argument would be revealed if, for example, conservatism equally predicted prejudice against "liberal atheists" and "atheists," and if, consistent with the ideological conflict model, liberalism equally predicted prejudice against "conservative Evangelicals" and "Evangelicals." Across two unpublished studies (total $N = 807$), this pattern of results held for target groups that are perceived as highly ideological (e.g., Evangelicals; atheists; gay men and lesbians) but not for groups perceived as relatively non-ideological (e.g., whites; hedge fund managers; women). Importantly, the effect of conservatism on prejudice against "liberal blacks" was stronger than the effect of conservatism on prejudice against "blacks," suggesting that ideological dissimilarity is not the only explanation for the effect of conservatism on anti-black prejudice. Thus, ideological dissimilarity can account for a large portion of dislike for certain groups, but that for other groups, other factors are also at play, including but not limited to, in the case of blacks, racial animosity.

Extending the Ideological Conflict Model to Other Individual Difference Variables

In addition to political conservatism, prejudice has also been tied to a number of other individual difference variables (see Hodson & Dhont, 2015, for a review). Recent studies have put these conclusions to the test in the context of the ideological conflict hypothesis. I review this evidence below.

Big Five personality traits. Low levels of openness to experience have been linked to prejudice toward a number of groups (Hodson & Dhont, 2015; Sibley & Duckitt, 2008); however, this research has largely focused on the relationship between openness and prejudice toward socially unconventional groups (e.g., ethnic and sexual minorities). If people high in openness are truly "open," then they should be less prejudiced toward both socially unconventional and conventional (e.g., Evangelical Christians; businesspeople) groups. However, if belief dissimilarity plays a role in the openness-prejudice relationship, then openness might have very different relationships with prejudice against socially conventional targets. A recent series of studies (Brandt et al., 2015) tested these possibilities and found that consistent with extant work, low openness is consistently associated with prejudice against unconventional groups. However, openness is either unrelated (Studies 1 and 2) or positively related (Studies 3 and 4) to prejudice against socially conventional groups, and these effects are mediated by perceived value dissimilarity.

A related series of studies examined the effects of each of the Big Five personality dimensions on prejudice toward an ideologically heterogeneous array of groups. Previous meta-analytic research examining prejudice against only disadvantaged and low-status groups found that low openness and low agreeableness strongly predict prejudice, but neuroticism, extraversion, and conscientiousness are not reliably related to prejudice (Sibley & Duckitt, 2008). In four unpublished studies (total $N = 7,543$), using large nationally representative and community samples, Crawford and Brandt (2017b) replicate Brandt et al.'s (2015) finding that the openness-prejudice relationship is moderated by the target's social conventionality and that this effect is mediated by dissimilarity. Importantly, however, low agreeableness is associated with prejudice toward a wide variety of groups, and is not consistently moderated by any factors tested, including target conventionality, likeability, or ideology. As in previous research, neuroticism, extraversion, and conscientiousness show no consistent relationships with prejudice toward this assortment of groups. In summary, these findings suggest that whereas the openness-prejudice relationship uncovered in meta-analyses is a product of target group choice, low agreeableness does truly seem to capture the "prejudiced personality," as it consistently predicts negative attitudes toward a heterogeneous set of targets.

Cognitive ability. Although some research suggests that low cognitive ability predicts prejudice, and that this relationship is mediated by socially conservative political attitudes (Hodson & Busseri, 2012; see Hodson & Dhont, 2015; Onraet et al., 2015, for reviews), this work has primarily focused on prejudice against left-leaning or left-aligned groups (e.g., gay men and lesbians; ethnic minorities; foreigners). Using the nationally representative 2012 ANES data set ($N = 5,914$), Brandt and Crawford (2016) show that cognitive ability (as measured with the WORDSUM battery) does not predict prejudice per se. Instead, target ideology, conventionality, and group membership choice moderate the ability-prejudice relationship, such that people low in ability dislike liberals, unconventional groups, and groups that have little choice over their group membership, whereas people high in ability dislike conservatives, conventional groups, and groups that have some choice over their group membership. Consistent with past work (e.g., Hodson & Busseri, 2012), these effects were mediated by socially conservative attitudes, but the effects reversed themselves for the high ability-prejudice relationship (i.e., greater social liberalism explained prejudice toward conservative groups).

Cognitive style. Cognitive styles associated with rigidity, dogmatism, and closed-mindedness have been associated with prejudice (e.g., van Hiel et al., 2004; see Hodson & Dhont, 2015, for a review). Price, Ottati, Wilson, and Kim (2015) developed an open-mindedness scale and found that low scores on this measure were associated with prejudice toward ethnic, religious, and sexual minorities, consistent with past work on the rigidity-prejudice relationship. However, this and past research examined only prejudice toward disadvantaged, low-status, liberal target groups. Crawford and Brandt (2017a) recently examined whether this new open-mindedness scale truly captures open-mindedness toward groups from across society or only toward disadvantaged, low-status, liberal groups. In an unpublished study ($N = 301$), they found that, whereas closed-mindedness predicted prejudice toward left-wing groups (replicating Price et al., 2015), it was unrelated to prejudice toward right-wing groups. Further, the effect of closed-mindedness on prejudice toward left-wing groups was mediated by perceived belief dissimilarity. Thus, open-mindedness does not appear to be the universal predictor of liking as Price et al. (2015) suggest; rather, it is another case of psychologists selectively choosing to study disadvantaged, low-status, liberal target groups and producing spurious correlations between individual difference measures and prejudice due to restriction in the range of targets assessed.

Religious fundamentalism. Religious belief, especially religious fundamentalism, has long been associated with prejudice (Allport & Ross, 1967; see Hunsberger & Jackson, 2005, for a review). As Brandt and van Tongeren (2017) recently point out, however, previous studies have included target groups that are likely seen as dissimilar to people who hold fundamentalist religious beliefs (e.g., gay men and lesbians; feminists; atheists; Blogowska & Saroglou, 2011; Hunsberger & Altemeyer, 2006; Jackson & Esses, 1997). Consistent with the ideological conflict model, Brandt and van Tongeren (2017) found in nationally representative and community samples that both people high and low in fundamentalism are prejudiced against groups seen as politically and religiously dissimilar (e.g., atheists and gay men and lesbians, and Catholics and Christians, respectively).

Disgust sensitivity. Disgust sensitivity predicts prejudice against disadvantaged and low-status groups, including immigrants, gay men and lesbians, Muslims, and poor people (Hodson & Costello, 2007; Inbar, Pizarro, Knobe, & Bloom, 2009; Terrizzi et al., 2010). Crawford, Inbar, and Maloney (2014) found that high disgust sensitivity is indeed associated with prejudice against groups perceived of as violating traditional sexual norms (e.g., pro-choice activists; feminists; gay men and lesbians), but that low disgust sensitivity is associated with prejudice against groups who uphold traditional sexual norms (e.g., pro-life activists; anti-gay activists). These findings are consistent with the belief dissimilarity mechanism underlying the ideological conflict model.

Implications of the Ideological Conflict Model on the "Prejudiced Personality"

Since Allport (1954) and Adorno et al. (1950), psychologists have been trying to determine the characteristics of the "prejudiced personality." Allport (1954, p. 68) observed that "One of the facts of which we are most certain is that people who reject one out-group will tend to reject other out-groups. If a person is anti-Jewish, he is likely to be anti-Catholic, anti-Negro, anti any out-group." Several modern scholars have taken up Allport's mantle to empirically identify the components of the prejudiced personality (or "generalized prejudice" as it is sometimes referred; Akrami et al., 2011). In their recent review, Hodson and Dhont (2015) argue that the prejudiced personality is one characterized by conservatism (particularly, authoritarianism), low openness and agreeableness, religiosity, heightened threat sensitivity, low cognitive ability, disgust sensitivity, and cognitive rigidity. Many of these contributing factors (e.g., psychological rigidity, conservatism, fearfulness) were emphasized by Allport himself (Hodson & Dhont, 2015, p. 3; 11).

But, as the present chapter has demonstrated, this approach is limited to an operationalization of prejudice restricted to socially disadvantaged, low-status, liberal target groups. An understanding of generalized prejudice must encompass an inclusive operationalization of prejudice—indeed, Allport's (1954, p. 68) explicit reference to "anti any out-group" demands it. From an ideological conflict model perspective, most of the individual difference predictors of prejudice that Hodson and Dhont (2015) identify fail to capture prejudice when applied to heterogeneous groups from across society (conservatism: Brandt et al., 2014; Crawford, 2014; right-wing authoritarianism: Crawford, Mallinas, & Furman, 2015; low openness: Brandt et al., 2015; Crawford et al., 2017; religiosity: Brandt & van Tongeren, 2017; threat and disgust sensitivity: Brandt et al., 2015; Crawford, 2014; Crawford et al., 2014; low cognitive ability: Brandt & Crawford, 2016; cognitive rigidity: Crawford & Brandt, 2017a).

So are there individual differences that truly capture the prejudiced personality from this broader, more inclusive understanding of prejudice? Only an ideological conflict model approach to intergroup attitudes can resolve this question. Some of this new research points toward possible candidates. Specifically, research on the personality-prejudice relationship (Crawford & Brandt, 2017b) shows across four studies that low agreeableness predicted prejudice toward groups from across the political spectrum and that this relationship was not moderated by important characteristics of the target group, or even related to worldview conflict. Crawford, Mallinas, and Furman (2015) also provide some evidence that obedience and submission to authority is the common denominator in political intolerance judgments, suggesting that value-neutral measures of authoritarianism may capture extreme forms of antipathy. Further, perceiving a group to be a threat to one's deeply held values (i.e., worldview conflict) seems to underlie prejudice across the political spectrum (Brandt et al., 2015; Brandt & van Tongeren, 2017; Crawford, 2014; Wetherell et al., 2013). Future research should use the ideological conflict model framework to explore other possible individual difference variables for their relation to a broad-based approach to prejudice. Good candidates would be constructs that purport to capture universal liking, such as Schwartz's (1992) Universalism value, and McFarland, Webb, and Brown's (2012) Identification With All Humanity scale.

Conclusion

In just a few short years, the ideological conflict hypothesis (Brandt et al., 2014) has already advanced our understanding of the individual differences that do and do not predict prejudice and the important role that value dissimilarity (i.e., worldview conflict) plays in people's judgments of others. Inconsistent with previous findings that certain types of individual differences encourage prejudice (e.g., political conservatism; openness; see Hodson & Dhont, 2015, for a review), these recent findings show that in almost all cases, characteristics of the target group moderate the relationships between these individual differences and prejudice. Studies inspired by the ideological conflict hypothesis replicate past research findings with the types of socially disadvantaged or marginalized groups social psychologists typically study—but they also show that these relationships are either non-significant or even reverse themselves for less-studied groups (e.g., conventional, high status, conservative, religious). That worldview conflict and value threats underlie prejudice across the political spectrum underscores the similarities in the way prejudice operates, regardless of the target group.

Social psychologists who study stereotyping, prejudice, and discrimination often have the well-meaning goals of reducing prejudice and uplifting groups who have been historically marginalized. These are goals that should not necessarily be abandoned. That said, such goals should not come at the expense of understanding the true scope of the antecedents, consequences, and manifestations of prejudice. To understand the psychological processes underlying intergroup negativity and prejudice, it is imperative that researchers explore prejudices toward a wider array of targets than they have traditionally. The ideological conflict hypothesis offers a way forward.

Note

1 Although "positive prejudice" (i.e., liking in-groups) can exist, similar to other accounts (e.g., Brown, 2010; Crandall & Eshleman, 2003), I focus on antipathy toward out-groups.

References

Adorno, T. W., Frenkel-Brunswick, E., Levinson, D. J. & Sanford, R. N. (1950). *The authoritarian personality*. New York: Harper.

Akrami, N., Ekehammar, B. & Bergh, R. (2011). Generalized prejudice: Common and specific components. *Psychological Science, 22*, 57–59.

Allport, G. W. (1954). *The nature of prejudice*. Reading: Addison-Wesley.

Allport, G. W. & Ross, J. M. (1967). Personal religious orientation and prejudice. *Journal of Personality and Social Psychology, 5*, 432–443.

Altemeyer, B. (1998). *The other "authoritarian personality."* In M. P. Zanna (Ed.), *Advances in experimental social psychology* (Vol. 30, pp. 47–91). New York: Academic Press.

Aronson, E., Wilson, T. D. & Akert, R. M. (2010). *Social psychology* (7th ed.). New York: Prentice Hall.

Blogowska, J. & Saroglou, V. (2011). Religious fundamentalism and limited prosociality as a function of the target. *Journal for the Scientific Study of Religion, 50,* 44–60.

Brandt, M. J., Chambers, J. R., Crawford, J. T., Wetherell, G. & Reyna, C. (2015). Bounded openness: The effect of openness to experience on intolerance is moderated by target group conventionality. *Journal of Personality and Social Psychology, 109,* 549–568.

Brandt, M. J. & Crawford, J. T. (2016). Answering unresolved questions about the relationship between cognitive ability and prejudice. *Social Psychological and Personality Science, 7,* 884–892.

Brandt, M. J., Reyna, C., Chambers, J., Crawford, J. & Wetherell, G. (2014). The ideological-conflict hypothesis: Intolerance among both liberals and conservatives. Current Directions. *Psychological Science, 23,* 27–34.

Brandt, M. J. & van Tongeren, D. R. (2017). People both high and low on religious fundamentalism are prejudiced towards dissimilar groups. *Journal of Personality and Social Psychology, 112,* 76–97.

Brown, R. (2010). *Prejudice: Its social psychology* (2nd ed.). Malden: Wiley-Blackwell.

Byrne, D. (1971). *The attraction paradigm.* New York: Academic Press.

Carmines, E. G. & D'Amico, N. J. (2015). The new look in political ideology research. *Annual Review of Political Science, 18,* 2015-216.

Chambers, J. R., Schlenker, B. R. & Collisson, B. (2013). Ideology and prejudice: The role of value conflicts. *Psychological Science, 24,* 140–149.

Crandall, C. & Eshleman, A. (2003). A justification-suppression model of the expression and experience of prejudice. *Psychological Bulletin, 129*(3), 414–446.

Crandall, C. S., Eshleman, A. & O'Brien, L. (2002). Social norms and the expression and suppression of prejudice: The struggle for internalization. *Journal of Personality and Social Psychology, 82,* 359–378.

Crawford, J. T. (2014). Ideological symmetries and asymmetries in political intolerance and prejudice toward political activist groups. *Journal of Experimental Social Psychology, 55,* 284–298.

Crawford, J. T. & Brandt, M. J. (2017a). *Open-mindedness only predicts liking of like-minded groups.* Manuscript in preparation.

Crawford, J. T. & Brandt, M. J. (2017b). *The "prejudiced personality": Low Agreeableness is associated with generalized prejudice, but low Openness is not.* Manuscript in preparation.

Crawford, J. T., Brandt, M. J., Inbar, Y., Chambers, J. R. & Motyl, M. (2017). Social and economic ideologies differently predict prejudice across the political spectrum, but social issues are most divisive. *Journal of Personality and Social Psychology, 112,* 383–412.

Crawford, J. T., Brandt, M. J., Inbar, Y. & Spälti, N. (2017). *A critical examination of the role of ideological (dis)similarity in political prejudice.* Manuscript in preparation.

Crawford, J. T., Inbar, Y. & Maloney, V. (2014). Disgust sensitivity selectively predicts attitudes toward groups that threaten (or *uphold*) traditional sexual morality. *Personality and Individual Differences, 70,* 218–223.

Crawford, J. T., Mallinas, S. R. & Furman, B. J. (2015). The balanced ideological antipathy model: Explaining the effects of ideological attitudes on intergroup antipathy across the political spectrum. *Personality and Social Psychology Bulletin, 41,* 1607–1622.

Crawford, J. T., Modri, S. A. & Motyl, M. (2013). Bleeding-heart liberals and hardhearted conservatives: Subtle political dehumanization through differential attributions of human nature and human uniqueness traits. *Journal of Social and Political Psychology, 1*(1), 86–104.

Crawford, J. T. & Pilanski, J. M. (2014a). The differential effects of right-wing authoritarianism and social dominance orientation on political intolerance. *Political Psychology, 35*(4), 557–576.

Crawford, J. T. & Pilanski, J. M. (2014b). Political intolerance, right and left. *Political Psychology, 35*, 841–851.

Dhont, K. & Hodson, G. (2014). Does lower cognitive ability predict greater prejudice? *Current Directions in Psychological Science, 23*, 454–459.

Duckitt, J., Bizumic, B., Krauss, S. W. & Heled, E. (2010). A tripartite approach to Right-Wing Authoritarianism: The authoritarianism-conservatism-traditionalism model. *Political Psychology, 31*, 685–715.

Duckitt, J. & Sibley, C. G. (2007). Right wing authoritarianism, social dominance orientation and the dimensions of generalized prejudice. *European Journal of Personality, 21*(2), 113–130.

Duckitt, J. & Sibley, C. G. (2010). Personality, ideology, prejudice, and politics: A dual process motivational model. *Journal of Personality, 78*, 1861–1893.

Eagly, A. H. (2016). When passionate advocates meet research on diversity, does the honest broker stand a chance? *Journal of Social Issues, 72*, 199–222.

Feldman, S. & Johnston, C. (2014). Understanding the determinants of political ideology: Implications of structural complexity. *Political Psychology, 35*, 337–358.

Gift, K. & Gift, T. (2015). Does politics influence hiring? Evidence from a randomized experiment. *Political Behavior, 37*, 653–675.

Graham, J., Haidt, J. & Nosek, B. A. (2009). Liberals and conservatives rely on different sets of moral foundations. *Journal of Personality and Social Psychology, 96*, 1029–1046.

Graham, J., Nosek, B. A. & Haidt, J. (2012). The moral stereotypes of liberals and conservatives: Exaggeration of differences across the political spectrum. *PLoS One, 7*, e50092.

Hare, C. & Poole, K. T. (2014). The polarization of contemporary American politics. *Polity, 46*, 411–429.

Heider, F. (1958). *The psychology of interpersonal relations*. New York: Wiley.

Hodson, G. & Busseri, M. A. (2012). Bright minds and dark attitudes: Lower cognitive ability predicts greater prejudice through right-wing ideology and low intergroup contact. *Psychological Science, 23*, 187–195.

Hodson, G. & Costello, K. (2007). Interpersonal disgust, ideological orientations, and dehumanization as predictors of intergroup attitudes. *Psychological Science, 18*(8), 691–698.

Hodson, G. & Dhont, K. (2015). The person-based nature of prejudice: Individual difference predictors of intergroup negativity. *European Review of Social Psychology, 26*, 1–42.

Hunsberger, B. & Altemeyer, B. (2006). *Atheists: A groundbreaking study of America's nonbelievers*. Buffalo: Prometheus Books.

Hunsberger, B. & Jackson, L. M. (2005). Religion, meaning, and prejudice. *Journal of Social Issues, 61*, 807–826.

Inbar, Y., Pizarro, D. A., Knobe, J. & Bloom, P. (2009). Disgust sensitivity predicts intuitive disapproval of gays. *Emotion, 9*(3), 435–439.

Inman, M. L. & Baron, R. S. (1996). Influence of prototypes on perceptions of prejudice. *Journal of Personality and Social Psychology, 70*, 727–739.

Iyengar, S. & Westwood, S. J. (2014). Fear and loathing across party lines: New evidence on group polarization. *American Journal of Political Science*, 59, 690–707.

Jackson, L. M. & Esses, V. M. (1997). Of scripture and ascription: The relation between religious fundamentalism and intergroup helping. *Personality and Social Psychology Bulletin*, *23*, 893–906.

Jost, J. T., Glaser, J., Kruglanski, A. W. & Sulloway, F. J. (2003). Political conservatism as motivated social cognition. *Psychological Bulletin*, *129*, 339–375.

Koleva, S. P., Graham, J., Iyer, R., Ditto, P. H. & Haidt, J. (2012). Tracing the threads: How five moral concerns (especially Purity) help explain culture war attitudes. *Journal of Research in Personality*, *46*(2), 184–194.

Lichtblau, E. (2016). U.S. hate crimes surge 6%, fueled by attacks on Muslims. Retrieved November 15, 2016 from www.nytimes.com/2016/11/15/us/politics/fbi-hate-crimes-muslims.html?hp&action=click&pgtype=Homepage&clickSource=story-heading&module=first-column-region&region=top-news&WT.nav=top-news.

Malka, A. & Soto, C. J. (2015). Rigidity of the economic right? Menu-independent and menu-dependent influences of psychological dispositions. *Current Directions in Psychological Science*, *24*, 137–142.

McFarland, S., Webb, M. & Brown, D. (2012). All humanity is my ingroup: A measure and studies of identification with all humanity. *Journal of Personality and Social Psychology*, *103*, 830–853.

Myers, D. G. (2013). *Social psychology* (11th ed.). New York: McGraw-Hill.

Onraet, E., van Hiel, A., Dhont, K., Hodson, G., Schittekatte, M. & De Pauw, S. (2015). The association of cognitive ability with right-wing ideological attitudes and prejudice: A meta-analytic review. *European Journal of Personality*, *29*, 599–621.

Price, E., Ottati, V., Wilson, C. & Kim, S. (2015). Open-minded cognition. *Personality and Social Psychology Bulletin*, *41*, 1488–1504.

Proulx, T. & Heine, S. J. (2010). The frog in Kierkegaard's beer: Finding meaning in the threat-compensation literature. *Social and Personality Psychology Compass*, *4*, 889–905.

Schwartz, S. H. (1992). Universals in the content and structure of values: Theoretical advances and empirical tests in 20 countries. *Advances in Experimental Social Psychology*, *25*, 1–65.

Sears, D. O. & Henry, P. J. (2003). The origins of symbolic racism. *Journal of Personality and Social Psychology*, *85*, 259-275.

Sibley, C. G. & Duckitt, J. (2008). Personality and prejudice: A meta-analysis and theoretical review. *Personality and Social Psychology Review*, *12*, 248–279.

Sidanius, J., Kteily, N., Levin, S., Pratto, F. & Obaidi, M. (in press). Support for asymmetric violence among Arab populations: The clash of cultures, social identity, or counter-dominance? *Group Processes and Intergroup Relations*.

Sidanius, J. & Pratto, F. (1999). *Social dominance: An intergroup theory of social hierarchy and oppression*. New York: Cambridge University Press.

Stangor, C. (2009). The study of stereotyping, prejudice, and discrimination within social psychology: A quick history of theory and research. In T. D. Nelson (Ed.), *Handbook of prejudice, stereotyping, and discrimination* (pp. 1–22). New York: Psychology Press.

Terrizzi Jr, J. A., Shook, N. J. & McDaniel, M. A. (2013). The behavioral immune system and conservatism: A meta-analysis. *Evolution and Human Behavior*, *34*(2), 99–108.

Terrizzi Jr, J. A., Shook, N. J. & Ventis, W. L. (2010). Disgust: A predictor of social conservatism and prejudicial attitudes toward homosexuals. *Personality and Individual Differences, 49*(6), 587–592.

Unger, R. (2011). SPSSI Leaders: Collective biography and the dilemma of value-laden action and value-neutral research. *Journal of Social Issues, 67,* 73–91.

van Hiel, A., Pandelaere, M. & Duriez, B. (2004). The impact of need for closure on conservative beliefs and racism: Differential mediation by authoritarian submission and authoritarian dominance. *Personality and Social Psychology Bulletin, 30,* 824–837.

Van Prooijen, J. W., Krouwel, A. P. M., Boiten, M. & Eendebak, L. (2015). Fear among the extremes: How political ideology predicts negative emotions and outgroup derogation. *Personality and Social Psychology Bulletin, 41,* 485–497.

Walker, L. E. A. (1995). Racism and violence against women. In J. Adelman & G. M. Enguidanos (Eds.), *Racism in the lives of women: Testimony, theory, and guides to antiracist practice* (pp. 239–250). New York: Haworth Press.

Waytz, A., Young, L. L. & Ginges, J. (2014). Motive attribution asymmetry for love vs. hate drives intractable conflict. *Proceedings of the National Academy of Sciences, 111,* 15687–15692.

Wetherell, G., Benson, O., Reyna, C. & Brandt, M. J. (2015). Perceived value congruence and attitudes toward international relations and foreign policies. *Basic & Applied Social Psychology, 37,* 3–18.

Wetherell, G., Brandt, M. J. & Reyna, C. (2013) Discrimination across the ideological divide: The role of perceptions of value violations and abstract values in discrimination by liberals and conservatives. *Social Psychological and Personality Science, 4,* 658–667.

Yzerbyt, V. & Demoulin, S. (2010). Intergroup relations. In S. T. Fiske, D. T. Gilbert & G. Lindzey (Eds.), *Handbook of social psychology* (Vol. 5, pp. 1024–1083). Hoboken, NJ: John Wiley & Sons.

8

RETHINKING THE RIGIDITY OF THE RIGHT MODEL

Three Suboptimal Methodological Practices and Their Implications

Ariel Malka, Yphtach Lelkes, and Nissan Holzer

The dominant psychological account of political ideology is an unflattering one for conservatives. Relative to liberals, they are said to be closed-minded, averse to novelty, highly attuned to threat, dogmatic, conformist, and disinclined toward complex thinking (Jost, Glaser, Kruglanski, & Sulloway, 2003). Perspectives along these lines—collectively dubbed the "Rigidity of the Right" Model (RR Model; Tetlock, 1984)—go back over half a century (Adorno, Frenkel-Brunswik, Levinson, & Sanford, 1950). After receiving sporadic attention for a number of years, they were revived and integrated in an influential review by Jost et al. (2003), who argued that people who are intolerant of uncertainty and sensitive to threat tend to have a cognitive-motivational affinity for right-wing ideology. It is fair to say that this viewpoint has become conventional wisdom within the psychological study of political ideology.

That this would strike many as an unsympathetic characterization of conservatives should not trouble anyone committed to accumulating knowledge through the scientific method. What does warrant greater attention, we presently argue, is that a non-negligible portion of the research considered supportive of the RR Model possesses one or more suboptimal methodological features and that the implications of these methodological issues for the RR Model have been insufficiently recognized. This, we contend, has resulted in a partial—but theoretically consequential—mischaracterization of the psychological origins of political ideology.

This chapter delineates three recurring suboptimal methodological practices within research on the psychological origins of political ideology and explores their implications by considering findings from studies in which they are not present. We offer a three-item checklist of methodological shortcomings and associated interpretive problems with the hope that scholars will use this checklist when (a) evaluating empirical findings relevant to the psychological origins of political ideology, and (b) selecting and operationalizing methodological moderators in meta-analyses of such findings. Although we believe that these methodological issues have tended to bias conclusions in support of the RR Model's central premise, we make no claim that ideological bias plays a role in any of them (cf., Duarte et al., 2015). We leave that as a matter for other scholars to debate.

The Three-Item Checklist

The three methodological issues that we highlight are

A   Content overlap between putatively pre-political measures and putatively political measures
B   Inadequate attention to the multidimensional structure—and, in particular, the central economic aspects—of political ideology
C   Inadequate attention to variation in political discourse exposure

The Rigidity of the Right Model

Many psychological perspectives on the origins of political ideology share a common theoretical core, which has been referred to as the Rigidity of the Right (RR) Model. The crux of this view is that a constellation of psychological attributes and evocable states—including dogmatism, closed-mindedness, intolerance of ambiguity, preference for order and structure, aversion to novelty and stimulation, valuing of conformity and obedience, and relatively strong concern with threat—leads to a preference for right-wing over left-wing political ideology. Three features of this general viewpoint are worth emphasizing.

First, the diverse attributes and states said to underlie conservatism may be efficiently described as falling within two broad families: uncertainty intolerance and threat sensitivity (Jost et al., 2003, 2007). Hibbing, Smith, and Alford (2014) argued that these various attributes and states may be distilled into a single construct, which they referred to as "negativity bias," but the manifestations of negativity bias in their model correspond closely with Jost et al.'s (2003) two families of pre-political characteristics. For expository purposes, we refer to these attributes and states collectively as Needs for Security and Certainty (NSC; cf., Hetherington & Weiler, 2009; Johnston & Wronski, 2015; Malka & Soto, 2015).

Second, the diverse attitudes and policy preferences said to comprise conservative vs. liberal ideology are often assumed to converge on a small number of core attributes. In Jost et al.'s (2003) model, these core attributes are opposition to change and tolerance of inequality. Putting these together, the central ideology-defining difference between conservatives and liberals is said to concern *change in the direction of equality promotion*; thus "liberals are invariably more

supportive than conservatives of initiatives that are designed to increase social and economic equality, such as welfare, social security, affirmative action,
universal health care, progressive forms of taxation, and same-sex marriage"
(Jost, Federico, & Napier, 2013, pp. 235–236). This is consistent with other
perspectives that conceptualize the core aspects of conservatism in terms of
preferences and values within particular policy domains, most commonly
economic and cultural (Carmines, Ensley, & Wagner, 2012; Treier & Hillygus,
2009). Across these conceptual frameworks, as in the RR Model, conservatism
(relative to liberalism) is defined as more culturally traditional and less economically redistributive.

Third, this is a viewpoint about an *organic* and *functional* relationship between a set of traits and states, on the one hand, and a broad, encompassing
social and economic ideology, on the other. As Thorisdottir, Jost, Liviatan, and
Shrout (2007) put it, "there is a special resonance or match between motives to
reduce uncertainty and threat, and the two core aspects of right-wing ideology,
resistance to change and acceptance of inequality" (pp. 179–180). This "special
resonance" between underlying psychological characteristics and political
ideology is sometimes described in connection with a system justification motive, or "motivation to defend, bolster, and justify existing social, economic, or
political institutions and arrangements" (Jost, Federico, & Napier, 2013, p. 236).
Noting various belief systems that are connected with right-wing politics, Jost
and Hunyady (2005) posited that while some of these belief systems "focus
purely on social and cultural issues, whereas others concern economic matters,"
the finding that they are intercorrelated "suggests that they may serve a similar ideological function, namely to legitimize existing social arrangements"
(pp. 260–261). Personality-based and situationally induced NSC are said to
yield a preference for preserving and justifying existing social and economic
arrangements, because doing so avoids destabilization of prevailing modes of
conduct and economic hierarchy. This, as the theory goes, satisfies needs to
avoid uncertainty and deal with threat. Such functional coherence between
personality attributes and both cultural and economic conservatism is the defining feature of the RR Model and can be traced to the central thesis of *The
Authoritarian Personality* "that the political, economic, and social convictions of
an individual often form a broad and coherent pattern ... and that this pattern is
an expression of deep-lying trends in his personality." (Adorno et al., 1950, p. 1).

Evaluating Research on the Psychological Origins of Political Ideology

We now describe three recurring methodological shortcomings within this
area of research and their implications for understanding the psychological
origins of political ideology. We begin with the long-recognized problem of
content overlap.

Content Overlap between Pre-political and Political Measures

Before reporting the results of their meta-analysis, Jost et al. (2003) noted that "too many measures of individual differences have conflated psychological and political variables in an attempt to measure a construct that is really a hybrid of the two" (p. 340). Indeed, the problem of content overlap has been present in many investigations of ideology's origins since the classic work of Adorno et al. (1950). Their F-Scale, intended to measure authoritarianism, overlapped in content with scales examined as correlates, such as measures of political-economic values and prejudice (e.g., Altemeyer, 1981; Hyman & Sheatsley, 1954). And as we will show below, this problem persists today in several widely cited studies on the psychological origins of ideology. Its recurrence reflects a guiding assumption in much of this research: that right-wing political opinion, threat sensitivity, novelty aversion, dogmatism, and prejudice all go together naturally as components of a *conservative syndrome* (e.g., Wilson, 1973). Quite problematically, measurement practices guided by this assumption are used to test the very idea that NSC characteristics relate to political conservatism.

Inclusion of NSC and related non-political content within political measures. The content overlap problem most often involves the inclusion within political measures of psychological content that is not directly political. Scales treated as indicators of conservative vs. liberal ideology often contain content pertaining to religious sentiment, cognitive rigidity, orientation toward authority, and/or intolerance, in addition to (mostly cultural) political content. The use of these scales as ideology measures is based on the *ex-ante* assumption that such traits and styles are an inherent part of conservatism vs. liberalism (cf., Crawford & Pilanski, 2014; Layman & Green, 2006). This is tautological when one is attempting to address the empirical question of whether, and to what degree, such traits and styles correlate with conservatism.

Consider, first of all, the F-Scale, which was the measure of conservatism in six of the findings summarized in Jost et al. (2003). In addition to socially conservative political content, it contains content condemning bad manners, expressing belief that people should "talk less and work more," asserting that everyone should "have complete faith in some supernatural power," and pertaining to a variety of other attributes that are reflective of rigidity, religious fundamentalism, and related characteristics (see Adorno et al., 1950, pp. 255–257, Table 7).

Next consider the Wilson-Patterson Conservatism scale (C-Scale). As Jost et al. (2003, p. 340) noted:

> Wilson and Patterson's (1968) Conservatism Scale (C-Scale)—which is the psychological instrument that has been most widely used to measure conservatism—combines nonpolitical stimuli that are meant to elicit

> general attitudes concerning uncertainty avoidance (e.g., modern art, jazz music, horoscopes) and stimuli that have explicitly political referents (e.g., death penalty, legalized abortion, socialism, religion).

But despite this acknowledgement, the Jost et al. (2003) meta-analysis included 40 findings (amounting to 26% of the findings summarized in their meta-analysis) involving the C-Scale as the conservatism measure. Testing a measure containing a substantial number of "nonpolitical stimuli that are meant to elicit general attitudes concerning uncertainty avoidance" (p. 340) as a correlate of uncertainty avoidance and threat sensitivity is, of course, tautological, and would be expected to inflate estimated associations between psychological and political variables (see Van Hiel, Onraet, & De Pauw, 2010).

Also less than ideal is the heavy reliance on Altemeyer's (1981) Right Wing Authoritarianism (RWA) scale as a measure of conservatism. This scale is now generally regarded as a measure of culturally conservative ideology (e.g., Duckitt, 2001) as its items do tap into culturally conservative content. But it is a particular kind of culturally conservative content involving an aggressiveness and paranoia directed at the unconventional; for example, longing for a leader who will "destroy the radical new ways and sinfulness that are ruining us" and expressing the urgent necessity of "smash[ing] the perversions eating away at our moral fiber and traditional beliefs." And like the F-Scale and the C-Scale, the RWA scale contains content pertaining directly to religiosity and fundamentalism, which ought to be viewed as correlates (rather than inherent components) of political ideology (e.g., Layman & Green, 2006).

The problem of content overlap has been widely recognized within political psychology (e.g., Sniderman & Tetlock, 1986; Stenner, 2005; Van Hiel et al., 2010), and one might be inclined to assume that the voluminous psychological literature guided by the RR Model since 2003 has largely used uncontaminated measures of political ideology. Unfortunately, there are many instances in which this is not the case. In a widely cited longitudinal study, for example, Block and Block (2006) included in their composite measure of ideology a political information scale, a political activism scale, and items assessing preferences regarding social stability, religion, and tolerance of political opponents. Those who knew more facts about politics, who engaged in more political activity, who were tolerant of political opponents, and who placed lower priority on social stability and religion, were coded as politically liberal. In a study of the origins of right vs. left political orientation, Kandler, Bleidorn, and Riemann (2012) included in their ideological conservatism measures position on "rebelliousness-conformity" and "tolerance-intolerance." These types of indicators should be treated as potential *correlates* of political views, with potentially complex ties to the latter—not as indicators of political conservatism itself (e.g., Brandt, Reyna, Chambers, Crawford, & Wetherell, 2014; Duckitt, 2001). Thorisdottir et al. (2007) documented intriguing differences in the origins of attitudes between Eastern and Western Europe, but they used a particular item to gauge an aspect of rightist political ideology that would have been better treated as a pre-political indicator: "Tradition is important to him. He tries to follow the customs handed down by his religion or his family." Similarly, Aspelund, Lindeman and Verkasalo (2013) measured political conservatism with value measures tapping openness to change and self-enhancement, measures that should be (and usually are) treated as indicators of "basic values" as opposed to political ideology (Caprara, Schwartz, Capanna, Vecchione, & Barbaranelli, 2006). Van Hiel et al. (2010) included "religiosity," "adherence to authoritarian parent-child relationships," and "dogmatism" among the variables "included as 'proxies' for socio-cultural conservative attitudes" (p. 1767) in a meta-analysis of behaviorally assessed predictors of social conservatism. While it is true that the dogmatism measure they used contains a good deal of political content, it is best described as a hybrid measure that combines a particular form of conservatism with non-political content (more on this below).

Inclusion of political content within pre-political measures. Sometimes political content is included in measures of putatively pre-political attributes. For example, associations between political group memberships (e.g., ideological and partisan groups) and the F-Scale—which blends cultural conservatism with non-political content—were long taken as support of the RR Model, based on the assumption that the F-Scale assessed rigidity (cf., Jost et al., 2003). Acknowledging problems with the F-Scale as a rigidity indicator, Rokeach (1960) developed a "dogmatism" scale, but unfortunately this measure contains political content, such as anti-Communist sentiment, pro-American nationalism, and a hawkish foreign policy posture. Those taking a hard-line cold war stance and expressing nationalism in this measure were assumed to be dogmatic, and dogmatism measured this way was examined as a correlate of (other) political attitudes. After a fleeting reference to this problem in a widely cited review, Stone (1980) proceeded to present evidence that right-wing and left-wing groups differ on the Rokeach dogmatism scale and then conclude primarily from this "that authoritarianism is a personality and attitudinal syndrome characteristic of right-wingers alone" (p. 14). The problematic reasoning here was thrown into sharp relief in a recent study by Conway et al. (2015). They noted correctly that the Rokeach dogmatism scale is a "measurement of dogmatism that captures domains on which conservatives are more dogmatic" (p. 4) and found that left-wingers were more dogmatic when the items were adjusted to query assertions of left-wing dogmatism (e.g., an environmental group tolerating diversity of opinion).

Inclusion of conservatism content within pre-political measures is not the most prevalent methodological flaw in personality-politics research, but it does lurk unnoticed in certain parts of the literature. For example, Jost et al. (2007, Study 3) used items assessing concern about crime victimization and the threat of terrorism (p. 1000) to study relations between threat sensitivity and conservatism. But these are two politicized threats associated with contemporary American conservatism (in contrast, for example, to climate change threat or threats from police violence, which are associated with contemporary American liberalism). Similarly, Thorisdottir and Jost (2011, Study 2) manipulated threat of terrorism to specifically examine "the effect of threat on political conservatism" (p. 785).

To summarize, when one looks into the measurement details of research cited in support of the RR Model, it is far too common to find NSC-related content in political measures, and one will sometimes find political content within what are supposed to be measures (or manipulations) of pre-political attributes (or psychological states). This would be expected to yield overestimates of the relationship between NSC and conservative political attitudes.

Inadequate Attention to the Multidimensional Structure—and the Central Economic Aspects— of Right vs. Left Political Ideology

When it comes to political policy, two dimensions of right vs. left conflict are most prominent: the economic dimension, having to do with views about government economic intervention and redistributive social welfare policy, and the cultural (or "social") dimension, having to do with views about traditional morality and treatment of cultural outsiders and transgressors (Benoit & Laver, 2006; Carmines et al., 2012; Duckitt & Sibley, 2009; Treier & Hillygus, 2009). Despite its well-established multidimensional structure, most research on ideology's psychological origins relies on a unidimensional operationalization of ideology. This implies, in a manner consistent with the RR Model, that cultural and economic forms of conservatism (vs. liberalism) cohere naturally due to common underlying psychological and biological influences (e.g., Alford, Funk, & Hibbing, 2005; Amodio, Jost, Master, & Yee, 2007; Jost et al., 2003). But, as Feldman and Johnston (2014) noted:

> [t]heoretical accounts of ideology must not assume what they seek to explain; namely, the foundations of ideological constraint in biological and psychological antecedents. Many of these recent studies have relied upon unidimensional operationalizations of ideology only to extrapolate their findings backwards to explain the effects of prepolitical orientations on multiple dimensions of ideology and thus on ideological constraint. In our view, this puts the proverbial cart before the horse. While such theories are both reasonable and well-grounded, they must hold up to closer empirical scrutiny.

Some work has indeed provided such scrutiny, by employing a multidimensional conceptualization of ideology when seeking to understand the psychological origins of political attitudes (Duckitt & Sibley, 2009; Feldman & Johnston, 2014; Johnston, Lavine, & Federico, 2017; Malka, Soto, Inzlicht, & Lelkes, 2014). Within psychology, this type of perspective dates back to the work of Eysenck (1954) and Middendorp (1978), but the Dual Process Model proposed by Duckitt and colleagues (e.g., Duckitt, 2001; Duckitt & Sibley, 2009) has perhaps been the most influential contemporary perspective along these lines. This model distinguishes a cultural ideological dimension said to be best operationalized by RWA and an egalitarianism-economic dimension said to be best represented by social dominance orientation (SDO). According to the Dual Process Model, high RWA is rooted in closed-mindedness, social conformity, and perceptions of the world as a dangerous place, along the lines of NSC; SDO, however, is rooted in dispositional tough-mindedness and a view of the world as a "competitive jungle."

Thus, like the RR Model, the Dual Process Model posits that NSC characteristics underlie attitudes regarded as conservative. But unlike the RR Model, the Dual Process Model posits that such NSC characteristics only underlie the cultural dimension, not the egalitarianism-economic dimension, the latter of which emerges from a distinct set of motivational goals. We will argue that, although SDO and economic attitudes ought not be treated interchangeably as in the Dual Process Model, the balance of evidence is consistent with the fundamental contention of this model that NSC does not yield a functional affinity for right-wing economic attitudes.

But first, why should one care? After all, as Hibbing et al. (2014) note, "modern polities deal with an amazing array of issues and categories and it is foolhardy to expect a single trait ... to account for all political variations" (p. 305). We contend that a failure of NSC to reliably predict economic conservatism would, in fact, constitute evidence against the RR Model. Economic matters are central to right-left policy competition within nations around the world (e.g., Bakker, Jolly, & Polk, 2012; Benoit & Laver, 2006; Huber & Inglehart, 1995; Lefkofridi, Wagner & Willmann, 2014; McCarty, Poole, & Rosenthal, 2008), as societies face fundamental trade-offs concerning the priorities of promoting growth and incentivizing productive activity, on the one hand, and providing for the needy, promoting economic equality, and harnessing economic activity for socially beneficial goals, on the other. According to the RR Model, those who especially prioritize security, threat avoidance, order, structure, and so on will, on average, be drawn to right-wing economic policies because those policies resist disruption of the economic hierarchy. Our view, quite simply, is that the balance of evidence runs against the RR Model when it comes to the ideologically central economic domain.

In considering this case, it is first of all important to recognize that most studies cited in support of the RR Model are unsuitable for examining the origins of economic attitudes. This is often because unidimensional conservative vs. liberal ideology measures or cultural conservatism indicators are used as the dependent variable (e.g., Fraley, Griffin, Belsky, & Roisman, 2012). Also, many studies assess a broad construct dealing with views about "equality"—such as SDO or other measures of generalized inegalitarianism—with implications for both cultural and economic forms of equality (e.g., Van Berkel, Crandall, Eidelman, & Blanchar, 2015). But there are now enough published studies with uncontaminated economic attitude measures to test whether the RR Model applies to the economic domain.

Six sources reported in Jost et al. (2003) dealt with economic attitudes, and several of these possessed problematic methodological features described in this chapter. The evidence from these six studies was inconsistent and inconclusive. Also, some studies omitted from the review showed null (Ray, 1973) or negative (Johnson & Tamney, 2001) relationships between NSC and economically right-wing views. But what does research since 2003 say about the link between NSC and economic attitudes?

One commonly used NSC indicator is "authoritarianism," which reflects "a set of personality traits associated with aversion to difference and conformity to authority" (Cizmar, Layman, McTague, Pearson-Merkowitz, & Spivey, 2014, p. 71). Unlike Altemeyer's RWA scale, measures dealing directly with valuing of obedience and uniformity gauge a trait that is devoid of political content and thus can be examined as a psychological predictor of political attitudes in a non-tautological way (Feldman & Stenner, 1997; Stenner, 2005). Analyses involving this type of authoritarianism measure show reliable relations with social conservatism but small and directionally inconsistent relations with economic attitudes (Cizmar et al., 2014; Clifford, Jewell, & Waggoner, 2015; Feldman & Johnston, 2014; Hetherington & Weiler, 2009; Napier & Jost, 2008; Stenner, 2005).

When one considers a broader range of uncertainty intolerance indicators, including openness to experience, uncertainty avoidance, and need for cognitive closure—it would appear that these measures have reliably correlated with cultural, but not economic, conservatism (e.g., Carney, Jost, Gosling, & Potter, 2008, Study 1; Chirumbolo, Areni, & Sensales, 2004; Crowson, 2009; Feldman & Johnston, 2014; Van Hiel, Pandelaere, & Duriez, 2004). Some studies have found (mostly with American samples) that uncertainty intolerance indicators relate to economic conservatism (e.g., Gerber, Huber, Doherty, Dowling, & Ha, 2010; Hennes, Nam, Stern, & Jost, 2012) and other studies have found mixed evidence in this regard across samples or measures (e.g., Cichocka, Bilewicz, Jost, Marrouch, & Witkowska, 2016; Clifford et al., 2015; Kossowska & Van Hiel, 2003). Meanwhile, the balance of evidence suggests that the related characteristic of low intelligence correlates with culturally right-wing but economically left-wing attitudes (Carl, 2015; Kemmelmeier, 2008; Morton, Tyran, & Wengström, 2011; Stankov, 2009). And Cichocka et al. (2016) found that preference for use of nouns in communication (theorized to "satisfy psychological needs for order, stability, and predictability," p. 3) correlated with social and "general" conservatism, but not with economic conservatism.

It is fair to say that threat sensitivity indicators have failed to reliably predict economic conservatism (Feldman & Huddy, 2014). As it turns out, some studies show links between threat sensitivity indicators and left-wing economic views (Gerber et al., 2010; Janoff-Bulman, Sheikh, & Baldacci, 2008, Study 2). Other studies show no relationship between threat sensitivity indicators and economic attitudes (Carney et al., 2008; Clifford et al., 2015; Crowson, 2009; Oxley et al., 2008).

Other research has examined changes in political attitudes following threatening events or threat manipulations (e.g., Bonanno & Jost, 2006; Hetherington & Suhay, 2011; Lambert et al., 2010; Nail & McGregor, 2009; Peterson & Gerstein, 2005). Although this work provides evidence that certain kinds of threats increase cultural or "general" conservatism, it has not provided reliable evidence that threat increases economic conservatism. Moreover, recent studies suggest that experimentally generated threats to control (Luguri & Napier, 2016), feelings of low economic status (Brown-Iannuzzi, Lundberg, Kay, & Payne, 2015), and disgust experience (Petrescu & Parkinson, 2014) might yield *left-leaning* economic preference.

The latter of these experiences, disgust, has been examined in the context of political ideology in quite a bit of recent research. Some research has demonstrated that inducing disgust leads to particular forms of cultural conservatism, especially regarding sexual morality (e.g., Inbar, Pizzaro, & Bloom, 2012). But, as described above, manipulated disgust might yield left-wing economic attitudes (Petrescu & Parkinson, 2014). Individual difference studies also suggest that disgust sensitivity relates to cultural but not economic conservatism (Inbar, Pizzaro, & Bloom, 2009, Study 2 (see footnote 2, p. 720); Smith, Oxley, Hibbing, Alford, & Hibbing, 2011, Online Supplemental Material; Terrizzi, Shook, & Ventis, 2010, Study 1)—consistent with findings that self-identified libertarians ascribe low moral significance to purity and other "binding" moral foundations (e.g., Graham, Haidt, & Nosek, 2009, Study 3; Iyer, Koleva, Graham, Ditto, & Haidt, 2012).

The balance of evidence described above is consistent with the view that while NSC indicators predict right-wing cultural attitudes, they do not reliably predict right-wing economic attitudes. Recently, Malka and colleagues carried out the largest cross-national study of these associations to date (Malka et al., 2014; Malka, Lelkes, & Soto, 2017). Using data from Wave 5 of the World Values Survey (WVS; 2005–2007), Malka et al. (2014) found that while a composite indicator of NSC reliably predicted culturally conservative attitudes, it was actually a small predictor of *left-wing* economic attitudes, on average. In a recent paper (Malka et al., 2017), this effect replicated within the Wave 6 WVS data set (2010–2014). In that paper, Malka et al. (2017) reported the zero-order correlations between NSC and two economic attitude measures for all Wave 5 and 6 samples with available data. One of the economic attitude measures assessed views concerning government responsibility for reducing economic inequality and promoting social welfare ("social welfare conservatism"), and the other assessed views about government vs. private ownership of business and industry ("ownership conservatism"). Across the two waves, only 5.3% of the within-nation correlations between NSC and social welfare conservatism were positive and statistically significant. Meanwhile, almost nine times as many of these within-nation correlations were *negative* and statistically significant (44.6%). The within-nation correlations between NSC and business ownership conservatism were positive and significant in 12.0% of the cases but negative and significant in 39.8% of the cases. Thus within-nations around the world, NSC more often went with left-wing than with right-wing attitudes in the ideologically central economic domain, although this association was typically small. In contrast, NSC often related to right-wing cultural views, such as traditional sexual morality. Like prior research, this suggests that when it comes to the cultural domain, there is a great deal of truth to the RR Model. However, given the centrality of economic matters to right vs. left political ideology around the world, these findings raise serious doubts about the RR Model's scope of applicability.

Inadequate Attention to Variation in Discourse Exposure

Most psychological studies aim to draw inferences about a large population from which study participants are sampled. But it is also true that most psychological studies are not conducted with a sample drawn randomly from a discernible population. The degree to which this mismatch yields misleading conclusions will vary based on a number of factors, including topic area. As for the topic of this chapter, it has been recognized that there are various forms of contextual variability in the relation between dispositions and political attitudes (Federico & Goren, 2009; Hibbing et al., 2014). However, as we argue in this section, researchers have underappreciated the implications of this contextual variability for the conclusions that can be drawn from particular research samples. In particular, we argue that inadequate attention to certain forms of contextual variability has biased conclusions in support of the RR Model.

Psychological samples tend to be "WEIRD"—Western, educated, industrialized, rich, and democratic (Henrich, Heine, & Norenzayan, 2010). This applies to most psychological studies on the origins of ideology. These studies are usually conducted with American samples or samples from other developed and democratic Western nations. Furthermore, many of these studies are conducted with samples whose characteristics would generally incline them toward a higher than average level of political involvement and knowledge: in particular, relatively high education or wealthy samples. And it is rare for variation across cultural or discursive context to be examined as a moderator of dispositional effects on political attitudes (cf., Duriez, Van Hiel, & Kossowska, 2005; Federico & Goren, 2009; Thorisdottir et al., 2007).

To understand how this could overstate support for the RR Model, it is necessary to focus on the construct of political engagement—or the tendency to follow politics, to be interested in politics, and to be politically knowledgeable (e.g., Abramowitz, 2010). As political scientists have long been aware, a unidimensional right-left organization of diverse political attitudes is mainly, if not exclusively, characteristic of politically engaged people (Converse, 1964). This is likely because politically engaged people tend to be committed to political identities (e.g., Huddy, Mason, & Aarøe, 2015) and to know information about what political positions are left-wing and what political positions are right-wing (e.g., Zaller, 1992). Those with political identities and the requisite exposure to political cues then employ "motivated reasoning" strategies (Kunda, 1990) to justify and bolster attitudes consistent with their political identities (e.g., Kahan, Peters, Dawson, & Slovic, 2013; Malka & Lelkes, 2010; Morgan, Mullen, & Skitka, 2010).

This has implications for the way in which basic dispositions translate into political attitudes. In particular, those high in political engagement often display the strongest relations between NSC and a unidimensional conservative vs. liberal ideology (e.g., Federico & Goren, 2009; Jost, Federico, & Napier, 2009). This in and of itself would suggest that evidence in support of the RR Model has been overstated by disproportionately sampling high political engagement groups, such as relatively educated and wealthy individuals, or, worse yet, political elites. But this problem is compounded when lack of attention to variation in political discourse is coupled with failure to take a suitable measure of economic political attitudes. Recently, two research groups have addressed this matter and proposed modifications to the RR Model based on their findings (Johnston et al., 2017; Malka et al., 2014; Malka & Soto, 2015).

To understand this new approach, consider a person with a high level of NSC. She will likely be inclined to adopt culturally conservative attitudes, in a manner consistent with the RR Model. But she might also experience a force compelling her to adopt left-wing economic attitudes, as shown in the previous section. This latter influence has been described by Johnston et al. (2017) as "instrumental"—those high in NSC should desire the material protection and stability that left-wing economic policies are intended to provide. But what if this person is exposed to a high volume of political information suggesting that right-wing cultural attitudes belong together with right-wing economic attitudes as part of a broad-based right-wing ideology? A good deal of survey evidence is now consistent with the view that she would adjust her economic attitudes to the right and that this would change the relationship between NSC and economic attitudes.

In Malka et al.'s (2014) cross-national investigation, NSC more often went with left-wing than with right-wing economic views. But there was a key exception to this pattern: among politically engaged individuals from ideologically constrained nations (in that they were characterized by a strong degree of right–left structuring of political attitudes), NSC displayed a small positive relation with right-wing economic attitudes. Coming from an ideologically constrained country (such as the United States) and having been exposed to a high volume of political discourse was associated with a reversal of the instrumental effect of NSC on left-wing economic views.

Similar findings were obtained by Johnston et al. (2017), who conducted relevant analyses with ten representative American samples and a diverse variety of NSC (what they referred to as "open" vs. "closed" personality) indicators. In the majority of cases, the relations between dispositional measures such as authoritarianism, need for cognitive closure, conservation vs. openness values, and conscientiousness had opposite effects on economic attitudes across those high and low in political engagement. In what Johnston et al. (2017) called the "reversal effect," NSC predicted right-wing economic views among those high in political engagement but left-wing economic views among those low in political engagement. Moreover, their findings from longitudinal data were consistent with opposite causal influences of NSC on economic attitudes across those high and low in political engagement—that is, the reversal effect. Thus, the findings presented in this section reveal how failure to account for variation in political discourse exposure can—especially when coupled with failure to cleanly measure economic attitudes—yield misleading conclusions about the psychological origins of ideology.

Summary and Conclusion

We have illustrated three common, and often overlooked, sub-optimal methodological characteristics of research considered supportive of the RR Model. We recommend that consumers of research on the psychological origins of ideology consider each of these when evaluating relevant empirical findings. First, we advise readers to gauge the extent to which the findings are impacted by *content overlap* between political measures and measures of pre-political attributes or manipulations of psychological states. Second, we recommend that readers take note of whether the *economic dimension* of ideological conflict—a central aspect of right vs. left political ideology in much of the world—is independently examined as a correlate or consequence of the psychological factor. Third, we advise readers to consider whether the study oversamples WEIRD individuals or otherwise fails to account for variation in discourse exposure.

As we have shown, consideration of these features will often temper conclusions in support of the RR Model. Inclusion of content pertaining to uncertainty intolerance, religiosity, religious fundamentalism, and the like within political measures, and/or inclusion of right-wing political content within NSC measures, will inflate estimates of the link between NSC and conservative ideology. Failure to examine effects and influences on a bare-bones measure of economic attitudes will conceal the inadequacy of the RR Model when it comes to the ideologically central economic domain. And failure to explore variation across discursive context and level of exposure to discourse will obscure the complex and discourse-contingent nature of the relationship between NSC and economic views.

A great deal of literature assumes the fundamental validity of the RR Model and cites studies as supportive of the RR Model when they in fact possess one or more of these methodological features. Therefore, we contend, it is worthwhile to go back to the cited literature and evaluate studies' methodologies based on this checklist instead of taking their conclusions at face value. The devil is often in the methodological details.

In light of these observations, we present four straightforward methodological recommendations for research on the psychological origins of ideology. First, studies should employ a multidimensional conceptualization of ideology and take clean "bare-bones" (e.g., Stenner, 2005) measures of economic and cultural attitudes. Political measures should not contain content pertaining to uncertainty intolerance, religiosity, and other related constructs when these political measures are being examined as correlates of such constructs.

Second, studies should include measures of political engagement and should test this as a moderator of the link between psychological characteristics and political attitudes. Regrettably, this practice has been uncommon in psychological research on the origins of ideology, despite consistent evidence that political engagement relates to organization of ideological attitudes on the right-left dimension (e.g., Abramowitz, 2010) and moderates the relations between dispositions and political attitudes (e.g., Federico & Goren, 2009). Exploring how effects of dispositions on specific political attitudes differ between those high and low in political engagement has potential to illuminate the complex and often competing social and psychological processes that shape political ideology.

Third, when possible, researchers should examine differences in the correlates and causes of ideological attitudes across nations that vary in levels of development, political institutions, and aspects of the political information environment. This goes hand in hand with examining political engagement as a moderator, as both would improve understanding of the conditional and context-dependent nature of links between psychological factors and specific political attitudes.

Our final recommendation pertains to meta-analyses on the psychological origins of political attitudes. This chapter has provided only a narrative review of prior research, and one might challenge it on the grounds that it did not quantitatively summarize prior findings. To this anticipated critique, we reply that a meta-analysis that includes findings obtained with the problematic methodological features described here would be expected to overstate support for the RR Model. We recommend that, within meta-analyses of findings on the psychological origins of ideology, researchers include tests of potential methodological moderators in line with the checklist presented here. This would involve computing study-level measures that quantify the extent to which a particular finding involves variables with content overlap, includes a political measure reflecting a particular type of content (e.g., economic, cultural, generalized egalitarianism, unidimensional right-left ideology), and comes from a WEIRD and/or highly politically engaged sample. A rigorous test of these moderators would shed light on the extent to which the conventional wisdom about the psychological origins of ideology is the product of less-than-ideal methodological and interpretive practices.

Acknowledgments

We are grateful to Christine Reyna and Jarret Crawford for their helpful comments on an earlier version of this chapter.

References

Abramowitz, A. I. (2010). *The disappearing center: Engaged citizens, polarization, and American democracy.* New Haven: Yale University Press.

Adorno, T. W., Frenkel-Brunswik, E., Levinson, D. J. & Sanford, R. N. (1950). *The authoritarian personality.* New York: Harper.

Alford, J. R., Funk, C. L. & Hibbing, J. R. (2005). Are political orientations genetically transmitted? *American Political Science Review, 99*(02), 153–167.

Altemeyer, B. (1981). *Right-wing authoritarianism.* Manitoba: University of Manitoba Press.

Amodio, D. M., Jost, J. T., Master, S. L. & Yee, C. M. (2007). Neurocognitive correlates of liberalism and conservatism. *Nature Neuroscience, 10*(10), 1246–1247.

Aspelund, A., Lindeman, M. & Verkasalo, M. (2013). Political Conservatism and Left–Right Orientation in 28 Eastern and Western European Countries. *Political Psychology, 34*(3), 409–417.

Bakker, R., Jolly, S. & Polk, J. (2012). Complexity in the European party space: Exploring dimensionality with experts. *European Union Politics, 13*(2), 219–245.

Benoit, K. & Laver, M. (2006). *Party policy in modern democracies.* London: Routledge.

Block, J. & Block, J. H. (2006). Nursery school personality and political orientation two decades later. *Journal of Research in Personality, 40*(5), 734–749.

Bonanno, G. A. & Jost, J. T. (2006). Conservative shift among high-exposure survivors of the September 11th terrorist attacks. *Basic and Applied Social Psychology, 28*(4), 311–323.

Brandt, M. J., Reyna, C., Chambers, J. R., Crawford, J. T. & Wetherell, G. (2014). The ideological-conflict hypothesis intolerance among both liberals and conservatives. *Current Directions in Psychological Science, 23*(1), 27–34.

Brown-Iannuzzi, J. L., Lundberg, K. B., Kay, A. C. & Payne, B. K. (2015). Subjective status shapes political preferences. *Psychological Science, 26*(1), 15–26.

Carmines, E. G., Ensley, M. J. & Wagner, M. W. (2012). Political ideology in American politics: One, two, or none? *The Forum, 10*(3), 1–18.

Caprara, G. V., Schwartz, S., Capanna, C., Vecchione, M. & Barbaranelli, C. (2006). Personality and politics: Values, traits, and political choice. *Political Psychology*, 27(1), 1–28.

Carney, D. R., Jost, J. T., Gosling, S. D. & Potter, J. (2008). The secret lives of liberals and conservatives: Personality profiles, interaction styles, and the things they leave behind. *Political Psychology*, 29(6), 807–840.

Chirumbolo, A., Areni, A. & Sensales, G. (2004). Need for cognitive closure and politics: Voting, political attitudes and attributional style. *International Journal of Psychology*, 39(4), 245–253.

Cichocka, A., Bilewicz, M., Jost, J. T., Marroush, N. & Witkowska, M. (2016). On the grammar of politics—or why conservatives prefer nouns. *Political Psychology*. doi:10.1111/pops.12327.

Cizmar, A. M., Layman, G. C., McTague, J., Pearson-Merkowitz, S. & Spivey, M. (2014). Authoritarianism and American political behavior from 1952 to 2008. *Political Research Quarterly*, 67(1), 71–83.

Clifford, S., Jewell, R. M. & Waggoner, P. D. (2015). Are samples drawn from Mechanical Turk valid for research on political ideology? *Research & Politics*, 2(4), 1–9. doi:10.1177/2053168015622072.

Converse, P. E. (1964). The nature of belief systems in mass publics. In D. Apter (Ed.), ·*Ideology and discontent* (pp. 206–261). New York: The Free Press.

Conway, L. G., Gornick, L. J., Houck, S. C., Anderson, C., Stockert, J., Sessoms, D. & McCue, K. (2015). Are conservatives really more simple-minded than liberals? The domain specificity of complex thinking. *Political Psychology*. doi:10.1111/pops.12304.

Crawford, J. T. & Pilanski, J. M. (2014). Political intolerance, right and left. *Political Psychology*, 35(6), 841–851.

Crowson, H. M. (2009). Are all conservatives alike? A study of the psychological correlates of cultural and economic conservatism. *The Journal of Psychology*, 143(5), 449–463.

Duarte, J. L., Crawford, J. T., Stern, C., Haidt, J., Jussim, L. & Tetlock, P. E. (2015). Political diversity will improve social psychological science. *Behavioral and Brain Sciences*, 38, e130.

Duckitt, J. (2001). A dual-process cognitive-motivational theory of ideology and prejudice. *Advances in Experimental Social Psychology*, 33, 41–113.

Duckitt, J. & Sibley, C. G. (2009). A dual-process motivational model of ideology, politics, and prejudice. *Psychological Inquiry*, 20, 98–109.

Duriez, B., Van Hiel, A. & Kossowska, M. (2005). Authoritarianism and social dominance in Western and Eastern Europe: The importance of the sociopolitical context and of political interest and involvement. *Political Psychology*, 26(2), 299–320.

Eysenck, H. J. (1954). *The psychology of politics*. London: Routledge & Kegan Paul.

Federico, C. M. & Goren, P. (2009). Motivated social cognition and ideology: Is attention to elite discourse a prerequisite for epistemically motivated political affinities. In J.T. Jost, A.C. Kay & H. Thorisdottir (Eds.), *Social and psychological bases of ideology and system justification* (pp. 267–291). New York: Oxford University Press.

Feldman, S. & Huddy, L. (2014). Not so simple: The multidimensional nature and diverse origins of political ideology. *Behavioral & Brain Sciences*, 37, 312–313.

Feldman, S. & Johnston, C. (2014). Understanding the determinants of political ideology: Implications of structural complexity. *Political Psychology*, 35(3), 337–358.

Feldman, S. & Stenner, K. (1997). Perceived threat and authoritarianism. *Political Psychology*, 18(4), 741–770.

Fraley, R. C., Griffin, B. N., Belsky, J. & Roisman, G. I. (2012). Developmental antecedents of political ideology a longitudinal investigation from birth to age 18 years. *Psychological Science, 23*(11), 1425–1431.

Gerber, A. S., Huber, G. A., Doherty, D., Dowling, C. M. & Ha, S. E. (2010). Personality and political attitudes: Relationships across issue domains and political contexts. *American Political Science Review, 104*(1), 111–133.

Graham, J., Haidt, J. & Nosek, B. A. (2009). Liberals and conservatives rely on different sets of moral foundations. *Journal of Personality and Social Psychology, 96*(5), 1029–1046.

Green, D. P., Palmquist, B. & Schickler, E. (2004). *Partisan hearts and minds: Political parties and the social identities of voters.* New Haven: Yale University Press.

Hennes, E. P., Nam, H. H., Stern, C. & Jost, J. T. (2012). Not all ideologies are created equal: Epistemic, existential, and relational needs predict system-justifying attitudes. *Social Cognition, 30*(6), 669–688.

Henrich, J., Heine, S. J. & Norenzayan, A. (2010). The weirdest people in the world? *Behavioral and Brain Sciences, 33*(2–3), 61–83.

Hetherington, M. J. & Weiler, J. D. (2009). *Authoritarianism and polarization in American politics.* New York: Cambridge University Press.

Hibbing, J. R., Smith, K. B. & Alford, J. R. (2014). Differences in negativity bias underlie variations in political ideology. *Behavioral and Brain Sciences, 37*(3), 297–307.

Huber, J. & Inglehart, R. (1995). Expert interpretations of party space and party locations in 42 societies. *Party Politics, 1*(1), 73–111.

Huddy, L., Mason, L. & Aarøe, L. (2015). Expressive partisanship: Campaign involvement, political emotion, and partisan identity. *American Political Science Review, 109*(1), 1–17.

Hyman, H. H. & Sheatsley, P. B. (1954). "The Authoritarian Personality"—A methodological critique. In R. Christie & M. Jahoda (Eds.), *Studies in the scope and method of "The Authoritarian Personality"* (pp. 50–122). Glencoe: Free Press.

Inbar, Y., Pizarro, D. A. & Bloom, P. (2009). Conservatives are more easily disgusted than liberals. *Cognition and Emotion, 23*(4), 714–725.

Inbar, Y., Pizarro, D. A. & Bloom, P. (2012). Disgusting smells cause decreased liking of gay men. *Emotion, 12*(1), 23–27.

Iyer, R., Koleva, S., Graham, J., Ditto, P. & Haidt, J. (2012). Understanding libertarian morality: The psychological dispositions of self-identified libertarians. *PloS One, 7*(8), e42366.

Janoff-Bulman, R., Sheikh, S. & Baldacci, K. G. (2008). Mapping moral motives: Approach, avoidance, and political orientation. *Journal of Experimental Social Psychology, 44*(4), 1091–1099.

Johnson, S. D. & Tamney, J. B. (2001). Social traditionalism and economic conservatism: Two conservative political ideologies in the United States. *The Journal of Social Psychology, 141*(2), 233–243.

Johnston, C. D., Lavine, H. G. & Federico, C. M. (2017). *Open versus closed: Personality, identity, and the politics of redistribution.* New York: Cambridge University Press.

Johnston, C. D. & Wronski, J. (2015). Personality dispositions and political preferences across hard and easy issues. *Political Psychology, 36*(1), 35–53.

Jost, J. T., Federico, C. M. & Napier, J. L. (2009). Political ideology: Its structure, functions, and elective affinities. *Annual Review of Psychology, 60*, 307–337.

Jost, J. T., Federico, C. M. & Napier, J. L. (2013). Political ideologies and their social psychological functions. *The Oxford Handbook of Political Ideologies*, 232–250.

Jost, J. T., Glaser, J., Kruglanski, A. W. & Sulloway, F. J. (2003). Political conservatism as motivated social cognition. *Psychological Bulletin, 129*(3), 339–375.

Jost, J. T. & Hunyady, O. (2005). Antecedents and consequences of system-justifying ideologies. *Current Directions in Psychological Science, 14*(5), 260–265.

Jost, J. T., Napier, J. L., Thorisdottir, H., Gosling, S. D., Palfai, T. P. & Ostafin, B. (2007). Are needs to manage uncertainty and threat associated with political conservatism or ideological extremity? *Personality and Social Psychology Bulletin, 33*(7), 989–1007.

Kahan, D. M., Peters, E., Dawson, E. C. & Slovic, P. (2013). *Motivated numeracy and enlightened self-government*. Yale Law School, Public Law Working Paper, No. 307.

Kandler, C., Bleidorn, W. & Riemann, R. (2012). Left or right? Sources of political orientation: The roles of genetic factors, cultural transmission, assortative mating, and personality. *Journal of Personality and Social Psychology, 102*(3), 633.

Kemmelmeier, M. (2008). Is there a relationship between political orientation and cognitive ability? A test of three hypotheses in two studies. *Personality and Individual Differences, 45*(8), 767–772.

Kossowska, M. & Van Hiel, A. V. (2003). The relationship between need for closure and conservative beliefs in Western and Eastern Europe. *Political Psychology, 24*(3), 501–518.

Kunda, Z. (1990). The case for motivated reasoning. *Psychological Bulletin, 108*(3), 480–498.

Lambert, A. J., Scherer, L. D., Schott, J. P., Olson, K. R., Andrews, R. K., O'Brien, T. C. & Zisser, A. R. (2010). Rally effects, threat, and attitude change: An integrative approach to understanding the role of emotion. *Journal of Personality and Social Psychology, 98*(6), 886–903.

Layman, G. C. & Green, J. C. (2006). Wars and rumours of wars: The contexts of cultural conflict in American political behaviour. *British Journal of Political Science, 36*(01), 61–89.

Lefkofridi, Z., Wagner, M. & Willmann, J. E. (2014). Left-authoritarians and policy representation in Western Europe: Electoral choice across ideological dimensions. *West European Politics, 37*(1), 65–90.

Luguri, J.B. & Napier, J. L. (2016). *Threats to personal control increase support for liberal economic (but not social) policies*. Paper presented at the annual meeting of the Society for Personality Psychology, San Diego, CA.

Malka, A. & Lelkes, Y. (2010). More than ideology: Conservative–liberal identity and receptivity to political cues. *Social Justice Research, 23*(2–3), 156–188.

Malka, A., Lelkes, Y. & Soto, C. J. (2017, in press). Are cultural and economic conservatism positively correlated? A large-scale cross-national test. *British Journal of Political Science*.

Malka, A. & Soto, C. J. (2015). Rigidity of the economic right? Menu-independent and menu-dependent influences of psychological dispositions on political attitudes. *Current Directions in Psychological Science, 24*(2), 137–142.

Malka, A., Soto, C. J., Inzlicht, M. & Lelkes, Y. (2014). Do needs for security and certainty predict cultural and economic conservatism? A cross-national analysis. *Journal of Personality and Social Psychology, 106*(6), 1031.

McCarty, N., Poole, K. T. & Rosenthal, H. (2008). *Polarized America: The dance of ideology and unequal riches*. Cambridge: MIT Press.

Middendorp, C. P. (1978). *Progressiveness and conservatism: The fundamental dimensions of ideological controversy and their relationship to social class*. New York: Mouton.

Morton, R., Tyran, J. R. & Wengström, E., (2011). Income and Ideology: How Personality Traits, Cognitive Abilities, and Education Shape Political Attitudes. Univ. of Copenhagen Dept. of Economics Discussion Paper 11(08).

Morgan, G. S., Mullen, E. & Skitka, L. J. (2010). When values and attributions collide: Liberals' and conservatives' values motivate attributions for alleged misdeeds. *Personality and Social Psychology Bulletin, 36*(9), 1241–1254.

Nail, P. R. & McGregor, I. (2009). Conservative shift among liberals and conservatives following 9/11/01. *Social Justice Research, 22*(2–3), 231–240.

Napier, J. L. & Jost, J. T. (2008). The "Antidemocratic Personality" revisited: A cross-national investigation of working-class authoritarianism. *Journal of Social Issues, 64*(3), 595–617.

Oxley, D. R., Smith, K. B., Alford, J. R., Hibbing, M. V., Miller, J. L., Scalora, M., Hatemi, P. K. & Hibbing, J. R. (2008). Political attitudes vary with physiological traits. *Science, 321*(5896), 1667–1670.

Peterson, B. E. & Gerstein, E. D. (2005). Fighting and flying: Archival analysis of threat, authoritarianism, and the North American comic book. *Political Psychology, 26*(6), 887–904.

Petrescu, D. C. & Parkinson, B. (2014). Incidental disgust increases adherence to left-wing economic attitudes. *Social Justice Research, 27*(4), 464–486.

Ray, J. J. (1973). Conservatism, authoritarianism, and related variables: A review and empirical study. In G. D. Wilson (Ed.), *The Psychology of Conservatism* (pp. 17–35). New York: Academic Press.

Rokeach, M. (1960). *The open and closed mind.* New York: Basic Books.

Smith, K. B., Oxley, D., Hibbing, M. V., Alford, J. R. & Hibbing, J. R. (2011). Disgust sensitivity and the neurophysiology of left-right political orientations. *PLoS One, 6*(10), e25552.

Sniderman, P. M. & Tetlock, P. E. (1986). Symbolic racism: Problems of motive attribution in political analysis. *Journal of Social Issues, 42*(2), 129–150.

Stankov, L. (2009). Conservatism and cognitive ability. *Intelligence, 37*(3), 294–304.

Stenner, K. (2005). *The authoritarian dynamic.* New York: Cambridge University Press.

Stone, W. F. (1980) The myth of left-wing authoritarianism. *Political Psychology, 2*(3–4), 3–19.

Terrizzi, J. A., Shook, N. J. & Ventis, W. L. (2010). Disgust: A predictor of social conservatism and prejudicial attitudes toward homosexuals. *Personality and Individual Differences, 49*(6), 587–592.

Tetlock, P. E. (1984). Cognitive style and political belief systems in the British House of Commons. *Journal of Personality and Social Psychology, 46*(2), 365.

Thorisdottir, H. & Jost, J. T. (2011). Motivated closed-mindedness mediates the effect of threat on political conservatism. *Political Psychology, 32*(5), 785–811.

Thorisdottir, H., Jost, J. T., Liviatan, I. & Shrout, P. E. (2007). Psychological needs and values underlying left-right political orientation: Cross-national evidence from Eastern and Western Europe. *Public Opinion Quarterly, 71*(2), 175–203.

Treier, S. & Hillygus, D. S. (2009). The nature of political ideology in the contemporary electorate. *Public Opinion Quarterly, 73*, 679–703.

Van Berkel, L., Crandall, C. S., Eidelman, S. & Blanchar, J. C. (2015). Hierarchy, dominance, and deliberation egalitarian values require mental effort. *Personality and Social Psychology Bulletin, 41*(9), 1207–1222.

Van Hiel, A., Onraet, E. & De Pauw, S. (2010). The relationship between social-cultural attitudes and behavioral measures of cognitive style: A Meta-Analytic Integration of Studies. *Journal of Personality, 78*(6), 1765–1799.

Van Hiel, A., Pandelaere, M. & Duriez, B. (2004). The impact of need for closure on conservative beliefs and racism: Differential mediation by authoritarian submission and authoritarian dominance. *Personality and Social Psychology Bulletin, 30*(7), 824–837.

Wilson, G. D. (1973). *The psychology of conservatism*. Oxford: Academic Press.

Wilson, G. D. & Patterson, J. R. (1968). A new measure of conservatism. *British Journal of Social and Clinical Psychology, 7*(4), 264–269.

Zaller, J. (1992). *The nature and origins of mass opinion*. New York: Cambridge University Press.

PART III

How Politicized Social Psychology Distorts Interpretation of Research

9

JUMPING TO CONCLUSIONS

Advocacy and Application of Psychological Research

Gregory Mitchell

The Market for Applications

Power posing (Hanna, 2010; Robinson, 2014), stereotype threat (Vedantum, 2012), fear induction through the naming of hurricanes (Associated Press, 2014), and sight as a better guide to musical quality than hearing (Vedantum, 2013) are just a few of the ideas that have recently made the jump from the pages of psychological journals to the public consciousness. With press releases from journals and universities feeding a content-hungry media, publishing houses looking for the next Gladwellian bestseller, governments embracing behavioral science (Wright, 2015), and courts increasingly open to evidence from social scientists (Monahan, Walker & Mitchell, 2008), psychologists have more opportunities than ever to educate the public on what they have learned about why people behave as they do.

The public, including many well-educated business leaders and policymakers, understandably accepts the science-based wisdom that social psychologists offer. That is what a progressive society surely does. What much of the public probably fails to appreciate, however, is that much of the psychological wisdom on offer is based on very limited bodies of research and that much of psychological science places little value on assessing the external validity of research. This unfortunate combination means that practically every application offered by a psychologist will involve numerous personal judgments about the social meaning and implications of the underlying research, about the likelihood of findings replicating, and about the costs of non-replication. Thus, the researcher who counsels women to stand with arms akimbo or engage in other power poses in the workplace to gain confidence, and perhaps gain better standing in the organization (see the TED talk at http://web.archive.org/web/20150408202457/http://www.ted.com/talks/amy_cuddy_your_body_language_shapes_who_you_are/transcript?language=en), must believe that her past findings will generalize to new settings and samples. This researcher also implicitly assumes that a lack of confidence on the part of women, or perceptions of a lack of confidence by people in power, plays some causal role in the outcomes of women in the workplace.

The underlying psychological research does not answer these questions, however; while several studies have examined power posing effects, none involve field studies looking at organizational consequences of power posing, and the observed effects are small and appear to be quite limited. In fact, in response to a failed replication of the power-posing research (Ranehill et al., 2015), Carney, Cuddy, and Yap (2015) speculate that the replication failure may have been due to the participants' awareness that the effects of power posing were being studied. If it is true that a lack of awareness of power-posing effects is a requirement for positive effects to appear, then we should question whether publicizing research on power posing can ever bestow benefits. Most importantly, no research has shown that power posing has an effect—good or bad—on corporate outcomes.

The power-posing example is not unique; in every application of psychological research, numerous judgments must be made about the likelihood of replication in new settings and new samples. Because every body of research and every psychological theory is subject to conditions and uncertainty about their scope or coverage, every application of research or theory will require many judgments about which variables are behaviorally potent and which are not. These judgments will inevitably draw on the researcher's own beliefs and values to inform the extrapolations required for the extension of research. The influence of these beliefs and values will rarely be made explicit, perhaps not even to the researcher herself, but such influence is inevitable. Just as a researcher's values and beliefs inevitably affect what topics are chosen for study and how those topics are studied, the same is true for any application of psychological research to a new domain. Some of those extensions will be more justifiable than others, and some will pose greater risks than others if extension turns out to be wrong. But whereas science provides procedures aimed at checking the influence of a researcher's own biases in collecting and interpreting data, science provides little check on researcher bias when it comes to applying research. As a result, applications leave considerable space for psychologists, wittingly or unwittingly, to become advocates for particular outcomes and particular ways of viewing the world.

The Space for Advocacy

When a study receives publicity, the community of scientists often scrutinizes the study for statistical errors, design flaws, and questionable inferences (e.g., Thorstenson et al., 2015), and sometimes an effort to replicate the study yields evidence of otherwise unobservable mistakes and even misconduct (e.g., Blanton & Mitchell, 2011; Singal, 2015). Because of shared standards for judging whether valid statistical and causal inferences have been made, consensus is often reached regarding the internal and statistical validity of a study's conclusions and whether the author used questionable research practices or placed debatable interpretations onto a data set.

A study's construct and external validity typically receive less attention because, unlike questions of statistical conclusion and internal validity, we lack shared norms for judging construct validity and external validity because of the context-specific nature of these qualities. Whereas one serious error may completely undercut a study's internal or statistical conclusion validity, a construct's operationalization may be valid for some purposes and invalid for others; a study may generalize to one group in one setting but not to other combinations of persons and situations.

We primarily assess construct and external validity through follow-up examinations aimed at assessing the limitations of the original result (Shadish, Cook & Campbell, 2002; Willems & Howard, 1980). Whether the speed of pushing or pulling a lever in response to "ice cream" and other words (as in Chen & Bargh, 1999) is a good operationalization of negative and positive attitudes toward the objects supposedly represented by those words depends on how these measurements relate to other attitude measures and other behaviors. Whether the average time for college students to push or pull a lever in response to the words "ice cream" reflects the negative or positive attitudes of others toward ice cream depends not only on the representativeness of this sample of persons but also of this situation for assessing ice-cream attitudes. We may predict that the dietary preferences of New York University undergrads differ greatly from the dietary preferences of middle-aged Southerners and that time of day would affect the responses obtained (e.g., perhaps assessing ice-cream attitudes in a laboratory setting late in the day yields different responses than assessing ice-cream attitudes in a cafeteria right before lunch), but we cannot know whether these predictions are correct without further study.

Choices made during the research process also affect construct and external validity, but these choices will often be undetectable by observers. Decisions to discard data and to not check for the influence of outliers affect not only the reliability of statistical conclusions but also the representativeness of the data (Blanton et al., 2009). The decision to emphasize one dependent measure over another after results are known impacts construct validity: Presumably all the dependent variables were chosen under a theory predicting that the construct of interest would have some impact, positive or negative, on each measure; the fact that the predicted relations were not found provides important information on the validity of the operationalizations chosen to represent the construct of interest (Fiedler, 2011).

This asymmetry in the evaluability of validities—internal validity is usually easier to asses than external and construct validities from the information presented in a research report—leads to a greater emphasis on internal validity in both pre-publication and post-publication peer review. Internal validity review imposes an important, but very limited, check on whether a finding will and should be treated as having applied value. Much research survives internal validity scrutiny, either because its flaws are unobservable or because the study is internally sound. Even when internal validity criticisms of a study are made, those criticisms may not stick. Because most publicized studies will have passed peer review, the authors will often argue that their critics are wrong or engage in post hoc justifications of design or analytical choices.

While internal validity review provides at best weak protection against unreliable studies being extended to other settings and samples, construct and external validity review impose practically no constraint on applications of psychological research. Occasionally, an operationalization or choice of research setting will be so problematic or debatable that critics will question construct and external validity even without the aid of additional data, casting doubt on the results, but these criticisms can usually be deflected by explaining the rationale for the choices or by pointing to other research in which the criticisms were shown to be impotent. Construct validity complaints can be addressed by claiming face validity, invoking a theory that guided the operationalizations, or pointing to future studies that will examine discriminant, convergent, and predictive validity. Concerns about the realism of the design can be addressed by invoking the design ethos of "psychological realism" paired with "experimental realism" (Wilson, Aronson & Carlsmith, 2010), under which it is assumed that the psychological processes activated by short, simple, even contrived, one-shot interactions with strangers or imaginary persons will not be meaningfully different from those activated in the everyday processes and interactions that motivated the study in the first place. The truth of these design assumptions is left for future studies that will establish moderators and mediators of the effects observed in the first study. Yet these follow-up studies typically do not make empirical comparisons between the laboratory settings and everyday settings of interest but rather create variations on the original research design. This path dependence in research design can lead to large bodies of research that purport to examine some real-world domain without ever actually studying the domain of interest or any persons inhabiting those domains (see, e.g., Landy, 2008). When field tests are eventually conducted, the results are often not pretty, especially not for social psychological research (Mitchell, 2012). My comparison of studies conducted on the same topic in the laboratory and field found that social psychology had among the lowest rates of replication in the field, and 20% of the correlations observed in social psychology laboratories exhibited opposite relations in the field (i.e., positive correlations became negative correlations and vice versa).

The larger point is that knowing one will face little external and construct validity scrutiny ramifies through the whole research and publication process, and not just at the back end to permit unheeded speculation about applications. The lack of knock-down construct and external validity critiques permits psychologists to create experimental situations and to operationalize variables in ways that are manageable rather than faithful to the real-world problem of interest. And psychologists have little incentive otherwise to engage in such validation research because it poses great risk to a research program and is not needed for publication in top journals. Accordingly, large and influential lines of research are sometimes built on surprisingly thin operationalizations of constructs that are examined using very limited research designs (see, e.g., Gawronski's, 2004, discussion of correspondence bias research, and Brandt, Reyna, Chambers, Crawford & Wetherell's, 2014, discussion of research on intolerance and political ideology).

Nor is the lack of validation research a hurdle to psychologists serving as expert witnesses in court, advising government agencies on policy or offering the public explanations of current events. The only real hurdle to psychologists extending their research findings to new settings and samples is the psychologist's own epistemic, political, and ethical values and their beliefs about the generalizability of the research (or willingness to suppress concerns about generalizability). The APA's Code of Ethics directs psychologists to avoid making false or deceptive statements to the public but offers no guidelines on when research is suitable for applications. Some psychologists call for special care in the publication of research bearing on socially sensitive topics, such as whether racial groups differ in intelligence (e.g., Hunt & Carlson, 2007), suggesting that applications of such research should proceed very cautiously. Some see an important role for psychologists in applying their research to socially sensitive topics, such as the causes of discrimination (Kang & Banaji, 2006), even when that research has yet to be subjected to external validation. Some argue that psychologists have a duty to assist with even morally questionable practices such as "enhanced interrogation" if doing so can increase efficacy or reduce harm (O'Donohue et al., 2014), while others argue that psychologists have an obligation not to assist morally questionable practices (Arrigo, DeBatto, Rockwood & Mawe, 2015). Ultimately, each psychologist is left to make her own determination about whether to apply her research to a legal proceeding, to testify before Congress or another body charged with formulating public policy, to commercialize the research, or to translate findings for a popular audience, drawing out the supposed implications of that research for the audience.

In making these applications, numerous judgments about extensions are inevitable. The research itself can only take the researcher so far. Ideally, the researcher would fill in the knowledge gaps by resort to robust theories covering the domain at hand and empirically derived base rates for behaviors from the domain, but, for the reasons discussed above, we often lack good, robust theories and good base-rate data to inform the applications. Social psychology is primarily a field that demonstrates that certain effects can be found under particular conditions—it is by and large a field of small, contingent effects of dubious external validity (Mitchell, 2012; Richard, Bond & Stokes-Zoota, 2003)—it is not a field devoted to gathering descriptive data from real-world settings. In the absence of validated theory and good data, the researcher will have to resort to default cognitive and motivational assumptions about how people think and behave to fill in gaps, with those on the political left likely embracing different assumptions than those on the political right (MacCoun, 1998; Redding, 2001; Tetlock & Mitchell, 1993, 2015).

For instance, when inferences about causation must be made, liberals and conservatives are likely to have different attributional sympathies and different beliefs about how people will respond to incentives to alter their behavior (e.g., Abramowitz, Gomes & Abramowitz, 1975; Ceci, Peters & Plotkin, 1985). Ambiguities in the available data also may be assimilated to pre-existing beliefs and theories, with liberals and conservatives likely to find different patterns and messages in the same data to different applications (e.g., Koehler, 1993; Mahoney, 1987). Furthermore, researcher values should affect the sorts of errors of application that researchers are more willing to risk. Because psychologists tend to be ideologically liberal, quite concerned about inequalities and oppression within society, and skeptical of the fairness of market in assigning outcomes, we should expect applications from psychologists that more often err on the side of those with less power. In short, just as we should be concerned about extracurricular influences on how researchers collect, analyze, and interpret data, we should be likewise concerned about extracurricular influences on applications of data.

There is one final large concern with applications: Because psychology tends to be dominated by researchers with left-leaning ideologies and sympathies (Duarte et al., 2015; Gross, 2013), the body of research surrounding politically charged questions, such as the role of gender in employment outcomes or whether liberals are more tolerant than conservatives, will likely reflect the motivational and cognitive assumptions of liberals more than those of conservatives. Thus, even a researcher who tries objectively to summarize a body of work, address and disclose its limitations fully, and then carefully assess what applied lessons can be drawn from this body of work may still reach biased conclusions. If the concern about bias within the full body of work is sufficiently severe, the only antidote is to draw no applications from the body of work until this risk is empirically assessed.

The Example of Implicit Bias Research

Pair surprising results with a timely topic and enthusiastic researchers ready to extend those results to real-world domains, and psychological research may quickly find its way into policy debates, agency rule-making, executive suites and boardrooms, and courtrooms. That has certainly been the case with implicit bias research. With the aid of several psychologists who believe that new implicit measures of psychological processes—particularly the Implicit Association Test (IAT) and the shooter bias paradigm—have opened the door to the subconscious and its many influences on behavior, a new understanding of the power of race and gender to bias behavior has entered public consciousness and public policy discussions.

In conjunction with activation of the first Project Implicit website in 1998 and publication of the first IAT results, Drs. Greenwald and Banaji held a press conference in which they declared that the race IAT reveals unconscious prejudice that affects "90% to 95% of people" (www.washington. edu/news/1998/09/29/roots-of-unconscious-prejudice-affect-90-to-95-percent-of-people-psychologists-demonstrate-at-press-conference/). Shortly thereafter, Dr. Greenwald appeared on an NBC News segment demonstrating the IAT as a measure of unconscious prejudice. In March of 2000, Drs. Banaji and Greenwald appeared on NBC's *Dateline* program discussing IAT research, with Dr. Banaji characterizing the test as an examination of how "fair are we being when we judge a person," and Dr. Greenwald giving an example of the wrongful shooting of a black suspect by police as an example of how the bias measured by the IAT can affect behavior. Since those early appearances, Drs. Banaji and Greenwald have given many statements for television shows, radio programs, and print articles about the IAT, what it measures, and the behavioral consequences of implicit bias as measured by the IAT. In their book published in 2013 for a general audience, Banaji and Greenwald write, after detailing disparities in housing, employment, healthcare, and imprisonment, that "it is reasonable to conclude not only that implicit bias is a cause of Black disadvantage but also that it plausibly plays a greater role than does explicit bias in explaining the discrimination that contributes to Black disadvantage" (Banaji & Greenwald, 2013, p. 209).

The public policy agenda behind Drs. Greenwald and Banaji publicity efforts is no secret. According to Dr. Banaji, "[t]he central idea is to use the energy generated by research on unconscious forms of prejudice to understand and challenge the notion of intentionality in the law" (Potier, 2004). To this end, Dr. Greenwald has given presentations at American Bar Association conferences aimed at educating lawyers on legal implications of the IAT research, and both Dr. Greenwald and Dr. Banaji have written articles for legal audiences (e.g., Greenwald & Krieger, 2006; Kang & Banaji, 2006; Kang et al., 2012).

Drs. Banaji and Greenwald (and others) have taken their education efforts to courts as well. Dr. Banaji testified about the possible influence of implicit bias on jurors in a death penalty case in New Hampshire, and Dr. Greenwald has now appeared as an expert witness in several legal cases (and in some of those cases, the present author submitted a responsive report discussing the limits of the IAT research), opining that implicit biases are pervasive, that human behavior is much less guided by explicit belief and conscious intentions than is often thought, that implicit bias is now scientifically established as a source of discriminatory behavior in organizations, that personnel systems that involve subjective personnel assessments are prone to influence by implicit bias, and, in some cases, that particular organizations lacked sufficient objective controls to prevent the influence of implicit bias. In none of these cases has Dr. Greenwald performed any case-specific empirical research to support his applications.

Other psychologists are similarly clear in their desire to bring public policy in line with what they see as the implications of implicit bias research. In an article in the *San Francisco Chronicle*, the social psychologist Jack Glaser concluded that

> most Americans (including many black Americans) have in their heads the stereotypes and feelings that cause them to regard black people differently. Consequently, there is discrimination in many important realms, including employment, lending, health care, etc. With policing, however, the discriminatory outcomes are immediately consequential, often dire—even fatal (www.sfgate.com/opinion/article/Biased-policing-is-real-and-fixable-5969332.php).

Another leading researcher on race and policing, Dr. Jennifer Eberhardt, told the *Los Angeles Times* that "[r]esearch shows that people associate 'blackness' with 'threat' in study after study … It's not something that is just about the police. It's not something that is just about white people. It's a function of how we're socialized" (www.latimes.com/local/crime/la-me-1206-banks-black-stereotypes-20141206-column.html).

It is not hard to spot the influence these publicity efforts are having. Both Google (https://googleblog.blogspot.com/2014/09/you-dont-know-what-you-dont-know-how.html) and Facebook (https://managingbias.fb.com/) have instituted internal programs aimed at combatting implicit bias. The National Center for State Courts, with the assistance of one of Drs. Greenwald and Banaji's law professor co-authors, started an initiative on implicit bias in the courts (www.ncsc.org/ibeducation), and this same law professor now regularly gives talks to law firms and companies about implicit bias (http://jerrykang.net/talk/implicit-bias-talks/). An implicit bias consulting industry has also sprung up to help companies overcome the problems posed by implicit biases, including consulting services provided by the nonprofit organization begun by the creators of the IAT (www.projectimplicit.net/consulting.html). These examples illustrate the impact implicit bias research is having on understandings of and efforts to prevent employment discrimination.

It is easy to find examples of influence on policing policy as well. For instance, in a speech given less than three months after Dr. Glaser's article appeared in the *San Francisco Chronicle*, James Comey, the director of the FBI, diagnosed the police brutality problem in a strikingly similar way. Director Comey pointed to research on implicit bias as revealing the "hard truth" that unconscious biases are pervasive and lead to different instinctive reactions to white and black suspects by police officers, sometimes with life-or-death consequences. According to Director Comey, law enforcement must recognize unconscious biases as "inescapable parts of the human condition" and design systems and processes for reducing their influence (www.fbi.gov/news/speeches/hard-truths-law-enforcement-and-race). In line with Director Comey's diagnosis of the problem, the Department of Justice funded development of the Fair and Impartial Policing Program, which provides training to police officers on how to recognize biases in themselves and control the effects of those biases on their behavior (www.fairimpartialpolicing.com/training-programs/). The program, which relies heavily on social psychological research on implicit bias (www. fairimpartialpolicing.com/bias/), counts among its many clients police forces that have been involved in a number of the high-profile incidents, including the Baltimore Police Department, the Bay Area Rapid Transit (BART) Police Department, and the Sanford, Florida, Police Department (www. fairimpartialpolicing.com/testimonials/).

Director Comey's remarks and the Fair and Impartial Policing Program illustrate two different ways in which implicit bias research is influencing public policy. In Comey's remarks, a psychological construct, implicit bias, is used as a general causal explanation for troubling incidents of police violence directed at black males. Director Comey understandably makes no effort to demonstrate that implicit bias caused each incident. Rather, he assumes that implicit bias research has generated a theory that has successfully predicted when police officers will and will not shoot suspects of different races under conditions similar to those involved in the incidents. He assumes, that is, that social scientists have already done the heavy lifting needed to establish that implicit bias is a pervasive negative force in police interactions with minority suspects but not in their interactions with white suspects. With this assumption in place, Comey can make use of implicit bias research to tell a particular kind of causal story (Stone, 1997), one that allows him to assign responsibility to the police officers (instead of their victims) without blaming or castigating the officers, because the harms the officers inflicted were inadvertent rather than intentional. As Stone (1997) discusses, this kind of causal story can be particularly attractive when a policy-maker seeks to impose reforms without alienating those affected by the reforms.

In the Fair and Impartial Policing Program, psychological research is used to provide concrete solutions to the general problem as diagnosed by Director Comey. The program assumes the truth of the causal story told by Comey and aims to help police overcome the negative consequences of bias using videos, demonstrations, and lectures derived from the research on bias. It is assumed (and strongly implied in the promotional materials for the program) that the training will have positive effects that transfer to the field. This assumption is supported, not by any research into the efficacy of the training, but by the fact that the exercises are based on published research and scientific principles drawn from that research (also, positive reactions to the program by participants figure prominently on the program's website as testimonials).

In less than two decades since the first IAT and shooter bias studies were published, the public dissemination of information about implicit bias research has had a remarkable impact on how the public thinks about thinking and behavior and how governments and companies respond to the risks of discrimination (see Forscher et al., 2016). What is even more remarkable is how speculative this whole public education and influence effort has been (see Mitchell & Tetlock, in press, for a history of implicit bias claims). Before even a single piece of data had been collected from any workforce or police force, social psychologists were describing implicit bias as the primary cause of racial and ethnic disparities in housing, employment, health, representation in government, and police mistreatment and gender disparities in employment and representation in government, and as more powerful than explicit stereotypes and old-fashioned racism and sexism.

Seventeen years after introduction of the IAT, only a handful of studies have examined the influence of implicit bias on real personnel decisions, and those studies have provided inconsistent and at best weak evidence that implicit bias has any impact on employment decisions (Oswald, Mitchell, Blanton, Jaccard & Tetlock, 2015). Similarly, only a handful of studies have examined the behavior of actual police officers on the shooter bias task, and those studies likewise fail to provide support for the applied claims made by social psychologists. For instance, contrary to Correll and colleagues' initial speculation that shooter bias would likely exist among police officers, a follow-up study by Correll et al. (2007) using a police officer sample found a difference in response times to white versus black targets but no bias in the shooting of unarmed black versus white suspects. And in a recent review of the literature, Correll, Hudson, Guillermo, and Ma (2014) concluded that police do not show bias on the shooter task. A recent meta-analysis of the shooter bias studies found no racial difference in false alarm rates (i.e., there was no significant difference in the number of black versus white unarmed targets) or sensitivity to threat (Mekawi & Bresin, 2015) for both police and layperson samples, though the review did find small differences in reaction times and shooting thresholds. The false-alarm data is most relevant to the claims by psychologists that raced-based implicit biases can explain unjustified police shootings. Also noteworthy is the lack of data showing that measures of implicit bias are good predictors of shooter bias (see Mekawi & Bresin, 2015, who did not even include implicit and explicit bias measures as moderators). Indeed, colleagues and I found in a meta-analysis of IAT predictive validity studies that measures of explicit racial bias were just as good at predicting reaction times to white and black targets as the race IAT (or rather, were equally as bad as the IAT, given that both kinds of measures performed poorly; Oswald, Mitchell, Blanton, Jaccard & Tetlock, 2013).

The psychologists advancing implicit bias as the explanation for various societal inequalities and harms jumped to that conclusion, apparently in the sincere belief that the data would eventually support that conclusion, but it has not. The accumulated data in fact now show that measures of implicit bias provide no more explanatory power than explicit bias, even for socially sensitive topics, and often provide less explanatory power. There is no reliable link between implicit bias in police officers and police violence against minorities, and there is no reliable link between implicit bias and employment evaluations or employment outcomes for women and minorities. If those behind applications of implicit bias to the law really are committed to "behavioral realism," to taking science seriously and making values secondary to science, as they say (Kang & Banaji, 2006, p. l065), then they must accept that implicit bias has not turned out to be the explanatory juggernaut it was optimistically expected to be.

Despite these now undisputed facts, the implicit bias construct continues to play an influential role in public debates, court cases, and the making of governmental and company policy. Millions of dollars are being spent on untested implicit bias training and consulting (Forscher et al., 2016; Lai et al., 2014; Lublin, 2014), money that could be devoted to exploring demonstrated sources of employment disparities and police misconduct in all their multi-determined complexity. Likewise, the crisis and commitment to change policing practices prompted by greater citizen surveillance and body cams revealing minority mistreatment is being squandered on implicit bias. How officers react to minority suspects of course plays a role in these troubling cases, but there is simply no reason to believe that the implicit processes studied by social psychologists can account for these incidents.

Getting the implicit bias cat back into the bag will require much more than conceding that the behavioral effects of implicit bias are small and that scores on an IAT are not reliable predictors of an individual's behavior (as Greenwald and colleagues have now conceded; Greenwald, Banaji & Nosek, 2015). Errors and omissions should be acknowledged to put a brake on further applications, including:

- The decision to treat as meaningful the zero-point on the IAT's scoring algorithms and to assign IAT scores to different categories that supposedly reflect low, moderate, and high levels of bias (see Blanton & Jaccard, 2006, 2008). As Blanton, Jaccard, Strauts, Mitchell, and Tetlock (2015) have shown, when one uses attitude-based or behavior-based markers of bias and examines what level of IAT scores match up with these empirically derived points of no bias, one finds that many IAT studies that treat the zero-point on the IAT as the point of no bias greatly overestimate the number of participants who actually show any bias and overestimate the magnitude of behavioral bias. These results cast doubt on the construct validity of the IAT and undercut the pervasiveness-of-bias claim that has been one of the key drivers of public attention to implicit bias research.
- Examining only behavior toward minority targets rather than treatment of a minority relative to a white target (or even worse, to exclude this

comparison from the research report despite having the data). Although Greenwald and Pettigrew (2014) argue that modern discrimination primarily takes the form of acts of in-group favoritism instead of acts of out-group derogation, Greenwald, Poehlman, Uhlmann, and Banaji (2009) excluded from their meta-analysis of correlations between IAT scores and criterion measures data on whether IATs predict acts of in-group favoritism. When we included that data in our meta-analysis, we found that IATs do not (Oswald et al., 2013).

- Using questionable criterion measures in research and meta-analyses, such as treating measures of brain activity as a measure of discriminatory behavior (see Blanton et al., 2009, and Oswald et al., 2013, for specific examples and extended discussion of these problems). Very few implicit bias studies employ realistic tasks. For instance, many shooter bias studies use keyboard responses as a stand-in for shooting or not shooting. Choosing to operationalization police-suspect interactions in this way appears to explain some of the early results that have turned out to be misleading (see Cox, Devine, Plant & Schwartz, 2014, who employed a more realistic research design and found no racial bias in the type of mistakes made).

- Devoting most research resources to the proliferation of new IATs instead of to research on construct validity in all its forms (convergent, divergent, and predictive) for key IATs, such as race and gender IATs. Project Implicit and the sharing of the code needed to produce and score IATs make it very easy to construct new IATs and collect data using those IATs. As a result, we have seen countless IATs created. Yet very few of the IATs have been subjected to sustained construct validity research. All too often, little examination is even made with respect to whether the particular exemplars chosen to represent the two categories being contrasted produce a unique set of results, even though we know that may be the case (e.g., the use of race-inflected names versus pictures of persons of different races leads to different results; Nosek, Greenwald & Banaji, 2007).

- The decision to focus on demonstrating effects instead of determining causes and possible solutions once the causes are found. Numerous factors that may serve as a check on any potential influence of implicit bias have been neglected, including such variables we should expect to find in many employment settings, police departments, and courtrooms, such as accountability for following fair procedures and achieving merited outcomes, group deliberation and the diversity of the group, and the possession of information beyond simply the appearance of a person or knowledge of race or gender via a name.

- The decision to exclude from the Project Implicit website IATs that do not produce patterns of bias consistent with the implicit bias causal story, such as the gender attitudes IAT on which men tend not to show bias against women but on which women show in-group bias, and to exclude from that website full disclosures regarding the lack of predictive validity for IATs and the general lack of external validation of IAT research. As the public face of IAT research, the Project Implicit website can greatly affect what the public knows about implicit bias research and believes about implicit bias. A useful exercise would be to have disinterested social scientists who have reviewed the IAT meta-analyses review the Project Implicit website to determine whether it conveys proper understandings of what we presently know about implicit bias and its effects, including whether the website omits details that are necessary for a proper understanding of the limits of the research.

Where from Here?

Disposing of the mistaken belief that implicit bias is a powerful and pervasive corrupter of behavior will be slow and difficult. How do we avoid more myth making of the kind that has occurred with the implicit bias construct?

One simple but important corrective would be to adopt a research design ethos that emphasizes mundane realism. The dominance of the psychological realism approach to research design, in which the researcher attempts to engineer a situation that activates the psychological processes of interest without simulating the real-world conditions under which the behavior of interest occurs, leads to much speculation and inevitable error about generalizability. Not coincidentally, the subfield of psychology whose lab results most reliably replicate in the field, industrial-organizational psychology, places great emphasis on faithful simulations of the target environment (Mitchell, 2012).

Another simple corrective would be to embrace the adage, "no single study captures the world." Despite the pressure to publicize every interesting result, even the best study cannot eliminate all questions about construct and external validity. No single study should be treated as if it has revealed immutable laws of human behavior, given the heterogeneity in treatment effects and unknown moderators that will accompany any psychological finding. As indisputable as that may seem, revisit the news stories that opened this chapter and examine how the research is portrayed, often in quotes from the researchers themselves. We are told that people in general perceive male-named hurricanes as more threatening than female-named hurricanes, that power posing has broad implications for anyone suffering from low self-esteem or a sense of powerlessness, and that oxytocin is the social glue that holds together families, communities, and societies. To any psychologist who understands how research of this type is done, those claims do not mean what they seem to say, but unfortunately, many non-psychologists may take those claims at face value and some may even act on those statements.

Until psychologists endorse a set of shared specific norms for evaluating construct and external validity (and concomitantly for when applications are appropriate and how applied advice is given), and until social scientists devote as much attention in post-publication review to construct and external validity critiques as to internal validity critiques, unsupportable claims are likely to persist. Although the recent attention paid to questionable research practices and reproducibility problems may lead to greater transparency and rigor in social psychology research, until more research is devoted to external validation, the applied value of social psychology should remain suspect. We have too many reasons not to trust the advice of social psychologists unless they can show that data on construct and external validity, not speculation, provide the basis for the applied advice.

References

Abramowitz, S. I., Gomes, B. & Abramowitz, C. V. (1975). Publish or politic: Referee bias in manuscript review. *Journal of Applied Social Psychology*, 5, 187–200.

Arrigo, J. M., DeBatto, D., Rockwood, L. & Mawe, T. G. (2015). The "good" psychologist, "good" torture, and "good" reputation—Response to O'Donohue, Snipes, Dalto, Soto, Margarakis, and Im (2014) "The ethics of enhanced interrogations and torture." *Ethics & Behavior*, 25, 361–372.

Associated Press. (June 2, 2014). *People don't fear hurricanes with female names.* Available at: http://nypost.com/2014/06/02/people-dont-fear-hurricanes-with-female-names-study/.

Banaji, M. R. & Greenwald, A. G. (2013). *Blindspot: Hidden biases of good people.* New York: Random House.

Blanton, H. & Jaccard J. (2006). Arbitrary metrics in psychology. *American Psychologist*, 61, 27–41.

Blanton, H. & Jaccard, J. (2008). Unconscious racism: A concept in pursuit of a measure. *Annual Review of Sociology*, 34, 277–297.

Blanton, H. & Mitchell, G. (2011). Reassessing the predictive validity of the IAT II: Re-analysis of Heider & Skowronski (2007). *North American Journal of Psychology*, 13, 99–106.

Blanton, H., Jaccard, J., Klick, J., Mellers, B. A., Mitchell, G. & Tetlock, P. E. (2009). Strong claims and weak evidence: Reassessing the predictive validity of the IAT. *Journal of Applied Psychology*, 94, 567–582.

Blanton, H., Jaccard, J., Strauts, E., Mitchell, G. & Tetlock, P. E. (2015). Toward a meaningful metric of implicit prejudice. *Journal of Applied Psychology*, 100, 1468–1482.

Brandt, M. J., Reyna, C., Chambers, J. R., Crawford, J. T. & Wetherell, G. (2014). Theideological-conflict hypothesis: Intolerance among both liberals and conservatives. *Current Directions in Psychological Science*, 23, 27–34.

Carney, D. R., Cuddy, A. J. C. & Yap, A. J. (2015). Review and summary of research on the embodied effects of expansive (vs. contractive) nonverbal displays. *Psychological Science*, 26, 657–663.

Ceci, S. J., Peters, D. & Plotkin, J. (1985). Human subjects review, personal values, and the regulation of social science research. *American Psychologist*, 40, 994–1002.

Chen, M. & Bargh, J. A. (1999). Consequences of automatic evaluation: Immediate behavioral predispositions to approach or avoid the stimulus. *Personality and Social Psychology Bulletin*, 25, 215–224.

Correll, J., Park, B., Judd, C. M. & Wittenbrink, B. (2002). The police officer's dilemma: Using ethnicity to disambiguate potentially threatening individuals. *Journal of Personality and Social Psychology, 83,* 1314–1329.

Correll, J., Park, B., Judd, C. M., Wittenbrink, B., Sadler, M. S. & Keesee, T. (2007). Across the thin blue line: Police officers and racial bias in the decision to shoot. *Journal of Personality and Social Psychology, 92,* 1006–1023.

Correll, J., Hudson, S. M., Guillermo, S. & Ma, D. S. (2014), The police officer's dilemma: A decade of research on racial bias in the decision to shoot. *Social and Personality Psychology Compass, 8,* 201–213.

Cox, W. T., Devine, P. G., Plant, E. A. & Schwartz, L. L. (2014). Toward a comprehensive understanding of officers' shooting decisions: No simple answers to this complex problem. *Basic and Applied Social Psychology, 36,* 356–364.

Duarte, J., Crawford, J. T., Stern, C., Haidt, J., Jussim, L. & Tetlock, P. E. (2015). Political diversity will improve social psychological science. *Behavioral and Brain Sciences, 38,* 1–13.

Fiedler, K. (2011). Voodoo correlations are everywhere—Not only in social neurosciences. *Perspectives on Psychological Science, 6,* 163–171.

Forscher, P. S. et al. (May 5, 2016). *A meta-analysis of change in implicit bias.* Unpublished manuscript. Available at: https://osf.io/b5m97/.

Gawronski, B. (2004). Theory-based bias correction in dispositional inference: The fundamental attribution error is dead, long live the correspondence bias. *European Review of Social Psychology, 15,* 183–217.

Greenwald, A. G., Banaji, M. R. & Nosek, B. A. (2015). Statistically small effects of the Implicit Association Test can have societally large effects. *Journal of Personality and Social Psychology, 108,* 553–561.

Greenwald, A. G. & Krieger, L. H. (2006). Implicit bias: Scientific foundations. *California Law Review, 94,* 945–967.

Greenwald, A. G. & Pettigrew, T. F. (2014). With malice toward none and charity for some: Ingroup favoritism enables discrimination. *American Psychologist, 69,* 669–684.

Greenwald, A. G., Poehlman, T. A., Uhlmann, E. L. & Banaji, M. R. (2009). Understanding and using the Implicit Association Test: III. Meta-analysis of predictive validity. *Journal of Personality and Social Psychology, 97,* 17–41.

Gross, N. (2013). *Why are professors liberal and why do conservatives care?* Cambridge: Harvard University Press.

Hanna, J. (2010). Power posing: Fake it until you make it. Available at: http://hbswk. hbs.edu/item/power-posing-fake-it-until-you-make-it.

Hunt, E. & Carlson, J. (2007). Considerations relating to the study of group differences in intelligence. *Perspectives on Psychological Science, 2,* 194–213.

Kang, J. & Banaji, M. R. (2006). Fair measures: A behavioral realist revision of "affirmative action", *California Law Review, 94,* 1063–1118.

Kang, J., Bennett, M., Carbado, D., Casey, P., Dasgupta, N., Faigman, D., ... Mnookin, J. (2012). Implicit bias in the courtroom. *UCLA Law Review, 59,* 1124–1186.

Koehler, J. (1993). The influence of prior beliefs on scientific judgments of evidence quality. *Organizational Behavior & Human Decision Processes, 56,* 28.

Lai, C. K., Marini, M., Lehr, S. A., Cerruti, C., Shin, J. L., Joy-Gaba, J. A., ... Nosek, B. A. (2014). A comparative investigation of 17 interventions to reduce implicit racial preferences. *Journal of Experimental Psychology: General, 143,* 1765–1785.

Landy, F. J. (2008). Stereotypes, bias, and personnel decisions: Strange and stranger. *Industrial and Organizational Psychology*, *1*, 379–392.

Lublin, J. S. (2014). Bringing hidden biases into the light—big businesses teach staffers how "unconscious bias" impacts decisions. *Wall Street Journal*. Available at: http://online. wsj.com/news/articles/SB10001424052702303754404579308562690896896.

MacCoun, R. J. (1998). Biases in the interpretation and use of research results. *Annual Review of Psychology*, *49*, 259–287.

Mahoney, M. J. (1987). Scientific publication and knowledge politics. *Journal of Social Behavior & Personality*, *2*, 165–176.

Mekawi, Y. & Bresin, K. (2015). Is the evidence from racial shooting task studies a smoking gun? Results from a meta-analysis. *Journal of Experimental Social Psychology*, *61*, 120–130.

Mitchell, G. (2012). Revisiting truth or triviality: The external validity of research in the psychological laboratory. *Perspectives on Psychological Science*, *7*, 109–117.

Mitchell, G. & Tetlock, P. E. (2017). Popularity as a poor proxy for utility: The case of implicit prejudice. In S.O. Lilienfeld & I. Waldman (Eds.), *Psychological science under scrutiny: Recent challenges and proposed solutions* (pp. 164–195). New York: John Wiley & Sons. doi: 10.1002/9781119095910.ch10.

Monahan, J., Walker, L. & Mitchell, G. (2008). Contextual evidence of gender discrimination: The ascendance of "social frameworks." *Virginia Law Review*, *94*, 1705–1739.

Nosek, B. A., Greenwald, A. G. & Banaji, M. R. (2007). The Implicit Association Test at age 7: A methodological and conceptual review. In J. A. Bargh (Ed.), *Social psychology and the unconscious: The automaticity of higher mental processes* (pp. 265–292). New York: Psychology Press.

O'Donohue, W., Snipes, C., Dalto, G., Soto, C., Maragakis, A. & Im, S. (2014) The ethics of enhanced interrogations and torture: A reappraisal of the argument. *Ethics & Behavior*, *27*, 109–125.

Oswald, F. L., Mitchell, G., Blanton, H., Jaccard, J. & Tetlock, P. E. (2013). Predicting ethnic and racial discrimination: A meta-analysis of IAT criterion studies. *Journal of Personality and Social Psychology*, *105*, 171–192.

Oswald, F. L., Mitchell, G., Blanton, H., Jaccard, J. & Tetlock, P. E. (2015). Predicting ethnic and racial discrimination with the IAT: Small effect sizes of unknown societal significance. *Journal of Personality and Social Psychology*, *108*, 562–571.

Potier, B. (Dec. 16, 2004). Making case for concept of "implicit prejudice": Extending the legal definition of discrimination, *Harvard University Gazette*. Available at: www. news.harvard.edu/gazette/2004/12.16/09-prejudice.html.

Ranehill, E., Dreber, A., Johannesson, M., Leiberg, S., Sul, S. & Weber, R. A. (2015). Assessing the robustness of power posing: No effect on hormones and risk tolerance in a large sample of men and women. *Psychological Science*, *26*, 653–656.

Redding, R. E. (2001). Sociopolitical diversity in psychology: The case for pluralism. *American Psychologist*, *56*, 205.

Richard, F. D., Bond, C. F., Jr. & Stokes-Zoota, J. J. (2003). One hundred years of social psychology quantitatively described. *Review of General Psychology*, *7*, 331–363.

Robinson, M. (June 26, 2014). 8 power poses that will make you more confident at work. *Business Insider*. Available at: www.businessinsider.com/power-posing-at-work-2014-6.

Shadish, W. R., Cook, T. D. & Campbell, D. T. (2002). *Experimental and Quasi-experimental designs for generalized causal inference.* Boston: Houghton Mifflin Co.

Stone, D. (1997). *Policy paradox: The art of political decision making.* New York: W.W. Norton & Co.

Tetlock, P. E. & Mitchell, G. (1993). Liberal and conservative approaches to justice: Conflicting psychopolitical portraits. In B. Mellers & J. Baron (Eds.), *Psychological perspectives on justice: Theory and applications* (pp. 234–255). Cambridge: Cambridge University Press.

Tetlock, P. E. & Mitchell, G. (2015). Why so few conservatives and should we care? *Society, 52,* 28–34.

Thorstenson et al., Thorstenson, C. A., Pazda, A. D. & Elliot, A. J. (2015). Retraction of "Sadness Impairs Color Perception." *Psychological Science, 26,* 1822.

Vedantum, S. (2012). How stereotypes can drive women to quit science. Available at: www.npr.org/2012/07/12/156664337/stereotype-threat-why-women-quit-science-jobs.

Vedantum, S. (2013). How to win that music competition? Send a video. Available at: www.npr.org/2013/08/20/213551358/how-to-win-that-music-competition-send-a-video.

Willems, E. P. & Howard, G. S. (1980). The external validity of papers on external validity. *American Psychologist, 35,* 387–388.

Wilson, T. D., Aronson, E. & Carlsmith, K. (2010). The art of laboratory experimentation. In S. T. Fiske, D. T. Gilbert & G. Lindzey (Eds.), *Handbook of social psychology* (Vol. 1, pp. 51–81). Hoboken: John Wiley & Sons.

Wright, O. (Sept. 16, 2015). Barack Obama to bring Whitehall's "nudge" theory to the White House. Available at: www.independent.co.uk/news/world/americas/barack-obama-to-bring-whitehalls-nudge-theory-to-the-white-house-10504616.html.

10

SOCIO-POLITICAL VALUES INFILTRATE THE ASSESSMENT OF SCIENTIFIC RESEARCH

Stephen J. Ceci and Wendy M. Williams

The dearth of diversity of viewpoints within the academy—and especially the lack of conservative political perspectives—has been identified by Duarte et al. (2015) as an impediment to teaching and research. A number of commentators have challenged this claim and/or its policy implications, such as the need to hire more conservative faculty. In this chapter, we describe an aspect of this issue that has escaped serious attention in recent decades; specifically, the infiltration of sociopolitical viewpoints into assessments of the quality of scientific contributions. We present three case studies consistent with Duarte et al.'s (2015) claim that socio-political viewpoints influence evaluations of scientific findings. These case studies illustrate that whether a manuscript is accepted for publication, a grant is funded, or a proposal is approved by an IRB is seemingly a function of the congruence of each work product with reviewers' socio-political agenda.

In our commentary on Duarte et al.'s target article in *Behavioral and Brain Sciences* (Ceci & Williams, 2015), we suggested the following three-part thought experiment. Part 1: Identify a socially or politically sensitive question, such as whether racial or gender differences in academic achievement are consistent with claims of a genetic basis. Part 2: Create two versions of an experiment that provides a test of this claim. Both versions should be identical in all ways (methodology, literature review, and statistical treatment). The sole difference between them should be in their findings. In one version, there should be a "liberal" finding: Results indicate that all of the observed racial/gender variance can be accounted for by nongenetic factors and therefore are consistent with sociocultural factors that are malleable. In the other version, there should be a "conservative" finding: A large fraction of the observed racial/gender gap cannot be explained by socio-cultural differences between racial/gender groups but is consistent with a genetic explanation. Part 3: Send one or the other of these two versions randomly to a large sample of researchers and ask them to review the manuscript for publication in a journal, or for presentation at a conference, or as background data for a grant application. Ask reviewers to read the version they were sent and then answer the usual questions that reviewers are asked, such as (a) How important is the research question? (b) How adequate is the literature review? (c) How rigorous is the methodology? (d) Is the statistical treatment appropriate? (e) Do the conclusions follow from the data? Also ask reviewers how often they review for journals or grant agencies and for how many years they have done such reviews. Finally, get a proxy for reviewers' socio-political orientation that minimizes demand characteristics that inhere when directly inquiring about political affiliation. For example, ask for reviewers' preferred solution to a societal problem that has established ideological viewpoints.

In our commentary on their target article, we predicted that such an experiment would reveal a political matching effect, with liberal reviewers down-rating the same methodology when it leads to a conservative finding (achievement gap consistent with genetic explanation) and conservative reviewers down-rating it when it leads to a liberal finding (data consistent with socio-cultural explanation of the racial achievement gap).

It may not be necessary to conduct this thought experiment because actual experiments and "experiments of nature" already exist that give us a good idea of what would be found. In this chapter, we describe three personal examples of experimental evidence that, taken together, suggest that scientific reviewers' socio-political attitudes can influence their decisions, and we discuss what this implies about the need for viewpoint diversity in the larger academy.

IRBs and Political Values

In 1985, Ceci, Peters, and Plotkin conducted an experiment that had an unusual history. Plotkin, a graduate student at the time, had an idea for an experiment involving gender and racial discrimination in hiring. He wondered whether white women and African-American applicants of both genders were bypassed in hiring for managerial posts in favor of less-qualified white males. In the early 1980s, there was ample evidence of racial "redlining" in housing, discriminatory mortgage-lending practices, and bias in hiring of black and female applicants for positions in construction, law enforcement, and firefighting. However, no one had examined whether there was bias in hiring high-level management posts, and there was some reason to hypothesize that there might not be. We proposed an experiment to our IRB in which we would send personnel officers at Fortune 500 companies a letter asking them to participate in our experiment but explaining that we could not give them any details about the nature of the experiment or when it would occur. (We proposed to tell them that it would occur sometime in the next 12 months but that we could not give them the exact date because doing so would compromise the study.) So, although we were interested in whether there was racial and gender bias in managerial hiring, we did not plan to mention this in our correspondence with these companies until after the experiment was completed. We proposed to ask these personnel officers to agree to receive one fake application for a managerial post they advertised over the course of the coming 12 months, and we pledged that they would not be asked to do anything other than what they ordinarily do when evaluating an application. We promised to immediately withdraw the fake application once they evaluated it and to fully debrief them about the nature of the study, and we promised complete confidentiality for them and their companies.

We drafted the human subjects protocol, attaching the cover letter we would send to Fortune 500 personnel managers, a copy of the fake applications that we planned to submit to these personnel officers in response to ads for managerial positions that their companies posted in the *Wall Street Journal*, and a description of the debriefing procedure and pledge of confidentiality. Some personnel officers would get a letter and résumé with a typical white male name, and others would be sent the same letter/résumé with a white woman or African-American male or female's name on it (signaled by ethnic names and organization membership). The dependent variables included length of time to respond to the fake applicant's letter and whether it included an invitation to interview. Our proposed use of deception (partially informed consent) coupled with full debriefing and a pledge of confidentiality seemed pretty innocuous as far as treatment of the personnel officers was concerned and was pretty tame compared to other social psychological experiments that were often approved (particularly 30 years ago, which is the era we are discussing here), so we expected a quick approval by our IRB. It was not to be.

Following several communications with the head of the IRB that asked us to respond to concerns raised by members of the IRB having to do with deception and debriefing, it became clear that our answers were unsatisfactory, and we eventually were invited to appear before the IRB and answer members' questions. This struck us as odd because other deception studies had been approved that had not met with requests for the investigators to appear before the IRB, but we agreed to do so. When two of us met with the full IRB committee, it became evident that their concerns had very little, if anything, to do with deception per se but with our study's potential political and financial consequences. One member of the IRB launched into a series of questions about an outcome we had not anticipated; she asked whether we had thought about how our findings, if they showed bias *in favor of* women and ethnic minorities (i.e., reverse discrimination), might set back initiatives for hiring members of these groups. The IRB chair thankfully responded that the socio-political ramifications of research were beyond the committee's purview and they should confine their consideration to our proposed treatment of the

faculty in our study may have inferred the purpose of the study and responded in a politically correct manner that did not reflect their actual preferences when they vote on real job candidates (www.huffingtonpost.com/wendy-m-williams/women-scientists-academic-hiring-advantage-is_b_7195312.html). We responded to all these claims and many others, explaining why they were incorrect. (See, for example, our responses at http://chronicle.com/article/Passions-Supplant-Reason-in/232989?cid=megamenu, and at: www.spsp.org/blog/strong-preference-for-hiring.) Here, we summarize our rebuttals.

Faculty guessed the purpose of the study. Commentators claimed that the faculty in our five experiments were aware we were studying sexist hiring and that they chose women applicants to appear politically correct. (Interestingly, similar criticisms were not leveled against studies with opposite findings, such as Moss-Racusin et al.'s, 2012.) Four sources of evidence refute this claim (and a fifth that has since come to our attention). First, in our article, we reported that 30 faculty members had been asked to guess what the study was about and none guessed correctly. They assumed that its purpose was to determine whether they preferred creative colleagues to analytical ones; gender was not on their radar. Second, in Experiment 5, faculty members were given only a single applicant to rate, male or female. They had no awareness that a mirror applicant had been sent to other faculty members with identical credentials but with the gender reversed. Thus, faculty members rating the male applicant could not have downgraded him to the observed 7.14 (on a 10-point scale) under an assumption that some unknown faculty member elsewhere in the United States would upgrade an otherwise-identical female applicant to the observed 8.20 (which, furthermore, is an absurdly tortured line of reasoning). Third, if faculty members were aware that our purpose was to find out whether they judge female applicants more favorably to identically qualified males, faculty members should have rated identical male and female applicants the same rather than reveal a lack of objectivity. But as we reported, fewer than 3% of faculty members rated the identical female and male applicants the same. Fourth, if respondents knew the purpose of the study, why in some conditions (e.g., when a single mother with two young children was pitted against a married father of two with a stay-at-home wife) was there no preference for the woman, or even a preference for the man? It seems implausible to argue that the faculty members knew the hypothesis but acted upon it only in some conditions. Since publishing our study, a fifth reason for rejecting this claim has been reported: When we followed this study with a new one in which we depicted a female applicant as very impressive but slightly less so than her male competitor (9.3 for the female vs. 9.5 for the male), faculty members strongly preferred to hire the male, thus refuting the claim that they were reflexively behaving in a politically correct manner.

The applicants were unrealistically academically strong, and therefore we cannot generalize to actual tenure-track finalists. Some argued that our three short-listed finalists were described as unrealistically academically strong (link). Finalists were rated between 9.3 and 9.5 on a 10-point scale (in which 10 is truly exceptional). It is true that we described the three finalists for the tenure-track position as very impressive, with strong letters of recommendation, and high ratings by the search committee. We did this because in our experience, short-listed finalists are usually highly impressive. In support of this claim, we quoted anecdotal evidence from respondents who spontaneously wrote that they usually had 100-plus applicants for each tenure-track position in their department, and the top 15 or 20 were undeniably excellent. In our own years of experience chairing search committees, we have had a similar experience, with our last search netting 267 applicants and the top 20 or so being uniformly considered to be very impressive.

We wrote in our article that if bias against one sex occurs, it is likely to occur under conditions of ambiguity, when one sex is depicted as ambiguously competent. Meta-analyses support this claim. For example, Koch, D'Mello, and Sacket (2015) found that gender-role congruity bias occurs when "individuating information" that describes applicants' competence is ambiguous or not clearly diagnostic of success. Sex bias in male-dominated fields, when diagnostic information about applicants' competence is available, is near zero ($d = 0.02$; Koch et al., pp. 130–131). In our experiments, we used two fields in which gender-role congruity could be an issue—engineering and economics—and found a preference for hiring women in both; in all tenure-track hiring in both male-dominated and gender-neutral fields, faculty members are given ample diagnostic information, including letters of reference, CVs, and publications, in addition to attending their job talks. Thus, biases that occur under conditions of ambiguity in male-dominated fields should not occur in academic hiring. In addition, in one of our experiments, we asked faculty members how impressive they judged these finalists to be, and they rated the men 7.14 (out of 10) and the women with the statistically identical credentials 8.2. So, although we depicted the finalists as highly impressive (9.3–9.5 out of 10), faculty members felt that they were less stellar and there was room for us to make them even more impressive. Finally, in one experiment, we used actual CVs from recent job applicants. We did not alter them to make them more impressive; we used them as they were, simply varying the gender of the names. Faculty still preferred the applicant with a female name on the CV by a 2-to-1 margin. Thus, for all these reasons, there is no basis for claiming that our results do not reveal pro-female hiring attitudes.

Passions over reason. We suspect that none of our rebuttals changed critics' minds, given the passion with which they attacked our findings (as well as us personally). In many online blogs and columns, critics used colorful language to deride us (referring to us as "crustaceans") and demean our work (e.g., "What we have here is not clear findings; it's mud" (http://chronicle.com/

article/The-Myth-That-Academic-Science/231413/). We were described as university fat cats who look down on untenured folks:

> These White professors who have 'made it' in academia do not see a major problem with the gender imbalance in STEM…Williams and Ceci's own biases lead them to believe that women and men belong to two discrete groups [making genderqueer and transgender scientists invisible]…Ignoring race, sexuality and other socio-economic factors is a power dynamic: White, senior academics can pretend that race doesn't matter, because racism does not adversely affect their individual progress. They can choose to believe that sexism is over because they have secured their tenure" (http://othersociologist.com/2015/04/16/myth-about-women-in-science/).

Lest one imagine that we have quoted the most passionate of our critics, we assure you we have not, and in an early HuffPost response, we listed myriad personally insulting comments that were posted—such as calling us incompetent and unscholarly (e.g., "*They are not serious scholars*"), sexists ("*Nothing like a good bit of sexism to keep Twitter well fed*"), right-wing homophobes, and secretly machinating to overturn affirmative action ("*Ceci and Williams are beloved of right-wing columnists. We need to approach their work with skepticism, as commentators have largely done*"; www.huffingtonpost.com/wendy-m-williams/women-scientists-academic_2_b_7480318.html).

Against this backdrop of ardent invectives, we held out little hope that we could convince critics that our methods were actually sound and that their claims lacked merit. However, this assault on our ideas provided an opportunity to conduct what Urie Bronfenbrenner (1979) used to call an "experiment by nature," which we turn to next. It reveals something we long feared, namely, that the objection to our work's methods has more to do with the message than the methods themselves.

Affirmative Action Hiring

Recently, we conducted an experiment that employed the same methods, materials, and procedures that we used in our tenure-track hiring study—the one that showed a 2-to-1 hiring preference for women applicants—that was so roundly criticized for its alleged methodological flaws. However, in this new study, instead of pitting identically competent men and women against each other for a tenure-track position, we pitted a slightly superior man (rated 9.5 out of 10) against a slightly inferior woman (rated 9.3). In a second condition, we pitted a slightly superior woman (9.5) against a slightly inferior man (9.3). We wondered whether gender would trump objective merit in faculty hiring preferences. It did not. Nearly all faculty members in this experiment preferred to hire the finalist with the 9.5 rating over the one with the 9.3 rating, regardless of the applicant's gender.

To some, this is good news; it implies that women are not hired when they are inferior to the men against whom they compete for tenure-track posts. Thus, it assuages concern that affirmative action has diluted the talent pool, as some have discussed (see Niederle, Segal, & Vesterlund, 2013). In fact, some proponents of affirmative action may use our findings to argue that it is not achieving its objective of hiring very impressive women in fields in which they are underrepresented, if a slightly more impressive man is available. Thus, we were not completely surprised to find that there were no criticisms of this new study, despite the fact that it employed the identical methods that were assailed by critics of our previous experiments. If our methods showing a hiring preference for women were fatally flawed (http://chronicle.com/article/The-Myth-That-Academic-Science/231413/), why did no one rush to pronounce these latest findings flawed? Perhaps this glaring gap is due to the second study being published in a less visible journal, although it has gotten a great deal of national media attention. (The Altmetric score for this second study is 172, i.e., the top 1%, reflecting very high media attention: https://frontiers.altmetric.com/details/4651833/twitter.) How odd that the chorus of naysayers has been so utterly silent. This outcome, as well as its thunderous sound of silence, illustrates once again how people's political agendas infiltrate their evaluation of science. In retrospect, we wish we had published this second study first and then, after seeing it favorably cited, published our former study showing pro-women hiring attitudes. It would be difficult for fans of one to be contemptuous of the other, although we have learned never to underestimate the creativity of our critics when it comes to their ability to retroactively justify criticisms as a function of the political valence of our most current findings.

Postlude

We have been studying controversial issues for over three decades. During this time, our guiding principle has been to follow the data wherever it takes us. Sometimes, our data have been amenable to the political right, as in the case of our finding that faculty prefer to hire women applicants for tenure-track posts (Williams & Ceci, 2015), our finding of gender neutrality in obtaining grants and journal acceptances (Ceci & Williams, 2011), and our finding of gender fairness both in remuneration and obtaining of tenure in most fields (Ceci, Ginther, Kahn & Williams, 2014). At other times, our data have tilted to the political left, as in our finding that affirmative hiring values do not result in lower-quality women professors being hired (Ceci & Williams, 2015) as well as in our finding that women have a harder time getting tenure in the field of biology, are less satisfied with their professorial positions in the social sciences, and receive somewhat different tenure advice than their male counterparts (Ceci et al., 2014).

One thing we learned from this three-decade enterprise is that zealots on both sides of the socio-political spectrum have a proclivity for denial, post hoc rationalization, and obfuscation. Because social scientists in the academy are preponderantly liberal, we assume that this orientation results in fewer right-leaning proposals getting funded and fewer right-leaning sets of findings being published in authors' journals-of-first-choice than is the case for more politically liberal authors. We base this assumption on the much greater likelihood of drawing all liberal reviewers for journals and grants. Consider: 58–66% of social science professors in the United States identify as liberals compared to only 5–8% who identify as conservatives; self-identified Democratic faculty members outnumber Republicans by ratios of at least 8 to 1 and often higher (Gross & Simmons, 2007; Klein & Stern, 2009); and in psychology, 84% of faculty members identify themselves as liberals vs. only 8% as conservatives.

This is the most troubling aspect of the left-right asymmetry in the contemporary social sciences. Liberal and conservative social scientists can both undoubtedly tell stories about the time their submissions were rejected based on biased reviews (www.huffingtonpost.com/2015/05/01/sexist-peer-review_n_7190656.html), or were rejected without review by a seemingly biased editor, or about the unusual steps taken in reviewing studies that tilt in one direction. Consider, for example, our *PNAS* article showing a preference for hiring women, which had to survive seven outside reviews plus an eighth full-length review by the editor—all in a journal in which the modal number of reviews is only two. Surveys suggest that conservative and moderate social scientists experience these rejections and delays more often than do liberals. Out of 506 members of the Society for Personality and Social Psychology, Inbar and Lammers (2012) found that only 5.5% described themselves as socially moderate or conservative. They found that conservative social-personality psychologists conceal their views out of a well-founded fear of negative repercussions, such as grant denials and hiring rejections. Out of 229 members of SPSP who responded to their survey, substantial percentages of liberals indicated that they would discriminate against conservative applicants in hiring, symposia invitations, journal reviews, and grant reviews (see Table 2 from Inbar & Lammers, 2012, p. 501). And there was a dose-response relationship; the more liberal these respondents were, the more they said they were willing to discriminate against conservatives on each question: paper reviews, $r(279) = -0.32$, $p < 0.0001$; grant reviews, $r(280) = -0.34$, $p < 0.0001$; symposium invitations, $r(277) = -0.20$, $p = 0.001$; and hiring decisions, $r(279) = -0.44$, $p < 0.0001$.

Given that people are better at identifying the flaws in other people's research than in their own, especially if those other people have dissimilar beliefs (e.g., Mercier & Sperber, 2011), the limited diversity in political viewpoints, particularly among social scientists, is concerning. Although we do not favor a political litmus test or quotas for faculty hiring, we do see merit in explicit acknowledgment and discussions to increase awareness of the costs associated with lack of viewpoint diversity in the academy—costs that include rejecting or delaying projects because of their political ramifications, as seen in our IRB study. As psychologists, who as a group study the processes underlying rational and optimal thinking, we can and must do better to ensure true fairness and openness of our discipline and the broader academy to the full range of political views, regardless whether or not they conform to our own personal agendas. The more politically restrictive we become, the farther we travel toward blindness and insularity and away from the most basic foundational principles of academic inquiry.

References

Bronfenbrenner, U. (1979). *The ecology of human development: Experiments of nature and by design*. Cambridge: Harvard University Press.

Ceci, S. J., Peters, D. & Plotkin, J. (1985). Human Subjects Review: Personal values and the regulation of social science research. *American Psychologist, 40,* 994–1003.

Ceci, S. J., Ginther, D. K., Kahn, S. & Williams, W. M. (2014). Women in academic science: A changing landscape. *Psychological Science in the Public Interest*. http://psi.sagepub.com/content/15/3/75.abstract?patientinform-links=yes&legid=sppsi;15/3/75. doi:10.1177/1529100614541236.

Ceci, S. J. & Williams, W. M. (2011). Understanding current causes of women's underrepresentation in science. *Proceedings of the National Academy of Sciences, 108,* 3157–3162.

Ceci, S. J. & Williams, W. M. (2015). Women have substantial advantage in STEM faculty hiring, except when competing against more-accomplished men. *Frontiers in Psychology, 6,* 1532. http://journal.frontiersin.org/article/10.3389/fpsyg.2015.01532/full. doi:10.3389/fpsyg.2015.01532.

Duarte, J. L., Crawford, J. T., Stern, C., Haidt, J., Jussim, L. & Tetlock, P. E. (2015). Political diversity will improve social psychological science. *Behavioral and Brain Sciences, 38,* 1–13. doi:10.1017/S0140525X14000430.

Gross, N. & Simmons, S. (2007). The social and political views of American professors. Available at: http://citeseerx.ist.psu.edu/viewdoc/download?. doi=10.1.1.147.6141&rep=rep1&type=pdf.

Haidt, J. (2001). The emotional dog and its rational tail: A social intuitionist approach to moral judgment. *Psychological Review, 108,* 814–834.

Inbar, Y. & Lammers, J. (2012). Political diversity in social and personality psychology. *Perspectives in Psychological Science, 7*(5), 496–503. doi:10.1177/1745691612448792.

Klein, D. & Stern, C. (2009). Groupthink in Academia: Majoritarian departmental politics and the professional pyramid. In R. Maranto, R. Redding & F. Hess (Eds). *The Politically Correct University* (pp. 79–98). Washington, D.C.: AEI Press.

Koch, A. J., D'Mello, S. D. & Sackett, P. R. (2015). A metaanalysis of gender stereotypes and bias in experimental simulations of employment decision making. *Journal of Applied Psychology, 100,* 128–161.

Mercier, H. & Sperber, D. (2011). Why do humans reason? Arguments for an argumentative theory. *Behavioral and Brain Sciences, 34*(2), 57–74.

Moss-Racusin, C., Dovidio, J., Brescoll, V., Graham, M. & Handelsman, J. (2012). Science faculty's subtle gender biases favor male students. *Proceedings of the National Academy of Sciences*, *109*(41), 16474–16479.

Niederle, M., Segal, C. & Vesterlund, L. (2013) How costly is diversity? Affirmative action in light of gender differences in competitiveness. *Management Science*, *59*(1), 1–16.

Williams, W. M. & Ceci, S. J. (2015). National hiring experiments reveal 2-to-1 preference for women on STEM tenure track. *Proceedings of the National Academy of Sciences*, *112*(17), 5360–5365. www.pnas.org/content/early/2015/04/08/1418878112. abstract.

11

THE BULLET-POINT BIAS

How Diluted Science Communications Can Impede Social Progress

Hart Blanton and Elif G. Ikizer

In June 1883, the literary and science magazine *The Chautauquan* presented readers with a question it had adapted from a paradox formulated over a century earlier by philosopher George Berkeley: "If a tree were to fall on an island where there were no human beings, would there be any sound?" The query's unnamed author went on to answer, "No. Sound is the sensation excited in the ear when the air or other medium is set in motion." This question has since been adapted to facilitate debates over whether objects themselves can exist independent of perception. This particular author's answer is both logically sound and consistent with immaterialism, a philosophical school of thought arguing that material objects have no reality independent of perception. This answer is also altogether unsatisfying. We all know that our lives can be affected by events that we will never see or hear. As material objects that can set consequential events in motion through falling, unseen and unheard trees exist. The same cannot be said of scientists.

To exist, a scientist must be heard. This fact can be missed from reading common definitions of "scientist." The Merriam Webster Dictionary (2016), for instance, defines a scientist as "a person who studies, specializes in, or investigates a field of science and does scientific work." This definition and others like it do not make clear that "scientific work" requires not just the application of theory, deduction, and observation but also acts of *communication*. In the words of the naturalist John Burroughs (1889), "...one man's science must be another man's science; all science is a whole; a pushing farther and farther of the lines of knowledge into nature" (p. 567). To join in this conversation, scientists must communicate; make noise.

This is not to say that the consequences of communicating will always be as intended or, for that matter, good. The concern animating the present analysis relates to the potential unwanted impact of scientific communication. Our thesis is that, by simplifying research to make it accessible to the public, researchers at times set events in motion that produce negative consequences. In the extreme case, simplified communications can exacerbate the very social problems researchers hope to address through their work. We begin this argument by considering the factors that produce simplified communications.

Simple Pressures

Public perception about what is and what is not "scientifically supported" by the medical, environmental, sociological, health, and psychological sciences can influence individual decision making and shape public policies. There is thus an urgent need for the world's scientists to have their voices heard, and most researchers see the media playing a critical role. Surveys of scientists indicate that, as a group, they view it as one of their public duties to inform and educate the public through their interactions with the media (Peter, 2013). Such interests are often facilitated by media relations specialists working at researchers' home institutions, their professional organizations, and the publishing houses that host their journals. With ever-growing competition in the "marketplace of ideas," successful media outreach can be critical, not just to the advancement of individual scientific careers, but to the survival of entire scientific disciplines (Rödder, Franzen & Weingart, 2012).

The resulting pressure put on the scientific community often is a positive force that promotes social progress. It can push scientists outside their comfort zones so that they inform the public about important scientific advances. Such incentives are often needed as scientists tend to suffer what Heath and Heath (2007) termed "the curse of knowledge." They know their topics so well that they often find it hard to adopt audience perspectives. To meet the goal of informing the public, they often must find ways to distill the knowledge in their heads to the fundamental take-away points that non-specialists can understand. Media relations specialists often help in this effort, as do a number of professional services (e.g., Basken, 2013), and the rewards for mastering public communication skills can be great. By learning to communicate effectively to science reporters, through the editorial pages of national news sources and on the stages at TED, scientists might be able to charge higher speaking fees, pursue lucrative consulting jobs, secure book deals, and enjoy the perks of minor celebrity. The incentives connecting scientists to the media also cut the other way—in a new media environment, where alternative new sources are only a click away, media outlets have become increasingly reliant on material generated by scientists who know how to grab and retain audience interest. Science sells; more so the more easily it is communicated.

All these factors can push scientists to tell simple stories that will engage and entertain the public. We thus propose the presence of a new bias. We define the *bullet-point bias* as the tendency to advance diluted but provocative scientific conclusions in the media. In social psychology, this bias tends to be manifest by the tendency to tell simple stories that focus the public's attention on strong, counterintuitive and often unseen forces. In social psychology, this often means turning public attention to such topics as (1) the power of the situation to drive human behavior, (2) the consequential role that the unconscious plays in shaping human judgments and decisions, and (3) the potent ability of social psychologists to exert power over unsuspecting humans, through non-obvious means.[1]

What's the Harm?

Given the benefits that can come when scientists effectively engage the media, we think most social psychologists view media attention in largely positive terms. Such a view is revealed by a recent call to action that Dan Gilbert (2016) delivered to the annual conference of the Society for Personality and Social Psychology. He argued that psychologists should put caution aside when communicating with the media, because

> ... our fear of being wrong often leads us to pass, to stay quiet, to let others who know far less than we do take our turns while we do further analysis of this complicated problem. What we don't seem to realize is that the world doesn't have the luxury of waiting for complete answers before it takes action.

Although Gilbert is not arguing explicitly for the need to simplify messages, his ready dismissal of the need to wait for "complete" (possibly more complex) answers to research questions in our minds highlights the value scientists at times might place on simply engaging the media. We are of a different orientation, more concerned with the damage that might be done when standards for engaging the media are lowered.

We begin with the premise that, by delivering simple, provocative claims through the media, social psychologists will increase their likelihood of getting attention and thus of influencing public perceptions. Whether this influence is for the good or bad, however, is a separate question. By delivering simple stories in the media, psychologists might promote public opinions that benefit society—*but not necessarily so*. Through their ability to connect and engage the public, simple storytellers can be expected to produce both more positive and more negative consequences than can complex (or silent) storytellers. Because positive consequences are often assumed (per Prof. Gilbert's thesis), we focus here on the negative. We highlight the potential negative effects that the bullet-point bias might have in society by focusing attention on two case studies. Both point to instances where simple, provocative media engagement might be impeding social progress.[2]

First Case Study: Simple Racism

Many scholars have suggested that the face of racism has changed from an earlier overt, intended, and "explicit" form to a more subtle, unwanted, and "implicit" form (e.g., Dovidio & Gaertner, 1998). Much of the justification for focusing on this new form of racism comes from observable changes in survey data. Whereas it was once common for white Americans to state that they do not to want black people to live in their own neighborhoods, attend schools in their district, or drink from the same fountains, the majority now reject such unambiguously racist sentiments (Quillian, 2006). But many scholars argue that these changes in self-report can promote overly optimistic views on racial attitudes, because they reveal changes in only explicit forms of racism that survey respondents willingly express. They do not tap the implicit forms that survey respondents might not perceive or wish to report. In response to the potential limitations of explicit measures, many psychologists have advanced a wide range of new measures that ostensibly measure implicit racial attitudes that survey instruments might be failing to assess (see Wittenbrink & Schwartz, 2007).

By far, the most popular and influential of these new measures is the Implicit Association Test (IAT). Modal response patterns on the IAT—particularly data collected from millions of respondents via a demonstration website hosted by Harvard University (https://implicit.harvard.edu/)—have been interpreted as providing evidence that a potent form of implicit racism is rampant in society. Such claims rest in large part on interpretations of the frequency distributions of race-related IAT measures. These distributions are reliably left-skewed, which has led IAT researchers to conclude that "any non-African American subgroup of the United States population will reveal high proportions of persons showing statistically noticeable implicit race bias in favor of [European Americans] relative to [African Americans]" (Greenwald & Krieger, 2006, p. 945). Such interpretations have traveled far beyond academic journals, and they are having particularly strong influence on discussions and debates occurring within legal journals, where IAT scholars have argued that the IAT taps into a potent form of hidden racism that current antidiscrimination law is ill-equipped to handle (e.g., Kang & Banaji, 2006).

Media Coverage

Equally strong statements have been advanced through the media. Any casual internet search of "implicit bias" and "racism" will yield hundreds of reports in all manner of new and traditional media outlets. In these, the IAT distribution is presented as proof that implicit racial bias is (1) prevalent, and (2) potent. Illustrative of common claims are statements made in the popular press book *Blindspot*, in which Banaji and Greenwald (2013) proclaimed:

> First, we now know that automatic White preference is pervasive in American society—almost 75 percent of those who take the Race IAT

on the Internet or in laboratory studies reveal automatic White preference ... Second, the automatic White preference expressed on the Race
IAT is now established as signaling discriminatory behavior. It predicts
discriminatory behavior even among research participants who earnestly
(and, we believe, honestly) espouse egalitarian beliefs. That last statement
may sound like a self-contradiction, but it's an empirical truth (p. 47).

They later added:

> ... given the relatively small proportion of people who are overtly
> prejudiced and how clearly it is established that automatic race preference
> predicts discrimination, it is reasonable to conclude not only that im-
> plicit bias is a cause of Black disadvantage but also that it plausibly plays a
> greater role than does explicit bias in explaining the discrimination that
> contributes to Black disadvantage (p. 209).

These simple, strong and provocative claims have all the hallmarks of bullet-
point bias, and they completely ignore a large and growing literature pointing
to the need for far greater caution. For one, meta-analyses suggest that this measure is at best weakly predictive of discriminatory behavior (e.g., Carlsson &
Agerström, 2016; Oswald, Mitchell, Blanton, Jaccard, & Tetlock, 2013, 2015).
Weak prediction is to be expected, in part, because IAT researchers have been
shown to impose statistically misidentified measurement and causal models
to their data (Blanton, Jaccard, Gonzales & Christie, 2006), and because IAT
scores are contaminated by a host of non-attitudinal factors, including but
not limited to a respondent's prior test-taking experience (Nosek, Banaji &
Greenwald, 2002), their self-presentation motives (e.g., Steffens, 2004) and a
range of more general skills related to intelligence, cognitive flexibility and
speed (e.g., Blanton, Jaccard, Gonzales & Christie, 2006; Mierke & Klauer,
2001; Rothermund & Wentura, 2001, 2004).

More worrisome, the interpretations of the IAT distribution at the center
of strong claims have not been empirically assessed (Blanton & Jaccard, 2006).
Researchers have no research basis for knowing what behaviors to expect of
someone who has an IAT score of, say, 1.5 (which would be sufficient by current scoring algorithms applied on the demonstration web page to merit a label
of "strong automatic preference for whites over blacks"), or how that person
would differ from someone with a score of −1.5 (meriting the label "strong
automatic preference for blacks over whites"). In fact, the only published study
to empirically examine the potential meaning of race-related IAT scores found
evidence that current scoring conventions wildly overestimate the number of
people at risk of acting in a discriminatory fashion. Blanton, Jaccard, Strauts,
Mitchell, and Tetlock (2015) reanalyzed data from published studies ostensibly showing that the IAT predicted "biased" behavior and found that even

individuals who acted in an egalitarian fashion in laboratory studies tended to have IAT scores suggestive of prejudicial attitudes. These scores also were common among individuals who showed out-group favoritism. These findings suggest that the simple media story about the IAT is a misrepresentation, as it leads to an overestimation of bias in society. That said, we of course acknowledge that IAT researchers would probably vigorously defend their simple media claims, just as they have defended their scientific conclusions (see, for example, Greenwald, Nosek & Sriram, 2006; Nosek & Sriram, 2006). Our concern here, however, is not with the veracity of their claims (or lack therefore). We focus here on the consequences.

The Justification: Doing Good

There is a case to be made for using the IAT to tell a simple, provocative story. Truth dilution in this domain might seem forgivable if, by grabbing and holding the public's attention, researchers raise awareness of implicit racial bias. This might promote individual-level changes and promote social progress. IAT researchers invoke such a justification. They suggest, for instance, that knowledge of the IAT might promote a form of "unconsciousness raising" that will lead people to examine and try to correct for their racial biases (e.g., Jost et al., 2009). "I regard awareness to be a singularly important experience because the problem lies in the lack of awareness," Professor Mahzarin Banaji told one media outlet.

> When good people discover their blind spots, they are inherently motivated to wish to change. I try to make use of that motive to do good and take it one step further—to ask about the extent to which people are willing to doubt their own intuitions.
>
> *(Henneman, 2014)*

This is a laudable goal.

The Risk: Doing Bad

Unfortunately, there is no strong empirical evidence that exposing people to their biases will change their behavior (see Forscher et al., 2016, for an exhaustive and pessimistic meta-analytic review of the effects of implicit bias interventions). Thus, by not "waiting for complete answers," implicit attitude researchers might be promoting public faith in interventions that simply will not work, which could result in massive misallocation of resources to combat bias. More worrisome, there is just as good a reason to think that this simple story is promoting the bad, not the good.

To understand the potentially deleterious effects of promoting a simple implicit bias story, it is useful to consider what discrimination looks like in a typical IAT study. Although there is little evidence in the aggregate that the IAT reliably predicts consequential forms of discrimination (e.g., Oswald et al., 2013, 2015), there is heterogeneity in the research literature and so some studies appear suggestive when viewed in isolation. By far, the most highly cited study to suggest a link between IAT scores and discrimination is a study by McConnell and Leibold (2001). They attempted to use the IAT to predict what now are commonly referred to as "microaggressions" (after Pierce, 1970). They arranged for participants to interact with a white and then a black experimenter, and they coded a wide range of nonverbal behaviors to try to assess interaction quality (based on ratings from the experimenters and independent judges). In between these two interactions, participants took an IAT designed to measure their anti-black, implicit attitudes. The researchers found that the IAT had modest but statistically significant correlations with a number of non-verbal indices, with their report suggesting that participants high on the IAT acted more nervously and were less warm, friendly, and comfortable when interacting with the black experimenter relative to the white experimenter.[3]

This study might show that the IAT predicted racial discrimination, but there is another compelling interpretation. Perhaps critical to this study was the fact that respondents completed the IAT immediately before they had contact with the black experimenter. Moreover, participants who performed poorly on the IAT were likely aware of this fact[4] and perhaps felt like they had "failed" the test. The possibility of such reactions is acknowledged by IAT researchers. For instance, *Blindspot* co-author Professor Anthony T. Greenwald stated that his first exposure to the IAT resulted in a "moment of jarring self-insight. ... I can't say if I was more personally distressed or scientifically elated to discover something inside my head that I had no previous knowledge of" (Hutson, 2013). If participants in McConnell and Leibold's study had the same jarring experience, it seems likely that distress was their more common reaction. Moreover, it was only after producing such distress that the experimenters replaced the white experimenter with the black experimenter. Participants who had done poorly might now worry that their racism was again being assessed, causing them to feel resentful, nervous, and uncomfortable in the second interaction—actions that would produce correlations in the direction these researchers found.

Even if a large methodological artifact was driving the results in McConnell and Leibold's (2001) study, one might argue that the anxiety created by the test can more often than not promote the "good" if it motivates positive interactions by whites. Data by Vorauer (2012) argues against such simple predictions. Similar to McConnell and Leibold, she had white Canadian participants interact with either a white or aboriginal work partner. She found that if whites had completed the race-relevant IAT prior to an interaction with the aboriginal, the interaction quality diminished. No such effect was evident if participants instead (1) completed an IAT that was unrelated to race, (2) completed an explicit rather than implicit measures of anti-aboriginal prejudice, or (3) if they interacted with a white instead of an aboriginal partner. These results suggest that the IAT produced some type of counterproductive evaluation apprehension, and Vorauer's mediation analyses supported this interpretation. These analyses indicated that the race-related IAT caused white participants to adopt a more cautious approach to their interactions with the aboriginal partner, which inadvertently led them to convey nonverbal signals of discomfort. These attempts to be non-biased are precisely the types of "microaggressions" that would be coded as evidence of prejudicial implicit attitudes in the McConnell and Leibold study.[5]

There is now a growing body of literature suggesting that attempts to address the potentially hyped influence of implicit bias on behavior will cause more harm than good. For instance, when researchers have instructed white participants to try not to act differently while interacting with a white versus black person, their nonverbal treatment of blacks appears more negative (to both white and black observers) as a result (Apfelbaum, Sommers & Norton, 2008). Simply instructing individuals to actively try to empathize with members of stigmatized groups in order to reduce their biases can produce such effects (Vorauer & Sasaki, 2009). These and other studies are giving clear signs that, by increasing the public concern about not appearing to be biased, psychologists might be increasing the risk that people will act in precisely the ways that "biased" individuals act when interacting with members of historically stigmatized groups (see Frantz, Cuddy, Burnett, Ray & Hart, 2004; Sasaki & Vorauer, 2013).

To date, no study has empirically examined what influence media coverage of implicit bias research might be having on intergroup relations. However, until research gives this a critical look, we think the more cautious and responsible approach to handling the media would be to avoid advancing provocative stories that might heighten a new form of worry; one that can exacerbate intergroup relations. Adding to our concerns on this topic, many articles on implicit bias not only engage the public with a provocative but questionable story about the powerful influence of implicit bias on behavior, but journalists quite often point readers to the IAT demonstration webpage. There, the majority will be given personalized feedback indicating to them that they have "automatic" biases against blacks and other minorities. The entire point to providing this feedback is to encourage people to suppress their hidden biases, but on the face of it, this is problematic. A large literature on ironic processes suggests that thought suppression commonly backfires (Wegner & Schneider, 2003). By encouraging individuals to monitor their thoughts to avoid unbidden and unwanted stereotypical and prejudicial thoughts, media reports and accompanying IAT diagnoses might be increasing the accessibility and influence of these same cognitions.

These are worrisome possibilities, and the desire to inhibit hidden racism is not the only pathway through which IAT media reports might result in an increase in "bad" behavior. Even individuals who avoid the trap of trying to inhibit their inner thoughts might be at greater risk of acting in a biased fashion. This can occur if people simply come to believe common arguments in media reports—that implicit biases are pervasive in society and held to some considerable degree by the majority of individuals. By going beyond the current data to encourage the public to think that implicit biases are common, media reports might be advancing normative claims that can lower the social constraints against acting in a biased fashion. Such unintended effects of communications have been demonstrated in research on social influence, where social marketing designed to reduce risky health behaviors and promote conservation have been shown to backfire if they inadvertently communicate to their audiences that bad behaviors are common (Blanton & Burkley, 2008; Cialdini et al., 2006).

Could similar effects occur from media reports emphasizing the prevalence of racial bias? A set of studies by Duguid and Thomas-Hunt (2015) is suggestive. They randomly assigned participants to read messages emphasizing either the high or low prevalence of gender stereotyping. Much as in social marketing domains, high-prevalence messages were found to increase gender stereotyping relative to low-prevalence messages. In one study, for instance, participants in the high-prevalence conditions rated women as less career- and more family-oriented, and these effects were found even when participants were instructed not to think stereotypically. A subsequent study had business managers read the transcript of a bogus interview of a male or female job applicant. This transcript was written such that the candidate engaged in actions that violated prescriptive stereotypes for women (by asking for higher compensation and better benefits). Managers in the high-prevalence condition were shown to be less interested in hiring the female candidate, and they judged her as less likable as compared to managers in the low-prevalence condition. No such effects were found when the candidate was male. These findings suggest that when people think that biases are common, the normative constraints that typically inhibit bias are reduced.

Summary

Researchers working on the IAT have advanced a simple, provocative story in the media that the extant literature does not support. In so doing, they may be promoting evaluation concerns and normative beliefs that promote prejudice and discrimination. It also bears mention that this same simple story is being used to promote legal and organizational reforms that might further exacerbate anxiety about not appearing biased (see Kang & Banaji, 2006). Before we consider how researchers might interact with the media in a more responsible fashion, we turn to our second case study. This comes from research designed to reduce racial disparities in health and education.

Second Case Study: Simple Solutions

The majority of real-world psychological interventions are multifaceted. Take, for instance, research guided by the Reasoned Action Model or its many variants (Fishbein & Ajzen, 2010). This model was designed to identify (1) the proximal determinant of volitional behavior (intention), (2) the intermediate determinants of behavior (perceived norms, attitudes, and perceived control), and (3) more distal expectancies and beliefs that influence behavior through their effects on the intermediate and proximal indicators. Given the multiple determinants of behavior highlighted in this model, interventions guided by this and similar frameworks tend to come at behavior from multiple angles—hitting any and all of the pathways that appear from pilot testing to be influencing behavioral decisions. Although strategies for doing this vary from study to study, researchers in this tradition also tend to pursue multiple strategies for influencing any single pathway. Such norms are common in the applied research community because, all things being equal, the stronger and more comprehensive the attempts to predict behavior, the greater the influence.

Contrasted with this heavy-handed and multifaceted approach are the theory-testing traditions common in experimental social psychology, for which the tradition has been to locate subtle manipulations that can exert surprising effects (e.g., Mook, 1983). A researcher who wishes to trigger cooperative behavior, for instance, might do so by embedding cooperation-related words in a word search (Bargh, Gollwitzer, Lee-Chai, Barndollar, & Trötschel, 2001). Another who wishes to activate racial stereotypes might embed a single self-rating of ethnicity in a questionnaire as a means of increasing race salience (Steele & Aronson, 1995). As Prentice and Miller (1992) argue, such seemingly inconsequential manipulations are common in experimental social psychology because they can provide strong rhetorical support for the theories being tested. Moreover, they do this even when the overall effect sizes obtained are small. When a laboratory effect defies intuition—the logic goes—it needn't be large to alter the way people think.

In the last decade, there has been a move to harness this same subtle approach to experimental manipulations, but this is being done for a much different purpose. In this "new science of wise psychological interventions" (Walton, 2014), the goal is to utilize laboratory methods to exert real-world changes in behavior (and see Yeager et al., 2014). A wise approach to psychological intervention embraces the same minimalist strategy of manipulation that experimental social psychologists typically puruse, but it does so out of a desire to generate large effect sizes. "Wise" researchers seek to isolate a single mechanism that might influence behavior, and they pursue a single, low-effort strategy of influencing behavior through this path. But small effects are not valued here. Valued are small interventions that produce large effects.

Consider, for purposes of illustration, a study by Taylor and Walton (2011) and the later intervention this work inspired (Sherman et al., 2013). These researchers focused on the way *stereotype threat* might contribute to academic achievement gaps (Steele & Aronson, 1995). Consistent with research in that area, they showed that a brief, ten-minute self-affirmation task—when delivered in an experimental laboratory—could help reduce the racial achievement gap commonly exhibited on a laboratory learning task. The subtle nature of their manipulation was very much in the spirit of Prentice and Miller (1992), in that a seemingly incidental manipulation influenced performance on what would seem to be an unrelated intellectual test. This type of effect can change views on what is possible and could inspire new approaches at intervention. If this result were handed over to most applied researchers, however, we think most would think of ways that the affirmations could be folded into a larger, multifaceted approach. Consider, for instance, an intervention Slavin and Madden (2006) designed. They developed a school-based program to reduce the minority achievement gap in middle school, called "Success for All." This program has many components, including but not limited to training of teachers, changes to the school curricula, and the introduction of tutors, classroom facilitators, and a parent-support network. Given past successes of this strategy, an educator might apply the findings in Taylor and Walton's (2011) study by finding ways of delivering affirmations through the many channels of influence built into this program. Such a strategy for adapting Taylor and Walton's finding might work, but it would not make for good journalism, nor would it constitute a wise intervention.

Walton (2014) contrasts the wise approach to intervention with approaches that are "multifaceted and expensive" (p. 73). Simplicity is the goal here. That point is driven home by a set of wise interventions implemented by Sherman et al. (2013) to apply the Taylor and Walton (2011) finding. Their intervention (Study 1) was carried out in middle-school classrooms, and it involved no more than having school students complete four or five brief self-affirmation exercises at the beginning of the school year (with each lasting ten minutes or less). Despite the seemingly trivial nature of these interventions, they reported that their approach stimulated higher grades among the Latino (but not white) students over the next *three-year* period. This is a remarkable finding, and it highlights the philosophy driving the wise approach: Use a strong theory to locate an easy way of generating large effects.

Media Coverage

Wise interventions yield provocative and at times shocking results, and so they also attract media attention. Ikizer and Blanton (2016) examined the studies featured in the tables of Taylor and Walton and found media coverage for 21 out of the 23 programs of research featured. Consider, for instance, media interest in the Sherman et al. (2013) studies. Coinciding with their publication, Stanford University posted a press release, titled "Simple Interventions Bridge the Achievement Gap between Latino and White Students" (Rigoglioso, 2013). Various media outlets then picked up this report, and it was promoted in numerous reports focusing on this one, seemingly simple trick for eliminating the academic achievement gap. As with media coverage of most other wise-intervention approaches, the articles we located tended to highlight the subtle, minimalist nature of the interventions and the large and sometimes dramatic effects they can produce.

From this vantage point, wise interventions often encourage simple stories—just by their very nature. The fault is not so much of media oversimplification but with media focus. By drawing attention to one, dramatic effect, media outlets can draw attention away from the more complicated reality surrounding that effect. With the Sherman et al. (2013) study, for instance, it stands to reason that despite the simple, strong power of the findings, an affirmation-based intervention offers at best a partial solution. Certainly, this approach is not sufficient for overcoming the damage done by common racial and ethnic differences in family income, education, and involvement; in the quality of the schools, teachers, and curriculum; and in family life experiences related to stress, nutrition, housing, and safety. In the *Review of Educational Research*, Yeager and Walton (2011) acknowledged that there are limitations to wise interventions that their studies do not highlight (see Cohen, Garcia, Apfel, & Master, 2006; Walton, 2014). But our concern is not with academic discussion but rather media coverage. In general, media reports focus public attention on the powerful aspects of wise interventions, not their boundary conditions. This strikes us as an issue relevant to much of social psychology. The long tradition within social psychology of pursuing subtle, surprising effects could be attracting media coverage across research areas that have the cumulative effect of promoting undue public faith in simple solutions to complex problems.

Much as with research on the IAT, much of the oversimplification surrounding media coverage of stereotype threat effects starts with simplified representations found in scientific journals. In these venues, stereotype threat and related affirmation interventions have, in the words of Jussim (2015), been "overstated, overpromoted, and oversold." He notes that research studies in this tradition give readers the appearance of "equating" the performance of racial and ethnic groups when they, in fact, do not. This misperception arises from researchers' reliance on covariate-adjusted analyses (where strong predictors of academic performance are statistically controlled). As a result, the seeming elimination of statistically significant effects of race or ethnicity on performance might occur, even when group means differ wildly (and statistically significantly; see Jussim, Crawford, Stevens, Anglin & Duarte, 2016; Sackett, Hardison & Cullen, 2005). This important caveat cannot be found in common media representations. In the press release for Sherman et al. (2013), for instance, the title of the report indicated that "Simple interventions *bridge* the achievement gap between Latino and white students" and the article reported that "the effects of 'stereotype threat' can be *overcome*" (emphases added). These statements suggest a far more dramatic result than was found by these researchers (who utilized covariate-adjusted analyses in the evaluation of their intervention). Although the researchers themselves did not make misleading statements in this article, it is worth noting that this press release came from their home institution, a place where many of the media exaggerations and misrepresentations of science originate (see Sumner et al., 2014).

Simple Blame

But what is the harm of overstating the power of social psychologists to solve social problems? Even if results are overstated, they might promote more favorable opinions of social psychology, which can result in stronger public and material support of our science. Thought of this way, simplified media accounts can benefit society indirectly, by benefiting a concerned science. But what are the direct effects? Consider again the study by Sherman et al. (2013). Their seemingly trivial intervention seems to have eliminated the achievement gap, and it did so by having Latino children engage minimal effort to self-affirm. If, as a result, the general public concludes that Latinos need to make only minor mental adjustments in order to overcome societal disadvantages, they might also adopt a more critical view of Latinos who fail to initiate such changes on their own. Supporting this concern, considerable research suggests that attributions of responsibility and the assignment of blame are driven by the ease with which negative events can be mentally "undone" (Spellman & Gilbert, 2014). When making such judgments about individuals who have experienced misfortune, perceivers seem to work backward from what they know to try to locate the voluntary actions that caused the outcome (e.g., Hilton & Slugoski, 1986; McClure, Hilton, & Sutton, 2007; McEleney & Byrne, 2006). Wise interventions, by drawing attention to "simple" fixes, might make it easier for the public to imagine simple ways the disadvantaged could have undone their misfortunes, had they tried. This process might reduce sympathy and raise blame.

That prediction was tested by Ikizer and Blanton (2016), who exposed white, online (Mechanical Turk) samples to actual media reports covering wise interventions designed to reduce racial inequalities (in education and health). They then measured the effect of such exposure on later ratings of responsibility and blame. In their first study, for instance, participants were randomly assigned either to read an article adapted from the Stanford University press release announcing the Sherman et al. (2013) study (Rigoglioso, 2013), which relied on a simple, "wise" approach, or to read an alternative article that followed this same format but that instead detailed the methods employed in the multifaceted "Success for All" program that Slavin and Madden (2006) created. They found that after this manipulation, those in the wise intervention condition more strongly endorsed the view that minority students can easily overcome relative disadvantages on their own, if they simply try. Their Study 2 showed that wise interventions not only promoted attributions of responsibility but also led to the assignment of blame—provided that the targets of the intervention were members of a historically disadvantaged group (African-Americans as opposed to UCSD students). Study 3 further revealed that such increases in blame were strongest among participants who were politically conservative, as opposed to liberal.

There is some irony to be found in this latter result. Considerable concern has been expressed about how "liberal bias" might be shaping research priorities and affecting the conclusions drawn (e.g., Haidt, 2011; Inbar & Lammers, 2012), particularly with regards to social psychological studies on racism and racial inequity (Tetlock, 2012). One manifestation of this liberal bias, it has been argued, is a tendency for social psychologists to emphasize the power of the situation (Swann & Jetten, 2016). Faith in the power of the situation is compatible with a liberal view of government that emphasizes the role it can play in reducing inequities. From Ikizer and Blanton (2016), however, it appears that media coverage of wise interventions designed to assist minorities can actually reinforce the "principled conservatism" view of social inequities, which places greater responsibility on the disadvantaged to solve their own problems (e.g., Christopher, Zabel, Jones, & Marek, 2008; Federico, & Sidanius, 2002).

Summary on Media Coverage of Wise Interventions

This second case study offers an interesting contrast to the first one on a number of dimensions. The first case promotes belief in an overly simple story about the causes of racism, which might thereby increase counterproductive concern about a social problem. The second case promotes belief in an overly simple story about how to overcome the effects of racism, which might thereby decrease productive concern about the need to fix a social problem. These two stories are thus mirror images of one another in certain respects, save one: Each points to the unwanted consequences that can result when psychologists promote overly simple stories in the media.

Implications and Reflections

Society advances when decisions are informed by science, but to inform society, scientists often need to simplify their message. This reality has caused some media scholars to try to determine when simplification becomes misrepresentation (Nelkin, 1995). Our concern was different from this. Although in the course of writing this chapter we did ponder what advice we might offer to researchers trying to gauge when a simple story becomes an inaccurate story, we ultimately concluded that no easy answers to this exist. Indeed, non-trivial measurement issues would arise if one took seriously the goal of measuring the (in)accuracy of scientific statements (e.g., Cronbach, 1955).

Impact over Accuracy

We thus moved to embracing a more modest agenda for psychologists seeking to communicate findings to the public. We think greater attention should be given to the *impact* that science communications have. We further think that these examinations should be grounded by two considerations. On the whole, simple and provocative stories will generate more interest and thus exert more influence on public opinion than complex and mundane stories. There is no reason, in principle, to think that this influence will always be negative. In fact, simple stories could at times lead to social progress by promoting self-fulfilling optimism for finding solutions to seemingly intractable problems. However, with greater influence comes a greater likelihood of both positive and negative effects and thus the need to engage in more critical analysis of media impact. This approach to media bias does not conflate the veracity of "bullet points" with their effects. Unlike the IAT research we reviewed, we do not contest the validity of any "wise intervention" we have reviewed. We think that in both cases, however, the research promotes media portrayals that are far less nuanced than the reality, and our concern is with the influence of these media portrayals.

To illustrate the value of this distinction between the truth and consequences of media coverage, we turn again to research on implicit racism. Research on this topic inspires great passion among scientists, because even individuals who disagree on their science share strong desires to find ways of reducing racial bias and inequities. We have registered our concerns that research teams oriented around the IAT fail to provide a strong empirical support for the many strong media claims they make, but what if this reality were to change? Suppose that implicit racism adopted stronger measurement and criterion-validation approaches and suppose that they ended up making a far stronger case for the very conclusions they currently are advancing in the media. This new (imagined) research indicates that implicit racial bias pervades American society, and modal levels of it found in the general public reliably bias people to engage in consequential forms of discriminatory behavior. In this hypothetical world, researchers would have far greater justification for telling precisely the stories current researchers already are telling. But this does not mean the consequences of their communication will be any less negative. In fact, negative consequences might increase.

Through their ability to back their strong claims with even stronger evidence than they currently have, communications advanced by implicit attitude researchers might generate less skepticism and message resistance in the general public. The unintended influences thereby magnify. Some will feel even more anxious about not expressing their hidden racist thoughts, and others will feel even less inhibited about expressing them. This analysis makes clear that the problem with simple stories is not only veracity but also impact. We would argue that there is no sound justification for advancing simple stories that are in fact inaccurate. This criticism is particularly relevant to the IAT example we reviewed. We add to this our own bias that we tend to view simple stories as less likely to be "complete," and so, simply through omission, they are less likely to be fully accurate than more complex, conditional, and nuanced stories. However, even when their stories are accurate, researchers are not absolved from considering the consequences of advancing simple, provocative stories in the public domains. This leads us to propose three broad questions that we think psychologists should consider whenever they might engage the media.

Three Questions

First, they should ask, *what statements are scientifically justified, and what are not?* If scientists conclude that enough is known to communicate with some certainty to the public, they can proceed with caution—and therein lies the first challenge. Not only do researchers have the largest "conflict of interest" when evaluating the veracity of their own research claims, but there are also media dynamics that will bias them against caution. We presented the tendency to engage the media with simple, provocative stories as a "bias" because we were able to identify both psychological and systemic forces that reward simple certainty. This is problematic because the media does not introduce the same checks and balances found in the broader science. When scientists communicate with one another, undue confidence by one researcher or by one research team will spark challenges from other researchers and other research teams. Over the long arc of history, where egos eventually die and strong ideas can live on, science should do a reasonable job of self-correcting. This analysis does not apply with the media, however. Media outlets have a short attention span, and they lack the ability to "undo" the impact of ideas, once released (Ross, Lepper, & Hubbard, 1975). The unfortunate conclusion we draw is that psychologists will too often err in the direction of communicating simple confidence when they should not.

In light of this bias, there is value in researchers pondering the second question: *What will be the likely effect of engaging the media (simply and confidently)?* One goal motivating us to write this chapter was that we wished to challenge default faith in the benefits of engaging media. That story is too simple. We think researchers who wish to do this should be asking themselves some basic questions. Who stands to benefit from this message? Will this message promote new social policies that will further society? Will this message encourage funding of inquiries into this question? Will this message help the field recruit new talent into the discipline? Researchers should not just ponder these questions, we think, but at times pursue answers through empirical analysis. We reviewed a number of studies that explore the undesired effects that might arise from engaging the public (Duguid & Thomas-Hunt, 2015; Ikizer & Blanton, 2016;

Vorauer, 2012), and we think more attention should be given to such inquiries. If questions about the impact of scientific communications are pursued more vigorously and critically, we think the conclusions researchers will draw from the first question (which will be biased toward certainty) will at times clash with the conclusions drawn in the second (which at times will point to problems).

What should be done when a scientifically justified communication produces undesired effects? We have a simple view on this: The bias of a free society has to be to move forward with communications that inform the public, even at cost. The threshold of certainty needed to justify the communication might rise when there are known risks, but there will come a point when certainty necessitates even risky communications. Far too many alternative dangers present themselves if scientists try to self-censor in order to "protect" the public from possessing an informed view of the world. They might consider ways of limiting their message, however. Active engagement of the media isn't always needed to advance knowledge that can promote social change. If one identifies a seemingly easy way to address minority underachievement, for instance, it is far more important to engage educators and policymakers than to entertain the public. More pointed messaging presents a partial solution to this issue.

That said, there is no controlling when scientific research might grab attention of the general public or the popular media, and this leads us to the third question that researchers should ask when they have detected or simply suspect ill effects of their messages: *Are there ways to counteract the unwanted effects of engaging the media?* Again, imagine a hypothetical scenario in which implicit attitude researchers have turned to stronger methods but ended up resting on the same conclusion. Their interactions with the media educate the public to the high prevalence of consequential racism to the general public. Even if this promotes racial bias in ways already discussed, researchers may be able to pursue messaging strategies in order to advance their findings in a manner that will offset the anticipated uptick in discrimination. Some research suggests, for instance, that speakers can override the unwanted impact of communicating that "bad" behaviors are common by adding positively framed messages that also praise uncommon and "good" ways of breaking from that norm (Blanton & Christie, 2003). In this spirit, implicit bias researchers might explore ways of conveying that although racial bias is common, there are positive steps to take. By adopting a positive tone that seeks to promote equality rather than inhibit racism, they might also minimize some of the evaluation apprehension that can lead to ironic racism. Of course, this is all speculation, and we readily admit that such framing of the implicit bias message might prove problematic for other reasons. This is an empirical question—one of many that might be worthy of study. We think that when researchers engage the public, they should consider empirical questions in this same spirit. They should critically evaluate the effects they have when they engage the public and the ways they counteract any undesired effects.

Science as Political Communication

As scientists move from this first question (of simply asking whether they know enough to communicate) to the second two (of asking what effects they have when they communicate and what can be done about it), the line between their science and their politics will blur. Any evaluation of the "good" versus "bad" consequences of engaging the media must be informed by the political views of the researcher. Many times these views will generate little controversy (e.g., "racism is bad and should be reduced"), but even in noncontroversial cases like these, it is important for scientists to be mindful of their personal politics and how it affects both their certainty and their approach to messaging (Suedfeld & Tetlock, 1992). We think they should examine the role they are seeking to play when they present their media communications as scientific in nature, if that message advances their politics.

For purposes of comparison, consider the role currently being played by the Black Lives Matter (BLM) movement. This is an American political movement we both support that arose out of a desire to draw attention to the systemic and often extreme forms of racism and bias found in U.S. society. Through political activities and protests and engaging the media, BLM seeks to sensitize the public to what it views as common, everyday forms of oppression that could otherwise go unnoticed. This goal of informing thus bears some similarity to goals that might motivate IAT researchers. So—one might argue—we are being inconsistent. Our critique of the way IAT researchers engage the media applies even more to the way BLM engages the media. If so, BLM might be exacerbating racial tensions far more than the IAT "movement" ever could. So perhaps we reject the way IAT researchers and BLM engage the media, or we should endorse both—but we should not endorse one and reject the other. But we do not contradict ourselves by doing precisely this. We evaluate BLM as a political movement, where actors are engaged in political communication for political purposes. As such, it is the priority of the communicators to decide what means they are willing to pursue and to what ends. We evaluate the IAT as a research tool, where communicators ostensibly are engaged in science communication. As such, it is the obligation of the communicators to treat the societal impact of their communications as an empirical question. How their impact comports with their politics is another matter.

Acknowledgments

We thank William B. Swann Jr. for comments on an earlier draft of this chapter.

Notes

1 We focus on how this bias influence might influence researcher decisions, but also relevant is how cautious, measured communicators might find their research findings simplified and oversold by media agents (see Brechman, Lee, & Cappella, 2009; Sumner et al., 2014; Young, Ioannidis & Al-Ubaydi, 2008).

2 Our focus is on communications with media that most typically occur after research has been published, but we also see reasons to be concerned with how a "long game" interest in media engagement might alter actual professional presentations. This can occur when research scientists simplify professional presentations in order to facilitate later media interest. (See Jussim, Crawford, Stevens, Anglin & Duarte, 2016, for relevant examples.)

3 These findings should be viewed with some caution, however. Blanton et al. (2009) re-analyzed the original data and found that key results were influenced by a single, middle-aged outlier in an otherwise all college-aged sample, and key results did not replicate across raters. Further, although the IAT was predictive of "relative" treatment of the white and black experimenters in the results reported, unreported was the fact that the majority of participants showed an out-group bias—treating the black experimenter more favorably than the white.

4 It is widely accepted that people can detect when they "fail" race-related IAT measures. In fact, the IAT demonstration website informs respondents that "No matter which IAT you took, if a speed difference between different pairings was so great as to be obvious to you, it would likely be labeled a 'strong' effect."

5 A later research team, Heider and Skowronski (2007), expressed concern that the order of events in McConnell and Leibold's (2001) study might have produced behaviors that created a false appearance of prejudicial attitudes. They thus pursued a straightforward replication where the IAT was administered weeks prior to the study. They reported a complete replication of McConnell and Leibold's study. However—consistent with our concern that the bullet-point bias at times encourages false reporting—Blanton and Mitchell (2011) found, upon re-analyzing Heider and Skowronski's original data, that parts of it had been fabricated (later confirmed by J. Heider; personal communication, September, 2014). When this fabrication was removed, the IAT was no longer predictive of behavioral bias. Although one must be careful not to overinterpret null results, it is possible that the second team failed to replicate findings from the first because the second addressed the artifact in the first. McConnell and Leibold (2001) thus found evidence of the IAT predicting bias, because the act of "failing" the IAT created it.

References

Apfelbaum, E. P., Sommers, S. R. & Norton, M. (2008). Seeing race and seeming racist? Evaluating strategic colorblindness in social interaction. *Journal of Personality and Social Psychology, 95(4)*, 918–932.

Banaji, M. R. & Greenwald, A. G. (2013). *Blindspot: Hidden biases of good people.* New York: Random House.

Bargh, J., Gollwitzer, P. M., Lee-Chai, A., Barndollar, K. & Trötschel, R. (2001). The automated will: Nonconscious activation and pursuit of behavioral goals. *Journal of Personality and Social Psychology, 81(6)*, 1014–1027.

Basken, P. (2013). Actor is honored for using improv to help scientists communicate. *The Chronicle of Higher Education.* Retrieved on January 5, 2016, at: http://chronicle.com/article/Alan-Alda-Is-Honored-for-Using/138673/.

Blanton, H. & Burkley, M. (2008). Deviance regulation theory: Applications to adolescent social influence. In M. Prinstein & K. A. Dodge (Eds.), *Understanding Peer Influence in Children and Adolescents.* (pp. 94–121). New York: Guilford Press.

Blanton, H. & Christie, C. (2003). Deviance regulation: A theory of identity and action. *Review of General Psychology, 7(2)*, 115–149.

Blanton, H. & Jaccard, J. (2006). Arbitrary metrics in psychology. *American Psychologist, 61*, 27–41.

Blanton, H. & Mitchell, G. (2011). Reassessing the predictive validity of the IAT II: Reanalysis of Heider & Skowronski (2007). *North American Journal of Psychology, 13*(1), 99–106.

Blanton, H., Jaccard, J., Gonzales, P. M. & Christie, C. (2006). Decoding the implicit association test: Perspectives on criterion prediction. *Journal of Experimental Social Psychology, 42*, 192–212.

Blanton, H., Jaccard, J., Klick, J., Mellers, B., Mitchell, G. & Tetlock, P. (2009). Strong claims and weak evidence: Reassessing the predictive validity of the race IAT. *Journal of Applied Psychology, 94(3)*, 567–582.

Blanton, H., Jaccard, J., Strauts, E., Mitchell, G. & Tetlock, P. E. (2015). Toward a meaningful metric of implicit prejudice. *Journal of Applied Psychology, 100*(5), 1468–1481.

Brechman, J. M., Lee, C. & Cappella, J. N. (2009). Lost in translation? A comparison of cancer-genetics reporting in the press release and its subsequent coverage in press. *Science Communication, 30*(4), 453–474.

Burroughs, J. (1889). The corroboration of Professor Huxley. *The North American Review, 149*(346), 567.

Carlsson, R. & Agerström, J. (2016). A closer look at the discrimination outcomes in the IAT literature. *Scandinavian Journal of Psychology, 57*, 278–287.

Chautauquan, The (1883). *Editor's table*, pp. 543–544.

Christopher, A. N., Zabel, K. L., Jones, J. R. & Marek, P. (2008). Protestant ethic ideology: Its multifaceted relationships with just world beliefs, social dominance orientation, and right-wing authoritarianism. *Personality and Individual Differences, 45*(6), 473–477.

Cialdini, R. B., Demaine, L. J., Sagarin, B. J., Barrett, D. W., Rhoads, K. & Winter, P. L. (2006). Managing social norms for persuasive impact. *Social Influence, 1*(1), 3–15.

Cohen, G. L., Garcia, J., Apfel, N. & Master, A. (2006). Reducing the racial achievement gap: A social-psychological intervention. *Science, 313*(5791), 1307–1310.

Cronbach, L. J. (1955). Processes affecting scores on "understanding others" and "assumed similarity." *Psychological Bulletin, 52*, 177–193.

Dovidio, J. F. & Gaertner, S. L. (1998). On the nature of contemporary prejudice: The causes, consequences, and challenges of aversive racism. In J. Eberhardt & S. T. Fiske (Eds.), *Confronting Racism: The Problem and the Response* (pp. 3–32). Newbury Park: Sage.

Duguid, M. M. & Thomas-Hunt, M. C. (2015). Condoning stereotyping? How awareness of stereotyping prevalence impacts expression of stereotypes. *Journal of Applied Psychology, 100*(2), 343–359.

Federico, C. M. & Sidanius, J. (2002). Racism, ideology, and affirmative action revisited: The antecedents and consequences of "principled objections" to affirmative action. *Journal of Personality and Social Psychology, 82*(4), 488–502.

Fishbein, M. & Ajzen, I. (2010). *Predicting and changing behavior: The reasoned action approach*. New York: Psychology Press (Taylor & Francis).

Forscher, P. S., Lai, C. K., Axt, J. R., Ebersole, C. R., Herman, M., Devine, P. G. & Nosek, B. A. (under revision). A meta-analysis of change in implicit bias. *Psychological Bulletin*.

Frantz, C. M., Cuddy, A. J., Burnett, M., Ray, H. & Hart, A. (2004). A threat in the computer: The race implicit association test as a stereotype threat experience. *Personality and Social Psychology Bulletin, 30*(12), 1611–1624.

Gilbert, D. (2016). *Talking to Humans: Is it a Good Idea?* Talk delivered at the 17th Annual Convention of the Society for Personality and Social Psychology, San Diego, CA. Retrieved on 2/1/2016 from www.danielgilbert.com/SPSP2016.pdf.

Greenwald, A. G. & Krieger, L. H. (2006). Implicit bias: Scientific foundations. *California Law Review, 94,* 945–967.

Greenwald, A. G., Nosek, B. A. & Sriram, N. (2006). Consequential Validity of the Implicit Association Test: Comment on Blanton and Jaccard (2006). *American Psychologist, 61*(1), 56–61.

Haidt, J. (2011). *The Bright Future of a Post-Partisan Social Psychology.* Presentation at the annual meeting of the Society for Personality and Social Psychology, San Antonio. Retrieved on 10/7/2014.

Heath, C. & Heath, D. (2008). *Made to stick: Why some ideas survive and others die.* New York. Random House.

Heider, J. D. & Skowronski, J. J. (2007). Improving the Predictive Validity of the Implicit Association Test. *North American Journal of Psychology, 9*(1), 53–76.

Henneman, T. (2014). You, biased? No, it's your brain. *Workforce.* Retrieved on January 5, 2016, at: www.workforce.com/articles/20242-you-biased-no-its-your-brain.

Hilton, D. J. & Slugoski, B. R. (1986). Knowledge-based causal attribution: The abnormal conditions focus model. *Psychological Review, 93*(1), 75–88.

Hutson, M. (2013). "Blindspot: Hidden Biases of Good People" by Mahzarin R. Banaji and Anthony G. Greenwald. Retrieved June 2016 from https://goo.gl/61SpkP.

Ikizer, E. G. & Blanton, H. (2016; in press). Media coverage of "wise" interventions can reduce concern for the disadvantaged. *Journal of Experimental Psychology: Applied.*

Inbar, Y. & Lammers, J. (2012). Political diversity in social and personality psychology. *Perspectives on Psychological Science, 7*(5), 496–503.

Jost, J. T., Rudman L. A, Blair, I. V., Carney, D. R., Dasgupta, N., Glaser, J. & Hardin, C. D. (2009). The existence of implicit bias is beyond reasonable doubt: A refutation of ideological and methodological objections and executive summary of ten studies that no manager should ignore. *Research in Organizational Behavior, 29,* 39–69.

Jussim, L. (2015). Is stereotype threat overcooked, overstated, and oversold? Why dilute a great story with actual facts? *Rabble Rouser Blog, Psychology Today,* retrieved on 1/15/2016 from http://bit.ly/1Q1IEJN.

Jussim, L., Crawford, J. T., Stevens, S. T., Anglin, S. M. & Duarte, J. L. (2016). Good morals gone bad: Can high moral purposes undermine scientific integrity? In J. Forgas, P. van Lange & L. Jussim (Eds.), *The Social Psychology of Morality* (pp. 173–195). New York: Routledge.

Kang, J. & Banaji, M. R. (2006). Fair measures: A behavioral realist revision of "affirmative action." *California Law Review, 94*(4), 1063–1118.

McClure, J., Hilton, D. J. & Sutton, R. M. (2007). Judgments of voluntary and physical causes in causal chains: Probabilistic and social functionalist criteria for attributions. *European Journal of Social Psychology, 37*(5), 879–901.

McConnell, A. R. & Leibold, J. M. (2001). Relations among the Implicit Association Test, discriminatory behavior, and explicit measures of racial attitudes. *Journal of Experimental Social Psychology, 37*(5), 435–442.

McEleney, A. & Byrne, R. J. (2006). Spontaneous counterfactual thoughts and causal explanations. *Thinking & Reasoning, 12*(2), 235–255.

The Merriam Webster Dictionary. (2016). Online. Retrieved on January 2, 2016, at: www.merriam-webster.com/dictionary/scientist.

Mierke, J. & Klauer, K. C. (2001). Implicit association measurement with the IAT: Evidence for effects of executive control processes. *Zeitschrift für Experimentelle Psychologie, 48*, 107–122.

Mook, D. G. (1983). In defense of external invalidity. *American Psychologist, 38*(4), 379–387.

Nelkin, D. (1995) *Selling Science: How the Press Covers Science & Technology* (2nd ed.). New York: WH Freeman.

Nosek, B. A., Banaji, M. R. & Greenwald, A. G. (2002). Harvesting implicit group attitudes and beliefs from a demonstration website. *Group Dynamics, 6*, 101–115.

Nosek, B. A. & Sriram, N. (2006). Faulty assumptions: A comment on Blanton, Jaccard, Gonzales, and Christie (2006). *Journal of Experimental Social Psychology, 43*, 393–398.

Oswald, F., Mitchell, G., Blanton, H., Jaccard, J. & Tetlock, P. (2013). Predicting ethnic and racial discrimination: A meta-analysis of IAT research. *Journal of Personality and Social Psychology, 105*, 171–192.

Oswald, F., Mitchell, G., Blanton, H., Jaccard, J. & Tetlock, P. (2015). Using the IAT to predict ethnic and racial discrimination: Small effect sizes of unknown societal significance. *Journal of Personality and Social Psychology, 108*(4), 562–571.

Pierce, C. (1970). Offensive mechanisms. In F. Barbour (Ed.), *The black seventies* (pp. 265–282). Boston: Porter Sargent.

Prentice, D. A. & Miller, D. T. (1992). When small effects are impressive. *Psychological Bulletin, 112*(1), 160–164.

Quillian, L. (2006). New approaches to understanding racial prejudice and discrimination. *Annual Review of Sociology, 32*, 299–328.

Rigoglioso, M. (2013). Simple interventions bridge the achievement gap between Latino and white students, Stanford researcher finds. *Stanford News.* Retrieved May 3, 2017, from: http://news.stanford.edu/news/2013/february/latino-achievement-gap-021413.

Rödder, S., Franzen, M. & Weingart, P. (2012). *The Sciences' Media Connection—Public Communication and Its Repercussions.* New York: Springer-Science.

Ross, L., Lepper, M. R. & Hubbard, M. (1975). Perseverance in self-perception and social perception: Biased attributional processes in the debriefing paradigm. *Journal of Personality and Social Psychology, 32*, 880–892.

Rothermund, K. & Wentura, D. (2001). Figure-ground asymmetries in the Implicit Association Test (IAT). *Zeitschrift fuer Experimentelle Psychologie, 48*(2), 94–106.

Rothermund, K. & Wentura, D. (2004). Underlying processes in the Implicit Association Test (IAT): Dissociating salience from associations. *Journal of Experimental Psychology: General, 133*, 139–165.

Sackett, P. R., Hardison, C. M. & Cullen, M. J. (2005). On interpreting research on stereotype threat and test performance. *American Psychologist, 60*(3), 271–272.

Sasaki, S. J. & Vorauer, J. D. (2013). Ignoring versus exploring differences between groups: Effects of salient color-blindness and multiculturalism on intergroup attitudes and behavior. *Social and Personality Psychology Compass, 7*(4), 246–259.

Sherman, D. K., Hartson, K. A., Binning, K. R., Purdie-Vaughns, V., Garcia, J., Taborsky-Barba, S., … Cohen, G. L. (2013). Deflecting the trajectory and changing the narrative: How self-affirmation affects academic performance and motivation under identity threat. *Journal of Personality and Social Psychology, 104*(4), 591–618.

Slavin, R. E. & Madden, N. A. (2006). Reducing the gap: Success for all and the achievement of African American students. *Journal of Negro Education, 75*(3), 389–400.

Spellman, B. A. & Gilbert, E. A. (2014). Blame, cause, and counterfactuals: The inextricable link. *Psychological Inquiry, 25*(2), 245–250.

Steele, C. M. & Aronson, J. (1995). Stereotype threat and the intellectual test performance of African Americans. *Journal of Personality and Social Psychology, 69*(5), 797–811.

Steffens, M. C. (2004). Is the implicit association test immune to faking? *Experimental Psychology, 51*(3), 165–179.

Suedfeld, P. & Tetlock, P. E. (1992). Psychologists as policy advocates: The roots of controversy. In P. Suedfeld, P. E. Tetlock, P. Suedfeld & P. E. Tetlock (Eds.), *Psychology and social policy* (pp. 1–30). Washington, D.C.: Hemisphere Publishing Corp.

Sumner, P., Vivian-Griffiths, S., Boivin, J., Williams, A., Venetis, C. A., Davies, A., … Chambers, C. D. (2014). The association between exaggeration in health related science news and academic press releases: Retrospective observational study. *BMJ (Clinical research ed.), 349*. PMID: 25498121.

Swann, W. B., Jr. & Jetten, J. (2016). Restoring balance and relevance to social psychology: Beyond the search for spinelessness and the legacy of behaviorism. *Unpublished manuscript.*

Taylor, V. J. & Walton, G. M. (2011). Stereotype threat undermines academic learning. *Personality and Social Psychology Bulletin, 37*, 1055–1067.

Tetlock, P. E. (2012). Rational versus irrational prejudices: How problematic is the ideological lopsidedness of social psychology? *Perspectives on Psychological Science, 7*(5), 519–521.

Vorauer, J. D. (2012). Completing the Implicit Association Test (IAT) reduces positive intergroup interaction behavior. *Psychological Science, 23*, 1168–1175.

Vorauer, J. D. & Sasaki, S. J. (2009). Helpful only in the abstract? Ironic effects of empathy in intergroup interaction. *Psychological Science, 20*(2), 191–197.

Walton, G. M. (2014). The new science of wise psychological interventions: Erratum. *Current Directions in Psychological Science, 23*(2), 154.

Wegner, D. M. & Schneider, D. T. (2003). The White Bear Story. *Psychological Inquiry, 14*(3/4), 326–329.

Wittenbrink, B. & Schwarz, N. (2007). An introduction to the assessment of attitudes with implicit measures. In B. Wittenbrink & N. Schwarz (Eds.), *Implicit measures of attitudes* (pp. 1–13). New York: Guilford Press.

Yeager, D. & Walton, G. M. (2011). Social-psychological interventions in education: They're not magic. *Review of Educational Research, 81*(2), 267–701.

Yeager, D. S., Purdie-Vaughns, V., Garcia, J., Apfel, N., Brzustoski, P., Master, A., … Cohen, G. (2014). Breaking the cycle of mistrust: Wise interventions to provide critical feedback across the racial divide. *Journal of Experimental Psychology: General, 143*(2), 804–824.

Young, N. S., Ioannidis, J. P. A. & Al-Ubaydli, O. (2008). Why current publication practices may distort science. *PLoS Medicine, 5*(10), e201.

PART IV

Political Discrimination in Social Psychology

12

PARANOID EGALITARIAN MELIORISM

An Account of Bias in the Social Sciences

Bo Winegard and Benjamin Winegard

> *Convictions are more dangerous enemies of truth than lies.*
>
> —Friedrich Nietzsche, 1878

In 1994, Richard Herrnstein and Charles Murray published *The Bell Curve: Intelligence and Class Structure in American Life*, a prodigious book documenting the increasing importance of general cognitive ability in the United States. Among other things, the book argued that intelligence is highly heritable (between 40% and 80%) and that it is a strong predictor of people's life outcomes, especially in complicated, post-industrial societies such as the United States. They also included two chapters (13 and 14) that addressed well-established racial disparities in intelligence test scores, suggesting those differences were at least partially caused by genes. Reactions to *The Bell Curve* were often furious and vitriolic. Scholars and media pundits impugned Murray's character. Many accused him of attempting to cloak his own prejudices behind pages of pseudoscientific graphs and equations (Fraser, 1995). His reputation was so thoroughly besmirched that many today still consider him a racist and an anti-poor classist and continue to bludgeon the effigy-like caricature of him that was created during the "Bell Curve wars."

Reactions to *The Bell Curve* were not unprecedented. Scientists and philosophers who forward theories that violate sacred social narratives are often attacked, sometimes viciously. Socrates was arrested and eventually given a death sentence for impiousness, and Galileo was denounced and ultimately arrested for publishing a dialogue that suggested that the earth revolved around the sun (in other words, for appearing to support heliocentrism). These examples may seem quaint today. We no longer have sacred concerns about state-sponsored gods or the order of the ether. But we do have sacred concerns about human nature and its relation to society.

In this chapter, we argue that such sacred concerns contribute to bias in social psychology, the social sciences, and among the intelligentsia (journalists, media members, professional pundits, and nonacademic intellectuals) more broadly. Although we do not think that bias is ubiquitous (i.e., we believe most research in social psychology is relatively free from bias), we do think that bias is rife in certain specific areas that touch upon the sacred concerns of scholars. We forward and explain what we have called the paranoid egalitarian meliorist model of bias (Winegard, Winegard, & Geary, 2015). We connect our model to the work of other scholars who have raised concerns about possible bias in the social sciences. And we conclude with possible remedies.

Before beginning, we want to make a couple of comments and cautions about the material we discuss below. First, we do not think that most social scientific research is flawed or marred by bias. In fact, we suspect that most social science is self-correcting through the processes that philosophers and analysts have discussed, such as institutional norms that value truth and replicability (Pashler & Wagenmakers, 2012; Popper, 1934/2002). We call this *normal science*. Normal science is not, of course, infallible, and at any one time, much of its contents may be erroneous. But those erroneous contents are ultimately winnowed out by the exigencies of the scientific method (cf., Kuhn, 1970; note that our definition of normal science differs from his). We do, however, think that some research areas in the social sciences are beset by systematic bias. And these are areas that touch upon sacred narratives about social equality. We call this *sacralized science* and discuss it in depth below.

Second, we discuss research and theory about sex and race differences. These are sensitive topics that often cause immediate visceral reactions and unthinking accusations. We do not take a position on the research or theories that we present. The topic of race differences in cognitive ability, for example, is complicated enough to require its own discussion in another forum. We do, however, take a strong position that researchers need to explore and debate these topics openly and without fear of censure or rebuke. The truth, whatever its ultimate nature, cannot be hidden behind a comforting veil in perpetuity. Therefore, it is essential that scientists, philosophers, and other scholars responsibly discuss *all* issues about human nature, including issues that may temporarily discomfit.

Bias in Psychology: The Talk

In 2011, Jonathan Haidt gave a talk at the annual meeting of the Society for Personality and Social Psychology (SPSP) on the dangers of increasing ideological uniformity in social psychology. Specifically, Haidt argued that social psychology was dominated by political liberals and that very few working psychologists were political conservatives (or were willing to openly admit that they were), possibly causing bias in the field. Almost immediately, psychologists and the media were buzzing with debate about Haidt's remarks (Tierney, 2011). Some praised Haidt's speech; others condemned it. Although previous researchers had voiced similar concerns about political bias in the social sciences (Redding, 2001; Tetlock, 1994), Haidt's speech might represent the crossing of a narrative Rubicon about bias. Before, it was possible to ignore; after, it was not. Other scholars began to echo Haidt's concerns (or voice concerns that they had raised before), and some conducted more formal research to discover the depths of the problem (Inbar & Lammers, 2012). This research largely confirmed Haidt's arguments at SPSP, finding that most social psychologists did identify as liberal (and especially as socially liberal).

The line of research and debate initiated by Haidt's speech culminated in a *Brain and Behavioral Sciences* article written by a team of scholars who had, along with Haidt, been drawing attention to potential biases in the social sciences (Duarte et al., 2015). Although the article does not contain all concerns raised by these scholars at one time or another (as we note), it is fairly comprehensive and what we consider a quasi-official statement of this line of thought about political bias.

In the article, Duarte and colleagues asserted that the dearth of conservatives in the social sciences can (and does) create bias in three ways: (1) it allows liberal values (sacred equality narrative, for example) to become enmeshed into social theory and method; (2) it causes many researchers to focus on topics that support sacred liberal narratives while avoiding topics that might contradict them; and (3) it encourages an incomplete and unappealing psychological profile of conservatism because most researchers who study conservatives are hostile toward their political beliefs.

Duarte and colleagues supported their arguments with many examples. Consider two. One, researchers have consistently lamented that stereotypes are inaccurate, unjust, and maladaptive products of a biased social brain (see Jussim, 2012). However, it turns out that many stereotypes are remarkably accurate. Because many stereotypes are about talent, skill, and inequalities among social groups, this line of research, according to Duarte et al., was not palatable to social liberals, who value equality, and could only be initiated by a conservative, Clark McCauley (McCauley & Stitt, 1978).

And two, many researchers in social psychology have argued that the political right is prone to prejudice and that it attracts a certain personality type that is often domineering and authoritarian (Jost, Glaser, Kruglanski, & Sulloway, 2003). However, some recent theorists have argued (and demonstrated) that people across the political spectrum are biased against others who espouse ideological beliefs that contradict their own (Brandt, Reyna, Chambers, Crawford, & Wetherell, 2014). Conservatives are biased against liberals, Democrats, gays and lesbians, atheists, and labor unions, for example, whereas liberals are biased against soldiers, businesspeople, and Christian fundamentalists. Social psychologists largely ignored liberal social prejudices because they were not salient to mostly liberal researchers. One's own biases are seldom regarded as biases; they are regarded as truths about the world.

Duarte and colleagues ended with a number of possible palliatives. Because a lack of political diversity is the fundamental cause of the disease that Duarte and colleagues bemoaned, most of their recommendations focused on increasing the number of conservatives, libertarians, and other non-liberals in social psychology. For example, they suggested that universities should formulate and adopt anti-discrimination policies (against conservatives), should create reach-out programs to attract non-liberals, and should conduct studies about obstacles and barriers non-liberal students might face in social psychology. (They made a number of other suggestions, but this provides a useful sample.)

We largely agree with Duarte and colleagues' argument that ideological uniformity in social psychology (and social science, more generally) is potentially deleterious and distorts science through biased peer reviews, grant reviews, and hiring processes. However, as we argue in this chapter, we believe that the focus on political party affiliation per se is misleading (something with which Duarte and colleagues would possibly agree). We believe that the major cause of sacralized science (systematically biased psychology) is the prevalence of what we have called paranoid egalitarian meliorists (PEMs) in social psychology, social science, and the intelligentsia more broadly.

Paranoid Egalitarian Meliorism

What is paranoid egalitarian meliorism (PEM)? *Egalitarianism* is the belief that all individuals and groups should be treated equally under the law and should be afforded relatively equal opportunities. *Meliorism* is the belief that, through concerted effort, humans can make the world better and alleviate suffering. Now, what about paranoid? Paranoid sounds bad, like something that happens after one has ingested too much of the wrong drug. But in our conception, the word is not pejorative. The name was inspired by a clever turn of phrase by Martie Haselton and Daniel Nettle (2006) about the evolutionary logic of cognitive biases.

Haselton and Nettle argued that most people are "paranoid optimists." They are fearful (paranoid) of potential environmental threats but romantic (optimistic) about their ability to shape the world. Although this contradictory personality structure has perplexed many poets and philosophers, it is quite sensible from an evolutionary perspective. It is good to be hopeful about the future and enthusiastic about the great accomplishments one might achieve because those beliefs motivate beneficial (from an evolutionary perspective) behaviors. And it is good to be fearful of potential environmental threats because it is often less costly to mistake an innocuous stimuli for a threat than to mistake a threat for an innocuous stimuli. This last point is best illustrated by considering an alarm system (Nesse, 2001).

A house alarm is designed to commit more false alarms than false negatives, because people don't want a house alarm that remains silent while their house is robbed. It is better, in other words, to have a house alarm that sometimes goes off when one's cat gets overly animated but *almost always* goes off when one's house is getting robbed than to have a house alarm that never goes off when one's animals race around the yard but that sometimes stays silent when burglars break in.

Paranoid egalitarian meliorists are similar to a house alarm; they are "programmed" to detect threats to *egalitarian* beliefs and policies—and they sometimes detect danger where there is none. Consider, for example, the reaction to an article published recently by Williams and Ceci (2015) about hiring decisions in science, technology, engineering, and mathematics (STEM) fields. In that article, Williams and Ceci found that faculty were significantly more likely to report wanting to hire a woman than a man when qualifications were equal (see Chapter 10, this volume, for discussion of this case in detail). Ferocious debate ensued, including many blogs and essays denouncing the authors of the article (Williams & Smith, 2015). The article probably tripped the sensitive alarm of many PEMs because it was interpreted as a threat to egalitarianism and as an excuse to ignore the plight of women in STEM fields who, according to many scholars and pundits, have been historically mistreated in defiance of the egalitarian principles most academics and intellectuals hold sacred. That is, the article was seen as suggesting that women in STEM fields are not oppressed or discriminated against, potentially fostering a dangerous complacency.

PEMs' sensitivity to threats to egalitarianism leads to the development of what we call cosmic egalitarianism (see Table 12.1 for definition of some key terms). Cosmic egalitarianism is the belief that all ethnic and cultural groups, social classes, and sexes are relatively equal on all socially desired traits. Cosmic egalitarianism protects egalitarian meliorism from potential challenges. If all groups and sexes are generally equal, then there are *no* good reasons for treating them differently. On the other hand, people might believe there are good reasons for treating groups and sexes differently if they are actually different. And that belief is a challenge to egalitarian meliorism. Suppose, for example, that society believes that women are more likely to wilt under pressure than men are. Many people might then argue and believe that men should be hired and promoted more often than women in police departments and other domains where pressure is a prominent feature of the job. Notice that this argument is not necessarily a good argument. The point here is not that the argument is correct or even persuasive but rather that people who are high in PEM are afraid that society might *accept* this argument if it is widely believed that men and women are different, which would undermine egalitarian meliorism.

TABLE 12.1 Key Terms in the Paranoid Egalitarian Meliorist (PEM) Framework

Term	Definition
Cosmic egalitarianism	The belief that all ethnic and cultural groups, social classes, and sexes are relatively equal on all socially desired traits
Egalitarian meliorism	The belief that all ethnic and cultural groups, social classes, and sexes should be treated equally and that applying knowledge and effort to solving social problems involving the mistreatment of these groups will lead to improvement in their treatment and to a more egalitarian society
Paranoid egalitarian meliorism	A strong belief in egalitarian meliorism coupled with a heightened sensitivity to potential threats to egalitarian meliorist principles. One response to this sensitivity is to develop a strong version of egalitarian meliorism that relies upon the belief in cosmic egalitarianism

Blank slatism, or the belief that humans are relatively malleable, is a popular form of cosmic egalitarianism, because it suggests that all groups, social classes, and sexes have equal potential (Horowitz, Yaworsky & Kickham, 2014; Pinker, 2002). Perhaps more importantly, blank slatism also encourages optimism about humans' ability to ameliorate and ultimately eliminate inequalities because it suggests that most (perhaps all) inequalities in talent and ambition among individuals, groups, and sexes are caused by socialization. However, other viable forms of cosmic egalitarianism exist. And not everyone who generally accepts some version of cosmic egalitarianism accepts blank slatism.

Unlike the house alarm example, the PEM view of bias in social science requires two stages of processing. The first stage is the detection (or nondetection) of threatening theories and/or data; and the second stage is the assessment of the theories and/or data. Consider an article about sex differences. In the first stage, a researcher would assess whether the article is a threat to cosmic egalitarianism (i.e., does it violate the principle that all groups, social classes, and sexes are biologically equal on all socially desired traits?). And in the second, the researcher would assess the article's (and other articles') arguments for and against a biological hypothesis of sex differences. Generally speaking, if a theory is detected as a threat, then it will be assessed unfavorably and ultimately rejected. That is, a theory that is assessed as a threat often triggers some form of motivated reasoning, which then dismisses the threatening theory (Kunda, 1990). Of course, it could also be the case that the theory is dismissed because it is viewed as inadequate empirically. Thus, the PEM perspective requires judicious application. Many scholars disagree with *The Bell Curve,* for example, because they think that it is empirically flawed, not because they object to the inquiry of the importance of intelligence in everyday life.

The PEM model predicts that certain areas of social science, because they potentially challenge egalitarianism, are *sacralized*. Sacralized domains of science are those in which the normal self-correcting mechanisms of science are distorted by sacred values (Cofnas, 2015). By sacred values, we mean those values "that a moral community treats as possessing transcendental significance" and that cannot be compared or traded with other values, including, even the pursuit for truth (Tetlock, 2003, p. 320; see also Atran, Axelrod & Davis, 2007). In these domains, empirical inquiries are limited because conclusions are preordained by the moral desires of the research community. Consider, for example, this empirical question: Are there genetically influenced cognitive differences among ethnic groups? One a priori reasonable conclusion of this scientific exploration—namely, that, yes, there are genetically influenced cognitive differences—is almost entirely barred from contemplation because it so strongly violates cosmic egalitarianism that it provokes disgust, anger, and hostility from many social scientists (see, e.g., Gottfredson, 2013; Sesardic, 2010).

If a conclusion is completely dismissed for extra-scientific reasons, then researchers are constrained not only by the evidence but also by cosmic egalitarianism. Instead of positing the simplest, most parsimonious explanations for data, they are forced to posit the simplest, most parsimonious explanations for data *that concord with a priori cosmic egalitarian principles*. Just as things are difficult to see when they are too close to the eye, so things are difficult to judge when they are too close in time; therefore, consider a more distant example. In the 1300s, if you were a philosopher, then you had to allow god and other metaphysical entities (souls, for example) a prominent role in your philosophical system. Perhaps there were simpler, more elegant systems—say, some form of materialism. But you could not forward a materialistic system because others would have rejected it and denounced you. Philosophy in the 1300s was not self-correcting because no one could challenge a cluttered system with a simpler system that removed the metaphysical muddle (Koterski, 2008).

Many of the writings about bias in the social sciences that have been published in the past few years focus on political ideology (e.g., Duarte et al., 2015). The PEM model suggests that this focus on political ideology, per se, is somewhat misguided. A straightforward hypothesis of the political ideology theory of bias is that researchers who forward theories and/or data that contradict any of the sacred tenets of liberalism (because the social sciences are overwhelmingly liberal) should be attacked, criticized, and maligned as much as researchers who forward theories and or data that violate the sacred tenets of cosmic egalitarianism.[1] The PEM model, on the other hand, predicts that the most vicious attacks will be reserved exclusively for those who threaten cosmic egalitarianism and that many of the attacks will come from conservatives and libertarians who also adhere to cosmic egalitarianism. Although this is obviously an empirical question, evidence suggests (see the next section) that the PEM model's predictions are accurate. Anecdotally, many scholars who have attacked various tenets of (modern political) liberalism (for example,

Matt Ridley, Lee Jussim, Thomas Sowell, Clark McCauley, and Steven Pinker) remain in good standing in the academy, despite some snipes and slander. On the other hand, those scholars who have threatened cosmic egalitarianism (for example, Charles Murray, J. P. Rushton, Arthur Jensen, Richard Lynn, and Linda Gottfredson) suffered relentless smear campaigns and remain outside of the academic mainstream (and are especially abhorred in fields such as social psychology and sociology; see, e.g., Barash, 1995; Fraser, 1995; Gottfredson, 2010, 2013; Miele & Jensen, 2002).

Evidence

Some evidence, both quantitative and qualitative, supports the above claims. Because many of these claims have not been tested, the evidence is more limited than is desirable. We are hopeful that our suggestions in this chapter will provoke more research on this topic.

First, there is evidence that many researchers in the social sciences are PEMs; and there is even stronger evidence that many researchers in specific domains of the social sciences (women's studies, much of sociology, for example) are PEMs. Although we have noted that we believe the focus on political ideology per se is at least *partially* misguided, there is almost certainly a positive relation between political liberalism and PEM. (In fact, the authors have constructed a PEM scale and have found that it is positively related to political liberalism [$r = 0.4$]; however, this does not mean that there aren't conservative PEMs. Further, PEM scores were uniquely predictive of participants' views of the racism of the criminal justice system and high-stakes tests, whereas liberalism, once PEM was controlled, did not predict such outcomes.) Therefore, it is *likely* that research domains comprised mostly of liberals are also comprised of many PEMs. Recent research suggests that the social sciences are indeed composed mostly of liberals. For example, Inbar and Lammers (2012) found that only 6% of social and personality psychologists identified as conservative. von Hippel and Buss (Chapter 2, this volume) found that a paltry 4 out of over 300 members surveyed voted for Mitt Romney in the 2012 election. This pattern pertains in the social sciences more broadly according to research by Gross and Simmons (2007), who found that the social sciences are more liberal than other disciplines and are even more liberal on social than economic issues. This makes sense because many liberal economic issues (e.g., the belief in activist government) are not *directly* tied to egalitarianism (many people believe more egalitarian outcomes occur with smaller, less-activist government), whereas social issues, such as same-sex marriage, are (if same-sex individuals cannot get married they are not being treated equally).

More granular analyses suggest that many researchers in the social sciences adhere to some form of cosmic egalitarianism or another, or at least repudiate the notion that there could be biological differences between human populations or the sexes. Geher and Gambacorta (2010) found that scholars in women's studies were more likely than scholars in other domains to believe that differences between men and women (and even hens and roosters) were caused by nurture, not nature. They did not exhibit the same beliefs about the differences between cats and dogs, presumably because cat/dog differences are ideologically irrelevant (that is, they are not perceived to threaten gender egalitarianism). Similarly, Horowitz, Yaworsky, and Kickham (2014) found that although many sociologists believed that there was at least a partial genetic cause to individual differences in intellectual ability, they *did not* think there was even a partial genetic cause to sex differences in certain skills such as communication and spatial reasoning (remember, cosmic egalitarianism applies most forcefully to *group* and not *individual* differences). Winegard, Winegard, and Deaner (2014) found evidence that supports this general pattern. They examined 12 popular sex and gender textbooks and coded their presentations of evolutionary psychology, a theoretical perspective that presents challenges to cosmic egalitarianism because it asserts that there are biological differences between men and women (see Tybur & Navarette, Chapter 14, this volume). They found that all 12 textbooks were rife with errors and distortions, generally painting an unflattering picture of evolutionary psychology as a rigid, patriarchal system of thought. They also found that sociology textbooks made more errors than psychology textbooks, suggesting that sociology might be more sacralized than the other social sciences, an observation that is consistent with the observations of other researchers (Martin, 2015).

Evidence also supports the contention that the attitudes of researchers can distort review processes, thus distorting science (creating a science that is not self-correcting because extra-scientific variables affect the scientific process). For example, Abramowitz, Gomes, and Abramowitz (1975) asked psychologists to review a manuscript to assess its suitability for publication. In both conditions, the manuscript's methods and analyses were held constant. In one condition, however, radical (protesting) students were described as more mentally healthy than a cross-section of students on the campus; and in the other, the protestors were described as less mentally healthy. Reviewers who were more liberal than others were stricter than less liberal reviewers when reviewing the manuscript that stated that the protesters were less mentally healthy than other students; and they were more lenient when reviewing the manuscript that stated that the protesters were more mentally healthy. We note that this evidence is imperfect since we are using liberalism as a stand in for PEMism when we believe the concepts are somewhat distinct. In a broader analysis of the peer-review process, Mahoney (1977) found congruent results, noting that reviewers were biased against articles that contradicted their theoretical perspectives.

Ceci, Peters, and Plotkin (1985) found similar results in assessments of Internal Review Board applications. Specifically, they submitted proposals that hypothesized either "reverse discrimination"—that is, discrimination against whites—or traditional discrimination—that is, against ethnic minorities. The rest of the application was held constant. The Internal Review Boards approved the "reverse discrimination" proposals less often.

Perhaps the most convincing supporting (but unfortunately unsystematic) evidence that PEM is relatively widespread in the social sciences and among the intelligentsia more broadly is the ceaseless and vitriolic attacks faced by scholars who directly challenged cosmic egalitarianism—especially as applied to human populations. Below, we examine the case of Nicholas Wade, a former science journalist for *The New York Times*. Readers should keep in mind that there are many similar cases, including J. P. Rushton, Charles Murray, Linda Gottfredson, Larry Summers, Richard Lynn, Jason Richwine, and Arthur Jensen, to name a few (Barash, 1995; Fraser, 1995; Gottfredson, 2010, 2013; Miele & Jensen, 2002).

In 2014, Nicholas Wade wrote the book *A Troublesome Inheritance: Genes, Race and Human History* (2014). In it, Wade made a sustained argument that race is a biologically real and useful concept; that there are small, but discernible differences between human populations; and that these differences are important to understand because they shed light on historical differences in the structures and functions of different human civilizations. Before proceeding, it is worth noting that Wade was very candid about some of the speculative aspects of his book, noting:

> The conclusions presented in these chapters fall far short of proof. However plausible (or otherwise) they may seem, many are speculative. There is nothing wrong with speculation, of course, as long as its premises are made clear. And speculation is the customary way to begin the exploration of uncharted territory because it stimulates a search for the evidence that will support or refute it (p. 15).

The response to Nicholas Wade's book was rapid and almost universally negative. After a laudatory review at *The Wall Street Journal,* a deluge of hostile reviews followed. Of course, there is nothing wrong with criticizing Wade's book, but many of the reviews assailed his character and insinuated, often not very subtly, that Wade was a disturbed thinker with unwholesome beliefs about the supremacy of the white race (Johnson, 2014). Furthermore, many of the reviews ignored what he actually said in his book, suggesting that reviewers either did not read it or that they perhaps wanted to besmirch him publicly as an example to deter others from publishing material that violates a sacred cosmic egalitarian narrative (viz., all ethnic groups are equal on all socially valued traits; Coop, Eisen, Nielsen, Przeworski, & Rosenberg, 2014). For example, Wade (2014) writes that "because there is no clear dividing line, there are no distinct races—that is the nature of variation within a species. Nonetheless, useful distinctions can be made" (p. 92). However, a number of scholars accused him of racial Platonism (i.e., the belief that racial groups are "pure" and distinct). Jennifer Raff (2014) noted that "if Wade is right and races are distinct biological categories...," which is not what Wade argued. And Sarah Tishkoff, geneticist and a signer of an open letter against *A Troublesome Inheritance*, asserted that "You may see that individuals cluster by major geographic regions. The problem is, there are no firm boundaries" (quoted from Callaway, 2014), which is exactly what Wade asserted, namely, there are no "distinct races," so, of course, there aren't any "firm boundaries" or boundaries between racial groups (i.e., most variation in human populations is clinal).

Nicholas Wade's case was essentially a repeat, with less effervescence, of the "Bell Curve wars" that we discussed in the introduction. Similar tales could be told about other researchers who flagrantly violated cosmic egalitarianism. Although more research needs to be conducted, it is noteworthy that scholars who violate other tenets of liberalism are not exposed to the same hostility as scholars who specifically violate cosmic egalitarianism. For just one example, Gary Kleck, a professor at Florida State University, has published many articles that argue that many gun-control policies are useless and that the influence of gun ownership on crime rates is effectively neutral (Kleck, 2015; Kleck & Patterson, 1993). Kleck has certainly earned the ire of many liberals who vigorously dispute his findings and arguments; however, he has not been removed from the domain of respectable discourse. Furthermore, within the discipline of economics, many conservative thinkers who *do not violate cosmic egalitarianism* but do argue against broader liberal policies, thrive, and some have written bestselling and relatively uncontroversial books (Krugman, 2009; Levitt & Dubner, 2009).

In general, it appears as if researchers who violate cosmic egalitarianism are made into an effigy and bludgeoned to send a very clear signal to other researchers: Do not trespass on this sacred value! As we noted, this creates a sacralized science that is not self-correcting because the standard rules of normal science—hypotheses forwarded, analyzed, provisionally accepted, or rejected largely on merits of evidence—do not hold in these domains (Cofnas, 2015). Importantly, we do not believe that the PEMs who denounce scholars who violate sacred narratives about human equality are acting in bad faith or cynically. As we noted above, PEMs are especially sensitive to threats to egalitarianism. Social scientists honestly believe that books like Wade's pose an immediate and alarming threat to egalitarianism; therefore, they believe that its author must have malicious motives. Why else would an educated person publish a book that has such obvious pernicious ramifications?

What is to be done?

Scholars who have recently addressed problems of ideological bias in social psychology have forwarded a number of potential solutions, many with which we completely agree (Duarte et al., 2015). Here, we briefly suggest and discuss two potential solutions we have not encountered elsewhere. So, quickly restated, one of the potent causes of bias in the social sciences, according to our hypothesis, is the widespread distribution of paranoid egalitarian meliorists (PEMs) in academia, especially *in the social sciences*. This leads to the development and sacralizing of some variant of cosmic egalitarianism, or the belief that all ethnic and cultural groups, social classes, and sexes are relatively equal on all socially desired traits. PEM is also prevalent among the intelligentsia more broadly. Potential solutions must address at least two problems (and we'll focus on only two). First, and perhaps most importantly, researchers need to learn to separate values from facts. This might seem obvious and easy, but it is neither. And second, misinformation and unfair calumniations from the intelligentsia need to be corrected and called out.

First, we think that every college undergraduate who is majoring in a social science should be required to take a class on critical, scientific thinking that focuses extensively on distinguishing facts from values. Cofnas (2015), in his excellent article on ideological bias in the social sciences, notes: "There seems to be a deep human impulse to conflate facts and moral values. For most people for most of history, popular beliefs were simply unquestionable, and those who challenged them were condemned as evil outsiders" (p. 2).

His observation certainly seems correct. Conflating facts and values is probably as natural as seeing the world of objects as one, two, maybe three, and then *many*. Humans do not have a natural sense of numbers as fine-grained as five, six, seven, thirteen. It requires formal education to develop such an understanding. Similarly, it will probably require formal training to develop a firm understanding of the distinction between facts and values. Murder is really, really bad. But humans may have certain adaptations that make them likely, under some circumstances, to murder others (Duntley & Buss, 2011). The first statement is a value; the second is a fact. And they have nothing to do with each other. Likewise, egalitarianism might be very, very good. But different human populations may differ on socially desirable traits, such as athleticism, intelligence, and self-control. The first is a value; the second, a fact. Rigorous formal training will not be a panacea, but it can probably help students understand this crucial distinction.

Second, scholars need to publicly correct the misleading and often mendacious media accounts of the state of our knowledge in various controversial domains such as psychometrics and genetics. Because PEM is widespread among the intelligentsia, researchers who challenge cosmic egalitarianism are often berated and misrepresented by media figures, journalists, and political pundits. This creates widespread misunderstanding in the public, tarnishes the reputation of scholars, and exerts pressures on universities to punish professors who stray from politically acceptable conclusions. For just one example, Snyderman and Rothman (1988) found a large disconnect between public presentations of research on intelligence and the *anonymous* opinions of experts in the field. This creates a bizarre, dualistic world in which public presentations of research about intelligence are so distorted that they barely resemble private opinions (Gottfredson, 2000). Within psychometrics, for example, it is widely and uncontroversially known that there is a roughly 15-point IQ score difference between American blacks and whites. The only debate is about the source of the difference—most researchers appear to believe that the difference is caused by both genes and the environment (Snyderman & Rothman, 1988). But when science and technology writer William Saletan (2007) wrote a couple of popular articles that addressed the possibility that some of the differences in intelligence among human populations might be partially genetic, he was absolutely excoriated, eventually publishing a kind of mea culpa. In other words, when researchers or journalists present relatively uncontroversial theories and data from the field, they are treated as unspeakable fiends by the media and casually dismissed by most of the public.

If more scholars directly refuted such misinformation and supported attacked scholars, basic truths about research might disseminate into the media. At the very least, the media would not be able to so quickly and efficiently ruin the reputations of scholars who defy the basic tenets of cosmic egalitarianism. Of course, there is a steep price to pay for this at the moment. An intellectual who is desirous of prestige (which is a quite understandable desire) knows to avoid certain topics. So, in a sense, this is a traditional commons dilemma. It would be better for everyone if more researchers forwarded the truth to the media and defended others for speaking it. But it is worse for each individual to do so. Perhaps the best one can hope for here is slow change. Some scholars, for example, have created a site for "heterodox" views in the academy, promoting the values of free speech and inquiry (Heterodox Academy at heterodoxacademy. org). The more these values are lauded, the better. And the more status academics confer on other academics for pursuing the truth regardless of the public relations consequences, the better. Scientists are just as self-interested as business tycoons. The important thing is to set up the right incentives.

Conclusion

We have argued that many social scientists are paranoid egalitarian meliorists (PEMs)—that is, they are egalitarian meliorists who are especially sensitive to potential threats to egalitarianism. Because of this, the social sciences have largely accepted a useful myth about humans that we called cosmic egalitarianism. Cosmic egalitarianism contends that all ethnic and cultural groups, social classes, and sexes are relatively equal on all socially desired traits. Researchers who violate the principles of this narrative are often scurrilously attacked. This creates domains within social science that are sacralized. Sacralized science is not self-correcting because scientifically extraneous values constrain acceptable hypotheses, limiting the unbridled competition for truth that is necessary for normal, self-correcting science. A variety of evidence supports this basic framework, but some of the best-supporting evidence is observational and informal and requires more extensive study. We are hopeful that scholars will fill this lacuna in our knowledge.

We suggested two potential solutions for the problems we diagnosed. First, we believe that universities should compel social science majors to take a class focused on critical thinking and the distinction between facts and values. And second, we urge scholars to correct constant media misinformation and to defend other scholars who are unjustly attacked by the intelligentsia. This would require immediate sacrifice, so it will probably be a slow process.

We should mention that we are probably both paranoid egalitarian meliorists. And it probably is not bad to be especially sensitive to threats to egalitarianism. History suggests that it is very difficult to create a society that upholds egalitarian values. But history also suggests that ideologues of all variety have used their well-meaning values to distort and suppress science. Freedom of inquiry, like freedom of speech, is often unpleasant in the immediate. But, in the long run, both allow the best ideas to prevail.

Note

1 It would go far beyond our modest intentions in this chapter to define modern liberalism, conservatism, and libertarianism in any comprehensive manner. However, we want to note that modern liberalism is not simply associated with a belief in equal treatment before the law (a belief shared by most conservatives); it is also associated with an emphasis on government spending on programs such as healthcare and welfare. Further, modern liberalism is associated with a belief in legal abortion, stricter gun-control laws, same-sex marriage, criminal justice reform, and immigration reform (Alterman, 2009; Krugman, 2009). Conservatism, on the other hand, is associated with the belief that markets should decide outcomes, that smaller government is better and that social spending often has unintended consequences that often hurt those it is intended to help (Levin, 2014; Sowell, 2007).

References

Abramowitz, S. I., Gomes, B. & Abramowitz, C. V. (1975). Publish or politic: Referee bias in manuscript review. *Journal of Applied Social Psychology, 5,* 187–200.

Alterman, E. (2009). *Why we're liberals: A handbook for restoring America's most important ideals.* New York: Penguin.

Atran, S., Axelrod, R. & Davis, R. (2007). Sacred barriers to conflict resolution. *Science, 317,* 1039–1040.

Barash, D. P. (1995). Book review: Race, evolution, and behavior. *Animal Behavior, 49,* 1131–1133.

Brandt, M. J., Reyna, C., Chambers, J. R., Crawford, J. T. & Wetherell, G. (2014). The ideological-conflict hypothesis intolerance among both liberals and conservatives. *Current Directions in Psychological Science, 23,* 27–34.

Callaway, E. (August 8, 2014). Geneticists say popular book misrepresents research on human evolution. *Nature News Blog* retrieved 9/28/15 from http://blogs.nature.

com/news/2014/08/geneticists-say-popular-bookmisrepresents-research-on-human-evolution.html.

Ceci, S. J., Peters, D. & Plotkin, J. (1985). Human subjects review, personal values, and the regulation of social science research. *American Psychologist, 40,* 994–1002.

Cofnas, N. (2015). Science is not always "self-correcting." *Foundations of Science, 21*(3), 477–492.

Coop, G., Eisen, M. B., Nielsen, R., Przeworski, M. & Rosenberg, N. (August 8, 2014). "A troublesome inheritance." *The New York Times Book Review* retrieved 9/27/15 from www.nytimes.com/2014/08/10/books/review/letters-a-troublesome-inheritance. html.

Duarte, J. L., Crawford, J. T., Stern, C., Haidt, J., Jussim, L. & Tetlock, P. E. (2015). Political diversity will improve social psychological science. *Behavioral and Brain Sciences, 38,* e130.

Duntley, J. D. & Buss, D. M. (2011). Homicide adaptations. *Aggression and Violent Behavior, 16,* 399–410.

Fraser, S. (Ed.). (1995). *The bell curve wars.* New York: Basic Books.

Geher, G. & Gambacorta, D. (2010). Evolution is not relevant to sex differences in humans because I want it that way! Evidence for the politicization of human evolutionary psychology. *EvoSJournal: The Journal of the Evolutionary Studies Consortium, 2,* 32–47.

Gottfredson, L. S. (2000). Equal potential: A collective fraud. *Society, 37,* 19–28.

Gottfredson, L. S. (2010). Lessons in academic freedom as lived experience. *Personality and Individual Differences, 49,* 272–280.

Gottfredson, L. S. (2013). Resolute ignorance on race and Rushton. *Personality and Individual Differences, 55,* 218–223.

Gross, N. & Simmons, S. (2007). The social and political views of American professors. Working paper Harvard University.

Haidt, J. (February 11, 2011). The bright future of post-partisan social psychology. *Edge* retrieved 9/25/15 from https://edge.org/conversation/the-bright-future-of-postpartisan-social-psychology.

Haselton, M. G. & Nettle, D. (2006). The paranoid optimist: An integrative evolutionary model of cognitive biases. *Personality and Social Psychology Review, 10,* 47–66.

Herrnstein, R. J. & Murray, C (1994). *The bell curve: Intelligence and class structure in American life.* New York: Free Press.

Horowitz, M., Yaworsky, W. & Kickham, K. (2014). Whither the blank slate? A report on the reception of evolutionary biological ideas among sociological theorists. *Sociological Spectrum, 34,* 489–509.

Inbar, Y. & Lammers, J. (2012). Political diversity in social and personality psychology. *Perspectives on Psychological Science, 7,* 496–503.

Johnson, E. M. (May 21, 2014). On the origin of white power. *Scientific American* at http://blogs.scientificamerican.com/primate-diaries/on-the-origin-of-white-power/.

Jost, J. T., Glaser, J., Kruglanski, A. W. & Sulloway, F. J. (2003). Political conservatism as motivated social cognition. *Psychological Bulletin, 129,* 339–375.

Jussim, L. (2012). *Social perception and social reality: Why accuracy dominates bias and self-fulfilling prophecy.* New York: Oxford University Press.

Jussim, L. (September 13, 2015). Political diversity will improve psychological science. Psychology Today at www.psychologytoday.com/blog/rabblerouser/201509/political-diversity-will-improve-psychological-science.

Kleck, G. & Patterson, E. B. (1993). The impact of gun control and gun ownership levels on violence rates. *Journal of Quantitative Criminology, 9,* 249–287.

Kleck, G. (2015). The impact of gun ownership rates on crime rates: A methodological review of the evidence. *Journal of Criminal Justice, 43*, 40–48.

Koterski, J. W. (2008). *An introduction to Medieval philosophy: Basic concepts.* Hoboken: Wiley-Blackwell.

Krugman, P. (2009). *The conscience of a liberal.* New York: W.W. Norton.

Krugman, P. (September 2, 2009). How did economists get it so wrong? *New York Times Magazine* retrieved from www.nytimes.com/2009/09/06/magazine/06 Economic-t.html.

Kuhn, T. (1970). *The structure of scientific revolutions* (2nd ed.). Chicago: University of Chicago Press.

Kunda, Z. (1990). The case for motivated reasoning. *Psychological Bulletin, 108*, 480–498.

Levin, Y. (2014). *The great debate: Edmund Burk, Thomas Paine, and the birth of the right and left.* New York: Basic Books.

Levitt, S. D. & Dubner, S. J. (2009). *Freakonomics: A rogue economist explores the hidden side of everything.* New York: William & Morrow.

Mahoney, M. J. (1977). Publication prejudices: An experimental study of confirmatory bias in the peer review system. *Cognitive Therapy and Research, 1*, 161–175.

Martin, C. C. (2015). How ideology has hindered sociological insight. *The American Sociologist, 47*(1), 115–130.

McCauley, C. & Stitt, C. L. (1978). An individual and quantitative measure of stereotypes. *Journal of Personality and Social Psychology, 36*, 929–940.

Miele, F. & Jensen, A. (2002). *Intelligence, race, and genetics: Conversations with Arthur R. Jensen.* Boulder: Westview.

Nesse, R. M. (2001). The smoke detector principle. *Annals of the New York Academy of Sciences, 935*, 75–85.

Pashler, H. & Wagenmakers, E. J. (2012). Editors' introduction to the special section on replicability in psychological science a crisis of confidence? *Perspectives on Psychological Science, 7*, 528–530.

Pinker, S. (2002). *The blank slate: The modern denial of human nature.* New York: Penguin Books.

Popper, K. (1934/2002). *The logic of scientific discovery.* New York: Routledge.

Raff, J. (May 21, 2014). Nicholas Wade and race: Building a scientific facade. Violent Metaphors blog retrieved 9/28/15 from http://violentmetaphors.com/2014/05/21/ nicholas-wade-and-race-building-ascientific-facade/.

Redding, R. E. (2001). Sociopolitical diversity in psychology: The case for pluralism. *American Psychologist, 56*, 205–215.

Saletan, W. (November 8, 2007). Created equal. *Slate* retrieved from www.slate. com/articles/health_and_science/human_nature/features/2007/created_equal/ liberalcreationism.html.

Sesardic, N. (2010). Nature, nurture, and politics. *Biology & Philosophy, 25*, 433–436.

Snyderman, M. & Rothman, S. (1988). *The IQ controversy, the media and public policy.* Piscataway: Transaction Publishers.

Sowell, T. (2007). *A conflict of visions: Ideological origins of political struggles.* New York: Basic Books.

Tetlock, P. E. (1994). Political psychology or politicized psychology: Is the road to scientific hell paved with good moral intentions? *Political Psychology, 15*, 509–529.

Tetlock, P. E. (2003). Thinking the unthinkable: Sacred values and taboo cognitions. *Trends in Cognitive Sciences, 7*, 320–324.

Tierney, J. (February 7, 2011). Social scientist sees bias within. *New York Times* retrieved from www.nytimes.com/2011/02/08/science/08tier.html?_r=4&ref=science.

Wade, N. (2014). *A troublesome inheritance: Genes, race and human history.* New York: Penguin.

Williams, W. M. & Ceci, S. J. (2015). National hiring experiments reveal 2:1 faculty preference for women on STEM tenure track. *Proceedings of the National Academy of Sciences, 11,* 5360–5365.

Williams, J. C. & Smith, J. (July 8, 2015). The myth that academic science isn't biased against women. *The Chronicle of Higher Education* at http://chronicle.com/article/The-Myth-That-Academic-Science/231413.

Winegard, B., Winegard, B. & Deaner, R. O. (2014). Misrepresentations of evolutionary psychology in sex and gender textbooks. *Evolutionary Psychology, 12,* 474–508.

Winegard, B., Winegard, B. & Geary, D. C. (2015). Too paranoid to see progress: Social psychology is probably liberal, but it doesn't believe in progress. *Behavioral & Brain Sciences,* e162.

13

POLITICAL EXCLUSION AND DISCRIMINATION IN SOCIAL PSYCHOLOGY

Lived Experiences and Solutions

Sean T. Stevens, Lee Jussim, Stephanie M. Anglin, Richard Contrada, Cheryl Alyssa Welch, Jennifer S. Labrecque, Matt Motyl, Jose Duarte, Sylvia Terbeck, Walter Sowden, John Edlund, and W. Keith Campbell

The primary goal of science is to better approximate the truth through a series of conjectures and refutations (see Popper, 1959, 1963). When reliable means of self-correction are in place, ideas and theories compete in a "marketplace of ideas" (see Williams, 2016), where successful theories withstand numerous skeptical and critical attempts to disconfirm, falsify, or refute them (Meehl, 1967, 1990a,b; Popper, 1959, 1963). Unfortunately, science is not always self-correcting (Ioannidis, 2012; Jussim, Crawford, Anglin, Stevens, & Duarte, 2016a). One source of failures to self-correct includes political biases, which can create support for ideologically appealing conclusions in the absence of scientific support (Duarte et al., 2015; Pinker, 2002; Redding, 2001; Tetlock, 1994). Because there are vanishingly few social psychologists who do not identify as progressive within the field of social psychology, we suspect that political biases will almost exclusively manifest as biases against scientists and ideas that are critical of progressivism.

To support these claims, this chapter

1 Reviews ways in which conservative politics have distorted and denied scientific findings.
2 Reviews the social psychological literature on political prejudice and intolerance.
3 Reports the personal experiences of political bias as reported by social psychological faculty and psychology graduate students.
4 Integrates the scientific literature on confirmation bias with research on political prejudice and the burgeoning scholarship revealing political biases and distortions in social psychology.
5 Identifies some ways to limit such biases.

Before proceeding further, we define progressivism and conservatism, the political ideologies primarily discussed in this chapter. The term "progressive" refers to those who identify with the political left and place a high value on increased egalitarianism. Importantly, this represents a departure from much of the social psychological literature on the topic that typically refers to such individuals as "liberal." We have chosen to employ the term "progressive" instead of "liberal" because the latter term has multiple and conflicting meanings, which depend on the country being considered. For instance, in the United States, "liberal" currently means support for the Democratic Party and implies that one is critical of capitalism, while in the United Kingdom, "liberal" implies that one holds a positive view of capitalism. The term "conservative" refers to those who identify with the political right and prioritize other values, such as loyalty and respect for authority and tradition, over increased egalitarianism.

Conservative Distortion of Science: Brief Examples

The history of science is replete with examples of politics impeding the progress of knowledge. Well-known historical examples include Copernicus, who, out of fear of retribution from the Church, delayed publication of his theory of heliocentrism until just before his death. And he was justified in doing so because Galileo was imprisoned by the Church for advocating that theory. Darwin also delayed publishing his *Origin of Species* out of similar fears. Both Copernicus and Darwin feared retribution from political and social conservatives. Furthermore, many well-known distortions of science appear to have been motivated by politically conservative opposition to scientific findings that produce social and technological changes. Thus, we begin with a brief review of some well-known examples of how political conservatives have distorted science.

Creation "Science," the Intelligent Design Movement, and the Religious Denial of Evolution

Evolution has long been controversial in some religious circles because it is routinely interpreted as a threat to Biblical accounts of the origin of human life. Indeed, to this day, only one-third of Americans believe in evolution via natural selection (Masci, February 12, 2016). Primarily as an effort to undermine the teaching of evolution in schools, the pseudo-science theories of "creation science" and "intelligent design" were created (Forrest & Gross, 2004) to create a veneer of scientific-iness (to borrow Stephen Colbert's "truthiness" term). This was then used to argue that these "alternative theories" should be presented along with evolution. Neither pseudo-science theory has produced a shred of empirical evidence appearing in any peer-reviewed journal, and neither has led to any discoveries of any new phenomena, nor inspired *any* scientists, including religious ones, to search for evidence supporting it (see Forrest & Gross, 2004; Gilchrist, 1997). This is because both theories are primarily transparent political attempts to limit the teaching of evolution in schools, not bona fide scientific theories.

The Denial of Global Warming

The denial of global warming and its associated risks provides another example of an active attempt to undermine scientific consensus in the service of an ideological agenda. Climate scientists have suspected that rising temperatures would present significant risks to people and population centers since the 1950s (Craig, 1957; Revelle & Seuss, 1957). The fossil fuel industry appears to have been aware of such risks by the late 1970s (see, e.g., Commoner, 1977; Longenecker, 1981; Oppenheimer, 1981), and by the 1990s, environmental concerns, particularly global warming, had become a prominent concern of climate scientists and environmental policymakers within the United States (see, e.g., Chafee, 1989; Davies, 1990; Gifford, 1990).

As these environmental issues rose to prominence, a coordinated movement opposing stricter environmental regulations emerged. Increased regulatory action on fossil fuel usage was considered a threat to capitalism in general and, more specifically, the profitability of the fossil fuel industry. In response to this perceived threat, the fossil fuel industry has been joined by other business allies (e.g., the auto industry) and conservative think tanks in promoting skepticism about global warming (Lahsen, 2005; Mulvey et al., 2015). Despite near-unanimous consensus among climate scientists that the threats to people and the planet posed by global warming require immediate attention (see, e.g., Anderegg, 2010; Cook et al., 2013; Doran & Zimmerman, 2009; Oreskes, 2004), the anti-environmental movement has successfully prevented policy changes, in part, by sowing unjustified doubts about the validity of the climate science.

McCarthyism

The establishment of the Iron Curtain following World War II and the emergence of the Soviet Union as a superpower, complete with nuclear capabilities, constituted a major threat to U.S. interests and security. One result was an anti-communist frenzy in the U.S., complete with black-listings, stigmatization, and ostracism of anyone with any links (including some that were quite tenuous) to any communist organization or individual in the 1940s and 1950s. We gloss this here as "McCarthyism" because McCarthy's hearings are so infamous, but the "Second Red Scare" (the first taking place after the Russian

Revolution of 1917) began well before McCarthy's hearings. Although much of this was well beyond the scope of science, the Red Scare affected faculty and students, as illustrated by these next two stories.

University of Michigan I: Faculty Inquisition and Firings

McCarthyism had a direct impact on the Institute for Social Research at the University of Michigan in the 1950s (see Hollinger, 1988), when the issue of whether a communist could possess intellectual integrity, a concept widely perceived as a prerequisite to academic freedom, emerged. Harlan Hatcher, president of the University of Michigan, was one of 37 university presidents to sign a statement establishing the Association of American Universities, an organization that contended it was not possible for a communist to possess academic integrity. Thus, communists could not be granted academic freedom or tenure, and known communists could be stripped of tenure and fired.

In May of 1953, Hatcher asked the Faculty Senate of the University of Michigan to endorse the Association of American Universities statement. E. Blythe Stason, the dean of the law school, contended that the statement contained language implying that a professor could be fired if they invoked the Fifth Amendment when asked about sympathies toward communism. The debate over endorsing the statement was tabled, and the Faculty Senate instead endorsed the American Association of University Professors' more conventional definition of academic freedom, which did not discriminate against communists. Despite this, Hatcher suspended three University of Michigan professors (Mark Nickerson, Clement Markert, and Chandler Davis) and began an internal investigation a year later after each of those faculty members invoked the Fifth Amendment when testifying in front of a Congressional subcommittee about their support for communism and their membership in the Communist party.

The Special Advisory Committee appointed to conduct the investigation focused on academic integrity as the central issue and made it clear that this meant a willingness to answer questions about one's political beliefs and sympathies. In the course of the University of Michigan's investigation, Markert was found to have integrity because he admitted that he had been a communist but left the party, something that he invoked the Fifth Amendment on when questioned about it by the Congressional subcommittee. He retained his faculty position. Nickerson also admitted to being a member of the Communist Party but did not report having left the party. Davis refused to answer any questions regarding his politics and denied that his academic integrity hinged on whether he was a communist. Hatcher fired both Nickerson and Davis. The Economics Department subsequently put on hold plans to hire Lawrence Klein, a former communist who had repudiated the party in public.

University of Michigan II: A Personal Reminiscence

In our request for stories of political biases (see below), Eugene Burnstein, now emeritus at the University of Michigan but who had been there since the 1950s as a graduate student, related this story:

> During my first semester of grad school at UM—in the glorious Doctoral Program in Social Psychology—I roomed with two older grad students, one in economics, the other in philosophy. Both were quite left-wing and active; one ran for Senator on the Progressive Party ticket (remember Henry Wallace?); the other gave talks and brought in speakers, some of whom were well-known members of the Communist Party (e.g., Gerhard Eisler). Both lost their teaching assistantships as a result.

Dr. Burnstein relayed this story from memory. After 60 years, it is possible that such memories are not perfect. Nonetheless, it is consistent with the spirit of the times.

Conclusions about Right-Wing Distortions of Science

We suspect that this brief but sordid history of right-wing distortions and misuse of science is familiar to many. These efforts were generally focused on advancing conservative policies and practices, or contesting reasonable, progressive ones, far more than on the conduct of science. In most of these cases, progressives have defended science from those who would misuse it or distort it. As such, many of those on the left may have developed a false sense of immunity (Pronin, Lin, & Ross, 2002) to their own intolerance of other ideas and their own propensities to distort science. Many may believe that the left has generally been more tolerant than the right and generally on the side advancing and defending academic freedom and scientific progress. The next three sections present some evidence that contrasts with such a belief.

Political Bias and Intolerance

Progressives and conservatives are often hostile to one another. The ICH argues that many people across the political spectrum are prejudiced against ideologically dissimilar others (Brandt, Reyna, Chambers, Crawford, & Wetherell, 2014). Conservatives tend to be hostile not just to progressives but also to groups known to be progressive, such as blacks, feminists, pro-choice advocates, and student protesters. Progressives tend to be hostile not just to conservatives but also to groups known to be conservative, such as white men, evangelical Christians, business leaders, and those who are pro-life (see Chambers, Schlenker, & Collisson, 2013; Crawford & Pilanski, 2013;

Wetherell, Brandt, & Reyna, 2013). Before reviewing the evidence indicating that social and personality psychologists are not completely immune to such psychological processes, we need to briefly address an important tangent.

Why Political Bias in Social Psychology Will Manifest as Progressive Bias

If, as we have just argued, the evidence shows that conservatives are just as politically prejudiced as progressives, how can it be that political prejudice within social psychology will almost exclusively manifest as bias against scientists and ideas that are critical of progressivism? The answer is simple: Most social psychologists identify as progressive (see Haidt, 2011; Inbar & Lammers, 2012; von Hippel and Buss, Chapter 2, this volume). For instance, in their survey of social psychologists, von Hippel and Buss found that, in the 2012 U.S. presidential election, 305 voted for Obama and only 4 voted for Romney. At the psychological level, we have no doubt that conservatives are at least as prone to political hostility and distortions as are progressives. However, within social psychology, the number of psychologists whose politics are right of center is so infinitesimal as to not warrant further discussion. What does warrant further discussion, however, is the evidence regarding whether this ideological monoculture has led to a hostile environment for *scientific* claims and evidence that contest left-wing values.

Political Prejudice in Social Psychology

Are progressive social psychologists prejudiced against (the rare) conservative colleagues and (the perhaps less rare) ideas that contest progressive narratives and values? Accumulating evidence from a variety of sources strongly suggests that at least some are. Inbar and Lammers (2012, Study 2) asked social psychological respondents how reluctant they would be to invite a conservative colleague to participate in a symposium, whether they would be reluctant to accept papers or fund grants taking a conservative perspective, and if when choosing between equally qualified candidates, they would be inclined to select the more liberal one over the more conservative one. Their scale ranged from 1 (not at all) to 7 (very much). Using scores above 4 as the cut off, they found that 15–43% of liberal social psychologists *endorse* (scores above the scale midpoint) discriminating against conservative colleagues in publication, grants, symposia, and hiring decisions. Another view, however, is that *any score above 1 (not at all)* constitutes *some* willingness to discriminate. Using this criterion, willingness to discriminate levels were 56%, 78%, 75%, and 78%, respectively, for the four questions (see also Honeycutt & Freberg, 2016).

Audit studies have yielded evidence that such discrimination actually occurs—articles and research proposals that advance liberal worldviews are more readily accepted than are those that contest such views (Abramowitz, Gomes & Abramowitz, 1975; Ceci, Peters, & Plotkin, 1985). And a literature is rapidly accumulating demonstrating that political biases have distorted social scientific claims about the role of evolution in social psychological functioning (Pinker, 2002; von Hipple & Buss, Chapter 2, this volume), the size and nature of sex differences (Eagly, 1995, 2013), the accuracy of stereotypes (Jussim, 2012; Jussim, Crawford, Anglin & Stevens, 2015), and the psychological characteristics of liberals and conservatives (Duarte et al., 2015).

Political prejudice may be quite powerful because it is not stigmatized in the way that other prejudices (e.g., race/ethnicity, sex, etc.) are. People, most likely including social psychologists, sometimes, and perhaps often, feel quite free to express those prejudices—viewing them as reasonable, rational, and justified (see Kristof, May 7, 2016; Kristof, May 28, 2016).

Living with Bias in Social Psychology

In this section, we relay personal stories of psychologists and students who believe they have had experiences that were possible manifestations of political biases. These are stories—anecdotal evidence—which, in some social science circles, are called "lived experience" (Tappan, 1997). These stories should not be interpreted in the same manner as experiments or surveys (although the ongoing scientific integrity and replicability crises suggest that caution is warranted in interpreting such research as well; Ioannidis, 2005, 2012; Jussim et al., 2016a; Open Science Collaboration, 2015). These stories, therefore, are presented here to *augment*, but not replace, other forms of scientific analysis.

Another way to look at these stories, however, is as smoke—as in, "where there is smoke, there is usually fire." When people have similar experiences, over and over, we think they are reasonable to express concern about the functioning of social psychology as an academic and scientific discipline. These experiences constitute examples of scientific dysfunction and integrity failures—typically involving obstacles to publication, admissions, hiring, funding, and the like.

Stories of Bias

Funding

This chapter's second and third authors (Jussim and Anglin) have worked together on developing a questionnaire to assess people's explicit willingness to compromise the principles of the scientific method to advance their political goals. As part of this project, a promising undergraduate submitted a grant proposal to an internal source at Rutgers. Jussim has advised over 20 of these undergraduate proposals, and nearly all of them have been fully or partially funded. This proposal, however, was not funded. There was not a hint of political bias in the review, which stated:

> I encourage the student researcher to dedicate more effort to explaining why this research question is meaningful to the field and how it fits into the broader body of knowledge. Meaningful research must emanate from previous work and in some way address a gap in the literature or offer a new perspective on understanding a problem. Moreover, I encourage the researcher to pay close attention to clearly defining the behavior (dependent variable) the research seeks to explain. It was unclear whether the research question dealt with the effect of ideology on psychologists' research methods or on their professionalism in dealing with colleagues.

Nonetheless, upon further reflection, Jussim began to suspect the proposal was not funded for political reasons. His judgment was that none of these criticisms were actually valid, and that it was, in fact, an excellent proposal, except for one thing. The funding proposal led off with the following paragraph:

> The field of psychology is dominated by liberals (Redding, 2001), and this political homogeneity can be problematic… In fact, content analysis of all the articles published in *American Psychologist* during the 1990s revealed that 97% had liberal themes (Redding, 2001). Furthermore, recent research suggests many social psychologists would blatantly discriminate based on politics. About 37% admitted that, given equally qualified conservative and liberal job applicants, the liberal candidate should be hired over the conservative candidate.
>
> *(Inbar & Lammers, 2012)*

This paragraph provided exactly what the reviewer called for (explaining how the work meaningfully linked to prior scholarship) and is an excellent review of the research conducted by Redding (2001) and Inbar and Lammers (2012). However, it frames the topic of political bias in science as a problem that exists predominantly among progressives. Jussim suspected that this framing was potentially problematic because:

1   Most faculty in the social sciences and humanities are progressive (see, e.g., Honeycutt & Freberg, 2016; Inbar & Lammers, 2012; Langbert, Quain, & Klein, 2016).
2   The proposal was reviewed by faculty in the social sciences or humanities.
3   And therefore, "research shows you are biased by your own politics" may have evoked hostility.

Jussim, Anglin, and the student then decided to perform an anecdotal experiment. The proposal was left intact and resubmitted with one and only one change. The opening paragraph on liberal bias was deleted and replaced with this:

> Conservatives are often more skeptical of scientific research than are liberals, and they are often more willing to sacrifice science to achieve political goals (Anglin & Jussim, in preparation). Furthermore, science has a long and checkered history of periodically being used and exploited as a tool to advance nefarious right-wing political agendas (e.g., social Darwinism; Nazi eliminationist practices; Herrnstein & Murray's [1994] claims about genetic bases of race differences in intelligence).

Although Jussim and Anglin were concerned that this was so blatantly and transparently "vamping for the camera" and would again be rejected, those concerns were not justified. The proposal was funded. Apparently, all those reasons the first proposal was supposedly "unclear," "failed to offer some new understanding," and failed to "fit into the broader field" (see the rejecting reviewer's comments) suddenly evaporated. Simply adding some trashing of Nazis, social Darwinists, and Herrnstein and Murray was, apparently, enough to render the resubmitted proposal interesting and important enough to fund.

Publication

Crawford, Jussim, Cain, and Cohen (2013) had a similar experience with the peer-review process. They performed a study showing that progressives were more biased than conservatives in their evaluations of scientific articles and submitted it for publication. The initial submissions were framed explicitly as examining whether political biases were symmetric (i.e., similar for conservatives or progressives) or asymmetric (larger for progressives or conservatives) and submitted for peer review. Because so much prior research emphasized bias and distortion among conservatives, the finding that biases were larger for progressives was seen by Crawford and colleagues as important "news" or even "counterintuitive news." Yet the paper was rejected by two separate journals.

Crawford et al. (2013) then performed a variation on the anecdotal experiment described above regarding funding. Although they still reported the pattern that progressives were more biased than conservatives in the tables and figures, they removed all text stating that progressives were more biased than conservatives and resubmitted it to another journal. The paper was accepted and is now published. It was, apparently, possible to *find* that progressives were more biased than conservatives and get published; it was, however, not possible for them to *say so* and get the paper published at the first two journals to which the paper was submitted.

More Bias Stories

Given these personal experiences, Jussim and this chapter's first author, Stevens, sent an email, titled "Call for personal experiences of political bias" to the listserv for the Society for Personality and Social Psychology (SPSP; email address: SPSP-openforum@ConnectedCommunity.org; full email text available on request).

The request generated 22 separate stories provided by 13 separate individuals[1]. These responses described a variety of experiences involving ideological hostility and discrimination and fell into two categories: (1) Experiences that describe a general *climate of hostility* toward non-progressive ideas, particularly politically conservative ideas, and (2) direct experiences of *hostility, derogation, or ostracism* toward non-progressives and, again, particularly political conservatives. We have altered possible identifying information to keep these lived experiences anonymous and have eliminated typos but have otherwise presented these stories unaltered from the original text sent to us.

Finally, one of the stories presented here is from a social psychologist who was originally an author of the chapter. However, just before we were ready to submit the chapter to the publisher, this social psychologist requested that his/her name be removed. The reason given was that s/he was working on some controversial topics and "I am beginning to worry [that] these upcoming papers may put my political commitments into question, and anything that suggests my political commitments deviate from the norm (e.g., this paper) may distract from what is most important: the scientific evidence."

Climate of Hostility Stories

Many of the experiences we present suggest that a good number of social psychologists assume that their colleagues and students are progressive, or that the validity of progressive ideas and values is so obvious that open derogation of political conservatives is acceptable. Some suggest that ideas that contest progressive narratives, which include but are not restricted to conservative narratives, warrant rejection without serious consideration. Each **boldface** subheader marks the beginning of a different story, with one exception. There is a single subsection at the end (**Additional short comments**) that is a collection of short stories from different sources.

"Justification" for Downgrading an Undergraduate

I was a graduate teaching assistant (TA) for one of the most overtly liberal professors in the psychology department at my university. She was hesitant about needing a TA because as she told me, past TAs "did not fit well" and "just didn't get it." I was confused when hearing this because my position simply required me to grade a bunch of papers for two sections of an abnormal psychology course. I was not sure how a graduate psychology student would not "get" how to grade right or wrong answers on assignments in a class that basically just covers what is in the DSM. It felt pretty straightforward to me, however, it did not take long to see what the issue was.

When this professor found out that I conducted diversity research, she instantly categorized me as a strong progressive and brought up topics accordingly. From environmental issues to the apparent disgrace of the delayed progress of progressive-minded changes to our university, it seemed like I became her best friend simply because I mentioned desiring a career researching effective methods for promoting diversity. I did not dare mention that I was not the liberal Democrat that she assumed me to be. Upon receiving the first assignment to grade, I started to gain a sense of why this professor was known for her political views.

Despite being a TA for an abnormal psychology class, all of the assignments I graded were about diversity and equality. While I am passionate about these topics, I did not see how they were appropriate for an abnormal psychology class. I was expecting to receive assignments on disorders, yet only one of the assignments assigned contained information relevant to the course topic. In a class that already has more information packed into it than can be taught in a single semester, I was surprised to see that so many assignments were completely unrelated to the course topic assigned. The questions in the written assignments (apart from the one previously mentioned) did not even make connections to information in the textbook.

Notably, in one assignment, a diversity paper, students were asked to read and write a response on two articles; one on racial equality and another on feminist research. I was instructed to grade the assignments based on effort. One question inquired about what the student would need to do in order to get their research ethics up to standards proposed by the article. One student did not agree with the article and simply put that they did not feel like they needed to meet those standards. I took off points on this particular response because the question did not ask an opinion on if they should meet those standards or if they agreed with them; the question simply asked what they would need to do in order to meet those proposed standards. This student made no effort to respond to the question that was asked.

I found out the next week via email that the student complained about the grade deduction. The professor emailed me with her response to the student, which left me speechless. I thought that she would have explained to the student the reason I had taken points off was for the student's answer. Yet, instead of explaining that the student did not attempt to answer the question, she explained that my response did not match the department's goal of promoting sociocultural awareness and producing enlightened students. There is no better description of my response to reading this email than flabbergasted. I had every right to deduct points from that assignment due to a lack of effort. Discovering that lowering a grade based on responses not being liberal enough was perfectly acceptable to her was not only baffling to me but worrisome. It made me wonder how many other professors are basing grades on such reasons.

Insulting review. "Personally, I know I have had manuscripts run into a bit of a liberal bias—specifically when I publish my work in evolutionary psychology (and more specially, in the sex difference in jealousy). In fact, when I proposed doing a Registered Replication Report, a reviewer suggested that evolutionary psychologists could not be trusted to do a proper data collection—the reviewer said she had no way to assure that I would not go to an evolutionary psychology conference and collect all of my data from there and not report that fact."

Hostile review. "My co-authors and I have had our share of negative reviews, but none so memorable as those of two manuscripts reporting studies of the relationship between religion and health. Attributing negative reviews to bias is self-serving, and motives, in particular, can be very difficult to discern. So, while I came away from these experiences strongly suspecting that anti-religious attitudes were at work, I am not certain. I should point out that I am otherwise a stranger to anti-religious bias, as I myself am not at all religious. And I am not aware of the religious views of my co-authors, as those were never something we discussed. So, I do not think I am particularly sensitive to the occurrence of anti-religion bias, accurately or not.

Case 1. With the first manuscript, one of three referees gave us the distinct impression that something other than the study itself was behind the critique. This impression was conveyed by selective attention, and selective inattention, to analyses, findings, and interpretations of findings that involved how positive health correlates benefits of religion predictors, to the neglect of other aspects of our manuscript. It also was based on comments implying that we had made stronger claims for the positive effects of religion on physical health that we were, in fact, making. I had the impression that the reviewer was fighting a battle with something other than our paper.

As an example of selective attention, consider that we had examined a set of psychosocial factors, of which religion was only one. Despite this, the reviewer focused exclusively on the findings that pertained to religion. Literally, all the criticisms that were aimed at the religion predictors could have been aimed at others. For example, the reviewer appeared to be convinced that unmeasured medical factors confounded the relationship linking a religion predictor to health outcomes. But this criticism would have been equally or even more appropriate for another psychosocial predictor, depressive symptoms. Depression has a somatic aspect that, at the measurement level, might reflect physical health status. Religious beliefs do not have this somatic aspect.

Another example of what seemed an undue focus on possible positive health correlates of religion concerns the Reviewer's efforts to reject the proposition that, in the reviewer's words, religion is a "major protective factor," and an "effective shield" against health problems, and the idea that religion would be "joining the ranks" of established biomedical predictors. We had never used those phrases and made no such claims in the manuscript. In fact, we had reported findings for three religion predictors, only one of which was in the direction suggesting that greater religiousness predicted better outcomes. A second religion variable suggested the opposite—that is, it indicated that greater religiousness predicted worse outcomes—and, for a third, there was no significant relationship. There was hardly a clear, consistent pattern of positive health correlates, so we did not make all that much of them, especially given there were other findings to report, including some involving non-religion-related predictors.

An example of selective inattention that also suggested the reviewer was reacting to something other than the manuscript itself concerns analyses he/she suggested we should have reported and the possible interpretations that he/she said we should have discussed: We had, in fact, reported and discussed these analyses and interpretations. The proposed analyses involved using certain variables as covariates, which analyses we had included/reported, and the suggested interpretation was that religion might not, in fact, be related to better health outcomes, a possibility that we had discussed. While reviewers can miss certain parts of a manuscript and the authors must take responsibility for clarity of expression, in this case the fact that they were missed was surprising since these "proposed" analyses (which we had already performed and reported!) and conclusions (which we had already offered!) formed the backbone of the reviewer's critique.

Normally, when referees seem unaware of portions of a manuscript, it might be attributed to a less than thorough effort on their part. But this was not generally the case here. This reviewer provided lots of detail, pointed to particular pages and tables in the manuscript, and made over a dozen citations of previously published papers on the health problems we had examined. In this regard, his/her review of the second/revised version of the manuscript was lengthier, more detailed, and contained more citations than the reviews of the initial version. It was also more negative. By contrast, the comments provided by the other two referees—who were of course privy to the first reviewer's comments—became briefer, had fewer details, and were more positive/complimentary.

Another part of the critique that aroused our curiosity was where the reviewer asked in what appeared to be a mocking manner, "Who can write a prescription for religious involvement?" This was in a set of comments concerning what was in his/her view the impossibility of implementing an intervention based on our religion findings. We were not sure why this was an issue. Research on psychology and health examines all manner of non-modifiable predictors, including age, gender, race, ethnicity, marital status, and socioeconomic status. And, in fact, components involving non-denominational religion/spirituality had been incorporated into psychosocial interventions for medical patients at the time our manuscript was reviewed. But there was nothing in what we wrote to indicate we were proposing that our study supported doing such interventions. Moreover, we reported significant effects involving age and participant gender, two factors no more amenable to intervention than religion, that did not draw this criticism.

Some of the other comments made by this reviewer felt like "piling on." For example, the focus of the literature cited in the review was on covariates that he/she felt we should have included but had not. What was interesting about this was that many of the specific variables reflect very rare events that had not occurred in our sample and therefore were irrelevant.

Another comment that felt the same way was the reviewer's assertion that, if anything, religion was a distal predictor whose impact on health outcomes had to be mediated by more proximal, biomedical factors. This was exactly what *we* were saying. The reviewer commented specifically on a hypothetical scenario in which religion might have effects on a health outcome through its influence on a biomedical mediator. He/she said that this type of process may have been going on in our data and referred to it as "confounding." It is important to note that this was not a discussion at a statistical level about the similarities in data patterns involving mediation and confounding; it was an account of what the reviewer thought might have really been going on in the study patients. In our response to this comment, we could only agree.

Similarly, there was the argument that apparent effects of religion were not and could not be "independent". Again, we agreed, since we suggested that effects of religion were likely mediated by biomedical factors. Overall, the reviewer went on at great length to provide a critique that looked like it had been a response to a paper other than the one we had submitted, in which religion was touted as a major, health-protective factor that operated independently of behavior and biology and could readily be modified by interventions.

I should point out that our sense that many of the reviewer's comments were inappropriate and might have reflected anti-religion bias is not a sour grapes response; the paper was ultimately published in the originally targeted journal.

Case 2. That was not the case in the second instance of a paper concerning religion and health seemingly arousing anti-religion bias, which was eventually published in a different journal. At the first journal, however, I again got an immediate sense that something was "off" about the reviewers' comments and, in this case, about the editor's comments as well. The paper was criticized for focusing on physical symptoms—this in a manuscript submitted to a journal that regularly publishes such research, as well it should, given the importance of symptoms in the lives of individuals, as an indicator of underlying disease, and as a driver of healthcare utilization and associated costs.

The paper also was criticized for not discussing its adherence to the standards for clinical trials; another odd criticism because this was a laboratory study examining a method for stress reduction in initially healthy participants. It also was criticized for being "sloppy" in treating the same variable as both an outcome and a predictor, which is in fact precisely the appropriate treatment of a mediator in a statistical mediation analysis such as we reported.

Overall, though, the main thrust of the reviewers' comments indicated that they required clarification of aspects of our methods and analysis, clarifications we could easily have provided. But the editor rejected the manuscript outright.

As a result of these experiences, I moved away from the study of religion. I felt there was a bias against it in certain quarters and that I did not want to put up with an additional obstacle to publishing and the added aggravation. Although this certainly was a compromise, I cannot complain too much as I did have an option that would allow me to avoid the problem, whereas others are not so fortunate.

A Curious Experience Serving on a University Diversity Committee

I was asked to join a university diversity committee in the early 2000s, and I accepted the assignment. I was one of very few Euro-Americans on the committee. I believe, though I do not know, that I was selected because my surname is sometimes mistakenly taken to be Latino; for example, it was on this basis that I once was invited to give a colloquium in a talk series at another university that was dedicated to diversity-related themes. Awkward.

As I recall the committee discussions, they were rather free-wheeling and not very well organized or systematic. I wondered about this, finding it a bit surprising since the committee chair was a well-respected academic dean. Also, attendance was highly variable; some well-known, distinguished faculty would attend a single meeting, make a comment or two during the discussion, and not be seen again at subsequent meetings. On the other hand, I had been on other university committees that also operated like this, so I was not shocked.

But I also found it curious that we were asked to convey any comments or suggestions following meetings by emailing the committee chair, rather than the committee as a whole. I remember sending one such email asking whether we should be discussing the value of promoting diversity of ideas in addition to that associated with social group memberships, the latter having dominated discussion during the meetings.

The university president joined the committee at one of the meetings. During the course of his comments, he addressed the way in which interest in "affirmative action" was being supplanted by that involving "diversity," in part as a response to the possibility of court decisions not favorable to the former. He conveyed the view that this was tactical, a matter of relabeling rather than reconceptualization. In doing so, he very explicitly said that we, the university, would not let legal considerations get in the way of our diversity-related goals.

At a subsequent meeting, the committee chair approached me before committee discussion began. She said she wanted to acknowledge and thank me for the emailed suggestions I had sent her. She seemed earnest, but at the same time I thought I detected something else, possibly an apologetic tone.

That was the last meeting of that particular committee. I was informed that it had been replaced by the formation of a new committee. I was not invited to join that second committee. In retrospect, I inferred that the first committee had been part of a preliminary screening process, intended to identify the most suitable individuals to serve on the actual committee. As far as I could tell, beyond the emails to the committee chair and whatever notes she took at meetings, there was no other concrete product of the first committee's activity. No report or recommendations of any kind. Of course, I cannot be sure of what actually happened.

Hostile Work Environment

One of the other PhD students in the lab is terribly hostile and often makes comments in person and on social media about evil conservatives, maintaining a firm "moral highroad," despite themselves vocally supporting left-wing leaders (e.g. Jeremy Corbyn; see Gilligan, July 18, 2015) who face frequent charges of anti-Semitism. The supervisor knows, I'm sure, that I don't attend any lab events because of this hostility—but doesn't say anything, maybe because he shares those political views.

Anticipation of Political Hostility Leads to Dropping a Research Topic

Most of my experiences in this realm have been at the research idea selection stage. There have been several occasions where I've stopped brainstorming or pursuing a research idea because I expected it would face too much unnecessary pushback at the review stage. The most vivid example of this was early in grad school when I came to a faculty member with an idea about studying the possibility of unintended psychological costs of affirmative action policies for intergroup relations. We mutually agreed that it's the kind of program that is better pursued when one has the comfort of tenure.

Professor Creates Politically Hostile Climate in Class and Then Doubles Down

During several classes, President Bush was constantly demonized, made the villain, or was the butt of jokes. In one class, the comments and innuendos were so disrespectful, I felt compelled to approach the professor after class and asked him to consider how those jokes might be offensive. Not taking me seriously, he made another joke and dismissed my comment as ridiculous. I think his attitude was "who in their right mind would ever support President Bush?" If this would have been any other topic raised by a student under the auspice of "offensive," I'm sure the professor would have taken my point more seriously.

Mocking among Colleagues

It was not uncommon in my meetings, especially during election cycles when political issues and candidates were particularly hot topics, for my more liberal colleagues to freely and frequently berate conservative politicians and the stances they supported. This was often manifested in a discussion of FOX News, which was a constant source of entertainment. There was a mutual understanding that the people on the network and the issues they spoke about were ridiculous and just ripe for jokes. As colleagues laughed together casually over these issues, it occurred to me how little they must realize how awkward it was to be present while holding a different viewpoint. Even though I've never been a big FOX News fan, it was difficult for me to listen to colleagues who I respect unintentionally belittle issues that I genuinely care about. Given the sociable tone of these comments (most were jokes) and my junior status in the department, I was hesitant to reveal my affiliation, fearing that I would appear overly sensitive and would be excluded in the future. However, I also struggled with how my lack of active participation in these conversations could have negative implications for my status in the department. In the best case, perhaps I appeared uninformed or too timid to speak about politics. If I had spoken up, however, actively alerting the group that there was one (or perhaps more!) among them who disagreed, it would have drastically changed the group dynamic in a way that was clearly unwelcome.

Social/political pressure to create the appearance of more support that progressive positions are "settled science" than really existed

These next two stories were provided by a former member of the Council of the American Psychological Association:

> There was a vote about saying that APA thinks gay couples are good parents. I thought the evidence was weak, especially given the idea of having a major society support that view as fact. I am all in favor of gay marriage and parenting, but did not think the evidence was at all compelling. I decided to abstain from the vote, but people all around me shouted at me to raise my hand so there would be a unanimous vote, and I am ashamed to say that I did so.
>
> Second vote was very similar, but on the damage done by Indian American school mascots. Again, I thought the evidence was thin—in fact, very thin in this case. But again, I voted that these mascots are harmful to students because they wanted an overwhelming vote on this issue.

Additional Short Comments on Various Forms of Hostility

"A grad student came by my office to complain about a recent string of stalls in the subway system, scoffing 'stupid Republican lawmakers' (the city is run by Democrats and the stalls were due to construction)."

"At a recent colloquium about moral decision-making, a professor joked about how we ought to study (Donald) Trump as a case of moral depravity."

"Any time the topics of narcissism, psychopathy, entitlement, or stupidity comes up, (Donald) Trump or (George W.) Bush are used as examples."

Direct Hostility, Derogation, or Ostracism

These next personal experiences document specific examples of hostility, derogation, or ostracism directed towards social psychologists who do not consider themselves progressives.

Outcast for Admitting to Having Voted Republican

I learned quickly upon starting graduate school that in the world of psychology, you are either liberal and fully agree with those around you, or you are outcast as a Republican. This concept became clear to me when I was working amongst a group of fellow graduate students. It all started with someone saying "I can't believe how people say they are pro-gay marriage yet vote Republican... that is so backwards." At first, one side of my lips curled up in a sly smile at the joke. However, when I looked up, I realized that it was not a joke at all.

For a second I hesitated saying anything, first because I was shocked that the statement was an actual belief, and second because I realized that opening my mouth could be social suicide in my department. After a deep breath and a quick thought of how I would probably regret my statement later, I opened my mouth and responded with, "Well, some people value other issues more than social issues. For instance, I am pro-gay marriage and pro-choice, yet I did not vote Democrat last election. To me, issues such as national security and international relations are more important when it comes to elections. I do not believe that the government should have control over those social issues anyways." After what felt like two full minutes of stares and blank faces, one of my classmates mumbled under his breath, "I still just don't get it." From that night on, I was no longer invited to study sessions, was essentially casted out amongst my colleagues in the office, and had various conversations that ended with my classmate (who was present that night) alluding to skepticism of my education, logic, sympathy, and intellect due to not agreeing on the same methods to attain true equality in the academic realm.

A few months later, I was talking with that same graduate student I had been studying with that night about how she was shocked to find out that her boyfriend did not consider himself to be a Democrat because he was so big on diversity. She quickly apologized to me after saying that. When I asked why she was apologizing, she quickly uttered that she thought I was a Republican. I was shocked because I had never claimed to be one around her. When I told her that I was more of a libertarian than anything else, she looked confused. I realized that she did not know what that meant. I explained that I was "fiscally conservative but socially liberal" to which she replied, "Well, that's all that really matters anyways." I am a bad liar so I doubt that I hid my jaw-dropping expression.

"Fucking Republican"

In grad school I was publicly called a "fucking Republican" by a faculty member. I saw other students' families insulted for the work they did (e.g., finance). There are other things I won't share that were worse. Being conservative or libertarian is a stigma you can hide, so most of the comments after I learned to keep my mouth shut publicly were more climate-based than directed at me. There are constant jokes about people on the right being idiots or evil. The default assumption [is that] you are liberal in any academic environment so nobody censors. I remember after one talk I went to where the speaker went off on Republicans for about 10 minutes. I had two liberal colleagues actually sympathize with me after that.

Silenced

It is very difficult to write this. I am worried that if someone I know will read it, they will be upset with me, and they will avoid me even more. Why would I worry about reporting to have faced prejudices? It started with my new job a couple of years ago. A new job, tenured post, life secured; fantastic. Also, my colleagues were nice. I am a very social person and outgoing and liked to attend all events to which I was invited. Everyone seemed supportive; they liked my research; it was great. A few months into the post, I noticed that many people often talked about politics rather than about their research. I kept out of these discussions. But then came the time of the primary presidential elections; one evening at a social event, I said: "I might vote for the Conservative party." I said, *I might,* because in fact I was not quite sure and would have liked to debate the issue. "Then you must be completely deluded," was the first response, "Then you are a fascist," someone else said to me. I was quite shocked and somehow not expecting that. And that was it. There were no further discussions, and since then I stopped being invited to social events. Ok, why would I care? It is a shame to not go to social events, but what was more worrying was that I also felt my work conditions were getting worse. That extra school funding, I didn't get it anymore, but that extra administrative load, I did get. Not only was social support withdrawn, but I also had the impression that internal research support and resources were also withdrawn. I wish I hadn't said anything. What do I do now when I am at a work meeting and the topic is politics as usual, and when it is said: "The Republican Party is terrible, selfish bastards who don't care for people. I wish more people were educated enough, so no one voted for them. They are awful, don't we all agree?" I don't dare to say anything anymore.

Unwelcome and Awkward

I belong to two labs in my department, supervised by two different professors. One lab is amazing and respectful and tolerant of differing opinions. The other, less so. It's been made clear that I'm not welcome to [the second] lab social events (or even informal academic events) because of my political beliefs. The supervisor meets with me infrequently and often makes some weird and irrelevant comment about me being a Conservative, even when it has no actual relevance to the discussion at hand.

Singled Out and Targeted

During a class discussion on social identity and self-categorization, out of nowhere, the professor aggressively asked me if I believed that the actions taken by President Bush in response to 9–11 (the invasion of Iraq) were any different than the actions taken by Mohammad Atta on 9–11(hijacking and crashing planes into the World Trade Center). This question was not posed to any other student in the class (none of the other students in the class, and in the program for that matter, were veterans). It was solely directed at me. This made me feel both uncomfortable and upset and I refused to answer the question.

Conservative = Nazi

Once I was asked at a summer school on social identity and group formation "why I was even there," because we discussed collective action, and conservatives, apparently, don't support activism. Another time I was told I had voted for "a Nazi Party" by voting for the Conservatives.

You Were in the Military? You Are a Bad Fit for This Lab

Following a 20-year career in the military, I entered graduate school to pursue a PhD in social psychology. During my first year, like most graduate students, I explored different labs to work in where I could participate in research that I found interesting while developing my skill set as a researcher. I ultimately found a lab that matched my interests. This lab had recently obtained a data set where the sample population was from the military, so given my military experience I began to work on a research project utilizing that data set.

Almost immediately, I began to feel as though my ideas were being discounted and discredited much quicker and more often than other students on the project, even though I had real tangible experience within the organization the group was studying. Although there is some truth to the stereotype that people who have served in the military politically lean to the "right," the real kicker in all of this is that I'm far from a hard-line conservative. Yes, some of my views would be considered politically conservative, however, other views I have would be considered by many to be very liberal/progressive. Nevertheless, within a few weeks of joining the lab, I was unceremoniously asked to not only leave the project but to leave the lab as well. When I asked about the reasoning behind my dismissal, I was told only that it appeared that I wasn't a good fit for the project/lab.

If You Are Conservative, I Am Not Your Friend

One of my colleagues and I went to the same university for our PhDs, she in philosophy, I in psychology. We had offices quite close to each other because my PhD was interdisciplinary and also involved philosophy. We went out for coffee a couple of times. I often came to her office, sat on her desk, and we discussed philosophy, laughed, and chatted. One day we went for ice cream and sat in the cafe for a long time discussing problems of philosophy and free will. It was cool. She wasn't my closest or best friend, but we were very good colleagues and wanted to keep in touch when we finished studying. We became friends on Facebook. After completing our PhDs, both of us got tenured positions at different universities. The cities were far away but we saw each other's updates on Facebook, and we also stayed in touch and exchanged stories through Facebook's private chat. Then came the 2015 U.K. general election, and the U.K. Conservative party won it. One Sunday morning, I was reading the newspaper and saw her name, the name of the woman I just described, my previous colleague, the friendly woman with whom I shared offices and went for coffee. She was in the news because of controversy over a web blog she wrote, titled "If you are a Conservative, I am not your friend" (Roache, May 8, 2015).

What?? … that morning I checked Facebook, and indeed, she had un-friended me. This was because I "liked" the Facebook page of the Conservative Party. And because, as she wrote in her article, "Life is too short, I thought, to hang out with people who hold abhorrent political views, even if it's just on-line." I was very upset about this, because you might think that this is virtual and thus does not matter, and I would agree that it would not have mattered if this was a person that I literally didn't know; but I did. In fact, we were friends before—in reality! I don't want to ever speak to her again and am now glad I am not "friends" with such an *intolerant* person.

Blog Critical of President Carter Disqualifies Applicant for Graduate Admission

I applied to several PhD programs in social psychology and was accepted by three. At one of these programs, the faculty had apparently seen my blog (an old blog that I canned later that year). Among posts about my recent marathon experience, I had posted about the mass resignation of all fourteen Jewish members of the board of advisors of the Carter Center, former President Jimmy Carter's nonprofit. They resigned because Carter's new book seemed to suggest that Palestinian terrorist bombings of Israeli civilian targets were justified until a Palestinian state was established, or a particular type of peace accord was accepted by Israel. In my blog post, I supported the board members and criticized Carter's apparent tolerance of terrorism. Then on a phone interview, a faculty member from the social psychology program directly asked me about this blog post (and no others). She also asked if I "really" felt that way about Jimmy Carter. She also openly stated that all of the faculty in the program had a problem with my post, except for her (it would've been 4–6 other professors), and that they all opposed my entry into the program.

From her questions, I got the impression that my politics needed to clarified and vetted before final decisions were made. They subsequently denied me admission, with no further interaction or visits (If it matters, this program was somewhat less selective and prestigious than the programs that accepted me). That was an extremely awkward phone call. I was blindsided, was not at all prepared to talk about politics or my precise feelings toward Jimmy Carter. It's the kind of thing that could not happen in a normal professional environment, and would give HR people nightmares if it did. During the call, I got the impression that they thought/were worried that I was a conservative.

Limitations and Qualifications to These Anecdotes

The evidence presented above was obtained from a non-representative, non-random sample and is qualitative and subjective. Although the Jussim and Anglin funding story and the Crawford et al. publication stories have been amply documented (e.g., the reviews are on record), the subsequent stories constitute the subjective experiences of those reporting them. Those stories include some unknown and unverified combination of facts and subjective perspectives. We have not sought to independently verify these stories with others present. As such, caution is warranted with respect to understanding what these stories mean. Some are so vividly recalled and presented that our own view is that they should be given high credibility, but, of course, even then we cannot be sure.

It is also important to note that the email sent to the SPSP listserv soliciting stories of political discrimination and hostility might be considered a leading question, emphasizing conservative more than liberal experiences with such biases. Given the well-documented preponderance of progressive social psychologists (Haidt, 2011; Honeycutt & Freberg, 2016; Inbar & Lammers, 2012; Langbert, Quain & Klein, 2016; von Hippel & Buss, Chapter 2, this volume), we thought it was reasonable to presume that ideological bias within social psychology is more often directed toward conservatives than progressives and, consequently, that we needed to work somewhat harder to communicate to conservatives that it was safe for them to share their experiences with us. Our email also offered anyone who submitted a personal experience the chance to collaborate on this chapter. We acknowledge that this could have led anyone responding to embellish or even make up a personal experience with ideological bias. Yet we felt our offer of collaboration was necessary to establish a sense of trust with conservative social psychologists so that they would willingly relay their personal experiences with ideological bias.

Nonetheless, these do constitute reports of subjective experiences and perceptions of political discrimination within social psychology by social psychologists. Are these anecdotes on the same firm scientific ground as experimental demonstrations of various forms of bias? Probably not, but that is the wrong question. Our view is that the right question is this: How consistent are these anecdotal stories with rigorous social scientific research on political biases?

Confirmation Bias and Political Prejudice

Motivated reasoning refers to biased information processing. It is driven by affect and goals unrelated to accurate belief formation (Kahan, 2011; Kunda, 1990). A specific type of motivated reasoning, confirmation bias, occurs when people seek out and evaluate information in ways that confirm their pre-existing views while downplaying, ignoring, or discrediting information of equal or greater quality that opposes their views (Ditto & Lopez, 1992; MacCoun, 1998; Munro & Ditto, 1997; Nickerson, 1998; Taber & Lodge, 2006; also referred to as myside bias, see Stanovich, West, & Toplak, 2013). Such biases occur across the political spectrum.

Confirmation Bias and Motivated Reasoning among Scientists

Scientists are not immune to confirmation biases and motivated reasoning (Ioannidis, 2012; Lilienfeld, 2010). Values influence each phase of the research process (Duarte et al., 2015). Reviewers' theoretical (Epstein, 2004; Greenwald, Pratkanis, Leippe, & Baumgardner, 1986; Mahoney, 1977) and ideological (Abramowitz et al., 1975) views can influence their evaluation of research reports, leading them to judge studies that oppose their beliefs more critically than studies supporting their views. Consequently, they are then less likely to recommend publication or funding of studies with undesired findings or hypotheses.

Potential Implications of Such Biases for the Social Psychological Research Literature

Political beliefs and values are one potential source of confirmation biases. To estimate the extent of such biases, we make the following assumptions. If political biases are nearly nonexistent (say, below 1%) the issue of politically distorted research would evaporate. However, given the ample evidence of politically distorted claims and conclusions throughout social psychology and other social sciences (Abramowitz et al., 1975; Ceci et al., 1985; Duarte et al., 2015; Jussim, 2012; Jussim et al., 2015; Jussim, Crawford, Stevens & Anglin, 2016b, Jussim, Crawford, Stevens, Anglin & Duarte, 2016c; Martin, 2015; Pinker, 2002; Redding, 2001; Schumm, 2015) and the additional evidence that confirmation biases more broadly distort social scientific conclusions (Ioannidis, 2012; Jussim et al., 2016a; Lilienfeld, 2010), our estimation starts with the assumption that such biases may not be trivial. What is a good operationalization of "not trivial"? First, we conservatively assume that only a small minority of articles are affected by political bias, either because the topic is not politicized or because our colleagues keep their biases at bay. For our first illustration, we assume only 10% of all articles are affected by political biases. Third, we assume such biases are just as likely among conservative as among progressive social psychologists.

Next, we must estimate the proportion of progressive versus conservative social psychologists. We again start with a conservative estimate of the proportion of social psychologists who are ideologically left—80% (the *lowest* of the figures obtained in the recent spate of studies assessing ideology among social psychologists; Buss & von Hippel, Chapter 2, this volume; Inbar & Lammers, 2012). Thus, our first estimation assumption means that, if we consider a group of 100 social psychologists, 80 would self-identify as progressive. Most of the remaining 20 would be moderates and libertarians, but, for simplicity purposes, we purposefully overestimate (based on survey results) that 10% are conservative. The overestimate of conservatives is a useful fiction here, because it biases our simulation as much as possible *against* finding biases in publication. Put differently, any lower estimate would indicate that the field's publications are *even more biased than our simulation suggests*.

Furthermore, we assume that each of our 80 progressives and 10 conservatives has published a single article. This, too, probably biases the results *against* finding political biases, because the most productive social psychologists, on average, are at the most prestigious institutions, and, for example, the psychology programs at Princeton, Harvard, Yale, and Stanford have exactly *zero faculty members who are registered Republicans* (Langbert et al., 2016). If, for example, the 80 progressives were, on average, 50% more productive than the 10 conservatives, given our assumptions, the level of biased publications would also increase by 50%.

Given these assumptions, of every 100 articles, we would expect eight to be progressively biased and one to be conservatively biased. Although the good news in this scenario is that 91% of the literature is unbiased, even these very low estimates of bias still lead to a literature that has eight times as many articles skewed by left-wing politics than by right-wing politics.

Table 13.1 also presents a variation of this analysis, making different assumptions about both the level of bias and about differences in progressives' and conservatives' propensities for bias. Specifically, we also present scenarios in which 20 and 50% of articles are subject to some degree of bias. For those who think the 50% figure is too high, consider this: It has been argued that even (and perhaps especially) "basic" research in social psychology without *obvious* ties to politics is actually *most* vulnerable to political biases (Funder, 2015). For example, the fundamental attribution error and the "power of the situation" both may seem to be fundamental phenomena revealed by basic research that is independent of ideology. In fact, however, both comport well with liberal worldviews that people are products of their conditions, rather than with conservative worldviews that hold people personally responsible for their behavior. We are not claiming that the 50% figure is true, but we do think it is worth considering how biased the literature would be *if it is true*.

In addition, Table 13.1 includes other scenarios regarding progressive/conservative differences in propensities for bias. Specifically, it also shows scenarios in which conservatives are twice as likely as progressives to be biased in their evaluations of manuscripts in ways that ultimately lead to biased publications. Even though we think the evidence shows progressives and conservatives to be similarly biased in their judgments of science (e.g., Anglin & Jussim, 2017; Ditto et al., 2016) and argument quality (Crawford, 2012; Crawford, Jussim, Cain, & Cohen, 2013), some literature suggests that conservatives tend to have more biases (e.g., Altemeyer, 1996; Jost, Glaser, Kruglanski, & Sulloway, 2003). Even if conservatives are indeed far more biased than are progressives, these scenarios

TABLE 13.1 Potential for Biased Research Due to Ideological Homogeneity per 100 Publications

Ideological Breakdown	% Of Biased Published Articles	Likelihood of Publishing Biased Research	# Of Progressively Biased Articles Per 100 Publications	# Of Conservatively Biased Articles Per 100 Publications
80 Progressives, 10 Conservatives	10	Right = Left	8	1
		Right = 2x Left	8	2
	20	Right = Left	16	2
		Right = 2x Left	16	4
	50	Right = Left	40	5
		Right = 2x Left	40	10

Note: This table assumes one publication per author.

show that there are good reasons to believe *the social psychological literature* will still suffer from far more left-wing than right-wing distortions because of the far greater number of liberals in the field.

Lastly, one more thing is worth keeping in mind. Specifically, 10% probably wildly overestimates the proportion of conservatives in social psychology, at least with respect to the types of social issues studied by social psychologists. Even Inbar and Lammers (2012) found only 3.9% of social psychologists self-identifying as conservative on social issues. von Hippel and Buss's data indicate a figure closer to 1%. Langbert et al.'s (2016) data shows that, at the most prestigious institutions, it is closer to zero. If we assume 5% conservatives in Table 13.1, each disproportion doubles, indicating literatures that are 8 to 16 times more biased in a left-wing direction. If we assume 2% conservatives, the bias estimates in the literatures in our simulation will range from 20 to 40 times more biased in favor of research advancing progressive values.

Conclusions

The scenarios we presented here oversimplify scientific processes. There is not likely to be a simple straight line between the ideological distribution of scientists and the frequency of ideologically biased publications in social psychology. Furthermore, given the widespread presence of colleagues with progressive perspectives, the few non-progressives in social psychology are likely to have a greater depth of understanding of progressive perspectives than do progressives of conservative perspectives (because progressives rarely have to seriously grapple with non-progressive perspectives). Nor has our simulation addressed the fact that there are usually multiple reviews of a single paper, or the dynamic interplay between editors, reviewers, and authors. Nonetheless, despite its oversimplification, our estimates have provided one potentially valuable contribution: They can at least be used to generate empirical hypotheses about the extent to which political biases might be tainting the scientific literature in social psychology.

Combating Political Discrimination and Encouraging Ideological Heterogeneity

The scientific literature indicates a climate of hostility toward non-progressive individuals, backgrounds, and ideas. The anecdotes presented here brought that climate to life with concrete examples of how it manifests. One might think, therefore, that we hold a deeply pessimistic view about our field's ability to combat such biases.

If so, however, one would be wrong. Over the last few years, as we have raised these issues in a variety of academic and scholarly contexts, we have been pleasantly surprised at the earnest openness and willingness to consider these ideas among many of our colleagues, including many progressives. Furthermore, a brief survey about the political orientation and political views of those 13 individuals[2] who submitted stories for this chapter revealed a fairly diverse group. Political orientation was assessed on a 7-point scale (very left/ progressive to very right/conservative). This scale also included response options for "other" and "not sure." Four of the 13 reported their political orientation as conservative (all four answered above the middle-of-the-road option at the midpoint of the scale), five reported their political orientation as progressive (all five answered with choices below the midpoint), and four reported their political orientation as other. We also asked if political views were left/progressive, centrist/moderate, right/conservative, libertarian/classical liberal, unclassifiable, or other. Three reported left/progressive views, two reported centrist/ moderate views, six reported libertarian/classical liberal views, and two reported other.

Some scientists clearly believe in the value of intellectual diversity as an important ingredient for advancing the quality of science rather than (or in addition to) as a tool for engineering social justice initiatives (e.g., Loeb, 2014). Furthermore, many may have been unaware of their own propensities for political biases, but, once revealed, are quite open to combating them. Furthermore, we are optimistic because, in fact, social psychologists have learned quite a lot about how to reduce intergroup hostility—all we need to do is apply our well-established principles to ourselves. For example, intergroup contact reduces prejudice (Pettigrew & Tropp, 2006), strongly arguing that, if the field embraces and welcomes non-progressives, many will discover that their exaggerated caricatures are not justified, and at least some of the hostility will be reduced. In that spirit, we next offer recommendations from two labs that have had some success in combating political biases and in encouraging non-leftist students to pursue social psychology.

Jussim's Social Perception Lab Policies and Practices

Inspired by Haidt's (2011) call for social psychologists to explicitly include political diversity in their diversity statements, Jussim has the following diversity statement on his page introducing opportunities for research for undergraduate and graduate students:

> Anyone, from any background whatsoever, regardless of race, gender, ethnic, religious, political, social class, sexual or gender orientation, and health or mental health status, and any other status or category not listed here is welcome in the Social Perception Lab (SPL) ...
>
> The Society for Personality and Social Psychology (SPSP) declared itself to have the goal of fostering: "the career development of students who come from underrepresented groups, i.e., ethnic or racial minorities,

first-generation college students, individuals with a physical disability, and/ or lesbian, gay, bisexual, or transgendered students."

I strongly endorse fostering the career development of such students. ... however, SPSP's statement clearly does not go far enough. Here is Jon Haidt's analysis of that statement:

> First, can we change "i.e." to "e.g.?" Why should it be i.e.? Do we really want to say to the public that this is the official list of groups that get benefits? Second, can we tack on a phrase like: "or who bring helpful and underrepresented perspectives in other ways?"

One of the main intellectual arguments for diversity is that people from diverse backgrounds will often (not necessarily all the time, but in general) have different experiences and therefore different perspectives to bring to bear on solving scientific and social problems. I agree. So, that sounds like we should make a particular point of trying to encourage and support the careers of people who actually think differently than most of us.

And who might those people? Two strong contenders are political non-liberals (including centrists, libertarians, and conservatives) and people who are highly religious....

Consequently, my view is that, for its own good (and regardless of my own particular political and religious beliefs), social psychology would greatly benefit from an influx of people whose political and personal beliefs are different than those of the overwhelming secular and left-wing majority of current social psychologists.

Certainly, the base rate of students in psychology with left-wing politics is quite high, and plenty of students in Jussim's lab have held such views. Nonetheless, as a result of this climate, he has also had two honors students who are Republicans (one of whom went on to a PhD in social psychology at an Ivy League university; the other recently started a master's program in forensic psychology—and is enthusiastically working on the extremely important problem of overturning wrongful convictions for serious crime). He has had a religious, right-of-center student who not only completed her PhD but has gone on to a terrific research career and to chair her department. His recent grad students have also included a politically inactive liberal (who nonetheless found studying political biases interesting and important) and a libertarian (also studying political biases).

Motyl's Lab Climate

Motyl believes there are two key elements to fostering a welcoming climate for all, regardless of their social or political identity. First, there must be a climate of respect. In respectful climates, people resist the temptation to take cheap shots for easy laughs in presentations by including pictures portraying people on the other side in a dehumanized way (e.g., Republican politicians morphed into chimpanzees or as demons with horns). In the occasional presentation where Motyl might include such pictures, he strives to ensure that he has a similar image of someone on his side (e.g., Democratic politicians morphed into chimpanzees or as devils with horns) and highlights the tendency for people to have mirror image stereotypes of people in different groups (e.g., Crawford, Modri, & Motyl, 2013; Graham et al., 2013). If we want people to feel like they belong, we cannot make a mockery of any particular subgroup of individuals without making a mockery of opposing groups. In other words, we must not poke fun at any group, unless we are doing so in a bipartisan, "equal opportunity" way.

Second, disagreement must be encouraged. This may be difficult because the inherent power asymmetry between students and professors may make students fearful that their professors will lower their grade or ridicule them in front of their peers if they disagree with them. To combat this, in initial meetings with advisees and student collaborators, Motyl explicitly encourages them to disagree with him. He tells them he has been studying social psychology longer than they have, but that largely means he is more familiar with (and perhaps biased by) the status quo in the field. They have fresher eyes and may see things differently than people further along in their careers. He also explicitly tells them that if intelligent people can study the same literature and still disagree, then the answer is not obvious. When the answer is not obvious, the research is then more interesting and important. More flippantly, he often insists that agreement is boring. Except agreement with that axiom, of course.

These two norms should help promote diversity along all lines, not just political lines. If we foster respect of different viewpoints, all people should feel more welcomed than in places where we tolerate intergroup bias and penalize those who do not conform. Ultimately, if we apply the same standard of evidence to papers that come to liberal conclusions as those that come to conservative conclusions, our field would likely study a broader range of the human experience and perhaps even be more replicable.

The Importance of Diversity of Thought

Science represents an attempt to reach the truth through a series of successive approximations. Ideas and theories compete in a marketplace of ideas where some attain greater success than others. One form of success in this marketplace is when an idea or theory attains increasing consensus or support. Yet consensus does not always imply veracity. Discord and disagreement are essential to the progression of knowledge and can motivate deeper thinking about the issues at stake (Crano, 2012). The potential benefits are numerous and include reducing the impact of confirmation bias (Mercier & Sperber, 2011), higher-quality group decisions (Crisp & Turner, 2011; Moscovici & Personnaz, 1980; Nemeth, 1995) and the production of novel solutions to a variety of problems (Crano,

2012; Mannix & Neale, 2005). In properly functioning scientific contexts, minority viewpoints constitute strength, not threats to scientific integrity. If the majority view is actually closer to the truth, then the validity and credibility of the majority view would be further strengthened by withstanding a forceful attempt at falsification by the minority (Popper, 1959, 1963). If the minority viewpoint is closer to the truth, in a well-functioning scientific context, data produced by that minority should lead to appropriate scientific self-correction. This sentiment is captured well by John Stuart Mill (1869/1989):

> He who knows only his own side of the case knows little of that. His reasons may be good, and no one may have been able to refute them. But if he is equally unable to refute the reasons on the opposite side, if he does not so much as know what they are, he has no ground for preferring either opinion... Nor is it enough that he should hear the opinions of adversaries from his own teachers, presented as they state them, and accompanied by what they offer as refutations. He must be able to hear them from persons who actually believe them...he must know them in their most plausible and persuasive form (p. 38).

Conclusions

Politicized science can have profound consequences. It becomes increasingly difficult for a field to protect against politicization when it lacks ideological diversity. While it is unreasonable to expect every field to have an equal representation of rival political viewpoints, it is not unreasonable to desire greater viewpoint diversity in fields that are overwhelmingly homogenous, particularly if that field, like social psychology, frequently investigates ideologically charged research topics. To rule certain political ideas out of bounds a priori because they represent the views of a rival ideology makes the field guilty of the very forces it desires to eradicate—namely, intolerance of others via prejudice and discrimination.

Notes

1 We have removed identifying information for the stories, but otherwise they are presented as submitted. Thus, in some places, the term "liberal" appears where we (Stevens and Jussim) would use the term "progressive."
2 Some of the individuals who submitted stories did take us up on the offer of co-authorship.

References

Abramowitz, S. I., Gomes, B. & Abramowitz, C. V. (1975) Publish or politic: Referee bias in manuscript review. *Journal of Applied Social Psychology* 5, 187–200. doi:10.1111/j.1559-1816.1975.tb00675.x.

Altemeyer, R. (1996). *The authoritarian specter.* Cambridge: Harvard University Press.

American Association of University Professors. (1940). 1940 statement of principles on academic freedom and tenure. Retrieved from www.aaup.org/report/1940-statement-principles academic-freedom-and-tenure, on May 25, 2016.

Anderegg, W. R. L. (2010). Expert credibility in climate change. *Proceedings of the National Academy of Sciences, 107,* 12107–12109. doi:10.1073/pnas.1003187107.

Anglin, S. M. & Jussim, L. (2017). Science and politics: Do people support the conduct and dissemination of politicized research? *Journal of Social and Political Psychology, 5,* 142–172.

Begley, C. G. & Ellis, L. M. (2012). Drug development: Raise standards for preclinical cancer research. *Nature, 483,* 531–533.

Brandt, M. J., Reyna, C., Chambers, J. R., Crawford, J. T. & Wetherell, G. (2014). The ideological-conflict hypothesis: Intolerance among both liberals and conservatives. *Current Directions in Psychological Science, 23,* 27–34.

Carter, E. & Murdock-Perriera, L. (May 12, 2016). Half truths about race on campus: The paths and dead ends to racial equality in higher education. Retrieved on July 6, 2016 from: https://medium.com/@evelyn.carter/half-truths-about-race-on-campus-7bd53128e88#.8gktmcyiy.

Ceci, S. J., Peters, D. & Plotkin, J. (1985) Human subjects review, personal values, and the regulation of social science research. *American Psychologist 40,* 994–1002.

Chafee, J. H. (1989). Testimony, the oil spill in Prince William Sound, Alaska, before the U.S. Senate Committee on Environment and Public Works. *101st Congress, April 19.*

Chambers, J. R., Schlenker, B. R. & Collisson, B. (2013). Ideology and prejudice: The role of value conflicts. *Psychological Science, 24,* 140–149.

Commoner, B. (1977). Appendix X, ERDA authorization fossil fuels, before a subcommittee of the U.S. House of Representatives Committee on Science and Technology. *94th Congress, February 17–25.*

Conover, P. J. & Feldman, S. (1981). The meaning of liberal/conservative self-identification. *American Journal of Political Science, 25,* 617–645.

Cook, J., Nuccitelli, D., Green, S. A., Richardson, M., Winkler, B., Painting, R., et al. (2013). Quantifying the consensus on anthropogenic global warming in the scientific literature. *Environmental Research Letters, 8,* 1–7.

Craig, H. (1957). The natural distribution of radiocarbon and the exchange times of CO_2 between atmosphere and sea. *Tellus, 9,* 1–17.

Crano, W. D. (2012) *The rules of influence: Winning when you are in the minority.* New York: St. Martin's Press.

Crawford, J. T. (2012). The ideologically objectionable premise model: Predicting biased political judgments on the left and right. *Journal of Experimental Social Psychology, 48,* 138–151.

Crawford, J. T. & Pilanski, J. M. (2013). Political intolerance, right and left. *Political Psychology.* doi:10.1111/j.1467-9221.2012.00926.x.

Crawford, J. T., Jussim, L., Cain, T. R. & Cohen, F. (2013). Right-wing authoritarianism and social dominance orientation differentially predict biased evaluations of media reports. *Journal of Applied Social Psychology, 43,* 163–174.

Crawford, J. T., Modri, S. A. & Motyl, M. (2013). Bleeding-heart liberals and hard-hearted conservatives: Subtle political dehumanization through differential attributions of human nature and human uniqueness traits. *Journal of Social and Political Psychology, 1*(1), 86–104.

Crisp, R. J. & Turner, R. N. (2011) Cognitive adaptation to the experience of social and cultural diversity. *Psychological Bulletin, 137,* 242–266.

Davies, C. J. (1990). Testimony, the environment, before the U.S. House of Representatives Committee on Ways and Means. *101st Congress, March 6.*

Ditto, P., Clark, C., Liu, B., Wojcik, S., Chen, E., Grady, R. & Zinger, J. (2016). *At least bias is bipartisan: A meta-analytic comparison of selective interpretation bias in liberals and conservatives.* Paper presented at the Society for Personality and Social Psychology Convention, San Diego, CA.

Ditto, P. H. & Lopez, D. F. (1992). Motivated skepticism: Use of differential decision criteria for preferred and nonpreferred conclusions. *Journal of Personality and Social Psychology, 63,* 569–584.

Doran, P. T. & Zimmerman, M. K. (2009). Examining the scientific consensus on climate change. *Eos, Transactions American Geophysical Union, 90,* 22–23. doi: 10.1029/2009EO030002.

Duarte, J. L., Crawford, J. T., Stern, C., Haidt, J., Jussim, L. & Tetlock, P. E. (2015) Political diversity will improve social psychological science. *Behavioral and Brain Sciences, 38,* 1–54.

Duckitt, J. (2001). A dual-process cognitive-motivational theory of ideology and prejudice. *Advances in Experimental Social Psychology, 33,* 41–113.

Eagly, A. H. (1995). The science and politics of comparing women and men. *American Psychologist, 50,* 145–158.

Eagly, A. H. (2013). *Sex differences in social behavior: A social-role interpretation.* Psychology Press.

Epstein, W. M. (2004). Informational response bias and the quality of the editorial processes among American social work journals. *Research on Social Work Practice, 14,* 450–458.

Forrest, B. & Gross, P. R. (2004). *Creationism's Trojan Horse: The wedge of intelligent design.* New York: Oxford University Press.

Funder, D. (2015). Towards a de-biased psychology: The effects of ideological perspective go beyond politics. *Behavioral and Brain Sciences, 38,* 25–26.

Gifford, R. R. (1990). Testimony, the environment, before the U.S. House of Representatives Committee on Ways and Means. *101st Congress, March 6.*

Gilchrist, G. W. (1997). The elusive scientific basis of intelligent design theory. *Reports of the National Center for Science Education, 17,* 14–15.

Gilligan, A. (July, 18, 2015). Jeremy Corbyn, friend to Hamas, Iran, and extremists. In *The Telegraph,* retrieved on July 11, 2016 from: www.telegraph.co.uk/news/politics/labour/11749043/Andrew-Gilligan-Jeremy-Corbyn-friend-to-Hamas-Iran-and-extremists.html.

Graham, J., Nosek, B. A. & Haidt, J. (2013). The moral stereotypes of liberals and conservatives: Exaggeration of differences across the political spectrum. *PLoS One, 7,* e50092. doi:10.1371/journal.pone.0050092.

Greenwald, A. G., Pratkanis, A., Leippe, M. R. & Baumgardner, M. H. (1986). Under what conditions does theory obstruct research progress? *Psychological Review, 93,* 216–229.

Gross, N. (2013). *Why are professors liberal and why do conservatives care?* Cambridge: Harvard University Press.

Gross, N. & Simmons, S. (2007) *The social and political views of American professors.* Working Paper presented at a Harvard University Symposium on Professors and Their Politics, October 6, 2007.

Haidt, J. (2011, January). "The bright future of post-partisan social psychology." Talk given at the annual meeting of the Society for Personality and Social Psychology. San Antonio, TX. Transcript available at http://people.stern.nyu.edu/jhaidt/postpartisan.html.

Hollinger, D. A. (1988). Academic Culture at Michigan, 1938–1988: The Apotheosis of Pluralism, Rackham Reports (1988–1989), 58–101. [Followed by responses from Philip E. Converse, James V. Neel, Martha J. Vicinus, Homer A. Neal, and Rudolf Arnheim, 102–140.]

Honeycutt, N. & Freberg, L. A. (2016). The liberal and conservative experience across academic disciplines: An extension of Inbar and Lammers. *Social Psychological and Personality Science*. doi:10.1177/1948550616667617.

Inbar, Y. & Lammers, J. (2012). Political diversity in social and personality psychology. *Perspectives on Psychological Science*, 7(5), 496–503.

Ioannidis, J. P. (2005). Why most published research findings are false. *PLoS Medicine*, 2, 696–701.

Ioannidis, J. P. (2012). Why science is not necessarily self-correcting. *Perspectives on Psychological Science*, 7, 645–654.

Jost, J. T., Glaser, J., Kruglanski, A. W. & Sulloway, F. J. (2003). Political conservatism as motivated social cognition. *Psychological Bulletin*, 129, 339–375.

Jussim, L. (2012). *Social perception and social reality: Why accuracy dominates bias and self-fulfilling prophecy*. New York: Oxford University Press.

Jussim, L., Crawford, J. T., Anglin, S. M. & Stevens, S. T. (2015). Ideological bias in social psychological research. In J. Forgas, K. Fiedler & W. Crano (Eds.), *Sydney symposium on social psychology and politics*. New York: Psychology Press.

Jussim, L., Crawford, J. T., Anglin, S. M., Stevens, S. T & Duarte, J. L. (2016a). Interpretations and methods: Towards a more effectively self-correcting social psychology. *Journal of Experimental Social Psychology*, 66, 116–133. doi:10.1016/j.jesp.2015.10.003

Jussim, L. Crawford, J. T., Stevens, S. T. & Anglin, S. M. (2016b). The politics of social psychological science: Distortions in the social psychology of intergroup relations. In P. Valdesolo & J. Graham (Eds.), *Social psychology of political polarization*. New York: Routledge.

Jussim, L., Crawford, J. T., Stevens, S. T., Anglin, S. M. & Duarte, J. L. (2016c). Can high moral purposes undermine scientific integrity? In J. Forgas, L. Jussim & P. A. M. van Lange (Eds.), *The social psychology of morality*. New York: Routledge.

Kahan, D. M. (2011). Neutral principles, motivated cognition, and some problems for constitutional law. *Harvard Law Review*, 125, 1.

Kristof, N. (May 7, 2016). A confession of liberal intolerance. *The New York Times*, retrieved on July 6, 2016 from: www.nytimes.com/2016/05/08/opinion/sunday/a-confession-of-liberal intolerance.html?rref=collection%2Fcolumn%2Fnicholaskristof&action=click&contentCollection=opinion&region=stream&module=stream_unit&versio=latest&contentPlacement=4&pgtype=collection.

Kristof, N. (May 28, 2016). The liberal blind spot. *The New York Times*, retrieved on July 6, 2016 from: www.nytimes.com/2016/05/29/opinion/sunday/the-liberal-blindspot.html?rref=collection%2Fcolumn%2Fnicholaskristof&action=click&contentCollection=opinion&region=stream&module=stream_unit&versio=latest&contentPlacement=10&pgtype=collection.

Kunda, Z. (1990). The case for motivated reasoning. *Psychological Bulletin*, 108, 480–498.

Lahsen, M. (2005). Technocracy, democracy, and U. S. climate politics. *Science, Technology and Human Values*, 30, 137–169.

Langbert, M., Quain, A. J. & Klein, D. B. (2016). Faculty voter registration in Economics, History, Journalism, Law, and Psychology. *Econ Journal Watch, 13*, 422–451.

Lilienfeld, S. O. (2010). Can psychology become a science? *Personality and Individual Differences, 49*, 281–288.

Loeb, A. (2014). Benefits of diversity. *Nature Physics, 10*, 616–617.

Longenecker, G. (1981). Memorandum in Clean Air Act oversight, presented to the U.S. Senate committee on Environment and Public Works. *97th Congress, June 30.*

MacCoun, R. J. (1998). Biases in the interpretation and use of research results. *Annual Review of Psychology, 49*, 259–287.

Mahoney, M. J. (1977). Publication prejudices: An experimental study of confirmatory bias in the peer review system. *Cognitive Therapy and Research, 1*, 161–175.

Mannix, E. & Neale, M. A. (2005) What differences make a difference? *Psychological Science in the Public Interest, 6*, 31–55.

Martin, C. C. (2015). How ideology has hindered sociological insight. *The American Sociologist, 47*, 115–130.

Masci, D. (February 12, 2016). On Darwin day, 5 facts about the evolution debate. *Pew Research Center,* retrieved on December 14, 2016, from: www.pewresearch.org/facttank/2016/02/12/darwin-day/.

Meehl, P. E. (1967). Theory-testing in psychology and physics: A methodological paradox. *Philosophy of Science, 34*, 103–115.

Meehl, P. E. (1990a). Why summaries of research on psychological theories are often uninterpretable. *Psychological Reports, 66*, 195–244.

Meehl, P. E. (1990b). Appraising and amending theories: The strategy of Lakatosian defense and two principles that warrant using it. *Psychological Inquiry, 1*, 108–141, 173–180.

Mercier, H. & Sperber, D. (2011) Why do humans reason? Arguments for an argumentative theory. *Behavioral and Brain Sciences, 34*, 57–74.

Mill, J. S. (1869/1989). *'On liberty' and other writings.* London: Cambridge University Press.

Moscovici, S. & Personnaz, B. (1980) Studies in social influence: V. Minority influence and conversion behavior in a perceptual task. *Journal of Experimental Social Psychology, 16*, 270–282.

Mulvey, K., Shulman, S., Anderson, D., Cole, N., Piepenburg, J. & Sideris, J. (2015). The climate deception dossiers: Internal fossil fuel industry memos reveal decades of corporate disinformation. *Union of Concerned Scientists,* retrieved on June 1, 2016, from www.ucsusa.org/sites/default/files/attach/2015/07/The-Climate-Deception-Dossiers.pdf.

Munro, G. D. & Ditto, P. H. (1997). Biased assimilation, attitude polarization, and affect in reactions to stereotype-relevant scientific information. *Personality and Social Psychology Bulletin, 23*, 636–653.

Nemeth, C. J. (1995) Dissent as driving cognition, attitudes, and judgments. *Social Cognition, 13*, 273–291.

Nickerson, R. S. (1998) Confirmation bias: A ubiquitous phenomenon in many guises. *Review of General Psychology, 2*, 175–220.

Open Science Collaboration. (2015). Estimating the reproducibility of psychological science. *Science, 349*(6251), aac4716. doi:10.1126/science.aac4716.

Oppenheimer, M. (1981). Testimony, Clean Air Act oversight, before the U.S. Senate Committee on Environment and Public Works. *97th Congress, July 1.*

Oreskes, N. (2004). Beyond the ivory tower: The scientific consensus on climate change. *Science, 306,* 1686. doi:10.1126/science.1103618

Pettigrew, T. F. & Tropp, L. R. (2006). A meta-analytic test of intergroup contact theory. *Journal of Personality and Social Psychology, 90,* 751–783.

Pinker, S. (2002). *The blank slate: The modern denial of human nature.* New York: Penguin Books.

Popper, K. R. (1959). *The logic of scientific discovery.* London: Hutchinson.

Popper, K. R. (1963). *Conjectures and refutations.* New York: Routledge.

Pronin, E., Lin, D. Y. & Ross, L. (2002). The bias blind spot: Perceptions of bias in self versus others. *Personality and Social Psychology Bulletin, 28*(3), 369–381.

Redding, R. E. (2001). Sociopolitical diversity in psychology. *American Psychologist, 56,* 205–215.

Revelle, R. & Seuss, H. E. (1957). Carbonates and carbon dioxide. *Memoirs of the Geological Society of America, 67,* 239.

Roache, R. (May 8, 2015). If you're a conservative, I'm not your friend. *Practical Ethics: Ethics in the News.* Retrieved on July 6, 2016, from: http://blog.practicalethics.ox.ac.uk/2015/05/if-youre-a conservative-im-not-your-friend/.

Schumm, W. R. (2015). Navigating treacherous waters—one researcher's 40 years of experience with controversial research. *Comprehensive Psychology, 4,* Article 24.

Stanovich, K. E., West, R. F. & Toplak, M. E. (2013). Myside bias, rational thinking, and intelligence. *Current Directions in Psychological Science, 22,* 259–264.

Taber, C. S. & Lodge, M. (2006). Motivated skepticism in the evaluation of political beliefs. *American Journal of Political Science, 50,* 755–769.

Tappan, M. B. (1997). Interpretive psychology: Stories, circles, and understanding lived experience. *Journal of Social Issues, 53,* 645–656.

Tetlock, P. E. (1994). Political psychology or politicized psychology: Is the road to scientific hell paved with good moral intentions? *Political Psychology,* 509–529.

Wetherell, G., Brandt, M. J. & Reyna, C. (2013). Discrimination across the ideological divide: The role of perceptions of value violations and abstract values in discrimination by liberals and conservatives. *Social Psychology and Personality Science, 4,* 658–667.

Williams, J. (2016). *Academic freedom in an age of conformity: Confronting the fear of knowledge.* New York: Palgrave Macmillan.

PART V

Towards a De-Politicized Social Psychological Science

14

INTERRUPTING BIAS IN PSYCHOLOGICAL SCIENCE

Evolutionary Psychology as a Guide

Joshua M. Tybur and C. David Navarrete

Why does our understanding of social psychological phenomena—such as why we have a moral sense, why we love some people yet hate others, and why we cooperate with others even when it's not obviously in our self-interest—pale in comparison to the precision with which we understand cellular division, plate tectonics, and semiconductors? It's not for a lack of effort, since thousands of social psychologists are furiously working to better understand these topics. It's probably not for lack of talent, since professional researchers must pass through several filters on their way from bachelor's degree to PhD to faculty position. Instead, progress is handicapped by a cold, hard fact: As far as sciences go, social psychology is as soft as a marshmallow. Our areas of inquiry are often grouped into folk categories (e.g., prejudice, morality, self-control) that may imperfectly carve nature at its joints. The phenomena we study are nebulous enough that we feel compelled to posit the existence of hypothetical, unobservable constructs that must be indirectly observed via idiosyncratic measures, which are readily compromised by unreliability or by fallacious interpretations of the constructs we're actually measuring (e.g., jingle and jangle fallacies; Uher, 2011). As such, the lack of set criteria for measurement and methodology introduces "researcher" degrees of freedom, which can lead the field down a bumpy detour of false positive findings. Progress is further impeded by the fact that researchers working in different social psychological subfields use different theoretical frameworks, many of which are so disconnected from each other that discoveries made in one sub-discipline can scarcely inform knowledge in another.

This type of gloomy assessment of psychology isn't novel. Indeed, Paul Meehl's (1978) blistering treatise on the slow progress of soft psychology has been required reading in many undergraduate and graduate courses in psychology for decades, and Meehl himself noted that many of his criticisms had already appeared in various critiques prior to 1978. And, although similar sentiments have been repeated in various forms through the years (Kelley, 2000; Krueger & Funder, 2004; Pinker, 2015; Tooby & Cosmides, 1992), the field has recently progressed in addressing some of the more problematic aspects of its softness. High-profile critiques of common research practices (Schimmack, 2012; Simmons, Nelson & Simonsohn, 2011) have tapped into researchers' indignation following prominent scientific fraud cases (e.g., those linked to Diederik Stapel and Dirk Smeesters), and journals and societies have adopted new standards designed to toughen up some of our soft contours.

Yet just as some leaks are being patched up, we've discovered a major rift that has been hiding in plain sight for decades: political bias (Duarte et al., 2015). It turns out that social psychologists are not just politically liberal—we are extremely, overwhelmingly, and shamelessly liberal. We are so dogmatically liberal that many of us admit to being willing to discriminate against political conservatives in professional contexts (Inbar & Lammers, 2012). Given the soft contours of social psychology, systematic ideological biases might mold our measurement instruments, our hypotheses, and our interpretations in a manner tailored to support individual researchers' political ideologies rather than clarify scientific puzzles (Duarte et al., 2015; Tetlock, 1998, 2007).

While p-curve analyses, Bayesian statistics, minimal standards for statistical power, meta-analyses, preregistration, and replication projects might address a subset of the challenges to social psychology, they are weaker medicines for addressing ideological biases that can shape the foundations of our research questions. So what type of strategy might we use to minimize our political biases? One approach might involve recruiting more political conservatives into our ranks—perhaps through affirmative action systems—so that they can gently remind us when our research reflects political goals rather than scientific ones (Duarte et al., 2015). We are skeptical of this approach (Tybur & Navarrete, 2015; see also Funder, 2015; Pfister & Böhm, 2015), both because of barriers to its implementation and because it appears better suited for nursing the illness's symptoms rather than addressing its epidemiological roots. Instead, we believe that the best way to neutralize political bias is to address a superficially unrelated critique offered by Meehl (1978)—by shoring up the softness in our theoretical foundations. And we believe that evolutionary psychologists can serve as an example for how successful attention to theory can attenuate political biases in research. To understand the contribution that evolutionary psychology can make to neutralize political bias, let's first consider evolutionary psychology's history and struggles with politics in science.

Evolution and Human Behavior

At the end of *On the Origin of Species*, Darwin (1859) suggested that his ideas of evolution by natural selection might one day form the foundation of psychological science. In its nascent state, though, Darwin's theory of evolution was not yet solid enough to support psychology; an evolutionary foundation for the psychological sciences required theoretical developments beyond those that Darwin was able to offer. This foundation was later built upon the insights of the Modern Evolutionary Synthesis (the integration of Darwinian evolution with Mendelian genetics), which can rightfully be referred to as a revolution in evolutionary behavioral science in its own right (Dawkins, 2009; Wilson, 1975). The Modern Synthesis implied a gene-centered view of the evolution of behavior, and it led to, among others, W. D. Hamilton's (1964) inclusive fitness theory and Robert Trivers's theories of reciprocal altruism (1971) and parental investment (1972), each of which organized the types of questions that evolutionary-oriented behavioral scientists could ask, and each of which provided examples of the types of cost-benefit analyses that can guide the evolution of functional organization. The identification of functional design as the most important criteria for identifying adaptations (Williams, 1966) provided scientists with a rough guide for detecting the signatures of natural selection in behavior, and the application of game theory to the costs and benefits of behavioral strategies shored up the underpinnings of this approach as a serious and rigorous enterprise (Axelrod & Hamilton, 1981; Maynard Smith, 1982; Maynard Smith & Price, 1973). These— and many other developments spurred by the Modern Synthesis—were summarized by E.O. Wilson in *Sociobiology: The New Synthesis* (1975), which described how evolutionary theory could be used to understand behavioral phenomena such as aggression, status hierarchies, parenting, and cooperation. The book was wildly successful—in 1989, the Animal Behavior Society voted it as the most important book on animal behavior ever published, and the ideas described in it now form the foundation of the field of animal behavior (Alcock, 2001).

Although most of *Sociobiology* was dedicated to understanding non-human behavior, Wilson's final chapter applied the same theoretical principles used to understand insects, birds, ungulates, and non-human primates to understanding humans. It aimed to connect insights from evolutionary theorists with those from sociologists, such as Erving Goffman, and cultural anthropologists, such as Claude Levi-Strauss. Wilson's short, 28-page evolutionary analysis of human behavior hinted at what would soon come from other scientists.

Following *Sociobiology*, several researchers went into greater depth in applying modern evolutionary theory to understanding human behavior. Don Symons's *The Evolution of Human Sexuality* (1979) and Martin Daly and Margo Wilson's *Sex, Evolution, and Behavior* (1978) laid the groundwork for much contemporary evolutionary research on mating. Daly and Wilson's *Homicide* (1988) articulated who should be expected to be the perpetrators and targets of aggression and when and why people should aggress. David Buss's (1989) landmark cross-cultural test of mate preferences tested some of the key predictions about mate preferences that could be generated using Trivers's Parental Investment Theory. And, perhaps most critically, John Tooby and Leda Cosmides offered a framework for understanding how proximate, cognitive mechanisms should be functionally organized to execute ultimate, evolutionary functions (Cosmides & Tooby, 1992, 1994; Tooby & Cosmides, 1990, 1992, 2005).

Whereas the theoretical insights described by E.O. Wilson (1975) now form the foundation of modern animal behavior research (Alcock, 2001), the approach offered by Tooby and Cosmides (or variations thereof; cf., Laland & Brown, 2011), while generative and accelerating in application, does not enjoy the same degree of success in mainstream research on aggression, morality, prejudice, cooperation, and other topics of interest to social psychologists. Why have researchers who study social behavior in humans been so much slower to adopt evolutionary theory than researchers who study social behavior in non-human animals? The reason lies partially in the ideology of scientific practitioners.

Early Resistance to Evolution and Human Behavior from the Left

Shortly after *Sociobiology* was published, 16 members of the so-called Sociobiology Study Group (some of them Wilson's Harvard colleagues, most of them self-described Marxists) published a letter, *Against Sociobiology* (Allen et al., 1975), in the *New York Review of Books*. The letter primarily targeted Wilson's final chapter on human behavior, which focused on, among other things, the relatively uncontroversial notions that (1) humans have remarkably large craniums compared to non-human primates; (2) humans engage in social exchange, which might facilitate status hierarchies; (3) human kinship systems are zoologically unique; (4) human language is rich and sophisticated compared to other animal communication systems; (5) tribalism and ethnocentrism appear to be common across human groups; and (6) human behavior is highly variable across societies, and cultures seem to evolve faster than do biological organisms. In response to these ideas, Harvard paleontologist Stephen Jay Gould, Harvard geneticist Richard Lewontin, and their letter co-authors argued that Wilson's work was in step with "the eugenics policies which led to the establishment of gas chambers in Nazi Germany" and that "Wilson joins the long parade of biological determinists whose work has served to buttress the institutions of their society by exonerating them from responsibility for social problems." Whereas the application of evolutionary principles to non-human animals transformed the study of animal behavior and won Wilson accolades, theoretically similar analyses of human behavior earned immediate scorn and condemnation, mostly from liberal political activists. Protesters picketed outside of Wilson's office and interrupted his lectures at Harvard. Most famously, at a public lecture at the American Association for the Advancement of Science, just two months after being awarded a National Medal of Science by U.S. President Jimmy Carter, he was assaulted by a group of left-wing activists, who seized the stage and dumped a pitcher of ice water on his head. Wilson expressed bewilderment at the political reaction to *Sociobiology*: "Having expected some frontal fire from social scientists primarily on evidential grounds, I had received instead a political enfilade from the flank" (Wilson, 2006, p. 338).

Protests against *Sociobiology* were largely unconcerned with Wilson's scientific accuracy. Instead, they focused on the degree to which Wilson's chapter on humans was superficially inconsistent with liberal political ideologies (Segerstråle, 2000). The most vocal critics of *Sociobiology* wanted any theoretical frameworks or testable hypotheses that sat uneasily with their ideologies silenced, and they wanted researchers whose science was seemingly inconsistent with a liberal political ideology banished from academia. To many of Wilson's critics, any type of evolutionary analysis of human behavior was political activism disguised as science; it was a thinly veiled attempt to justify economic inequality, sexism, and racism as the inevitable outcome of evolutionary processes.

That said, many of Wilson's critics did not sincerely believe that Wilson and others who dared to apply evolutionary theory to human behavior were politically conservative themselves. Instead, they objected to the idea that some evolutionary scientists weren't *liberal enough*—or at least they weren't sufficiently radical to steer their science in a direction that was clearly consistent with a liberal ideology, even if such a direction did not follow the flow of scientific progress (Segerstråle, 2000). Further, some believed that right-wing groups and politicians could seize upon sociobiology as scientific justification for enacting policies that discriminate against minority groups and inhibit social mobility. Of course, other critics did assume—and continue to assume—that evolutionary scientists like Wilson are conservative ideologues promoting evolutionary theory to support a nefarious right-wing political agenda. For example, Anne Innis Dagg (2005) wrote, "Darwinian psychologists seem to have a right wing bias" (p. 187), and she questioned whether the evolutionary behavioral sciences are "truly scientific if (they) so readily reflect political rather than academic precepts" (p. ix). Similarly, Hilary and Steven Rose (2000) wrote, "The political agenda of evolutionary psychology is transparently part of a right-wing libertarian attack on collectivity, above all the welfare state" (p. 8). It is unclear whether such examples reflect Dagg's and the Roses' true beliefs about evolutionary behavioral scientists, or if they are strategic rhetorical attacks designed to stigmatize their targets regardless of the veracity of their statements. Either way, how accurately did Wilson's critics, protesters, and accosters describe his political agenda? How accurate were critics like Dagg, Rose, and Rose? As it turns out, not at all.

Political Evolutionary Scientists

Wilson later described having walked into a political arena for which he was wholly unprepared:

> In 1975, I was a political naïf: I knew almost nothing of Marxism as either a political belief or a mode of analysis, I had paid little attention to the dynamism of the activist left, I had never heard of Science for the People.
>
> *(Wilson, 2006, p. 339)*

In sharp contrast with his self-described Marxist Harvard colleagues Stephen Jay Gould and Richard Lewontin, Wilson eschewed politics in favor of studying insects—primarily ants—and his primary goal was to understand whether and how a common theoretical perspective could explain the behavior of animals across taxa. As Richard Dawkins (2009) later put it, evolution was and remains "the only game in town," and *Sociobiology* was the output of years of research into a general theoretical framework for understanding the evolution of animal behavior. Wilson had little familiarity with political debates, and he had no desire or expectation for *Sociobiology* to inform or support anyone's personal ideology. If forced into a political coalition, he would have fit much more comfortably with liberal rather than conservative groups. In addition to his contributions to evolutionary biology, he coined the term "biodiversity," is a secular humanist, and is an influential environmental conservationist.

At least one of Wilson's contemporaries expressed surprise at Wilson's political naiveté. John Maynard Smith remarked, "I cannot believe Wilson didn't know that (*Sociobiology*) was going to provoke great hostility from American Marxists, and Marxists everywhere" (Wilson, 2006). Maynard Smith certainly had some insight into the minds of Marxists. He, one of the 20th century's most heavily cited and influential evolutionary biologists, was far from the type of right-wing ideologue that critics of evolutionary theory pictured. Indeed, he was a former member of the Communist party who only left the party after the USSR began brutalizing Eastern Europe. Maynard Smith's left-wing bona fides were outdone by Robert Trivers, another titan of the early days of sociobiology who, shortly after developing parental investment theory, the theory of reciprocal altruism, and parent offspring conflict theory, joined the far left Black Panther Party and became a close friend of Black Panther founder Huey P. Newton. If forced to pick three "founders" of sociobiology, one could reasonably select Wilson, Maynard Smith, and Trivers. Far from being covert agents of the political right, these three ranged from left-of-center to perhaps far-left-of-center in their personal lives, and their political profiles should have swiftly neutered any accusations of conservative political biases in their science. Of course, these three were not the only scientists using an evolutionary perspective to understand behavior; hundreds of other researchers would later follow in their scientific footsteps. What about the politics of those who adopted some of the core principles summarized by Wilson to study topics traditionally under the purview of social psychologists—what about the politics of contemporary evolutionary psychologists?

Evolutionary Psychologists' Political Attitudes

Evolutionary psychology differs from sociobiology in many ways (Tooby & Cosmides, 2005), but it carries much of sociobiology's political baggage. Books have been published outlining evolutionary psychologists' purported political sins (i.e., political conservatism). The blogosphere is rife with criticisms of evolutionary psychologists' ideological motivations. Consider, for example, Jezebel.com blogger Lindy West's summary of evolutionary psychology: "I don't want to hate evolutionary psychology, but I do. I hate it. It's a field of study that could be legitimately interesting, if it weren't constantly being twisted into a justification for backward (and, frankly, un-evolved) anti-feminist bullshit." Most evolutionary psychologists can recall concerns regarding the political motivations and implications of their work expressed by departmental colleagues, conference talk audiences, or anonymous article reviewers. A personal communication from evolutionary psychologist Doug Kenrick regarding a submission to *Journal of Personality and Social Psychology* in the 1980s can serve as a nice example. In recommending rejection for Kenrick's paper, which used evolutionary theory to generate hypotheses about mate preferences, the reviewer wrote: "As a feminist and a scholar, I feel duty-bound to protect the unwary journal readership from this type of inherently sexist scholarship."

Our personal observations contrast sharply with both published and whispered suggestions that evolutionary psychology research is motivated by conservative principles. The evolutionary psychologists we know seem just as likely as non-evolutionary social psychologists to support policies that reduce institutional biases against groups (e.g., allowing gay men and lesbians to marry or reducing or eliminating the War on Drugs, which disparately impacts ethnic minorities), to show antipathy toward conservative politicians, and, in the U.S., to attend political rallies for Democratic political candidates.

Survey data corroborate our personal observations. Much as was the case with sociobiology, stereotypes that evolutionary psychologists are politically conservative are based more in fantasy than reality. Consider a 2005 survey of 168 PhD students across six U.S. psychology departments (Tybur, Miller & Gangestad, 2007). After reporting their stances on a number of political issues and their political party affiliation, participants selected which of six perspectives (one of which was evolutionary) best described the theory they used to guide their research. Results suggested that young evolutionary psychologists were just as liberal as their non-evolutionary colleagues. Only two of the 31 evolutionary psychologists (6.5%)—compared with 21 out of the 137 non-evolutionary psychologists (18.1%)—identified as Republican or Libertarian. None of the 31 evolutionary psychologists—compared with 12 of the 137 non-evolutionary psychologists—preferred George W. Bush in the 2004 Presidential election. Evolutionary and non-evolutionary psychologists did not differ on a composite of items measuring political compassion (e.g., endorsement of government-funded healthcare; endorsement of raising the minimum wage) or wealth redistribution (e.g., endorsement of privatizing social security and implementing a flat tax), and evolutionary psychologists actually scored more liberally on issues related to individual rights (e.g., marriage equality, abortion rights). The overwhelming liberalness of evolutionary psychologists is mirrored by the overwhelming liberalness of evolutionary anthropologists (Lyle III & Smith, 2012), who have also been critiqued as using science to justify a pernicious conservative political agenda.

The fact that evolutionary psychologists are in fact similarly liberal as non-evolutionary psychologists offers some hope for social psychologists concerned with potentially contaminating effects of their own liberal biases. After all, if evolutionary psychology research is so divorced from liberal advocacy that it is sometimes mistaken as reflecting a conservative political agenda, then evolutionary psychologists are doing a pretty good job of attenuating personal political influence on their research. So how do evolutionary psychologists accomplish this? How do they separate their personally liberal politics from their research? Their views on science might provide some clues. Although evolutionary and non-evolutionary psychologists held similar political views, Tybur et al. (2007) found that they viewed science differently. Evolutionary psychologists more strongly endorsed a composite of items measuring appreciation of "strong science" (example items including "We must use strong scientific methods to truly understand social problems like racism, sexism, and sexual assault," and "Science is the best tool for understanding how the world works"), and they less strongly endorsed a composite of items measuring skepticism toward scientists' ideological motives (example items including "Science is often used as an excuse to support the status quo," and "Many academic papers reflect how the author wishes the world was rather than how it actually is").

Differences between evolutionary and non-evolutionary psychologists in orientations toward science could reflect self-selection, with students who are more invested in strong science finding an evolutionary framework more appealing, and students who are less prone to conflating scientific theories with researcher ideologies finding evolutionary approaches to studying human behavior less objectionable. Or they could reflect the kind of training that evolutionary psychology PhD students receive, with more of an emphasis on cumulative scientific progress across a number of disciplines (e.g., anthropology, biology, ethology). Regardless of their source, these differences offer an explanation for why liberal evolutionary psychologists entertain and test many hypotheses that are inconsistent with liberal political intuitions. That explanation lies in the potential protective effect of a strong theoretical framework for guarding against ideological biases.

Strong Theory as a Buffer between Ideology and Science

Relative to researchers from other disciplines, social psychologists face a challenging task: They aim to use scientific methods to understand topics for which they often have ideological opinions in their personal lives. Whereas a geologist's political ideology has little to say about the epoch a rock layer is dated as, a social psychologist's political ideology might scream out opinions regarding topics such as the natures of sex differences, race-based prejudice, and differences between liberals and conservatives. Further, even if a geologist has moral intuitions regarding the age of a rock, the ability for these intuitions to shape methods or results would be shackled by the dispassionate links between geology and chemistry (e.g., radiometric dating). In contrast, many social psychological methods and theories are untethered from other disciplines, and the lack of cross-scientific verification can give researchers more degrees of freedom to unwittingly introduce ideological biases into their research. Evolutionary psychologists have fewer ideological degrees of freedom; when well formulated, their hypotheses are directly or indirectly connected to—and do not easily violate—a body of knowledge gleaned from molecular genetics, quantitative genetics, ethology, parasitology, and evolutionary game theory, among other disciplines. Such integrative consilience is an important feature of strong theory. Hence, even if an individual evolutionary psychologist has strong moral intuitions regarding, say, how men and women should be treated, these intuitions can be readily divorced from the dispassionate predictions regarding sex differences in mate preferences, coalitional psychology, and aggression implied by evolutionary theory.

Strong theory, then, might be especially critical in the study of topics for which researchers have personal, ideologically based intuitions. While social psychologists have been successful in designing experiments, introducing cognitive processes to the study of behavior, and developing theories used to understand isolated social psychological phenomena (Van Lange, 2013), they have been less successful in developing the types of strong theories that can connect social psychological phenomena with other disciplines (and, indeed, even other phenomena within social psychology)—the types of strong theories that can attenuate the political biases that social psychologists might be especially vulnerable to (Duarte et al., 2015). Many of the theories that have been generated within social psychology have been critiqued as ultimately restating the phenomena that the theory aims to explain, or as unable to be verified, enriched, or refuted by other scientific disciplines (Pinker, 2015).

Consider Social Identity Theory, which was developed by social psychologists to explain intergroup bias. A key proposition underlying Social Identity Theory states that people have a need to see themselves in a positive light and as members of a distinct social group, and that this need underlies intergroup bias. The theory ends here, without an explanation of why humans would have a need to see themselves in a positive light, and without cross-disciplinary verification that this assumption is correct. The foundation of Social Identity Theory looks a little shakier when vetted using insights from evolutionary biology and research from other areas of social psychology, which suggest that, rather than being an ultimate goal in itself, self-esteem is a *means* to an end—it is the phenomenological gauge of social inclusion versus exclusion or social value to others (Kurzban & Aktipis, 2007; Leary, 1999; Leary & Baumeister, 2000). Other theories similarly end with assumptions that humans have needs to maintain a positive self-image, a perception of control, a perception of order, etc., and, in doing so, they similarly conflate ultimate explanations—*why* questions, which could connect social psychology with the broader study of animal behavior and could shatter or fortify key theoretical assumptions—with proximate ones (*how* questions—see Scott-Phillips, Dickins, & West, 2011, for an overview of this issue).

Whither Non-evolutionary Psychology?

Let's assume that the best way to attenuate ideological bias is to shore up social psychology's theoretical foundations. To do this, would we need all social psychologists to become evolutionary psychologists? We are unable to think of a theory outside of evolutionary theory that (a) has led such an overwhelmingly liberal group of scholars (evolutionary psychologists) to conduct research on human behavior without clearly liberal biases, (b) can be used to draw predictions and interpret data across the jungle of phenomena investigated by social psychologists (e.g., aggression, mating, cooperation), and (c) can link social psychology to disciplines within and outside of psychology. That said, a strategy aimed at convincing all social psychologists to suddenly become evolutionary psychologists might be less plausible than an affirmative action program designed to get conservatives to join the ranks of social psychology departments. Why is this? At first glance, an evolutionary perspective shouldn't be a hard sell to social psychologists, most of whom would accept the core tenets of modern evolutionary theory as fact, would accept that humans sit perched on one twig on the tree of life, and would accept that the human brain is an organ that has been shaped by natural selection.

A closer look reveals at least four barriers that social psychologists face in adopting evolutionary theory. First, many undergraduate and graduate psychology programs provide no training in evolutionary theory, and textbooks are rampant with factual errors concerning basic evolutionary principles (Park, 2007; Winegard, Winegard, & Deaner, 2014). Second, non-evolutionary psychologists sometimes mistakenly believe that evolutionary theory is inherently untestable or is unable to generate falsifiable hypotheses (Conway III & Schaller, 2002; Jonason & Schmitt, in press; Ketelaar & Ellis, 2000). Third, people easily adopt the naturalistic fallacy—the belief that something that *is* informs what *ought* to be (or, put differently, the existence of something like sex differences implies that the sexes should be treated differently). Fourth, evolutionary psychologists can appear to be a rival academic coalition with a different ideology (e.g., a phantom conservative ideology) competing for journal space, grant funding, and PhD students. And, as should be especially clear to social psychologists, humans tend to view rival coalitions negatively.

These barriers might prevent social psychologists from joining the Human Behavior and Evolution Society *en masse*, but they need not prevent social psychologists from taking advantage of the ideology-buffering effects of evolutionary theory. Indeed, we feel that four easily implemented changes to so-cial psychologists' orientations and training programs—changes inspired by the barriers that we propose inhibit the adoption of evolutionary theory by social psychologists—could contribute to attenuating ideological bias within the field.

Change 1: Increase Education in Biology and Anthropology

Many of the behaviors that social psychologists investigate have analogues or homologues in other animals. Chimpanzees engage in coalitional aggression. Several social species have dominance hierarchies. Some species engage in co-ercive mating behaviors (Thornhill & Palmer, 2001). The mating systems of many bird species are characterized by monogamy and paternal investment systems similar to those in humans. Indeed, the theories used by ornithologists in understanding the dynamics of bird mating might be especially useful in understanding topics pertaining to human mating and parenting, including courtship, mate guarding, extra-pair sex, and paternal investment (Thornhill & Gangestad, 2008). Further, careful reviews of the anthropological literature challenge many lay assumptions about the nature of human nature, especially in terms of mating, parenting, and aggression (Pinker, 2003, 2011; Sear, 2016). Given the thoroughly Western contexts through which most social psychologi-cal research and training occur, greater exposure to research on human culture and behavior in other contexts could greatly enrich social psychological research programs (Apicella & Barrett, 2016; Henrich, Heine, & Norenzayan, 2010).

Of course, the environments of evolutionary adaptedness (EEA; see Tooby & Cosmides, 1990) differ across traits, both within and between species, and a thorough understanding of bird behavior alone will not provide a thorough understanding of human behavior. Nevertheless, adding coursework in animal behavior and anthropology (and, specifically, behavioral ecology) can provide young social psychologists with some background in the evolutionary theories used to explain behavior across species. Such coursework could provide re-searchers with models for formulating and testing hypotheses derived from evo-lutionary theory—hypotheses that might be superficially inconsistent with the liberal ideological positions that most social psychologists have in their personal lives. Further, many of our "non-evolutionary" colleagues hesitate to famil-iarize themselves with evolutionary theory based on the idea that evolutionary hypotheses are less testable than non-evolutionary hypotheses. Exposure to the ubiquitous testing of evolutionary hypotheses across other disciplines could demonstrate the usefulness of evolutionary theory, which is, in fact, one of the best hypothesis-generating machines in the history of science (Dawkins, 2009).

Even with a background in evolutionary theory, though, and even with examples of testable and generative evolutionary hypotheses, future social psy-chologists might shy away from applying evolutionary theory to their research if they fall prey to the pernicious naturalistic fallacy. Hence, we suggest some specialized training on recognizing and avoiding this pitfall.

Change 2: Increase Familiarity with the Naturalistic Fallacy

Virologists can study some pretty nasty stuff, from diseases that kill children to those that cripple adults. These scientists are not accused of tacitly endorsing child murder by studying viruses, though—few people would infer, for example, that someone studying the evolution of HIV has a pro-HIV agenda or is trying to justify the existence of HIV. But when the topic of study concerns more morally valenced topics (e.g., prejudice, sexual coercion), people—even trained academics—more easily lapse into the naturalistic fallacy and assume that hypotheses drawn from evolutionary theory would justify the existence of the phenomenon being investigated. Such assumptions can cut scientific inquiry off at the knees, and they can lead investigators interested in morally charged topics to consider only hypotheses that superficially coincide with their own moral stances. Training young researchers about the naturalistic fallacy (the mistake of deriving "ought" from "is") and its potentially corrupting influence on scientific investigations can open an array of social psychological hypotheses and tests that might otherwise be ignored based on ideological reasons.

Consider Darwin's description of how his waning faith in God was shattered when he learned of the Ichneumonidae, a parasitic wasp whose reproductive cycle involves injecting a host insect's body with eggs, which later hatch and eat the host body from the inside. The behavior of Ichneumonidae was nothing that could have been predicted from Darwin's religious education—indeed, the creature's mere existence seemed at odds with the idea of a beneficent Lord. Now, entomologists are able to understand the Ichneumonidae using a gene-centric view of evolution; their scientific understanding can easily be compartmentalized from personal feelings regarding the parasite's cruelty. Social psychologists could be trained to better use the theoretical tool kit that dominates scientists' understandings of non-human animal behavior while compartmentalizing their own personal feelings about the phenomena they study. Our future understanding of behaviors that people find morally abhorrent (e.g., sexual coercion, infidelity, murder, bullying) can be enriched if the next generation of students is trained to understand that understanding and explaining a behavior need not imply endorsing or justifying that behavior.

Whereas basic coursework in animal behavior and anthropology (Proposed Change #1) would need to be outsourced to departments with expertise in these areas, training in the naturalistic fallacy could be included in any introductory psychology graduate seminar. Teaching students that scientific hypotheses should not be conflated with moral stances might encourage the adoption of naturalistic explanations (e.g., evolutionary or genetic), which might in turn encourage generating and testing useful hypotheses that would otherwise be rejected due to ideological biases.

Change 3: Link Sub-theories Back to Evolutionary Theory

Again, if we start with the relatively uncontroversial premises that (1) evolutionary processes have shaped all life on earth, including humans; (2) human brains, like all other organs, have a structure that has been molded by natural selection; and (3) all social behavior results from processes embedded within the brain, then theories in social psychology should ultimately be compatible with evolutionary theory, even if they are not explicitly referenced as "evolutionary" theories. As an example, consider Terror Management Theory (TMT), which some researchers have proposed to ground in evolutionary theory. The evolutionary account goes as such: In humans, a "survival instinct"—an evolved motivational system that causes all organisms to seek to avoid their own deaths—produced a gargantuan suite of psychological mechanisms functioning to buffer against the putatively debilitating anxiety that accompanies human recognition of mortality (Pyszczynski, Greenberg & Solomon, 1997). This type of exercise undergone by TMT researchers—specifying the evolved functions of the psychological processes proposed by the theoretical perspective—can be useful for many social psychological theories; it can allow for a kind of theoretical cross-checking with the state of the art in evolutionary psychology. In this case, there are principled grounds on which to doubt key aspects of TMT, specifically the idea that natural selection has shaped a "survival instinct" in any species, our own included. Evolutionary psychology has long demonstrated that thoughts and feelings are best conceptualized as emerging from computational systems designed "for" solving discrete problems (Tooby & Cosmides, 1992). An "avoiding death" imperative could result in any practical guidance for adaptive behavior (Paulhus & Trapnell, 1997); it offers no content for psychological mechanisms, e.g., what stimuli to respond to in avoiding death and how to respond to such stimuli (Navarrete & Fessler, 2005). Organisms do not safely navigate through complex environments because a single "orientation for death-avoidance behavior" is programmed into their nervous systems. Instead, they have myriad modular mechanisms for navigating through distinct situations, each of which can threaten life in a different way. Whereas avoiding falling off cliffs (Gibson & Walk, 1960) or avoiding aerial predators (Lang et al., 2000) are tasks that natural selection can design motivational mechanisms to solve (e.g., those that output fear of heights or freezing in response to aerial shadows, respectively), avoiding death, per se, is not. Thus, general motives (e.g., "survive") that can seem self-evident from folk perspectives are likely emergent property of a collection of discrete mechanisms, each designed to neutralize particular kinds of dangers (Holbrook, 2016).

Applying this type of exercise to other theories in social psychology could have two beneficial effects. First, theories can be refined and improved upon (and such improvements should be a goal of a progressing science of social psychology). Second, theories motivated more by ideological biases would perform less well when inspected under the light of an apolitical evolutionary analysis.

Change 4: Resolve Coalitional Issues

Social psychologists often propose evolutionary hypotheses—including the above-mentioned account of TMT (Pyszczynski et al., 1997), Conley's (2011) Pleasure Theory, and Eagly, Wood, and Diekman's (2000) Social Role Theory— or they assume some evolved function of the mind, even if that function is largely out of step with basic adaptationist principles (e.g., Kanazawa, 2010; cf., Penke et al., 2011). Others rely upon evolutionary theories of cooperation (e.g., indirect reciprocity; see Van Lange, Balliet, Parks, & Van Vugt, 2014). Even so, we suspect that many social psychologists open to using evolutionary theory in their research would bristle at the thought of being labeled an "evolutionary psychologist." Part of this coalitional resistance likely stems from the naturalistic fallacy and assumptions that evolutionary psychologists endorse some of the phenomena they study (e.g., social dominance, sexual coercion, physical formidability, etc.), and that they are part of some rival political coalition.

Research has long shown that political partisans resist persuasion from information perceived as supporting rival coalitions and more readily accept evidence perceived as supporting the policies advocated by their own political group (e.g., Tetlock, 1999). This pitfall is sometimes referred to as the moralistic fallacy—the tendency to deny the validity of propositions perceived as having implications inconsistent with one's moral matrix (the mistake of deriving "is" from "ought"). The moralistic fallacy might be especially problematic for liberals with high cognitive ability—exactly the demographic that characterizes social psychologists. In a study of political partisans at Yale, Dan Kahan (2013) found that participants who scored highest in cognitive ability and thoughtfulness were the most likely to display ideologically motivated cognition by doubting the validity of facts inconsistent with their worldview. In contrast with the popular notion that thoughtful, deliberative reasoning is a bulwark against error, Kahan's results suggest that ideologically motivated reasoning serves to promote individuals' interests in forming and maintaining beliefs advertising coalitional loyalty. Such group signaling interpretations of political conflict are consistent with "moral warfare" literature (Boyd & Richerson, 1985; Tooby & Cosmides, 2010), and they further underscore the importance of developing scientific practices that allow thoughtful, intelligent liberals to divorce themselves from factors that turn naturalistic explanations of behavior into divisive symbols of social identity and coalitional competition.

Concluding Thoughts

As social psychologists, we face challenges unique from those encountered by physicists, chemists, and geologists. Relative to practitioners of other sciences, we study phenomena that are hard to measure, hard to predict, and hard to understand, and our field is thus ignominiously referred to as a "soft" science. Rather than bristle under this label, we should embrace it as a challenge inherent to studying topics that are easily obscured by their complexity and by our own biases as individuals with stakes in and opinions about the topics we research. One weapon in the fight against this challenge should be strong theory, which can provide the kind of foundation that Darwin suggested would eventually guide psychology. As social psychological research increasingly springs from this kind of theoretical foundation and decreasingly leaks from practitioners' personal political biases, we will move forward to being the best soft scientists we can be.

References

Alcock, J. (2001). *The triumph of sociobiology*. Oxford: Oxford University Press.

Allen, E., et al. (1975). Against sociobiology. *New York Review of Books, 22*, 184–186.

Apicella, C. L. & Barrett, H. C. (2016). Cross-cultural evolutionary psychology. *Current Opinion in Psychology, 7*, 92–97.

Axelrod, R. & Hamilton, W. D. (1981). The evolution of cooperation. *Science, 211*, 1390–1396.

Boyd, R. & Richerson, P. J. (1985). *Culture and the evolutionary process*. Chicago: University of Chicago Press.

Buss, D. M. (1989). Sex differences in human mate preferences: Evolutionary hypotheses tested in 37 cultures. *Behavioral and Brain Sciences, 12*, 1–14.

Conley, T. D. (2011). Perceived proposer personality characteristics and gender differences in acceptance of casual sex offers. *Journal of Personality and Social Psychology, 100*, 309–329.

Conway III, L. G. & Schaller, M. (2002). On the verifiability of evolutionary psychological theories: An analysis of the psychology of scientific persuasion. *Personality and Social Psychology Review, 6*, 152–166.

Cosmides, L. & Tooby, J. (1992). Cognitive adaptations for social exchange. In J. Barkow, L. Cosmides & J. Tooby (Eds.), *The adapted mind: Evolutionary psychology and the generation of culture* (pp. 164–228). New York: Oxford University Press.

Cosmides, L. & Tooby, J. (1994). Origins of domain-specificity: The evolution of functional organization. In L. Hirschfeld & S. Gelman (Eds.), *Mapping the mind: Domain-specificity in cognition and culture* (pp. 85–116). New York: Cambridge University Press.

Dagg, A. I. (2005). *"Love of shopping" is not a gene: Problems with Darwinian psychology*. Montreal: Black Rose Books.

Daly, M. & Wilson, M. (1978). *Sex, evolution and behavior*. Belmont, CA: Brooks Cole.

Daly, M. & Wilson, M. (1988). *Homicide*. New York: Aldine.

Darwin, C. (1859). *On the origin of species*. London: John Murray.

Dawkins, R. (2009). *The greatest show on earth: The evidence for evolution*. New York: Simon and Schuster.

Duarte, J. L., Crawford, J. T., Stern, C., Haidt, J., Jussim, L. & Tetlock, P. E. (2015). Political diversity will improve social psychological science. *Behavioral and Brain Sciences, 38*, 1–13.

Eagly, A. H., Wood, W. & Diekman, A. B. (2000). Social role theory of sex differences and similarities: A current appraisal. In T. Eckes & H. M. Trautner (Eds.), *The developmental social psychology of gender*, 123–174. Hove: Psychology Press.

Funder, D. (2015). Towards a de-biased social psychology: The effects of ideological perspective go beyond politics. *Behavioral and Brain Sciences, 38*, 25–26.

Gibson, E. J. & Walk, R. D. (1960). The "visual cliff." *Scientific American, 202*, 64–71.

Hamilton, W. D. (1964). The genetical evolution of social behavior. *Journal of Theoretical Biology, 7*, 1–52.

Henrich, J., Heine, S. J. & Norenzayan, A. (2010). The weirdest people in the world? *Behavioral and Brain Sciences, 33*, 61–83.

Holbrook, C. (2016). Branches of a twisting tree: Domain-specific threat psychologies derive from shared mechanisms. *Current Opinion in Psychology, 7*, 81–86.

Inbar, Y. & Lammers, J. (2012). Political diversity in social and personality psychology. *Perspectives on Psychological Science, 7*, 496–503.

Jonason, P. K. & Schmitt, D. P. (in press). Quantifying common criticisms of evolutionary psychology. *Evolutionary Psychological Science.*

Kahan, D. M. (2012). Ideology, motivated reasoning, and cognitive reflection: An experimental study. *Judgment and Decision Making, 8*, 407–424.

Kanazawa, S. (2010). Evolutionary psychology and intelligence research. *American Psychologist, 65*, 279–289.

Kelley, H. H. (2000). The proper study of social psychology. *Social Psychology Quarterly, 63*, 3–15.

Ketelaar, T. & Ellis, B. J. (2000). Are evolutionary explanations unfalsifiable? Evolutionary psychology and the Lakatosian philosophy of science. *Psychological Inquiry, 11*, 1–21.

Krueger, J. I. & Funder, D. C. (2004) Towards a balanced social psychology: Causes, consequences, and cures for the problem-seeking approach to social behavior and cognition. *Behavioral and Brain Sciences, 27*, 313–328.

Kurzban, R. & Aktipis, C. A. (2007). Modularity and the social mind: Are psychologists too selfish? *Personality and Social Psychology Review, 11*, 131–149.

Laland, K. N. & Brown, G. R. (2011). *Sense and nonsense: Evolutionary perspectives on human behaviour.* Oxford: Oxford University Press.

Lang, P., Davis, M. & Ohman, A. (2000). Fear and anxiety: Animal models and human cognitive psychophysiology. *Journal of Affective Disorders, 61*, 137–159.

Leary, M. R. (1999). Making sense of self-esteem. *Current Directions in Psychological Science, 8*, 32–35.

Leary, M. R. & Baumeister, R. F. (2000). The nature and function of self-esteem: Sociometer theory. *Advances in Experimental Social Psychology, 32*, 1–62.

Lyle III, H. F. & Smith, E. A. (2012). How conservative are evolutionary anthropologists? *Human Nature, 23*, 306–322.

Maynard Smith, J. & Price, G. (1973). The logic of animal conflict. *Nature, 246*, 15–18.

Maynard Smith, J. (1982). *Evolution and the theory of games.* Cambridge: Cambridge University Press.

Meehl, P. E. (1978). Theoretical risks and tabular asterisks: Sir Karl, Sir Ronald, and the slow progress of soft psychology. *Journal of Consulting and Clinical Psychology, 46*, 806–834.

Navarrete, C. D. & Fessler, D. M. T. (2005). Normative bias and adaptive challenges: A relational approach to coalitional psychology and a critique of Terror Management Theory. *Evolutionary Psychology, 3*, 297–325.

Park, J. H. (2007). Persistent misunderstandings of inclusive fitness and kin selection: Their ubiquitous appearance in social psychology textbooks. *Evolutionary Psychology, 5*, 860–873.

Paulhus, D. L. & Trapnell, P. D. (1997). Terror management theory: Extended or over-extended. *Psychological Inquiry, 8*, 40–43.

Penke, L., Borsboom, D., Johnson, W., Kievit, R. A., Ploeger, A. & Wicherts, J. M. (2011). Evolutionary psychology and intelligence research cannot be integrated the way Kanazawa (2010) suggested. *American Psychologist, 66*, 916–917.

Pfister, H. & Böhm, G. (2015). Political orientations do not cancel out, and politics is not about truth. *Behavioral and Brain Sciences, 38*, 34–35.

Pinker, S. (2003). *The blank slate: The modern denial of human nature.* London: Penguin.

Pinker, S. (2011). *The better angels of our nature: The decline of violence in history and its causes.* London: Penguin.

Pinker, S. (2015). Political bias, explanatory depth, and narratives of progress. *Behavioral and Brain Sciences, 38*, 35–36.

Pyszczynski, T., Greenberg, J. & Solomon, S. (1997). Why do we need what we need? A terror management perspective on the roots of human social motivation. *Psychological Inquiry, 8*, 1–20.

Rose, H. & Rose, S. (2000). Introduction. In H. Rose & S. Rose (Eds.), *Alas poor Darwin: Arguments against evolutionary psychology* (pp. 1–13). London: Harmony Books.

Schimmack, U. (2012). The ironic effect of significant results on the credibility of multiple-study articles. *Psychological Methods, 17*, 551–566.

Scott-Phillips, T. C., Dickins, T. E. & West, S. A. (2011). Evolutionary theory and the ultimate–proximate distinction in the human behavioral sciences. *Perspectives on Psychological Science, 6*, 38–47.

Sear, R. (2016). Beyond the nuclear family: An evolutionary perspective on parenting. *Current Opinion in Psychology, 7*, 98–103.

Segerstråle, U. C. O. (2000) *Defenders of the truth: The battle for science in the sociobiology debate and beyond.* Oxford: Oxford University Press.

Simmons, J. P., Nelson, L. D. & Simonsohn, U. (2011). False-positive psychology un-disclosed flexibility in data collection and analysis allows presenting anything as significant. *Psychological Science, 22*, 1359–1366.

Symons, D. (1979). *The evolution of human sexuality.* New York: Oxford University Press.

Tetlock, P. E. (1998). Social psychology and world politics. In S. Fiske, D. Gilbert & G. Lindzey (Eds.), *Handbook of social psychology* (4th ed., pp. 865–912). New York: McGraw-Hill.

Tetlock, P. E. (1999). Theory-driven reasoning about possible pasts and probable futures: Are we prisoners of our preconceptions? *American Journal of Political Science, 43*, 335–366.

Tetlock, P. E. (2007). Psychology and politics: The challenges of integrating levels of analysis in social science. In E. T. Higgins & A. Kruglanski (Eds.), *Social psychology: Handbook of basic principles.* New York: Guilford.

Thornhill, R. & Gangestad, S. W. (2008). *The evolutionary biology of human female sexuality.* Oxford: Oxford University Press.

Thornhill, R. & Palmer, C. T. (2001). *A natural history of rape: Biological bases of sexual coercion.* MIT Press.

Tooby, J. & Cosmides, L. (1990). The past explains the present: Emotional adaptations and the structure of ancestral environments. *Ethology and Sociobiology, 11*, 375–424.

Tooby, J. & Cosmides, L. (1992) Psychological foundations of culture. In J. Barkow, L. Cosmides & J. Tooby (Eds.), *The adapted mind* (pp. 19–136). Oxford: Oxford University Press.

Tooby, J. & Cosmides, L. (2005). Conceptual foundations of evolutionary psychology. In D. M. Buss (Ed.), *The handbook of evolutionary psychology* (pp. 5–67). Hoboken: John Wiley & Sons.

Tooby, J. & Cosmides, L. (2010). Groups in mind: The coalitional roots of war and morality. In H. Høgh-Olesen (Ed.), *Human Morality & Sociality: Evolutionary & Comparative Perspectives* (pp. 91–234). New York: Henrik Palgrave MacMillan.

Trivers, R. L. (1971). Evolution of reciprocal altruism. *Quarterly Review of Biology, 46,* 35–57.

Trivers, R. L. (1972). Parental investment and sexual selection. In B. Campbell (Ed.), *Sexual Selection and the Descent of Man, 1871–1971* (pp. 136–179). Chicago: Aldine-Atherton.

Tybur, J. M., Miller, G. F. & Gangestad, S. W. (2007) Testing the controversy: An empirical investigation of adaptationists' attitudes toward politics and science. *Human Nature, 18,* 313–328.

Tybur, J. M. & Navarrete, C. D. (2015). When theory trumps ideology: Lessons from evolutionary psychology. *Behavioral and Brain Sciences, 38,* 40–41.

Uher, J. (2011). Individual behavioral phenotypes: An integrative meta-theoretical framework. Why "behavioral syndromes" are not analogs of "personality." *Developmental Psychobiology, 53,* 521–548.

Van Lange, P. A. M., Balliet, D. P., Parks, C. D. & Van Vugt, M. (2014). *Social dilemmas: The psychology of human cooperation.* Oxford: Oxford University Press.

Van Lange, P. A. M. (2013). What we should expect from theories in social psychology truth, abstraction, progress, and applicability as standards (TAPAS). *Personality and Social Psychology Review, 17,* 40–55.

Williams, G. C. (1966). *Adaptation and natural selection: A critique of some current evolutionary thought.* Princeton: Princeton University Press.

Wilson, E. O. (1975). *Sociobiology: The new synthesis.* Cambridge: Belknap Press.

Wilson, E. O. (2006). *Naturalist.* Washington, D.C.: Island Press.

Winegard, B. M., Winegard, B. M. & Deaner, R. O. (2014). Misrepresentations of evolutionary psychology in sex and gender textbooks. *Evolutionary Psychology, 12,* 474–508.

15

POSSIBLE SOLUTIONS FOR A LESS POLITICIZED SOCIAL PSYCHOLOGICAL SCIENCE

Lee Jussim and Jarret T. Crawford

As the chapters in this volume illustrate, there are a number of ways by which politics can potentially distort social psychological science (see also Duarte et al., 2015). That said, we do not believe that this is inevitably the case. In this chapter, we highlight the ways in which social psychologists can mitigate any inappropriate influences of their politics on their research.

The Ideological Skew Is Massive

Social psychologists are disproportionately liberal. We use the term "liberal" here as shorthand for anyone left of center, ranging from mainstream Democrats to Marxists. The point is not that all leftists are the same but to highlight the almost complete absence of an extremely large portion of the political spectrum from social psychology.

The ratio of liberals to all others combined ranges from about 8:1 to nearly 100:1, depending on exactly how the ratio is estimated. Jonathan Haidt first pointed out this extraordinarily lopsided skew at the 2011 meeting of the Society for Personality and Social Psychology (SPSP). However, he did so by calling for a show of hands (out of about 1,000 attendees), and only four or five admitted to being conservative. This evoked considerable pushback (see the comments on Haidt, 2011) on the grounds that this "show of hands" was not scientific. Inbar and Lammers (2012) then surveyed social psychologists and found a skew not quite as extreme but still extraordinarily lopsided (about 8:1). This, too, evoked some criticism (Skitka, 2012). Inbar and Lammers (2012) assessed SPSP members (who are not a representative sample of social psychologists) and asked questions only about discriminating against conservatives and research taking conservative positions, not about discrimination against liberals and research taking liberal positions.

von Hippel and Buss (Chapter 2, this volume) more recently surveyed members of the other major professional group of social psychologists—the Society for Experimental Social Psychology (SESP). They found SESP members voted nearly 100:1 for Obama over Romney—a result closer to Haidt's (2011) more extreme "show of hands" demonstration. Honeycutt and Freberg (2016) found that in the social sciences and humanities, self-identified liberals outnumber self-identified conservatives about 8:1, a result closer to Inbar and Lammers (2016) finding. When Langbert, Quain, and Klein (2016) examined actual behavior—political party registration—rather than self-reported political identity—they found that, across a wide range of disciplines, Democrats outnumbered Republicans in psychology over 17:1.

Furthermore, Honeycutt and Freberg (2016) did ask respondents about their willingness to discriminate against liberal faculty and ideas—and found that liberals were vastly more willing to discriminate against conservatives than against liberals. There was a mirror-image pattern among conservatives, who were much more willing to discriminate against liberals than against conservatives. At a psychological level, this means conservatives and liberals were personally about equally willing to endorse discriminating against their ideological opponents in academia. Of course, it would be a mistake to interpret this as indicating "equal" levels of discrimination in academia. Conservatives are such a small minority in most humanities and social science fields that conservative discrimination against liberal academics likely has few practical ramifications.

Regardless of whether the skew is 8:1 or 100:1 or somewhere in between, the data of a massive skew toward political liberalism in social psychology in particular, and many other social sciences and humanities more generally, has become overwhelming. Until data demonstrating otherwise is observed, the conclusion that social psychology is massively ideologically skewed is the only one consistent with the data from a variety of sources.

Consequences of the Ideological Skew

There is also a growing consensus that this extreme ideological skew undermines the quality of social psychological science and related disciplines by (1) narrowing the questions deemed important enough to ask or interesting enough to publish; (2) stigmatizing certain topics because they fail political or moral litmus tests; (3) implicitly importing political values and agendas into the very names of constructs and into which side of two-sided scales are emphasized; and (4) biasing and distorting the claims and conclusions reached, even on the basis of sound data (all the chapters in this book; Duarte et al., 2015; Jussim, Crawford, Anglin & Stevens, 2015a; Jussim et al., 2016a; Jussim, Crawford, Anglin, Stevens & Duarte, 2016b; Jussim, Crawford, Stevens & Anglin, 2016c; Martin, 2015; *Nature*, 2017; Redding, 2001; Tetlock, 1994).

This is not a healthy state of scientific affairs. Science in general, and social psychology in particular, is already grappling with a series of methodological and statistical threats, variously known as the "replicability crisis," threats to "scientific integrity," "p-hacking," widespread use of a great variety of questionable and suboptimal methodological and statistical techniques, and widespread failure of peer review to prevent any of this (Bakker et al., 2012; Gelman, 2016; Open Science Collaboration, 2015; Simmons, Nelson, & Simonsohn, 2011). The last thing social psychology needs is a powerful set of norms and motivations to undermine the validity and credibility of its science even further.

Solutions

The above arguments notwithstanding, the ratio of liberals to nonliberals is unlikely to change much in the near future. So let's presume the long-term continuation of a field in which liberals make up the vast majority, and let's assume that you, gentle reader, are yourself a practicing social psychologist who happens to be liberal. What can *you* do to limit political biases from distorting your cherished field? Many of the contributions to this volume offered quite specific and concrete suggestions, and they are reviewed next.

What Can You Do Right Now? Summary of Recommendations

One proposed solution is to increase political diversity in social psychology (Duarte et al., 2015; Stevens et al., Chapter 13, this volume). This, in our view, will have two laudable benefits.

Political discrimination is immoral. The first is moral. Social psychology should not generally be in the business of discriminating against people because of their politics. Teachers and mentors, especially, have a responsibility to create a supportive atmosphere for students who wish to pursue social psychology as a career path, regardless of their personal beliefs and values. Of course, as we put it elsewhere (Crawford et al., 2015, p. 44): we are not arguing faculty should be coddling "…Nazis, KKK members, terrorists, anti-Semites, racists, Creationists, or other political-religious extremists…"

At the same time, however, both scientific research (e.g., Westfall, Van Boven, Chambers & Judd, 2015) and anecdotal reports of real-world personal experiences (Stevens et al., Chapter 13, this volume) show that partisans often exaggerate their opponents' positions. This may manifest as leftist academics justifying political discrimination literally by equating mainstream conservatives with "Nazis." Put differently, some of our colleagues have given us reason to doubt their ability to distinguish between nonliberals (and even liberals who follow the evidence when that evidence contests liberal values) and actual Nazis. For example, when the first author of this chapter attended a Rutgers

Psychology Diversity Committee meeting and argued for incorporating political diversity into a formal diversity statement, he was immediately accused by a faculty member of holding a view tantamount to welcoming Nazis (see also the "Conservative = Nazi" story in Stevens et al., Chapter 13, this volume).

One of the distinguishing features of totalitarian political extremists (such as Nazis and communists)—is their near total disregard for actual facts and evidence (Pinker, 2002). And that is our main standard: If students are open to having their views of facts changed by evidence, their politics probably do not justify excluding them from entry into social psychology (or any scientific field). If they are not open to evidence, then they are probably not fit to be scientists, regardless of their personal politics.

Political diversity will likely improve validity by rejuvenating neo-Popperian falsification and Mertonian skepticism. The second set of reasons all involve improving the quality of social psychological science itself. Some of the clearest, strongest findings in psychology are "politically incorrect":

1   Stereotype accuracy is one of the largest and most replicable findings in social psychology (Jussim et al., 2016a).
2   Intelligence, as measured by standardized cognitive ability tests, predicts not only school achievement but other important life outcomes (Neisser et al., 1996).
3   Intelligence has a powerful genetic basis (Plomin, 2015).
4   Self-fulfilling prophecies are weak, fragile, and fleeting (Jussim, 2012).
5   Effects of individuating information on person perception are massive relative to stereotyping effects (Kunda & Thagard, 1996).
6   Even though sex differences on most characteristics are small or nonexistent, on a slew of stereotypical traits—physical strength, aggressiveness, nonverbal skills, spatial abilities—they are substantial (Hyde, 2005; Eagly, 2013).
7   More than a standard deviation separates some ethnic/racial groups in average standardized test score performance. This difference cannot be explained away by culturally biased tests or by stereotype threat (Neisser et al., 1996).

"Now," you might be thinking, "haven't they just contradicted their whole argument? If the field is so biased, how can it have produced so many solid yet politically incorrect findings?"

There is a one-word answer: skepticism. In general, our left-leaning colleagues subject politically unpalatable findings to far more skeptical scrutiny than they subject politically palatable findings to (for reviews, see Eagly, 1995, 2013; Jussim, 2012; Jussim, Crawford, & Rubinstein, 2015b; Pinker, 2002; and most of the chapters in this volume). But the strongest and most valid scientific claims, especially about controversial issues, will withstand even withering criticisms. Politically correct findings, even if they turn out to be true, are often less likely to be on as firm an evidentiary basis, because they have been subject to far less critical scrutiny.

Put differently, we embrace and are calling for a renewal of Popperian falsificationism and Mertonian skepticism. We use the term "neo-Popperian falsificationism" to refer to a modern adaptation of Popper's notion that scientists should seek to falsify their theories (Popper, 1959). There are limits to pure falsificationism. Predictions can fail for many reasons that do not invalidate the underlying theory (e.g., the methods were poor). Scientists are so good at coming up with reasons (some might say "excuses")—which, sometimes, will be quite valid—for why some hypothesis was not confirmed that it is almost impossible to conclusively falsify *any* theory in psychology (Meehl, 1990).

Nonetheless, even if falsification can never be absolute, certainly predictions can be disconfirmed for any particular study. We refer to emphasizing and valuing the seeking of such falsifying conditions as "neo-Popperian falsification." And when predictions are consistently disconfirmed for some theory, or perhaps merely not consistently confirmed, it becomes reasonable to doubt the validity of the theory as stated. Furthermore, even if theories can never be conclusively falsified, in the face of repeated disconfirmations of key predictions by methodologically strong studies, the burden of proof shifts to theory advocates to provide evidence demonstrating their claims are actually true. Strong neo-Popperian falsification is, perhaps, most starkly distinguished from the implicit confirmationism (efforts to "prove" one's preferred hypotheses, also known as confirmation bias) that has often pervaded social psychology (Jussim et al., 2016b).

Neo-Popperian falsificationism is itself rooted in longstanding calls for scientific skepticism—calls which seem to have been mostly ignored and even devalued at least in psychological science. One can see this in a former president of the *Association for Psychological Science*'s essay attempt to lambast science reformers and those "targeting" findings they consider suspect for attempted (and often failed) replications (Fiske, 2016). We think such lambasting is deeply misguided; if anything, psychology needs more, not less, skepticism.

We understand how scientists may not like having the claims they have staked their careers on threatened and challenged by science reformers, as such claims threaten their eminence (Gelman, 2016). One way to think of this issue is with the following question: Do we want an *eminence-based science or an evidence-based science?*

Our answer is simple and clear—validity hinges on evidence, not eminence. John Stuart Mill (1859/2014) was one of the first to make an argument for the value of skepticism for getting at the truth when he argued that even ideas we consider wrong should be taken seriously, for three reasons: (1) We may be sure we are right yet still be wrong; (2) even if we are mostly right, the opposing idea may have some truth as well, and only by engaging the alternative will we ever discover how we are even partially wrong; and (3) even if the alternative is completely wrong, the understanding of what is right is strengthened and sharpened by being compelled to engage with why some idea is wrong.

Merton (1942/1973) then argued that organized skepticism is one of the core norms of science. Although subsequent work has suggested that Merton presented more of an ideal than a norm (Mulkay, 1976), our view is that it is an ideal worth reinvigorating. Specifically, *most* important scientific claims *should* be subject to intense skepticism and scrutiny. In this way, unjustified claims will be sifted out from the justified claims. It is precisely because the evidence was so strong for the seven politically incorrect findings described above that they were able to withstand intense skeptical scrutiny. The criticism *forced* the strength of the findings to emerge.

On the other hand, a slew of claims in social psychology that were congenial to the left-leaning politics of the field have not withstood skeptical examinations of the underlying empirical evidence. Stereotype threat is settled science to an inner circle of advocates (e.g., Spencer, Logel, & Davies, 2016; Walton & Spencer, 2009), but not to many others (Flore & Wicherts, 2014; Jussim et al., 2016b; Sackett, Hardison, & Cullen, 2004; Stoet & Geary, 2012). The power of implicit prejudice is settled science to its proponents (e.g., Banaji & Greenwald, 2013; Jost et al., 2009), but not to other social psychologists (e.g., Blanton et al., 2009; Blanton & Mitchell, 2011; Oswald, Mitchell, Blanton, Jaccard, & Tetlock, 2013).

Similarly, stereotypes were once declared to be the "default" basis of person perception (Fiske & Neuberg, 1990), even though the evidence even at the time showed that the effects of individuating information were vastly larger (see reviews of evidence published in the 1970s and 1980s by Jussim, 2012; Kunda & Thagard, 1996). Self-fulfilling prophecies were once the darling of social psychology, touted as powerful and pervasive sources of social inequalities (Gilbert, 1995; Snyder, 1984), until the fullness of the evidence revealed that they are generally weak, fragile, and fleeting (see Jussim, 2012, for a review of the soaring claims and the weak evidence).

What is going on here? We speculate that the core problem is that flawed theories, questionable empirical studies, and wild overselling of findings are far *less* likely to meet with the type of intense skeptical scrutiny so important for a thriving science, *if* those theories, studies, and findings lead to conclusions liberals endorse. People often subject claims they endorse to less critical scrutiny than they subject claims they oppose (e.g. Nickerson, 1998); and scientists are not immune to this bias (Jussim et al., 2016b; Lilienfeld, 2010).

Skepticism is crucial to a thriving science (Merton, 1942/1973), and one way to strengthen that skepticism (and the concomitant thriving) is to embrace the inclusion of nonliberals into social psychology. Social psychology itself provides ample reasons to be confident that embracing political diversity will improve social psychological science. First, psychologists routinely claim to value "diversity" because diversity of perspectives is so valuable to science (Medin & Lee, 2012). Although this is usually presented as an argument for demographic diversity, which is a laudable goal, the type of "diversity of perspective" most lacking in social psychology is political diversity.

Second, research on minority influence (Crano, 2012) shows that there are two beneficial scientific outcomes when a minority attempts to change the majority's view: (1) The minority is wrong, but by mounting a strong challenge, it leads the majority to provide even stronger and clearer evidence that it was correct all along; or (2) the minority is right, and eventually accumulates such a mountain of evidence that it wins over and corrects the majority's initially incorrect view. Increasing political diversity should therefore work to improve social psychology because nonliberals will probably be far more skeptical of claims that advance cherished liberal perspectives than will liberals. They may not always be correct, but that skepticism will force advocates to either produce strong data or retreat from their strong claims.

What proactive steps can be taken to increase social psychology's political diversity? Duarte et al. (2015) suggested that psychological organizations and individual universities, departments, and laboratories issue diversity statements inclusive of nonliberals. Stevens et al. (Chapter 13, this volume) offer two examples of labs with such statements, and their experiences successfully attracting nonliberal students. It is quite striking how such a small step can actually help break down (perhaps unintentional) local barriers to the inclusion of nonliberals in social psychology.

Brandt and Spälti (Chapter 3, this volume) make this argument when they suggest that people consider alternative perspectives and norms and seek out potential moderators that might weaken or even reverse one's preferred conclusions. Mitchell (Chapter 9, this volume) highlights how study after study and review after review *fails* to support claims about powerful influences of implicit prejudice on real-world outcomes. He also juxtaposes this pervasive failure with a veritable cottage industry of "experts" selling interventions to combat what may be minor or even nonexistent biases in the real world of corporations, courts, and police.

The famous evolutionary biologist Stephen Jay Gould (1994) described a "scientific fact" as something "… confirmed to such a degree that it would be perverse to withhold provisional assent." We agree and would add this corollary: Anything *not* so well established that it would *not* be perverse to withhold provisional assent is *not* a scientific fact. Our view is that interventions should not be sold to the public until scientific facts, in the Gouldian sense, are established. The contribution to this volume by Blanton and Ikizer (Chapter 11) goes a step further, arguing that there is ample reason to believe that leaping to interventions before the science is well established, or on the basis of oversimplified communications even about valid findings, may sometimes (and perhaps often) do more harm than good.

Science then is a process of accumulation of evidence, especially of evidence subjecting claims to skeptical tests. Is some hypothesis *generally* confirmed or disconfirmed? Do higher quality studies *disconfirm* it, whereas lower quality ones "confirm" it? Does it hold even after accounting for publication biases and questionable research practices? By answering questions such as these, we can begin to hone in on actual (as opposed to illusory) and stronger (as opposed to weaker) scientific truths.

These ideas can be fairly readily and directly incorporated into researchers' personal practices, without any need to "wait" for social psychology to embrace an influx of nonliberals. If you were to try to falsify rather than confirm some hypothesis (say "conservatives are more rigid than liberals"), we speculate that that would often lead you to different research questions and, possibly, a different design of the study as it did when Crawford (Chapter 7, this volume) sought to disconfirm the hypothesis that conservatives were inherently more prejudiced than liberals.

Increase your exposure to politically diverse views. Galinsky et al. (2015) argue that one can improve one's own thinking by embracing a diversity of experiences, and they particularly highlight the value of visiting foreign countries as a spur to creativity. Brandt and Spälti (Chapter 3, this volume) make a similar argument about political diversity. They advocate exposing oneself not to caricatures of what "the other side" believes (for social psychologists, this will usually be conservatives and libertarians) but to people and outlets that embrace nonliberal views. As John Stuart Mill (1859/2014) wrote:

> Nor is it enough that he should hear the arguments of adversaries from his own teachers, presented as they state them, and accompanied by what they offer as refutations. That is not the way to do justice to the arguments, or bring them into real contact with his own mind. He must be able to hear them from persons who actually believe them; who defend them in earnest, and do their very utmost for them (p. 35).

Concretely, Brandt and Spälti recommend a little simple ideological "stepping out"—read articles by people and outlets that *do not share your worldview.*

Awareness of political biases. Tybur and Navarrete (Chapter 14, this volume) specifically recommend that students be trained to understand the naturalistic fallacy, and we agree. The naturalistic fallacy refers to confusing what is with what should be. In its most toxic, anti-scientific form, it involves stigmatizing scientists who produce empirical support for some proposition that those doing the stigmatizing find politically offensive. This variant is slightly more subtle than the classic naturalistic fallacy, because it involves confusing the production of scientific evidence that supports some factual claim about the world with personally advocating a particular moral worldview. The evidence reviewed in von Hippel and Buss's chapter (Chapter 2, this volume) with respect to gender differences and attractiveness would seem to also be a paradigmatic case (see also Eagly, 1995).

However, political biases can manifest in a slew of other logical fallacies, as well. Social psychology usually includes training in methods and statistics but rarely in reasoning and logic. Winegard and Winegard (Chapter 12, this volume) recommend students be required to take at least one class on critical thinking. Logicallyfallacious.com is an excellent introduction to many logical fallacies and how to avoid them (if you have never heard of, e.g., the "If by whiskey fallacy" or the "hypnotic repetition" fallacy—both of which are doozies—we strongly recommend this site).

Furthermore, familiarizing oneself with the now substantial literature demonstrating political biases in social psychology and related disciplines (Duarte et al., 2015; Jussim et al., 2016c; Jussim, Crawford, Stevens, Anglin & Duarte, 2016d; Jussim et al., 2015a; Martin, 2015; Pinker, 2002; Redding, 2001) is likely to heighten one's awareness of one's own tendencies toward such biases. We take a benevolent and optimistic view of most of our colleagues—with relatively few exceptions, we think many would strongly prefer to strengthen their science by limiting their biases. Therefore, when researchers familiarize themselves with real-world examples of such biases, many may become highly motivated to limit such weaknesses in their own work.

It is important to note here that just because the conclusions support liberal narratives does not mean that they are incorrect! Both authors of the present chapter, and many of the authors contributing to this volume, have published findings and arguments that, at least sometimes, are consistent with liberal worldviews. The natural world—and especially the social psychological world—rarely uniformly conforms to left-wing or right-wing ideals.

Implicit attitudes and prejudice may exist, but that does not mean they powerfully predict important real-world outcomes (Mitchell, Chapter 9, this volume). Liberals may hold fewer *racial* prejudices than do conservatives, but they are far more prejudiced against Evangelical or fundamentalist Christian groups. Indeed, we would speculate that one strong indicator that a particular researcher's work is biased would be if that researcher almost always (or always!) produces work that seems to vindicate a particular ideological perspective. Indeed, if *your* research always vindicates a particular ideological view, you might want to do some serious scientific soul searching and consider some of the philosophy of science emphasizing skepticism (Merton, 1942/1973), falsification (Popper, 1959) and strong inference by considering and testing plausible alternative hypotheses (Platt, 1964).

Work from a strong theory. Tybur and Navarrete (Chapter 14, this volumne) raise the possibility that starting with a sufficiently powerful theory preempts political biases. They focus on evolutionary theory as a paradigmatic case, and, given all the controversies and even protests that work has evoked, we find this argument (mostly) persuasive (especially because the proponents are themselves generally just as liberal as other social psychologists). There are, however, other contenders for strong theory, such as irrefutable statistical principles, including regression to the mean, aggregation (reduces error), and the law of large numbers (see Fiedler, 2017, for examples of how these statistical principles can be used to generate predictions about human behavior). Similarly, Fiedler (2017) argues that basing predictions on strong, well-established empirical phenomena also seems like a promising avenue for reducing bias in theorizing. Examples might include similarity attraction (Montoya & Horton, 2012) and the power of individuating information in person perception (Jussim, 2012). On the other hand, however, social psychologists have been in the business of denying, denigrating, dismissing, or underplaying the power of individuating information ever since Locksley, Borgida, Brekke and Hepburn (1980) first discovered it (see Jussim, 2012; Jussim et al., 2015b, for reviews of such efforts), so we are not quite as confident as Fiedler that this will necessarily reduce such biases.

For social psychologists interested in studying social phenomena from an evolutionary standpoint, however, this is a terrific recommendation. Furthermore, it seems likely that many of the rest of us would be surprised at how many deep, and often counterintuitive, insights and predictions about *social behavior* can and have been generated and often (though not always) confirmed based on evolutionary theory (e.g., Pinker, 2002). Therefore, it is possible that a greater incorporation of evolutionary ideas into social psychology would not only limit its propensity for politically motivated biases but would also provide a richer theoretical understanding of basic social phenomena. Nonetheless, this recommendation's benefits are limited to those questions that are evolutionary.

Embedded values, research questions, and questionnaire design. Duarte et al. (2015) pointed out that ideological values are sometimes embedded in the very measures social psychologists use. As a case study, they reviewed research by Feygina et al. (2010), who predicted that people scoring high on system justification would engage in the "denial of environmental realities." But their measures of denial were hopelessly problematic. For example, one of their constructs was "Denial of the possibility of an ecological crisis." Such a construct could be measured, for example, by an item that (1) first unambiguously defined what "ecological crisis" means, and (2) asked respondents whether they believed such a crisis was possible or impossible. People who responded with "impossible" would appropriately be viewed as denying the possibility of such a crisis.

But this is not how they measured denial. Instead, they asked, "If things continue on their present course, we will soon experience a major environmental catastrophe," and Feygina et al. (2010) claimed that people who disagreed with this were "denying the possibility of an ecological crisis." As Duarte et al. (2015) wrote: "The core problem with this research is that it misrepresents those who merely disagree with environmentalist values and slogans as being in 'denial'" (p. 4).

Both Reyna (Chapter 6, this volume) and Malka, Lelkes, and Holzer (Chapter 8, this volume) provide broad reviews of just how researchers go astray in this way and show how such biases lead to unjustified and invalid psychological conclusions. Reyna focuses specifically on the problem of embedded values; Malka et al. focus on the related problem of "overlap" in the content of pre-political versus political measures, which we see as a variant on the same problem. When researchers show that people who score high on measures of conservatism are also more "fearful" (or dogmatic or rigid) but the measures of conservatism themselves assess "fearfulness" (or dogmatism or rigidity), it should come as no surprise (because it is tautological) to discover that conservatives "are" more fearful (or dogmatic and rigid).

Fortunately, they also have some specific recommendations for how to limit such weaknesses. Consistent with the present chapter's emphasis on skepticism and falsificationism, Reyna recommends that researchers eschew one-sided scientific questions ("are conservatives more biased than liberals") for two-sided or more open-ended up questions ("who is more biased, liberals or conservatives" or, even better, "When are liberals more biased than conservatives, and when are conservatives more biased than liberals? And when are both groups unbiased?"). Brandt and Spälti's (Chapter 3, this volume)Table 1 is an excellent tool for helping researchers think through the many alternatives to one-sided or preferred hypotheses.

Reyna also strongly warns against the use of "proxy" measures—and makes a cogent argument for why they often do not measure what researchers intend them to measure. She puts this point quite bluntly, "If Construct X is the construct of interest, measure it, not Construct Y." Similar problems plagued the Implicit Association Test (IAT; Greenwald et al., 1998), which measures reaction time but is often interpreted as a measure of prejudice; early versions of the symbolic racism scale (Kinder & Sears, 1981), which at least partially measured conservative political beliefs (Sniderman & Tetlock, 1986), and the measures described previously in this section used by Feygina et al. (2010) to measure "denial" of environmental realities.

Reyna also issues a clarion call to *stop* interpreting minor movements along scales as being "high" versus "low" on some dimension. Researchers can divide any sample into "high" and "low" by performing a median split or comparable division. But if most of the scores cluster on the low end, then most people are "low." (She notes that this is a very common problem with measures of authoritarianism; we distort the meaning of results if we refer to people as "high" in authoritarianism when, in fact, they are on the low end of the scale, even if half the sample scores even lower.)

To Reyna's list, we would add one more –cognitive pretesting of questions (Krosnick, 2004). Such a procedure involves one-on-one pretesting, with a skilled interviewer presenting draft questions to a respondent and asking the respondent to rephrase the question using entirely different words. Such a procedure is invaluable for catching questions that the researcher wants interpreted one way but which participants interpret another (see Reyna's example about liberal and conservative differences in interpretation of questions about "affirmative action"). As such, it can also help reduce the unintentional infiltration of researcher values and ideologies into the very wording of questions and the interpretation of the responses.

Malka et al. (Chapter 8, this volume) take researchers to task for giving lip service to the need to separate measures of supposed correlates or predictors of political attitudes from the attitudes themselves. Obviously, the solution is greater attention to the linkage between construct development and question design. Similarly, they argue that a slew of understudied social and individual difference factors, ranging from economic beliefs to political activism to use of non-WEIRD samples (Henrich, Heine, & Norenzayan, 2010) are crucial to gaining both a more balanced and a more valid understanding of the sources of political ideology.

Checklists. Washburn, Morgan, and Skitka (2015) offer an excellent checklist of considerations to mitigate political biases in psychological research. Specifically, they recommend (1) making sure all theoretically relevant hypotheses are appropriately tested, even those inconsistent with one's prior beliefs; (2) providing "if-then" statements for your hypotheses, derived a priori from theory; (3) designing studies so that they can test alternative hypotheses; and (4) being open to adversarial collaboration, in which scholars with competing hypotheses have input on study design, data analysis, and interpretation. Their checklist starts with an honest self-assessment: What do I want to happen and why? Ceci and Williams (Chapter 10, this volume) and Stern (Chapter 4, this volume) show just why this question is so crucial—when passions run high on an issue, scientific objectivity often flies out the window. Jussim et al. (2016b) offer additional recommendations, such as carefully reviewing the literature, blinding researchers to the nature of the data even in the data analysis phase, and deliberately seeking evidence inconsistent with one's hypotheses rather than simply searching for evidence to support one's hypotheses.

Transparency. Surely, there will be good theoretical or empirical reasons to develop hypotheses that are consistent with liberal perspectives. If so, pre-registering those hypotheses can render the final research product more persuasive. Good data practices can guard against claims that one p-hacked, cherry-picked, or HARKed one's way to his/her conclusions.

Critically consider generalizability. Mitchell (Chapter 9, this volume) offered several recommendations for tempering our interpretations of lab-based research, critically considering their generalizability and external validity. Further, simply because an effect has been demonstrated does not mean it is robust or even valid. As numerous failures to replicate well-known studies have shown, extant evidence may be plagued by questionable research practices (Open Science Collaboration, 2015). Other contributors also encourage honest and clear interactions with the media (Blanton & Ikizer, Chapter 11; Winegard & Winegard, Chapter 12).

Conclusions

Researchers have been raising concerns about political biases distorting psychology for decades (e.g., Meehl, 1971; Redding, 2001; Tetlock, 1994), with little or no effect. Is this time different? We are cautiously optimistic that it is. Alarms raised about common statistical and methodological practices (e.g., Cohen, 1962; Meehl, 1967) had also been ignored until recently. Social psychology is going through an extraordinary and unique period of self-reexamination of its practices, and a science reform movement has gained considerable momentum and traction (e.g., Open Science Collaboration, 2015; Simmons, Nelson, & Simonsohn, 2011), complete with a new organization, the Society for the Improvement of Psychological Science (http://improvingpsych.org/).

When Haidt (2011) first broached the topic of political bias to an audience of 1,000 social and personality psychologists, the response was mostly a deafening silence, along with some breezy dismissals (Gilbert, 2011; Jost, 2011). By 2015, however, when we (Duarte et al., 2015) published our call for political diversity in *Behavioral and Brain Sciences*, nearly all of the 33 commentators conceded most of our main points.

Now, this volume, which has addressed the problem of political bias in a myriad of ways—from research design and interpretation, to media communication, to personal experiences with discrimination—includes a total of 32 authors. Editorials in both *Nature* (2016) and *The New York Times* (Kristof, 2016) have called for greater political tolerance in academia and in science. Clearly, a substantial and perhaps growing minority of social psychologists and other social scientists have come around to viewing the problem of political bias as serious and actionable.

The time has come for us to clean up our scientific act. The chapters in this volume provide ample evidence of the need to do so and a rich set of ideas for how to do so. We look forward to the creation of a sounder social psychological science as more of our colleagues take these messages to heart.

References

Bakker, M., van Dijk, A. & Wicherts, J. M. (2012). The rules of the game called psychological science. *Perspectives on Psychological Science, 7,* 543–554.

Banaji, M. R. & Greenwald, A. G. (2013). *Blindspot: Hidden biases of good people.* New York: Delacorte Press.

Blanton, H. & Mitchell, G. (2011). Reassessing the predictive validity of the IAT II: Reanalysis of Heider & Skowronski (2007). *North American Journal of Psychology, 13*, 99–106.

Blanton, H., Jaccard, J., Klick, J., Mellers, B., Mitchell, G. & Tetlock, P. E. (2009). Strong claims and weak evidence: Reassessing the predictive validity of the IAT. *Journal of Applied Psychology, 94*, 567–582. doi:10.1037/a0014665.

Cohen, J. (1962). The statistical power of abnormal-social psychological research: A review. *Journal of Abnormal and Social Psychology, 65*, 145–153.

Crano, W. D. (2012) *The rules of influence: Winning when you are in the minority.* New York: St. Martin's Press.

Crawford, J. T., Duarte, J. L., Haidt, J., Jussim, L., Stern, C. & Tetlock, P. E. (2015). It may be harder than we thought, but political diversity will (still) improve social psychological science. *Behavioral and Brain Sciences, 38*, 45–58.

Duarte, J. L., Crawford, J. T., Stern, C., Haidt, J., Jussim, L. & Tetlock, P. E. (2015). Political diversity will improve social psychological science. *Behavioral and Brain Sciences, 38*, 1–54.

Eagly, A. H. (1995). The science and politics of comparing women and men. *American Psychologist, 50*(3), 145–158.

Eagly, A. H. (2013). The science and politics of comparing women and men: A reconsideration. In M. K. Ryan & N. R. Branscombe (Eds.), *The Sage handbook of gender and psychology* (pp. 12–28). London: Sage.

Feygina, I., Jost, J. T. & Goldsmith, R. E. (2010). System justifications, the denial of global warming, and the possibility of "system-sanctioned change." *Personality and Social Psychology Bulletin, 36*(3), 326–338.

Fiedler, K. (2017). What constitutes strong psychological science? The (neglected) role of diagnosticity and a priori theorizing. *Perspectives on Psychological Science, 12*, 46–61.

Fiske, S. T. (2016). A call to change science's culture of shaming. *APS Observer.*

Fiske, S. T. & Neuberg, S. L. (1990). A continuum of impression formation, from category-based to individuating processes: Influences of information and motivation on attention and interpretation. *Advances in Experimental Social Psychology, 23*, 1–74.

Flore, P. C. & Wicherts, J. M. (2014). Does stereotype threat influence performance of girls in stereotyped domains? A meta-analysis. *Journal of School Psychology, 53*, 25–44.

Galinsky, A. D., Todd, A. R., Homan, A. C., et al. (2015). Maximizing the gains and minimizing the pains of diversity: A policy perspective. *Perspectives on Psychological Science, 10*, 742–748.

Gelman, A. (2016). What has happened down here is the winds have changed. Retrieved on 1/19/17 from: http://andrewgelman.com/2016/09/21/what-has-happened-down-here-is-the-winds-have-changed/.

Gilbert, D. T. (1995). Attribution and interpersonal perception. In A. Tesser (Ed.), *Advanced Social Psychology* (pp. 99–147). New York: McGraw-Hill.

Gilbert, D. T. (2011). Comment on Haidt's "Bright post-partisan future of social psychology." *The Edge.* Retrieved on 1/20/17 from: https://www.edge.org/conversation/jonathan_haidt-the-bright-future-of-post-partisan-social-psychology.

Gould, S. J. (1994). Evolution as fact and theory. Retrieved on 1/20/17 from: www.stephenjaygould.org/ctrl/gould_fact-and-theory.html

Greenwald, A. G., McGhee, D. E. & Schwartz, J. L. (1998). Measuring individual differences in implicit cognition: The implicit association test. *Journal of Personality and Social Psychology, 74*(6), 1464–1480.

Haidt, J. (2011). *The bright future of post-partisan social psychology.* Retrieved from www. edge.org/3rd_culture/haidt11/haidt11_index.html.

Henrich, J., Heine, S. J. & Norenzayan, A. (2010). Beyond WEIRD: Towards a broad-based behavioral science. *Behavioral and Brain Sciences, 33*(2–3), 111–135.

Honeycutt, N. & Freberg, L. (2016). The liberal and conservative experience across academic disciplines: An extension of Inbar and Lammers. *Social Psychological and Personality Science,* 1–9. doi:10.1177/1948550616667617.

Hyde, J. S. (2005). The gender similarities hypothesis. *American Psychologist, 60,* 581–592.

Inbar, Y. & Lammers, J. (2012). Political diversity in social and personality psychology. *Perspectives on Psychological Science, 7,* 496–503.

Jost, J. T. (2011). Ideological bias in social psychology? *The Situationist.* Retrieved on 1/20/17 from: https://thesituationist.wordpress.com/2011/03/02/ideological-bias-in-social-psychology/.

Jost, J. T., Rudman, L. A., Blair, I. V., et al. (2009). The existence of implicit bias is beyond reasonable doubt: A refutation of ideological and methodological objections and executive summary of ten studies that no manager should ignore. *Research in Organizational Behavior, 29,* 39–69.

Jussim, L. (2012). *Social perception and social reality: Why accuracy dominates bias and self-fulfilling prophecy.* New York: Oxford University Press.

Jussim, L., Crawford, J. T., Anglin, S. M. & Stevens, S. T. (2015a) Ideological bias in social psychological research. In J. Forgas, W. Crano & K. Fiedler (Eds.), *Social psychology and politics* (pp. 91–109). New York: Taylor & Francis.

Jussim, L., Crawford, J. T. & Rubinstein, R. S. (2015b) Stereotype (In)accuracy in perceptions of groups and individuals. *Current Directions in Psychological Science, 24,* 490–497.

Jussim, L., Crawford, J. T., Anglin, S. M., Chambers, J., Stevens, S. T. & Cohen, F. (2016a) Stereotype accuracy: One of the largest relationships and most replicable effects in all of social psychology. In T. Nelson (Ed.), *Handbook of prejudice, stereotyping, and discrimination* (2nd ed, pp. 31–63). Hillsdale: Erlbaum.

Jussim, L., Crawford, J. T., Anglin, S. M., Stevens, S. M. & Duarte, J. L. (2016b). Interpretations and methods: Towards a more effectively self-correcting social psychology. *Journal of Experimental Social Psychology, 66,* 116–133.

Jussim, L., Crawford, J. T., Stevens, S. T. & Anglin, S. M. (2016c). The politics of social psychological science: Distortions in the social psychology of intergroup relations. In P. Valdesolo & J. Graham (Eds.), *Social psychology of political polarization* (pp. 165–196). New York: Routledge.

Jussim, L., Crawford, J. T., Stevens, S. T., Anglin, S. M. & Duarte, J. L. (2016d) Can high moral purposes undermine scientific integrity? In J. Forgas, L. Jussim & P. van Lange (Eds.), *The social psychology of morality* (pp. 173–195). New York: Taylor and Francis.

Kinder, D. R. & Sears, D. O. (1981). Prejudice and politics: Symbolic racism versus racial threats to the good life. *Journal of personality and social psychology, 40*(3), 414–431.

Kristof, N. (2016). A confession of liberal intolerance. *New York Times,* May 7, 2016. Retrieved on 1/20/17 from: www.nytimes.com/2016/05/08/opinion/sunday/a-confession-of-liberal-intolerance.html?_r=0.

Krosnick, J. A. (2004). Suggestions on think-aloud cognitive interviewing to pretest questionnaires. Unpublished manuscript.

Kunda, Z. & Thagard, P. (1996). Forming impressions from stereotypes, traits, and behaviors: A parallel-constraint-satisfaction theory. *Psychological Review*, *103*(2), 284–308.

Langbert, M., Quain, A. J. & Klein, D. B. (2016). Faculty voter registration in economics, history, journalism, law, and psychology. *Econ Journal Watch*, *13*, 422–451.

Lilienfeld, S. O. (2010). Can psychology become a science? *Personality and Individual Differences*, *49*, 281–288.

Locksley, A., Borgida, E., Brekke, N. & Hepburn, C. (1980). Sex stereotypes and social judgment. *Journal of Personality and Social Psychology*, *39*, 821–831.

Martin, C. (2015) How ideology has hindered sociological insight. *American Sociologist*, (published online March 14, 2015). doi:10.1007/s12108-015-9263-z.

Medin, D. L. & Lee, C. D. (May/June 2012). Diversity makes better science. *Observer*, *25*. Retrieved on 11/30/15 from: www.psychologicalscience.org/index.php/publications/observer/2012/may-june-12/diversity-makes-better-science.html.

Meehl, P. E. (1967). Theory-testing in psychology and physics: A methodological paradox. *Philosophy of Science*, *34*, *103–115*.

Meehl, P. E. (1971). Law and fireside inductions: Some reflections of a clinical psychologist. *Journal of Social Issues*, *27*, 65–100.

Meehl, P. E. (1990). Appraising and amending theories: The strategy of Lakatosian defense and two principles that warrant it. *Psychological Inquiry*, *1*, 108–141.

Merton, R. K. (1942/1973). The normative structure of science. In N. W. Storer (Ed.), *The sociology of science* (pp. 267–278). Chicago: University of Chicago Press.

Mill, J. S. (1859/2014). *On liberty*. Toronto: Harper Perennial Classics.

Montoya, R. M. & Horton, R. S. (2012). A meta-analytic investigation of the processes underlying the similarity-attraction effect. *Journal of Social and Personal Relationships*, *20*, 64–94.

Mulkay, M. (1976). Norms and ideology in science. *Social Science Information*, *15*, 637–656.

Nature (editorial, 2017). Break out of the echo chamber. *Nature*, *540*, 7.

Neisser, U., Boodoo, G., Bouchard Jr., T. J., et al. (1996). Intelligence: Knowns and unknowns. *American Psychologist*, *51*, 77–101.

Nickerson, R. S. (1998) Confirmation bias: A ubiquitous phenomenon in many guises. *Review of General Psychology*, *2*, 175–220.

Open Science Collaboration. (2015). Estimating the reproducibility of psychological science. *Science*, *349*(6251), aac4716. doi:10.1126/science.aac4716.

Oswald, F. L., Mitchell, G., Blanton, H., Jaccard, J. & Tetlock, P. E. (2013). Predicting ethnic and racial discrimination: A meta-analysis of IAT criterion studies. *Journal of Personality and Social Psychology*, *105*, 171–192.

Pinker, S. (2002) *The blank slate*. New York: Penguin.

Platt J. R. (1964). Strong Inference. *Science 146*, 347–353.

Plomin, R. & Deary, U. (2015). Genetics and intelligence differences: Five special findings. *Molecular Psychiatry*, *20*, 98–108.

Popper, K. R. (1959). *The logic of scientific discovery*. London: Hutchinson.

Redding, R. E. (2001) Sociopolitical diversity in psychology: The case for pluralism. *American Psychologist*, *56*, 205–215.

Sackett, P. R., Hardison, C. M. & Cullen, M. J. (2004). On interpreting stereotype threat as accounting for African American-White differences on cognitive tests. *American Psychologist*, *59*, 7–13.

Simmons, J. P., Nelson, L. D. & Simonsohn, U. (2011). False-positive psychology undisclosed flexibility in data collection and analysis allows presenting anything as significant. *Psychological Science, 22*, 1359–1366.

Skitka, L. J. (2012). Multifaceted problems: Liberal bias and the need for scientific rigor in self-critical research. *Perspectives on Psychological Science, 7*, 508–511.

Sniderman, P. M. & Tetlock, P. E. (1986). Symbolic racism: Problems of motive attribution in political analysis. *Journal of Social Issues, 42*(2), 129–150.

Snyder, M. (1984). When belief creates reality. *Advances in Experimental Social Psychology, 18*, 247–305.

Spencer, S. J., Logel, C. & Davies, P. G. (2016). Stereotype threat. *Anuual Review of Psychology, 67*, 14.1–14.23.

Stoet, G. & Geary, D. C. (2012). Can stereotype threat explain the gender gap in mathematics performance and achievement? *Review of General Psychology, 16*, 93–102.

Tetlock, P. E. (1994) Political psychology or politicized psychology: Is the road to scientific hell paved with good moral intentions? *Political Psychology, 15*, 509–529.

Walton, G. M. & Spencer, S. J. (2009). Latent ability: Grades and test scores systematically underestimate the intellectual ability of negatively stereotyped students. *Psychological Science, 20*, 1132–1139.

Washburn, A. N., Morgan, G. S. & Skitka, L. J. (2015). A checklist to facilitate objective hypothesis in social psychology research. *Behavioral and Brain Sciences, 38*, 42–43.

Westfall, J., Van Boven, L., Chambers, J. R. & Judd, C. M. (2015). Perceiving political polarization in the United States: Party identity strength and attitude extremity exacerbate the perceived partisan divide. *Perspectives on Psychological Science, 10*, 145–158.

INDEX